AVIATION

An historical survey from its origins
to the end of the Second World War

Charles H Gibbs-Smith

Based on the author's *The Aeroplane: an historical survey* published
1960 by HMSO

First published 1970 by HMSO
Second edition 1985

This edition published 2003 by NMSI Trading Ltd, Science Museum,
Exhibition Road, London SW7 2DD

British Library Cataloguing-in-Publication Data
A catalogue record for this publication is available from the British
Library

Printed in England by the Cromwell Press
Designed by Jerry Fowler

ISBN 1 900747 52 9

Website http://www.nmsi.ac.uk

Contents

Introduction

This work originally appeared in 1960 as *The Aeroplane: An historical survey*. It has now been rewritten in the light of subsequent research, and brought to a close at the end of World War II, a time which saw the practical start of the jet age. As before, the intention has been to record the origin, birth and final establishment of the aeroplane in our civilisation, where it came to inaugurate – as Sir George Cayley had truly foretold – 'a new era in society'.

Of the scope and treatment adopted, I would first say that I have again devoted what might be felt an over-preponderance of space to the origins and early days of the aeroplane; that is to say, up to World War I. But I still feel that it is the early development of ideas, then the slow technological climb from Cayley to the Wright brothers, and the final achievement of the practical powered flying machine – followed by the oddly slow progress it made in Europe during the period 1902–09 – that should be firmly established in their general features, in order properly to lay the foundations of the aviation history to come. The later periods are, in any case, well covered by others.

Regarding, almost with nostalgia, the earlier state of aeronautical history – with its amorphous personal recollections, the tentative recording of events, and its often semi-fictitious chronicles – it is nevertheless gratifying to see how the subject has now become established as an important branch of technological history, with large numbers of books appearing on every aspect of the subject. These works often cover parts of the field in the greatest detail; whole books, for example, have been written about the aircraft manufactured by one firm, or one type of machine (such as the bomber) used by a single country; and there are even books dealing with individual makes of aeroplane, along with articles in periodicals which delve ever deeper into the minutiae of construction, development and performance. But my purpose has been quite different: it has been to describe the historical origins upon which the vast industry of modern aircraft manufacture has been raised. I therefore deal with later flying more briefly, in order to keep the whole subject in historical perspective. Regarding my fuller treatment of the early periods of ideas, endeavours and achievements, I would say that I have attempted, broadly speaking, to deal with them mainly from the evolutionary standpoint, concentrating upon the main formative influences.

Expressing thanks to all those who have aided me would involve, for the second time, a very long list of names; I have already paid tribute to many of them in the original version of the book. But I would again express my sincere thanks to the Director of the Science Museum, Sir David Follett, and to his colleagues Miss Margaret Weston, Mr Brian Lacey, and Commander Walter Tuck, for all their encouragement and many kindnesses. Then I would like to express deep gratitude to my friends at the Royal Aircraft Establishment at

Farnborough, especially Dr Percy B Walker, CBE, formerly Head of the Structures Department; Dr Dietrich Küchemann, CBE, FRS, Head of the Aerodynamics Department, and John Bagley, AFRAeS, of the same department. To my colleague Mrs Beryl Edginton I owe an ever increasing debt for her many labours in connection with my books, not the least of which is the laborious task of checking and reading the proofs. Finally in Her Majesty's Stationery Office itself, there are many old and new friends to thank for their extreme good nature and ever-willing cooperation with someone who must certainly rank as one of their most demanding and most enraging authors; but particular mention should be made of Mr David Napthine, Deputy Head of the Layout Section, who has so admirably designed this book, both in its original form,[1] and as it appears today.[2]

Not being happy with the somewhat 'spotty' appearance of the text illustrations in the previous work, I decided greatly to increase their number, and place them in 'page groups' throughout the historical narrative.[3] Most of the drawings which illustrate aircraft prior to about 1910 are taken from original documents. Mr Napthine and I then felt that it would preserve a certain essential harmony of appearance if we could continue this 'idiom of line' throughout the history. I had – in the original work – been allowed to use a number of the highly talented (sic) drawings made by Mr Douglas Rolfe in the USA; but I now required nearly double the number that I had originally used. It is therefore with especial gratitude that I here record the generous permission to use this large number of the Rolfe drawings, accorded me by The Condé Nast Publications Inc., of New York City, publishers of *Air Progress* magazine.

Every historian, no matter what his subject, must seek aid and advice from a variety of authorities within the field he explores. But every historian must also, and inevitably, make mistakes, as well as overlooking misprints. As before, I would finally appeal to readers to kindly inform me of any mistakes they find. Where it is a question of my facts being thought incorrect, I must ask to be provided with reliable documentary evidence of any alterations which they feel should be made.

Notes

1 *The Aeroplane: an historical survey*, published 1960.
2 The first edition of *Aviation: an historical survey*, published 1970.
3 The current edition uses almost all the line drawings from the previous editions, but most of the halftone images have been replaced with new pictures.

Preface to Second Edition

Since the stocks of the first edition of this book were exhausted there has been a continuing demand for copies, and the Science Museum decided that it should be reprinted.[1]

For some time before his death in December 1981, Charles Gibbs-Smith had started preparing for a fully revised second edition. Unfortunately his own notes were too fragmentary, and the burden of completing his work too onerous, to permit of this complete revision; so the decision was taken in conjunction with the production staff of HMSO that revisions would be kept to a minimum. A significant number of minor corrections have been made, particularly in Sections 2, 3 and 10 with the help of Professor Clive Hart and of Philip Jarrett.

Beyond that, the main change has been the deletion of numerous references to the projected Volume II – tentatively entitled *Early Aviation History: Studies and Problems* – which was intended by Charles Gibbs-Smith as a compendium on miscellaneous topics which had attracted his attention. In the event, the most important parts of this work were subsumed into his study of the influence of the Wright Brothers on the European pioneers, which was published as *The Rebirth of European Aviation 1902–1908* in 1974; and other items were published separately. However, there remained a series of studies on a topic of particular concern to Charles Gibbs-Smith: various claims advanced in recent years for powered flight before the Wright Brothers. I have thought it right to add a brief summary of this work, on pages 283–7.

I know that Charles would have wished any second edition of his book to contain acknowledgement of the help received from a number of people: Tom Crouch, Tony Elsworthy, Clive Hart, Gene Husting and Philip Jarrett would certainly have been among that number.

JOHN A BAGLEY
Curator, National Aeronautical Collection
Science Museum, London
January 1984

Note

1   This 2003 edition omits the quotations on flying, bibliography and conversion tables featured in the 1985 edition.

Prologue

The earliest-known illustration in history of a powered aircraft: c. 1325. It is a string-pull helicopter model, shown in a Flemish manuscript in the Royal Library at Copenhagen (No. 3384.8). This type of 'toy' – called by the French a 'moulinet à noix' (see page 16) – can be clearly plotted through the succeeding centuries; from it evolved the contra-rotating model of Launoy and Bienvenue (1784), which was copied by Cayley (1796) and published by him (1809), through which it became the direct ancestor of every helicopter flying today.

The practical realisation of voyaging through air and space has been a truly international achievement, in which some ten or more great nations have taken most honourable part, each making vital contributions to the development of the balloon, the airship, and the aeroplane. Disputes, claims and counter-claims should find no place in this great company.

The birthplace of civilisation would naturally have provided the breeding ground for many of the world's basic inventions: thus the ancient Chinese made three fundamental contributions in the field of aeronautics and propulsion when they invented the kite (*c.* 1000 BC), gunpowder (ninth century AD), and the rocket (*c.* AD 1100). The kite was the archetypal aeroplane wing, as well as the world's first aerial vehicle; for man-lifting kites were certainly in use in China within a few centuries of the invention of the kite, their first application being in the service of military observation. All three of these inventions found their way along the trade routes of the ancient world, and appeared in Europe during the Middle Ages.

The ancestry of the airscrew is obscure, but although the Chinese may have evolved it, the European airscrew did not originate in China, but appeared first in the uniquely European form of post (or tower) windmill, and was in widespread use by the thirteenth century. The passive role of the windmill's sails became an active propulsive airscrew by the fourteenth century, in the form of what were at first thought of as windmill toys, but were in fact pure helicopters of the string-pull type.

So, by the end of the fourteenth century, we had in Europe the two inventions which were to form the core, so to speak, of the powered aeroplane – the rigid inclined wing of the kite, and the active propulsive airscrew – not to be combined in one structure for some five centuries, but active in separation, and ready to come together when the historical processes had reached their appropriate stages of evolution.

As might be expected, the luxuriant explosion of art, science and letters which we call the Italian Renaissance brought forth the first man of great attainments to describe the flight of birds, to speculate on aviation and to design ornithopter flying machines (Leonardo da Vinci, 1485–1510).

Meanwhile, by way of some saints and many sinners, the idea of air-mindedness was to be nourished by brave and foolhardy men who fitted themselves with wings, and jumped to death or mutilation from high places.

Visions of military destruction from the air soon followed, and were first focussed and set down by a priest of Baroque Portugal (de Lana, 1670); and it was another Portuguese priest who took the first tentative steps towards gliders and hot-air balloons in model form (Gusmão, 1709).

As the eighteenth century was celebrated as the Age of Reason, and as France was the land of Diderot and Voltaire, it was properly in character for the French to accomplish the enclosure of a 'cloud in a bag', and for the first time to travel through the air in great gas balloons sustained by hot air or hydrogen (the Montgolfier brothers, and Charles, 1783). Soon after, came the practical parachute and the first human drop from the air (Garnerin, 1797).

As the Industrial Revolution was initiated in Britain during the same century, it was appropriate that the applied science of aerodynamics, and the first formulation of the practical flying machine – as well as the prefiguring of the aeroplanes to come – should be accomplished in the land of Isaac Newton and James Watt (Cayley, 1799–1809; Henson, 1843; Wenham, 1866).

In the meantime, France and Britain had both envisaged the elongated, powered and dirigible balloon (Meusnier, 1785; Cayley, 1809–16). Then, after a long interval, France took the lead, and brought to fulfilment the first tentative airship (Giffard, 1852), and the first near-practical airship (Renard and Krebs, 1884).

It was almost inevitable that France, with her lasting interest in aerial affairs, would also come to exploit the aeroplane products of the British 'race of shopkeepers', and to establish for some years an aeronautical ascendancy of experimentation, exploitation and panache (Du Temple, *c.* 1857; Le Bris, 1857–68, Pénaud, 1871; Tatin, 1879). It was also inevitable that the tradition of British speculative physics should again reassert itself by producing the first aeroplane model with superposed wings (Stringfellow, 1868), and by proving the superior lifting qualities – with the aerodynamic *raison d'être* – of double-surface cambered wings (Phillips, 1884, 1891).

Brave efforts to build and fly full-sized powered and piloted aeroplanes in France, Russia and Britain met with minimal success, only to the degree that, by various means, these machines were launched from the ground and into the air; but none of them could sustain themselves, and so could not fly (Du Temple, *c.* 1874; Mozhaiski, 1884; Ader, 1890; Maxim, 1894).

The all-important engines – which were later to make practical flying possible – grew from a French invention, the gas engine (Lenoir, 1866); and then took root and flourished in the atmosphere of well-patronised practicality then prevalent in the states of the German princelings, which thus saw the invention of the four-stroke petrol engine (Otto, 1876); its brilliant application to automobilisme was also brought about by Germany (Benz, 1885; Daimler, 1886).

It was the unified and emergent Germany, with her thoroughness and pertinacity, which produced the first man to mount magnificently into the air, to ride the wind on gliders, and directly to inspire the next generation of pioneers to master the craft of mechanical flight (Lilienthal, 1891–96).

Finally, the vigorous upsurge of pioneering energy, enterprise and practical experimentation, traditionally associated with the New World, made it appropriate that the ultimate triumph of achieving the practical powered aeroplane should take place in the United States of America (the Wright brothers, 1899–1908).

To bring about this practical flying machine, a number of parallel streams of endeavour and invention had to be born, to develop, and to coalesce, before the Wright brothers could apply their creative faculties to achieve a satisfactory mechanism. These streams were: (1) the science of aerodynamics; (2) the technology of structures and aeroplane configuration; (3) fuel technology; (4) engine technology; (5) airscrew design; (6) flight control.

Thus the age-old dream that human beings would fly through the air by mechanical means was ultimately brought about by citizens of the great nations of the modern world, all working towards a common end, and for the common good of humanity; for the spur of war played little part in it.

The airship finally came to fruition in the first years of the twentieth century through the efforts of a Brazilian, a German and a group of Frenchmen (Santos-Dumont, 1899 and on; von Zeppelin, 1900 and on; the designers and builders of the Lebaudy, 1902 and on).

The first type of powered aircraft in the Western world was the helicopter toy, powered by the pull of string wound on its rotor spindle; this first appeared in the fourteenth century, in Flanders. Ever since then, a continuous history of these models can be traced in Europe, with two in particular (Launoy and Bienvenu, 1784; Cayley, 1796) being much publicised, and leading direct to the development of the modern helicopter, the first of which just to take off freely and vertically under its own power, with a man on board, was Cornu's in France (1907). It was in Germany that the first successful helicopter was flown (Focke-Achgelis, 1936), aided by the influence of the helicopter's 'halfway house', the Cierva Autogiro (1923). Then an ex-patriate Russian, working in the United States, introduced the helicopter as a practical vehicle to the world (Sikorsky, 1942), since when it has taken its place as one of the most important types of flying machine in both peace and war.

The reaction propulsion of aircraft – by jets of one kind or another – was first envisaged in France (Montgolfier, 1783); the first jet aeroplane was designed in France, but not built (De Louvrié, 1865); the first rocket-propelled and piloted aeroplane was the product of Germany (Von Opel et al., 1928) which was prophetic rather than practical. Then the whole vast realm of jet propulsion, by turbo jet engines, was pioneered by Germany and Britain in the first two successful flights with such engines designed by von Ohain (1939), and Whittle (1941), the latter – because of Germany's defeat in World War II – being left to lead the world, and directly to inspire the United States.

Space travel, in the person of the artillery rocket, was born in China about AD 1100; it was first mightily employed against an adversary by Tipu Sultan's army in India (1798–99), which immediately led to the successful reinvention and exploitation of the European war rocket by Britain (Congreve, c. 1805; Hale, 1867).

Powerfully stimulated en route by French science fiction (Jules Verne, 1863 and on), the rocket remained in both the armouries and the imagination of the world – but for the most part ineffectually – until an American pioneered the use of the liquid fuel rocket, which was the direct ancestor of modern space-flight (Goddard, 1926 and on). This work was then enthusiastically taken up in Germany, whose scientists (in 1944) launched a successful long-range rocket bomb which was the immediate parent of all the space vehicles of today. It was Russia – with her interest in space flight reaching back to Ziolkowsky in the nineteenth century –who achieved the first spaceship to orbit our Earth and carry its pilot (Gagarin, 1961), and who sent the first woman into space (1963). Finally, the dream of centuries came true when American astronauts first set foot on the Moon (Armstrong and Aldrin, 1969).

The conquest of space, following the conquest of the air, has been accomplished by the greatest of the world powers; not, perhaps as a League of Nations, or as the United Nations, but as member states working in amicable rivalry one with another, each of them intent on aims and objects far beyond the confines of parochial nationalism; but here it was war that set the pace.

'Per ardua ad astra' – 'through hardship to the stars' – is a fitting motto to sum up the aspirations of brave and far-sighted men from the earliest days of civilisation to the present day – and beyond.

1 Dreams, myths and devices

The idea of human flight has engaged the waking and sleeping thoughts of men from the time when they developed visual imagination and began to regard the birds with envy. With the envy came the ambition to emulate. For flying has never appeared to its devotees as a mere method of transportation, faster or more convenient than travel by land or sea; nor was it finally achieved by any pressure of economic need. Aviation has drawn its strength from an appeal to the emotions; an appeal to the longing for escape, or to the desire for exhilaration and power. Some have simply seen it as a symbol of aspiration. Desire for rapid locomotion came later.

'O that I had wings like a dove,' wrote the Psalmist, 'for then I would fly away and be at rest.' And a modern writer speaks of when 'he closes his hands over the controls, and little by little in his bare palms he receives the gift of this power'.

In time there came prophecy to accompany desire, prophecy of achievement in both war and peace: in 1670 de Lana wrote of his proposed 'aerial ship': 'Where is the man who can fail to see that no city would be proof against surprise ... houses, fortresses, and cities could thus be destroyed, with the certainty that the aerial ship could come to no harm, as the missiles could be hurled from a great height.' And Tennyson 'dipt into the future, far as human eye could see, Saw the Vision of the world, and all the wonder that would be; Saw the heavens fill with commerce, argosies of magic sails, Pilots of the purple twilight, dropping down with costly bales'.

Realising that the prophecies were nearing fulfilment, the early pioneers were beset by more rational doubts concerning the uses that mankind might make of flying. And so both faith and hope – more technically informed – were added to prophecy, in a striving to temper the winds of Fate. In 1894 Octave Chanute was to write:

> So may it be; let us hope that the advent of a successful flying machine, now only dimly foreseen and nevertheless thought to be possible, will bring nothing but good into the world; that it shall abridge distance, make all parts of the globe accessible, bring men into closer relation with each other, advance civilisation, and hasten the promised era in which there shall be nothing but peace and good-will among all men.

Even though the dream of mechanical flight had haunted its slaves over millennia, it could not be realised until modern technology had evolved a powerful and reliable prime mover of small relative weight; and until there emerged a science of aerodynamics and structures, and a technique of pilotage. As it turned out, the foundations of aerodynamics (laid in 1799–1809) preceded the prime mover by a century, and had to mark time while a host of misguided and eccentric characters ran riot over the field of aviation in the nineteenth century, while a few wise men strove to keep it on the right lines of development. But we should now go back for a moment to the origins of flying, and also consider some remarkable aeronautical devices which man came to invent in the early epochs of his history.

Nature has not always suggested the basic tools of civilisation – *vide* the wheel, for example – but here can be no doubt that it has been the bird which has provided the chief inspiration for men to fly. Only later came the less dynamic inspiration of the clouds, whose passive flotation was to appeal to the less adventurous spirits. Hence there arose the basic division of human flight into aviation (heavier-than-air flight) with its aviators, and aerostation (lighter-than-air flight) with its aeronauts. But even the latter, after the invention of the balloon in 1783, became irked at being at the mercy of the winds, and went on to develop the 'navigable balloon', or airship. It is also interesting to note that the teeming squadrons of the insect world have never played a significant part in inspiring men to fly, probably owing to their being too small to allow of any effective rapport with human beings. Nature, of course, numbers other airmen among her creatures, the most accomplished of whom is the bat, followed by such far less talented exponents as the flying fish and flying squirrels, both of which are, however, only gliders: but none of these was important in aviation until the bat came to influence a handful of workers in the nineteenth century.

Earth – and heaven – has been peopled by aerial creatures of the imagination since the earliest days of recorded time: and the makers of myth, religion and legend often invoked the power of flight to transport their heroes, gods and holy men through the sky. Sometimes the voyages were made in cars or chariots, with or without the help of birds and other beasts; sometimes the passengers were provided with wings; and occasionally the sacred aeronauts were simply invested with the power of levitation. All such celestial activity encouraged the will to fly; and from the earliest times there was no lack of prophets who arose to forestall the conquest of the air, as well as the blessings and calamities that would attend it. Thus Egypt came to have her winged deities; Assyria her winged bulls; and Arabia her flying carpet, of mysterious origin. The Far East had not only many levitated beings and bird-gods, but flying chariots, some equipped with paddle wheels. Classical Greece and Rome produced such familiar figures as the winged god Mercury, the winged horse Pegasus, and the flying chariot of Triptolemus. Then came the angels and *putti* of Christianity, the former – through countless thousands of pictures – providing a constant stimulus to air-mindedness throughout the centuries, for cleric and layman alike.

Worth their weight in gold for the creation and maintenance of air-mindedness, were also the aerial legends that grew up in Europe. And the modern airman's legend *par excellence* is, of course, that of Daedalus and his son Icarus, which was possibly based on an early attempt at flight: Daedalus, who had constructed the Cretan labyrinth for King Minos, later incurred the King's wrath: so Daedalus made wings for them both to escape from Crete, where they were imprisoned; but he warned Icarus not to fly near the sun:

Figure 1.1 *The classic airman's myth of Daedalus and Icarus, showing Icarus crashing; from a woodcut of 1493.*

Icarus disobeyed, and the sun melted the wax which glued together his wings, causing him to crash to his death in the sea (Figure 1.1). Daedalus made a safe landing in Sicily. Almost as picturesque was the legendary journey of Alexander the Great to view the heavens by means of gryphons harnessed to his chariot, the beasts being persuaded to fly upward by meat fixed out of reach above them (Figure 1.2). There is also our own national story which tells how the legendary King Bladud of England – founder of Bath and father of King Lear – overtaxed his powers of necromancy by trying to fly over London with artificial wings, and was killed in the attempt (*c.* 852 BC).

Remaining over from the early days of civilisation, and still in use in various parts of the world, are a number of what might be called 'aeronautical devices'. First came the arrow and the boomerang, whose ages are incalculable: the arrow is, of course, only an aeronautical device by virtue of the stabilising effect of the feather(s), which are aerofoils. But the boomerang is virtually a power-launched rotating glider, and a highly remarkable aircraft at that, which returns to the man who launches it, if it misses its target: the aerodynamics of the boomerang are of considerable complexity, and it taxes the mind to imagine how such a device could have been developed by comparatively primitive tribes.

Figure 1.2 *Alexander the Great drawn through the air by gryphons; from a woodcut of 1506.*

The kite – which is really a tethered glider – is a device of great antiquity in the East, being known in China for probably a thousand years BC, and becoming known in Europe certainly by the thirteenth century[1]: it is the true ancestor of the aeroplane, and has played an important part in the history of flying. The kite was first to take part in aeroplane flight when it formed the wings of Cayley's first model glider in 1804.

How the European type of post (or tower) windmill – with its horizontal spindle and vertical sails – came into being, is still a mystery. The earliest known illustration of one is in the Windmill Psalter in the British Museum, and is dated *c.* 1290 (Figures 1.3 and 1.4); but, so far, it has no ancestors, although it must have come into use much earlier, and appears to be indigenous to Europe. For the Middle Eastern windmills, along the trade routes to China, seem always to have had vertical spindles and horizontally-set sails, half of which were boxed in so that the wind would strike only the blades on one side. This 'paddle' system would accord with the fact that paddle-wheel propulsion – and hence passive paddle-wheel rotation – were well known in China at an early date; and the principle, along with many other ideas and inventions, travelled westwards over the trade routes. But there is no trace of the transit, or arrival in Europe, of the upright type of mill, with its horizontal spindle. This familiar form of European windmill is the passive ancestor of the active aircraft airscrew; and it is interesting to note that certainly by the early fourteenth century, the passive 'airscrew' of the windmill had already become an active airscrew in the form of the string-pull toy helicopter. It was these toys – rather than the full-size windmills from which they were derived – which were the immediate ancestors of the modern aircraft airscrew – the first airborne use of which was on Blanchard's balloon of 1784 – and of the modern helicopter.

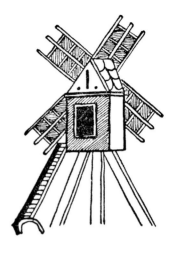

Figure 1.3 Earliest illustration of a European windmill: c. 1290.

Notes

1   As the ancient Chinese are known to have used man-lifting kites, the kite is – strictly speaking – the first man-carrying aircraft of history, but without the ability to travel from place to place.

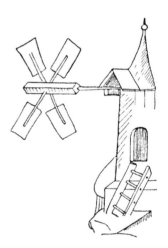

Figure 1.4 European windmill: c. 1410.

2 From classical antiquity to the end of the sixteenth century

Although classical mythology produced some intriguing figures equipped for flying, such as the winged horse Pegasus, as well as the airman's classic legend of Daedalus and Icarus, the civilisations of ancient Greece and Rome seem to have been singularly uninterested in aeronautical matters. Only the figure of Archytas of Tarentum emerges mistily about 400 BC: he is said to have made a wooden dove, which may have been propelled, when hung from a whirling arm, by a jet of steam.

There follows an astonishing interregnum of nearly 1500 years, during which time, if there were recorded events of men with wings, they do not survive, except for vague statements of an apocryphal nature.

Then emerge the historical figures of 'Abbas b. Firnas, an Arab savant who covered himself with feathers and attempted a flight in Spain, around 875; and of Eilmer,[1] a Benedictine monk who jumped off the tower of Malmesbury Abbey about 1010. He had equipped himself with wings, and is reported to have flown about 200 metres before crashing and breaking both legs: he is said to have regretted not fitting a tail surface. Then in 1162 the so-called 'Saracen of Constantinople' became famous by jumping to his death from a tower: he wore a voluminous cloak with stiffening battens forming sail-like wings. In all probability, there were many of these brave but foolhardy 'tower jumpers' who lived and died, and whose names have slowly faded out of history: they at least had the courage of their conviction that men must one day fly (Figure 2.1).

Aeronautical speculation – both on lighter- and heavier-than-air flying – was indulged in by a Franciscan monk, Roger Bacon (1214–92), whose work *De mirabili potestate artis et naturae* (written *c*. 1250, but first printed in Paris in 1542) contains references to hollow globes of copper filled with 'aetherial air', which would float in the atmosphere; and a flying machine in which a man would sit and propel himself by turning a mechanism of some kind: but such vague speculations must have been made by many a learned monk over the centuries but not written down; or having been committed to paper, were destroyed or lost to view, as indeed Roger Bacon's were lost for some centuries.

Then, at the end of the thirteenth century there suddenly appears, as already stated, the familiar form of the windmill with a horizontal spindle, which seems to spring into Europe fully developed, without origins or antecedents (Figures 1.3 and 1.4), but it must have been in use long before this illustration was made.

In 1326–27, there was produced a remarkable illuminated manuscript by Walter de Milemete (*De nobilitatibus, sapientiis et prudentiis regum*), now in the library of Christ Church, Oxford, which

Figure 2.1 Modern illustration of one of the 'tower jumpers' of early history.

Figure 2.2 First illustration in the Western world of an aircraft (a kite), and a bomb: 1326–27.

contains an unfinished drawing of what might fairly be called the first true aircraft in the Western world (Figure 2.2); it is a kite being flown over a beleaguered city, with a finned bomb hanging from it. The kite is the first known illustration of a type which grew increasingly familiar in Europe during the fourteenth and fifteenth centuries. It has a large, rigid, plane-surface head made of parchment, and a long, flexible cloth tail. Detailed instructions about how to build and fly one are found in a manuscript in Vienna, dated about 1430. Whether such kites were ever built large enough to carry a bomb in battle is perhaps doubtful but, if so, three knights (as shown in the illustration) could well have been needed to control them.

The earliest printed illustration of a kite of the familiar diamond type (imported from the East Indies) appears in a Dutch book of 1618.

The first illustration of a helicopter toy appeared in the first quarter of the fourteenth century – say c. 1320–30 in a Flemish psalter now at Copenhagen (see figure on page 7), with its four-bladed rotor derived from windmill sails: this type of little model, of which the most sophisticated of the early examples is that at Le Mans came to be called by the French, 'moulinet à noix' ('noix' referring to the pulley-wheel of a spindle): it is the earliest form of the active airscrew, and the direct ancestor of every helicopter flying today. The simpler toy, with an 'air-screw' solely rotated by the wind, was called a 'moulinet à vent' (see Figure 2.3), and possibly dates back as early as the helicopter toy. Both were probably invented in the twelfth century, soon after the introduction of the classic tower type of windmill in Europe. Apart from the kite and the doll, these toys must have the longest continuous history of any plaything in history.

Then, about 1420, we find in the well-known manuscript of the engineer Giovanni da Fontana, in the Staatsbibliothek at Munich (Cod. iconogr. 242) an illustration of the first rocket 'aeroplane'; it is a model bird with outstretched wings, and the efflux emerging from the tail (Figure 2.4): hereafter winged rockets appear at intervals.

Figure 2.3 Early representation of a simple airscrew toy ('moulinet à vent'): c. 1485.

The early history of the rocket is still somewhat unclear, although it is generally believed that it originated in China and reached Europe via the Mongols and Arabs. (See Chapter 2 of *History of Rocketry and Space Travel*, W von Braun and Frederick I Ordway, 1966.)

It is impossible to judge what it was that Regiomontanus (Johann Müller) made between about 1460–75; but it was described alternatively as an artificial eagle or as an 'iron fly'; it was probably a small model of some kind, and might easily have been a glider-model built by trial and error. There were probably a number of such models made through the years which remain unrecorded.

In 1496, an old cantor of Nuremberg broke an arm in trying to fly.

In 1498 – after some previous attempts – the Italian mathematician, G B Danti, who had attached wings to his arms, was seriously injured when he made a tower jump at Perugia. A few years later, in 1507, the Italian 'emigrant' John Damian, Abbot of Tungland, tried to fly with wings from the walls of Stirling Castle in Scotland; the record states that he 'fell to the ground and brak his thee bane', at which we would count him lucky.

Now – in the midst of the Italian Renaissance – there had just arisen the greatest all-round genius of history, to whom flying was a major obsession.

Leonardo da Vinci (1452–1519) provides an absorbing chapter in aeronautical history. He was the first man of high scientific attainments to investigate the problems of flight, and although a few of his aeronautical notes and drawings may have been lost, the bulk seem to have survived and it is fairly clear where his ambitions and achievements lay. Most of his work dealt with flapping-wing aircraft (ornithopters), based on bird and bat flight; and his concern with the human imitation of birds amounted to 'the most obsessing, most tyrannical of his dreams', in the words of one biographer. As a result of his emotional, rather than rational, approach to flying he did not on the whole subject it to the disciplined scrutiny he applied to other of his scientific activities. Perhaps it was the symbolic urge to escape and to conquer the air which led him to cling so tenaciously to the ornithopter idea, and neglect the idea of the fixed wing glider in all but a few of his later drawings. His obsession with the ornithopter was peculiarly fruitless owing to two factors: (a) his belief that the wings of such an aircraft 'have to row downwards and backwards ... write of swimming in the water (he says) and you will have the flight of the bird through the air'; and (b) that human muscles could properly power a machine. A bird cannot beat its wings backwards. The tradition that Leonardo launched a full-size ornithopter is without foundation, because any flight test based on downward and backward wing movements would have immediately wrecked the machine, with serious results for its pilot. As for human muscle as a power plant, Leonardo – if he had not been subject to his overpowering ornithopter obsession – could easily have arrived at the conclusion that a man's muscles could never have propelled even the lightest of his suggested machines, let alone the huge and cumbersome contraptions his fancy

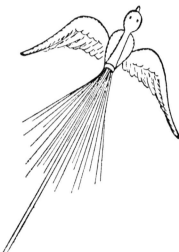

Figure 2.4 First illustration in history (by Fontana) of a rocket-propelled 'aeroplane' (i.e. a model bird): c. 1420.

ultimately drove him to; only today, with the ultra-light materials now available, has it become possible to make the briefest of man-powered flights. Leonardo designed various prone-position types of ornithopter and a standing-position type, most of them to be powered by combined arm and leg movements via machinery of fascinating but misplaced ingenuity. But there were times when his acute mind seems to have tired of its emotional tyrant, and he has left sketches of two aircraft types which show a completely different approach. One is an ornithopter powered by a bow-string mechanism (to be rewound by the pilot when in flight); the other has the outer wing-panels flapping down at a greater angle than the inner – a device which under modern conditions, and with the knowledge of how a bird is propelled, might be successful. Leonardo also designed some prophetic aeronautical instruments and devices,[2] including a flap-valve system of wing construction for ornithopters, a head-harness working an elevator (which anticipated Lilienthal's body harness), a retractable undercarriage, and various finned projectiles. Until the discovery of medieval helicopter models, the helicopter was thought to have been the invention of Leonardo, whose machine was a helical screw operated probably by clockwork. But he did invent the parachute – in the form of a pyramidal tent – with a pole from the apex to the jointure of the shroud lines (Figure 2.5). Both Leonardo's helicopter and parachute were recorded as almost thumbnail sketches, and unfortunately he did not return to them. There was then a device, of which Leonardo may have been the inventor, for turning a roasting spit, which consisted of a properly bladed propeller on a shaft, rotated by hot air rising from the fire. If he had envisaged the blades being turned by a prime mover and displacing air, instead of the air turning the blades, he would have pioneered the proper airscrew. Leonardo also made studies of the air and its forces, which included investigations concerning the centres of gravity and pressure; and he understood the principles of streamlining, but only seems to have applied them to bodies moving in water. Curiously enough, it was after the main force of his ideas on the ornithopter were spent that he wrote his remarkable book on bird flight, *Sul Volo degli Uccelli* (1505), without, however, solving the problem of bird propulsion. Finally, late in life, he made some thumbnail sketches of a man clinging to a flat board which is seen in gliding descent like a falling leaf, a concept which might have led to vital changes in his outlook and to a mature concept of the glider. It is such glimpses of his mind working unhampered on the problems of flight that cause posterity to regret that he did not concentrate on the fixed-wing glider, a type of aircraft of which he might well have been the pioneer (Figure 2.6).

Leonardo's remarkable work in aeronautics deserved to play a major role in the centuries of experimentation that followed; but owing to the culpable stupidity of his executor Francesco Melzi, it had no direct influence on the history of flying, and was not even known to the world until the last quarter of the nineteenth century, more than 100 years after the rediscovery of the parachute and the

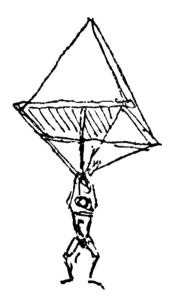

Figure 2.5 First design for a parachute, by Leonardo da Vinci: c. 1485.

Figure 2.6 Standing-type ornithopter, designed by Leonardo da Vinci: c. 1485–1500. (Science & Society Picture Library)

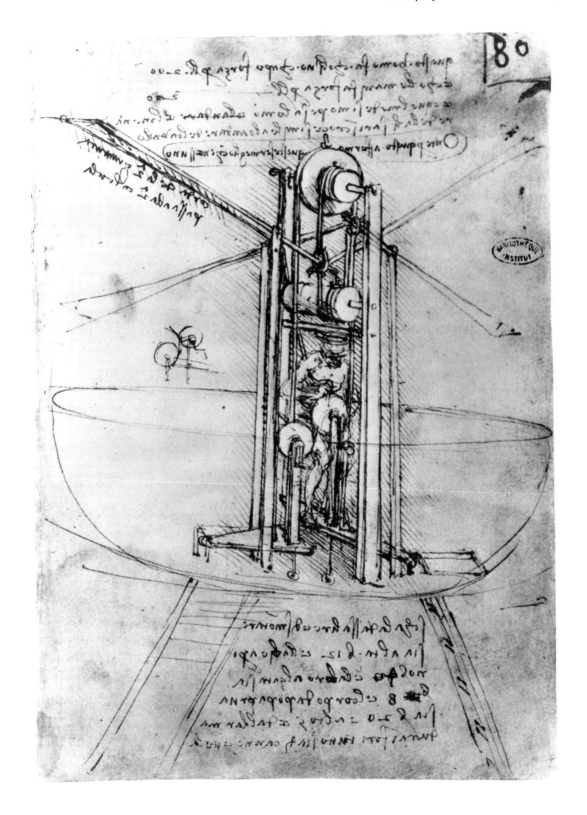

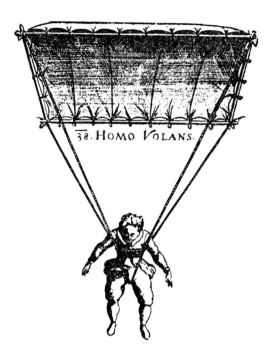

Figure 2.7 Design for a sail-derived parachute by Veranzio: c. 1595.

helicopter, and when aerodynamics was already an advanced study. If his researches had been published sooner – as he wished them to be – his achievements and mistakes would have spurred on others to experiment, correct, and develop, and his genius would have provided a powerful inspiration throughout the centuries.

With the death of Leonardo in 1519 there follows nearly a century's pause in serious aeronautical thinking.

In 1536 an Italian clock-maker, Bolori, was killed when attempting to fly from the Cathedral of Troyes in France.

About the year 1595 there was published in Venice a work entitled *Machinae novae* by Fausto Veranzio, in which he described and illustrated a 'homo volans', which provided the first published illustration of a parachute in history (Figure 2.7): unlike Leonardo's device, Veranzio's was clearly derived from a ship's sail, and it is interesting to note that the most obvious ancestors of the parachute – the sunshade or umbrella – took no part in either of the first two parachute designs to appear in the west, although they were directly to inspire the first viable parachutes which were to appear in the eighteenth century.

Notes

1 Owing to a mis-reading of the manuscript, Eilmer appears in earlier histories as Oliver of Malmesbury. Similarly, 'Abbas b. Firnas appears as Armen Firman in earlier books.
2 Tradition also credits Leonardo with the invention of the hot-air balloon, but this is not true. See my *Leonardo da Vinci's Aeronautics*.

3 The seventeenth century

Figure 3.1 European plane-surface kite, from Bate's Mysteryes of Nature and Art: *1634.*

Before describing the chief contributors to aeronautics during this century, there is a small but important item to note in 1618, when there occurs the first illustration – in a Dutch engraving – of what we have come to think of as a standard type of diamond-shaped kite, complete with tail.[1]

This enlightened century produced some interesting figures in the world of 'flying'. In 1638 two books were published in England, both works on the moon, by Francis Godwin, Bishop of Hereford (1562–1633), and by another bishop, John Wilkins, Bishop of Chester (1614–72), a founder member of the Royal Society. Godwin's book, published posthumously in 1638, was Man in the Moone, and told the story of the hero Gonsales who trained wild swans – tied to a framework – to transport him to the moon. Wilkins' work, Discovery of a New World, first published anonymously in 1638, was a speculation on the moon being inhabited. This was followed in 1640 by his Discourse concerning Flying, and in 1648 by Mathematical Magick: the former dealt with aerostation and the latter with various means of flying, i.e. with the spirits of angels, with the help of fowls, with wings fastened to the body, and with a flying chariot. These were the speculations of a shrewd man, but were not significant in history.

One of the few records of an actual model aircraft being built, concerns Tito Livio Burattini (born in Agordo, 1617), who settled in Poland about 1644. In 1647 he is said to have made working models of a flying machine, with four pairs of wings in tandem (the two middle pairs for lifting, the bow pair for propulsion, and the stern pair for propulsion and lift) with a tail unit for control: this is said to have been worked by springs, and to have raised a cat. Burattini is said also to have made a full-size version of this machine in 1648, but the account is probably untrue.

The most interesting figure in the seventeenth century, aeronautically speaking, was the great English scientist Robert Hooke (1635–1703) who, independently of Borelli, came to the conclusion that human muscles are not strong enough to provide the power for flying, and that an engine was essential. He appears to have made an ornithopter model operated by some spring device in 1655 which, as he said 'rais'd and sustain'd itself in the Air': this form of words probably, at the time, referred to travel through the air, and not helicopter flight. He then appears to have worked out designs for a man carrier. This is by far the most tantalising of 'cases', and one wonders if some sketch – as yet unrecognised – may not survive among his papers.

The German mechanic Johann Hautsch of Nuremburg, who is known mainly for his manumotive road carriage and his contribution to fire-fighting machinery, is also credited with building a flying carriage about 1660, but no details of this device are known. In 1673,

Figure 3.2 European winged dragon-form kite: 1665.

one Charles Bernouin, a surgeon from Grenoble, is said to have flown from a tower at Regensburg in Germany using sail-like wings and rocket assistance, but to have then broken his neck flying at Frankfurt-on-Main.

Reports of attempted flights by tower jumpers occur quite regularly during the century. Among the less successful were the Italian painter Guidotti who fell through a roof at Lucca around 1600, and the anonymous Russian peasant who was severely beaten for failing to fly in 1680. On the other hand, Ahmed Hezârfen is celebrated in Turkey for a claimed flight of several kilometres to a successful landing in the marketplace at Scutari around the mid-century.

A small item of light relief occurs during this period in the Marquess of Worcester's *Century of Inventions* (1663) where, under invention number 77, one reads: 'How to make a man fly; which I have tried with a little Boy of ten years old in a Barn, from one end to the other, on a Haymow'.

Among the most constantly reproduced pictures in aviation history is that of the French locksmith Besnier (Figure 3.3), who attempted to fly at Sablé in 1678 with an apparatus working on a similar principle to that of the waterbird's webbed feet. He is said to have made many careful experiments, and finally soared over a house and landed safely; this probably means he descended from the roof of the house. The apparatus he used must clearly have been more sophisticated and many times larger than that shown, which is a concept similar to that of the flap valve. It would just be possible for a man to make a floundering glide without coming to grief, if the 'machine' parachuted him down, which would seem to be the explanation of those survivals and maimings with which fortune favoured a few.

In this connection it should be recorded that Francis Willughby, who died in 1672, unwittingly helped to perpetuate the idea of the man-powered ornithopter when, in his posthumously published *Ornithologiae libri tres* (1676), he said that it was a man's legs which

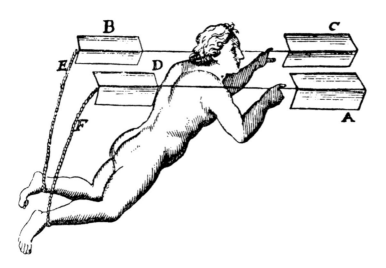

Figure 3.3 Fanciful representation of Besnier attempting to fly at Sablé: 1678.

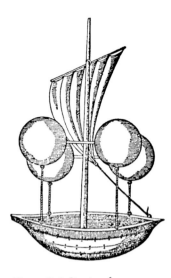

Figure 3.4 Design for an aerial ship, by de Lana: 1670.

were comparable in strength to a bird's wings, and not his arms; therefore the human makers of wings must harness leg power to them.

The man who did most to discourage the 'tower jumpers', and other experimenters with man-powered wings, was Giovanni Alphonso Borelli (1606–79), professor of mathematics at Messina, and later at Pisa. His *De motu animalium* was published posthumously at Rome in 1680, and became a major milestone in history; for in this work, Borelli proved that the musculature for a man – as compared with a bird – was inadequate for lifting himself and his apparatus, and flying. Today, with the ultra-light materials available, and the advanced knowledge of aerodynamics, man-powered flight is just physically possible; but up to a few years ago, it certainly was not; and Borelli's cold water on such schemes was badly needed. 'It is impossible', he wrote, 'that men should be able to fly craftily, by their own strength.'

In 1657–59, a Jesuit named Gaspar Schott published his *Magia universalis naturae et artis*, in which he went over the ground of speculation on aerostation, but did not contribute anything to ideas on aviation. Much more important was another book concerned with aerostation by the Jesuit Father Francesco de Lana de Terzi published in Brescia in 1670. This work – *Prodromo overo saggio* (etc.) – contained de Lana's design for, and description of, his aerial ship; this consisted of a vessel supported by four copper spheres which were to be emptied of all air, and hence rise: but de Lana did not appreciate that these spheres would be collapsed by atmospheric pressure (Figure 3.4). His descriptions of aerial bombing, and airborne invasion, by his ship, are among the classic anticipations of modern warfare.

In 1650 there had appeared the first edition of Cyrano de Bergerac's *Histoire comique, on Voyage dans la Lune*, with the first English translation appearing in 1659: Cyrano is of interest in that his fantasy methods of travel to the moon were ingeniously conceived. One of these methods was to strap round himself bottles of dew, which the sun would soak up, and take him up too: another was an inadvertent voyage in his aerial car after soldiers had fixed fireworks – presumably rockets – to it, and sent it up into space.

Notes

1   The first to be found in Britain is in *Bate's Mysteryes of Nature and Art* (1635), shown in Figure 3.1. The fully-developed winged wind-sock type of dragon-kite is shown in Figure 3.2, which was published as late as 1665.

4 The eighteenth century

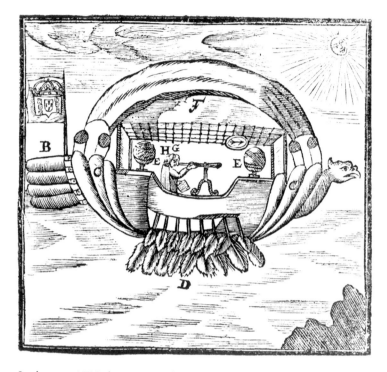

Figure 4.1 *The well-known and much-ridiculed illustration of Gusmão's* Passarola: *1709.*

In the year 1709 there occurred a somewhat mysterious event. One of the best known of aeronautical engravings shows an apparently ridiculous contraption called the *Passarola* (Great Bird), which until recently has been treated as pure fantasy. But the evidence now suggests that some well-meaning artist drew from hearsay an actual aircraft – a small model glider in the form of a bird. It was made by a Brazilian, Father Laurenço de Gusmão (1686–1724) and launched at Lisbon, perhaps achieving a tentative flight (Figures 4.1 and 4.2). He seems first to have constructed an inevitably earthbound full-size aircraft, and then made the model to rescue his reputation: its most interesting feature was an upper hood, or 'parachute' cover, a device to give more lift, which rested on a frame when the machine was not flying, and would immediately have the wind catch it from the underneath when flight commenced. A similar device was to be

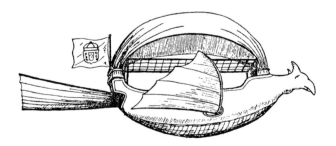

Figure 4.2 *Reconstruction by the present writer of how the* Passarola *probably appeared.*

employed by Trouvé in 1870. Gusmão also seems certain to have achieved a primitive model hot-air balloon.

In northern Europe, the Swedish mystic Emmanuel Swedenborg somewhat surprisingly suggested an aeroplane design in 1714 (it was published in *Daedalus Hyperboreas* in 1716), which consisted of a car fixed below a huge wing-canopy, which could be reefed like a sail, and propelled by flappers made on the duck's webbed-foot principle, and worked by 'a spiral spring'. There was to be a pendulum device projecting below the craft to give it automatic stability, and a sort of beetle-like shield above the wings, for no very good reason. Coming from a man of such eminence, this idea is interesting, but is – except for the pendulum stability – without much merit historically.

Despite the teachings of Borelli, the 'tower jumpers' still flourished, and perhaps the most famous of them all was the Marquis de Bacqueville, who attempted, about 1742, to fly the River Seine in Paris, with wings fixed to his arms and legs: he seems to have taken off from a riverside house and to have floundered down on to a washerwoman's barge, breaking his legs. The 'paddles' shown in the illustration are clearly some simplification, and are on far too small a scale, of the equipment used for this foolhardy but brave attempt at flight. The belief that a certain John Childs tried to fly in England, and then from a tower at Boston (USA) in 1757, is now known to be untrue, and was based on a misinterpretation of early records.

The kite first came into its own as a vehicle for scientific research – a role it was thereafter to fulfil for more than 150 years – in the year 1749 when the Professor of Astronomy at Glasgow University, Alexander Wilson, measured the temperature of clouds at about 3000 feet by means of a thermometer attached to a train of four or five paper kites; Wilson also seems to have antedated both Franklin and Jacques de Romas in the utilisation of kites for the study of atmospheric electricity. It was in 1752 that Benjamin Franklin made his celebrated experiment with a kite in a thunderstorm, in which he was nearly killed by the current.

The model helicopter – in use certainly since the fourteenth century as a toy – has recently been claimed by the Russian authorities to have been revived in 1754 with a twin contra-rotating rotor model operated by clockwork, made by the well-known scientist Michael Vasilyevitch Lomonosov, which is said to have flown successfully: but we have no documents. In 1768 the French mathematician, A J P Paucton, in his *Théorie de la Vis Archimède*, suggested a man-carrying and man-powered helicopter with two helical screws (*ptérophores*), one to sustain it and the other to propel it: it was never built. But, oddly enough, this must rank as the first specific suggestion for horizontal aerial propulsion by an airscrew.

There was discovered in 1921 in the Staatsarchiv of Thuringia, at Greiz, a collection of remarkable diagrams, giving the detailed design for an aeroplane, by Melchior Bauer, and drawn in 1764: it was to consist of a four-wheeled car for the pilot, fixed by struts to a large braced and dihedrally set low-aspect-ratio wing above it, and

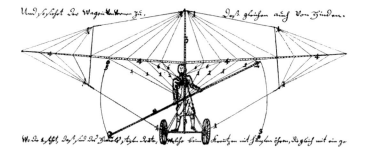

Figure 4.3 Design for a fixed-wing aeroplane, with flap-valve rocker for propulsion, by Bauer: 1764.

manually propelled from the car by means of a rocking system of flappers hinged on to a single large frame extending on both sides of the machine; this was to be rocked, so that when the port side of the frame was rising (with its flaps down), the starboard side was descending, with its flaps up, thus producing a rearward thrust (Figure 4.3). It is not impossible that Bauer had read, or heard of, the account of Swedenborg's machine.

In 1772, a Canon Desforges, of Étampes, built and tested – inevitably without success – a wickerwork 'voiture volante', which

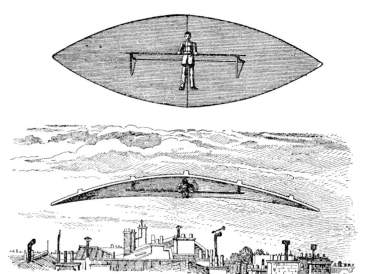

Figure 4.4 Meerwein's glider-cum-ornithopter: 1781.

was equipped with manually operated wings both for sustentation and propulsion, and topped by a huge canopy of fabric to help support it in the air. He had himself launched from the Tour Guinette at Étampes, and luckily suffered only minor injuries.

There was one outstanding pioneer of the pre-balloon era in the person of Karl Friedrich Meerwein, architect to the Prince of Baden, who in 1781 experimented with what one may call a glider-ornithopter (Figure 4.4), which he described in his pamphlet *L'Art de voler à la Manière des Oiseaux* (1784). Meerwein calculated that 126 square feet of wing surface would support him, and he apparently made one or two short glides – probably combined with

Figure 4.5 Engraving of Jean-Pierre Blanchard by J Newton, after an original work by R Livesay of Blanchard: 1785. (Science & Society Picture Library)

flapping – which, in the absence of any tail or other auxiliary surfaces, would have been only tentative in the extreme, but highly creditable. Meerwein lay prone beneath the wings of his machine, and could bring about some up-and-down movements of the wings by means of a mechanism which was only briefly specified.

Jean-Pierre Blanchard (Figure 4.5) was to become of great importance in aerostation, but his first appearance in 1781 was as builder of an amphibious 'vaisseau volant', which looked like a huge tented houseboat, and was equipped with large manually operated flappers on rods, and a huge rear rudder: needless to say, it stayed firmly on the ground in 1782 (and later) when it was tested. In the same year Blanchard made a creditable full-size manually operated helicopter, which although ingenious, also remained earthbound.

The works of aerial fiction and satire which appeared in the eighteenth century were widely read, and they too played their part in encouraging airmindedness. Joseph Addison wrote of flying in the *Guardian* (1713), Swift in *Gulliver's Travels* (1726), Samuel Brunt in *A Voyage to Cacklogallinia* (1727), R O Cambridge in *Scribleriad*

(1751), Robert Paltock in *The Life and Adventures of Peter Wilkins* (1751), Ralph Morris in *The Adventures of John Daniel* (1751), Doctor Johnson in *The Rambler* (1752) and *Rasselas* (1759), *La Follie in Le Philosophe sans Prétention* (1775), Hildebrand Bowman in *Travels* (1778), and Restif de la Bretonne in *La Découverte Australe* (1781). These and many others dealt with a variety of flying men, women, and machines, providing excellent reading and sometimes shrewd prophecy. Of particular interest was Restif's work, whose illustrations show winged men with what seem like parachutes above their heads, which are in fact auxiliary wings, which could be opened and closed at will; and the winged males and females (Glums and Gawries) whose expert flying is described by Paltock (Figure 4.6).

The invention of the practical balloon in 1783 was to have a profound effect on aviation, both as direct incentive and rival method of aerial navigation, and as a testing ground for various aeronautical devices such as the propeller and the parachute. Balloon flying also led to the consideration and application of aero engines to transform the

Figure 4.6 Flying Gawry, from Paltock's Peter Wilkins: *1751.*

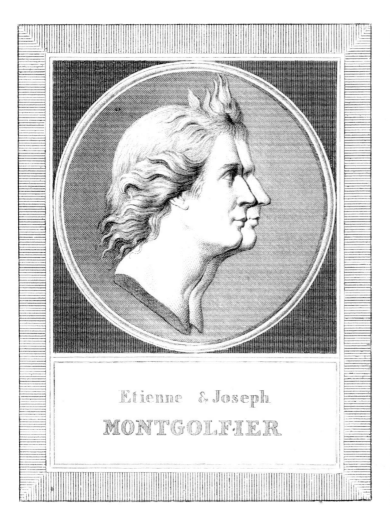

Etienne & Joseph
MONTGOLFIER

Figure 4.7 Jacques-Etienne and Joseph-Michel Montgolfier. Engraving by Robert Delaunay taken from a bas-relief by Jean Antoine Houdon in 1783. (Science & Society Picture Library)

Figure 4.8 An ascent by a Montgolfier balloon carrying a sheep, a duck and a cock at the Palace of Versailles in September 1783, depicted in an engraved plate by John Lodge for the European Magazine: *1783. (Science & Society Picture Library)*

Jn.ᵉ Lodge sc.

'sphericals' of different kinds into dirigibles; and to the building up of a wide-ranging personnel accustomed to travelling through the air.

In 1766, Henry Cavendish isolated hydrogen for the first time; described it as an element; and produced it in a sizeable quantity. He was followed by Joseph Black and Tiberius Cavallo (in England) who respectively suggested and carried out experiments to show the lifting power of hydrogen, the latter with hydrogen-filled soap bubbles. Then, working along totally different lines, the brothers Étienne and Joseph Montgolfier (Figures 4.7 and 4.8), paper-makers of Annonay, near Lyons, hit on the lifting power of hot air, without knowing why it lifted, and – after private experiments – made the first public demonstration with a small hot-air balloon of 11-metre diameter in the market place at Annonay on 5 June 1783. When news of this ascent reached Paris, it was decided there to improve on the Montgolfiers' efforts – the Parisian scientists also did not know what had raised the Montgolfier balloon – and the result was that J A C Charles decided to use hydrogen for his balloon. First off for an aerial journey with men on board, however, was a Montgolfiere on 21 November 1783, at Paris (Figure 4.9); then soon after, also at Paris, the first man-carrying hydrogen balloon set off on 1 December 1783; and ballooning was thus launched into the world. And so, after centuries of imaginative striving and speculation by the flappers, it was the floaters who first took to the air by courtesy of a 'cloud enclosed in a bag'. Man at last could be airborne at will.

In 1784, within a year of the first balloon ascents, the airscrew was revived for the helicopter model, and also first applied to forward propulsion. The model demonstrated on 28 April, in Paris by Launoy and Bienvenu consisted of two two-blade fabric rotors contra-rotating on the ends of a short pole, worked by a wound bow-drill mechanism (Figure 4.10): it was this model which – through Cayley's copy of it in 1796 – led direct to all subsequent helicopter development. Meanwhile, following the attempt by Vallet to propel a river boat with an airscrew in 1784, the indefatigable Blanchard had fitted a small six-bladed airscrew to the car of the balloon in which he took up the Royal Academy's Doctor John Sheldon on 16 October 1784 from Chelsea (London): he called it a 'moulinet', or little windmill, and rotated it ineffectually by hand; but nevertheless, this was the first application of the airscrew to a full-size man-carrying aircraft (Figure 4.11). Next year (1785) saw General Meusnier's prophetic design for an airship, to be manually driven by three huge airscrews, but never built.

Last among the pioneers of heavier-than-air flight at this time were such men as A -J Renaux, who designed[1] an ornithopter in 1784; Gérard, who in the same year designed a similarly futile 'flapper', but realised that an engine would be essential (he is wrongly credited with the proposal to apply rocket propulsion); and a certain Monsieur Ariès who was reported to have flown – meaning glided – at Embrun, also in 1784. It is not impossible that Ariès and others, equipped with rigid wings, or stiff-ribbed cloaks, succeeded in making some short floundering 'parachute' glides. The 'tower jumpers' and visionaries, no matter how misguided they may now seem, all played their part in sustaining the tradition, and furthering the cause, of flight.[2]

Figure 4.9 Model of the Montgolfier hot-air balloon: 1783. (Science & Society Picture Library)

It was Jean-Pierre Blanchard (1753–1809) who pioneered the use of the parachute from balloons when he started, in 1785, the questionable practice of sending down animals on small parachutes to entertain the crowds. But it was Jacques Garnerin (1770–1825) who on 22 October 1797, made the first human descent: using a large ribbed parasol-like canopy, he ascended at Paris under a balloon, and released himself over what is today the Parc Monceau at a height of about 3000 feet. The parachute, which was taken up closed, opened out as designed, and the descent was a great success (Figure 4.12). Dollfus describes this act of deliberate experimentation as 'un des grands actes d'héroisme de l'histoire humaine'; and it was praised in similar terms by Wilbur Wright. 'Cette modeste coupole d'étoffe' has since saved more than 200,000 human lives. Parachute drops thereafter became a standard showman's act throughout the nineteenth century, the parachute often being taken up by hot-air balloons, a cheap operation in which the balloon was quickly recovered when its air had cooled.

It is interesting to note that the idea of jet propulsion – reaction propulsion – entered aeronautics within a week or two of the first balloon ascents in 1783; aptly enough, the first suggestion came

Figure 4.10 Contra-rotating model helicopter by Launoy and Bienvenu (modern reconstruction): 1784.

Figure 4.11 First use of an airscrew (it actually had six blades) on a full-size aircraft, by Blanchard, on his balloon: 1784. (Science & Society Picture Library)

Figure 4.12 First human parachute descent from the air, by Garnerin: 1797.

from Joseph Montgolfier himself, in a 'mémoire' delivered to the Academy of Lyon in October 1783, in which he said: 'We have sought power in the same fire which serves to keep the vessel aloft. The first which presented itself to our imagination is the power of reaction (la puissance de réaction), which can be applied without any mechanism, and without expense:' he went on: 'it consists solely in one or more opening in the vessel on the side opposite to that in which one wishes to be conveyed.' This is the first technical statement in history on the subject of the jet propulsion of aircraft.

The first balloon with this Montgolfier system of propulsion – which, of course, would be totally ineffective owing to the lack of pressure – was the huge Montgolfier balloon built by Father Miolan and M. Janinet (Figure 4.13) in 1784, which was destroyed by the unruly crowd on 11 July 1784, when it failed to ascend from the Luxembourg Gardens at Paris.

There were a number of other suggestions for 'jet' propelling balloons – by rockets, compressed air, etc. – made during the years before the outbreak of the French Revolution in 1789 as well as an increasing number thereafter.

No further events of importance took place before France was engulfed in her Revolution of 1789. What may be called the 'pre-history' of aviation had now ended. With the more peaceful Industrial Revolution in Britain rapidly bringing forth new ideas, new techniques, and new men, it might have been supposed that a new spirit would infuse the whole tradition of flying experiments; but with

Figure 4.13 Caricature showing an accident (presumably a fire) in July 1784 involving a balloon made by Miolan and Janinet. (Science & Society Picture Library)

the exception of one great man – Sir George Cayley, who was to stand almost alone for half a century – this was not so.

Due perhaps to the universal unrest of that time, with major wars being fought the world over, the only novel innovation in aeronautics, apart from the parachute, was to be found in the first use of balloons for military observation by the French army at Maubeuge in 1794. It is also of interest to note that in some fantasy projects of the Napoleonic era, of which engravings survive, not only are balloons shown as troop transports for the invasion of England, but kites are seen being flown by the English, each manned by a soldier with a gun – a curious prevision of Fighter Command.

Before closing this section, one other device must be mentioned as being in full-scale use in the Orient, ready – as it were – to invade Europe and so lead in direct evolution towards the conquest of space. The war rocket had been introduced into India from China, and at the end of the century was a major weapon in the hands of Tipu Sultan's troops who were fighting Wellington's army in Mysore. Although the pyrotechnic rocket had been in constant use throughout Europe for generations, and war rockets had been used sporadically on the Continent, it was reports of Tipu's military rockets which caused Sir William Congreve to start his experiments and about 1805 to produce the first modern rocket missile.

Although in no way concerned with flying, there was of course much basic scientific research carried out in the eighteenth century which was later to prove important to aviation. One sphere, of particular applicability, comprised the studies in aerodynamics in the service of ballistics and windmills made by various investigators.

Notes

1 The words 'designed', 'suggested' or 'proposed', without mention of a model or full-sized machine being built, imply that only drawings and/or descriptions were produced.

2 An engraving of 1784, which shows men descending from a balloon, each wearing a 'habit aerostatique' – a kind of parachute cloak – along with manual paddles, is credited to Thibault de Saint-André; but this 'event' did not take place.

5 Cayley, and the first half of the nineteenth century

'The true inventor of the aeroplane and one of the most powerful geniuses in the history of aviation' are the words used by a modern French authority, Charles Dollfus, to describe Sir George Cayley (1773–1857), a scholarly Yorkshire baronet who until recently was comparatively unknown to historians of applied science. This curious state of affairs has now been righted by the researches of the late J E Hodgson, of Dollfus, of Captain J L Pritchard, and of the present writer, who have secured universal agreement in regarding Cayley as the basic originator of the modern aeroplane.

Cayley, who lived and did most of his research work at Brompton Hall, near Scarborough, first had his aeronautical imagination fired by the invention of the balloon in 1783 – when he was ten – and his active concern with flying lasted until he died in 1857. In the year 1796 he made a helicopter model on the lines of that invented by Launoy and Bienvenu – without knowing its origin – a device he later modified and improved, and which received wide publicity from the time Cayley published it in 1809; it led directly to the whole of subsequent helicopter development (Figure 5.1). Within a few years, with no previous workers to guide him or suggest the lines of approach, he arrived at a correct and mature conception of the modern aeroplane, and so laid the secure foundations upon which all subsequent developments in aviation have been built. He had, of course, paid careful attention to the work of Robins and Smeaton with whirling arms (eighteenth century) who pioneered the study of air resistance in relation to ballistics and windmills; but none of these investigators ever conceived the application of their researches to aircraft. It was typical of Cayley's genius that, with the central idea of flight in mind, he sought data in whatever fields he saw were relevant, and applied them to his own problems: thus in 1804 he turned to the whirling arm – first used by Robins in 1746 – and obtained valuable results which he applied to aircraft wings. Cayley first formulated the basic problem of mechanical flight in these words: 'to make a surface support a given weight by the application of power to the resistance of air'. On a silver disc (Figure 5.2) now preserved in the Science Museum, and dated 1799, is an engraved diagram showing the forces of lift, drag and thrust. The disc also bears, on the other side, an initialled sketch of a fixed-wing glider, with the wing shown in sharp perspective, and the fuselage below in which the pilot is seen sitting: the machine is fitted with a tail-unit comprising vertical and horizontal control surfaces, and a pair of manually operated flappers in lieu of an airscrew. We have here, in the last year of the eighteenth century, the aeroplane of today in embryo: it marks the start of a new epoch and the true beginnings of practical aviation. In the same year Cayley made a general arrangement drawing of his machine (Figure 5.3).

Figure 5.1 Cayley's version of the 1784 Launoy and Bienvenu helicopter model: 1796.

Figure 5.2 Silver disc engraved by Cayley with sketch for his fixed-wing aeroplane.

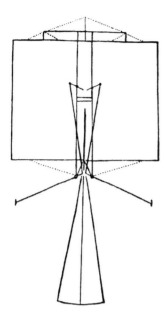

Figure 5.3 Cayley's drawing of his fixed-wing design, the first modern-configuration aeroplane in history: 1799.

In 1804, after this remarkable man had realised the true aerodynamic significance of the kite, he made the first proper and successful aeroplane of history. It was a five-foot-long model glider with a kite-form main plane set on a pole at a 6 degree angle of incidence, a tail unit attached by a universal joint – to act as a combined rudder and elevator control – and a movable weight to adjust the centre of gravity (Figure 5.4). In 1809 he constructed a full-sized glider with a wing area of 200 square feet which was flown successfully, unmanned, as well as being tested carrying a boy for a few yards at a time.

It was in 1809–10 that Cayley published his triple paper 'On Aerial Navigation', in *Nicholson's Journal*, a paper which laid the foundations of aerodynamics and flight control, upon which the whole vast science of flying is founded. He was precipitated into publishing this epoch-making work by hearing – and believing – in 1809 that Jacob Degen had flown unaided by muscle-power, which, of course, he had not.

In 1843 Cayley published a design for a highly ingenious convertiplane, which seems to be directly inspired by the drawings of a young man named Robert Taylor, Cayley never acknowledging his debt to Taylor – the only dishonest act of his long life: incidentally, Cayley turned Taylor's monoplane convertiplane into a biplane, and thus created the first biplane design in history, and the first twin-airscrew design.

After constructing further models, he returned in later life to achieve full-size triplane gliders; the first, in 1849, was flown free in ballast, and also tentatively flown (including being towed) with a boy aboard; the second in 1853, when his reluctant coachman was sent across a small valley at Brompton in the first gliding flight of history; both of these machines had fixed (but adjustable) tail units, inherent longitudinal and lateral stability, and a separate pilot-operated elevator-cum-rudder. In 1852, Cayley had published in the *Mechanics Magazine*, for all to see, the design – with a brilliant description of how to fly it – of a fixed-wing glider (Figure 5.5); but no-one took any notice of it, and it was not even mentioned at any of the meetings of the Aeronautical Society, which was founded in 1866.

In the course of his long life Cayley revealed a mind similar to Leonardo da Vinci's, and in many ways as remarkable. The more we discover about Cayley, the more fully may we endorse the opinion that he was the true inventor of the aeroplane, and the founder of the science of aerodynamics. More specifically, he was the first man in history:

Figure 5.4 Cayley's sketch of his first experimental model glider, with its kite wing: 1804.

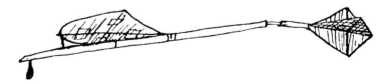

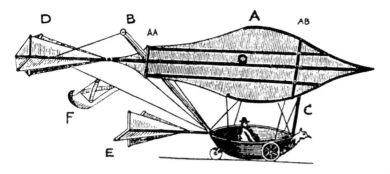

Fɪɢ. 1

Figure 5.5 Cayley's published design for a fixed-wing glider, to be launched from a balloon, with inherent longitudinal and lateral (roll) stability, and cruciform tail unit for flight control: 1852.

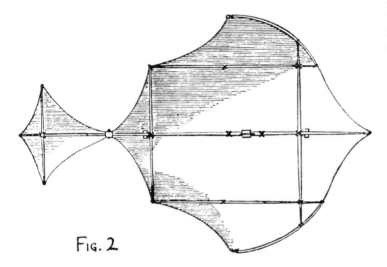

Fɪɢ. 2

(a) to divorce the system of thrust from that of lift, and so inaugurate the concept of the modern fixed-wing powered aeroplane;

(b) to use a whirling arm for aeronautical research;

(c) to use model gliders for aerodynamic research;

(d) to design, build, and successfully make to fly, proper aeroplanes (unpowered) in the form of both model and full-size man-carrying machines supported by fixed wings, stabilised by an adjustable tail unit and wing dihedral, and controlled by a combined elevator and rudder;

(e) to formulate and to publish the basic aerodynamics of the fixed-wing aeroplane, including longitudinal and lateral stability (by means of both the dihedral angle and pendulum construction), and to apply this to both model and full-size man-carrying aeroplanes;

(f) to suggest, build and make to fly man-carrying multiplane (triplane) gliders;

(g) to realise the presence of a region of low pressure on the upper surface of a wing, and its lifting power;

(h) to surmise that a cambered aerofoil gives greater lift than a flat one;
(i)   to investigate the movement of the centre of pressure;
(j)   to formulate, and demonstrate in practice, flight control by means of elevator and rudder;
(k) to suggest, build, and incorporate in a full-size aeroplane, a separate and adjustable tailplane-cum-fin, and pilot-operated elevator-cum-rudder;
(l)   to design, build, and apply a light cycle-type undercarriage;
(m) to investigate aeronautical streamlining; design a solid of least resistance; and use instruments to test streamlining;
(n) to properly understand and describe the basic technique of bird flight;
(o) to suggest an internal combustion engine for aircraft propulsion;
(p) to design a developed form of convertiplane: this was, apart from his 1796 helicopter model, the only significant invention he derived from another inventor (i.e. Robert Taylor).

In addition, although he did not invent the aircraft airscrew, Cayley was fully conversant with its principles, and incorporated it in his ideas for propelling both aeroplanes and airships, as well as considering ornithoptering 'winglets' analogous to the propelling wing tips of a bird.

Cayley also paid great attention to the dirigible airship (Figure 5.6): he realised that the practical difficulties of constructing powered aeroplanes would postpone success for many years and be preceded by the airship. 'I think', he wrote in 1846, 'that balloon aerial navigation [airships] can be done readily, and will probably in the order of things come into use before mechanical flight can be rendered sufficiently safe and efficient for ordinary use.' He was right: the first airship, designed by Giffard, flew tentatively in 1852.

Not only did Cayley achieve towering merit in aeronautics, his favourite sphere; but, fortunately for posterity, he was careful to publish his brilliant theories and conclusions, and so led directly to all subsequent research and development in aviation. His articles were translated into French, and thus fertilised the French inventors of the 1850s and 1860s. It was William Henson who conferred on him in 1846 the simple and definitive title of 'the Father of Aerial Navigation'.

As if all this were not enough, Cayley researched and invented indefatigably in many other fields, mechanical and social, such as land reclamation, unemployment relief, artificial limbs, theatre architecture, railways, lifeboats, finned projectiles, optics, and electricity. He also contributed to applied science two other major 'firsts' of lasting importance by inventing the expansion air engine (colloquially called the hot-air engine) about 1805; and the caterpillar tractor in 1825, which has equipped agriculture and warfare with one of their most important means of locomotion. His social work was further made

notable by his founding of the original Regent Street Polytechnic in 1838, thus greatly furthering technological education.

To round off the picture of this Georgian giant, it is interesting to record that Cayley was a poet in some of his spare moments, a Whig in politics (and even served for a short time as MP for Scarborough), a devout Unitarian by religion, and a devoted husband and father. It is interesting to note that he was the great-great-great grandfather of the present Duchess of Kent (formerly Miss Katharine Worsley).

'Aerial navigation', wrote Cayley in 1809, 'will form a most prominent feature in the progress of civilisation.' He would not have been disappointed.

Although Cayley published his first researches into heavier-than-air flight in 1809–10, he could not persuade the scientific world to take the idea of mechanical flight seriously – neither then nor at any time during his long life. But within two decades of his death his true greatness was recognised, and his 1809–10 paper was republished in England and France (1876 and 1877). In 1809 he had written of 'the art of flying, or aerial navigation as I have chosen to term it for the sake of giving a little more dignity to a subject bordering upon the ludicrous in public estimation'. This neglect and contempt prevented any vigorous follow-up of his basic researches, and retarded the development of aerodynamics for a generation, leaving only Cayley himself to press on, accompanied – with the exception of Henson and Stringfellow – by a series of eccentrics, showmen, and near-charlatans.

Figure 5.6 An early design for a dirigible airship by Sir George Cayley: 1817. (Science & Society Picture Library)

Other inventors: 1800–1850

Before describing the work of Henson and Stringfellow we must turn back to the 'curiosities' of the first half of the century. The 'flappers', although a dying race, still persisted both in theory and practice, and we find in 1801 the French General Resnier de Goué – at the age of 72 – testing an ornithopter based on a design he had made as long ago as 1788, with which he made a flapping dive from the picturesque ramparts of Angoulême into the River Charente, without injury. He later made another attempt, over land, and broke a leg. He was a fine and courageous old man.

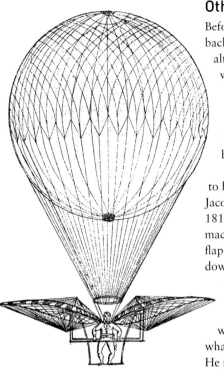

Quite the most notorious experimenter of the time – who seems to have had an excellent publicity sense – was the Swiss clockmaker Jacob Degen (1756–1846) who lived in Vienna. Between 1807 and 1817, he built and tested his ornithopter, which was an ingenious machine of 130-square-feet wing area with the wings made on the flap-valve principle of opening on the upstroke and closing on the downstroke. At first he tested it hung against a counterweight, but then – particularly in 1809 – he attached a hydrogen balloon to it which, whilst he exerted his full strength on the ornithopter, gave him a 90-lb lift, with the result that he and his apparatus (which weighed about 160 lb) were enabled to be raised off the ground in what became in this century the sport of balloon jumping (Figure 5.7). He managed to gain a wide reputation for having flown unaided, the balloon not being mentioned, and seldom thereafter illustrated: it was a report to this effect that directly precipitated Cayley's epoch-making paper of 1809–10. In October of 1812 Degen was injured by the crowd in Paris after failing to satisfy them, and he was – somewhat unfairly – described as a 'miserable charlatan'. Degen was, in fact, a serious and devoted experimenter, however mistaken his ideas; and in one field, the helicopter, he was well to the fore, and in 1816 made a small clockwork-driven model with contra-rotating rotors.

Figure 5.7 Degen's ornithopter suspended from a balloon, which supported most of the weight: 1809.

In 1811, using a copy of Degen's machine, but minus the balloon, Albrecht Berblinger (the Tailor of Ulm) flapped miserably off the Adlerbastei at Ulm and into the River Danube, from which he was rescued without having seriously injured himself.

In 1810, an English portrait painter, Thomas Walker, had published *A Treatise on the Art of Flying by Mechanical Means*, a specious work which tried to revive interest in ornithopters; it illustrated his own design for one, in which the pilot used arms and legs to flap the wings, and of which he stated a successful model had been made. But Walker was to have a strong influence on posterity; for in 1831 he published a new edition of his book in which he illustrated a novel idea, that of a tandem fixed-wing monoplane with propulsive flappers amidships (Figure 5.8). This probably influenced D S Brown toward the same configuration in 1874 and, through him, Langley[1] and Blériot. Walker also looked forward to the day when aircraft would be used for exploration and the carrying of mail.

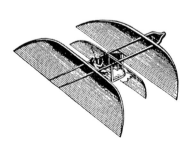

The ornithopter tradition died hard, as said above, and in 1818 the French Count Adolphe de Lambertye designed – but did not

Figure 5.8 Design for a fixed-wing tandem monoplane, with amidships flapper propulsion, by Walker: 1831.

build – a Blanchardesque monster with beating wings, but added a touch of prophetic ingenuity in suggesting a helical-screw helicopter to ply between his aerial vessel and the ground. F D Artingstall, fired by the progress of contemporary railway locomotives, varied the ornithopter theme by the first attempt to make a full-size two-wing ornithopter powered by steam: when suspended from the ceiling (in 1829 or 1830), it flapped itself violently to pieces, and then the boiler exploded. With a second machine, with four wings beating alternately, the boiler also exploded, and that was an end of his experiments.

A novel 'aeronautical' vehicle, which at least worked in a wayward fashion, was made and tested by George Pocock, and was called a 'char-volant', or kite-drawn carriage; it consisted of a kite flown from a horseless carriage, and allowed to draw the latter along, provided there was not too much 'difference of opinion' between the wind direction and the steering-gear of the carriage:[2] the 'char-volant' made a successful journey on the road between Bristol and Marlborough in 1827. Pocock's preoccupation with kites had previously led to his precarious achievement of man-carrying kites which, about 1825, took up amongst others, Pocock's daughter Martha, a passenger who was to become the mother of W G Grace, the cricketer.

Among the popularisers of the helicopter were the Italian Vittorio Sarti, who designed but did not build, a contra-rotating device in 1828; and an English carpenter, David Mayer, who went as far as constructing a large man-powered helicopter in the same year, which naturally remained grounded, but whose lack of performance was euphemistically described by its inventor as 'very flattering, though not perfectly successful'. But the most remarkable development in the helicopter field took place when, in 1842, W H Phillips completed and flew successfully a helicopter model driven by steam jets from the rotor tips – like Hero's aeolipile – the jets being the result of the combustion of charcoal, nitre, and gypsum: it flew up fast and crossed two fields. Phillips showed a replica of this model at the 1868 Exhibition held by the Aeronautical Society at the Crystal Palace. Next year (1843) saw an English engineer named Bourne construct and fly successfully some small model helicopters comprising feathers stuck in corks, à la Cayley, but driven by watch springs. In 1845, an inventor named Cossus described, but did not build, a full-size steam-driven helicopter composed of a large central rotor (for lift), flanked by two small ones whose angles could be varied in order to propel and steer the machine.

One of the most outstanding and influential aeroplanes in history was never built, and the model made from it could not fly. This was the Aerial Steam Carriage, designed in 1842–43 by William Samuel Henson (1812–88) and first published in April 1843, after its patent was granted (see Figure 5.9). Owing to W S Henson having an astute publicity agent named Frederick Marriott, romantic imaginative engravings, which closely followed the superb patent drawings, were published the world over; and, due to the excellence of the design, continued to be published throughout the century, and beyond.

Figure 5.9 The first airscrew-driven aeroplane design, by Henson, which had far-reaching influence in history: 1842–43. (Science & Society Picture Library)

It was the first design in history for a fixed-wing airscrew-propelled aeroplane of modern configuration, which incorporated the following:

- Wire-braced monoplane configuration, with rectilinear main wings, fuselage, and tail unit comprising elevator and rudder;
- Engine, in fuselage, driving two pusher airscrews;
- Tricycle undercarriage;
- Double-surfaced cambered wings, built up with spars and shaped ribs, which was to become standard practice from 1908 onwards.

Henson intended the machine to have a span of 150 feet, a wing area of 4500 square feet, and a steam engine of 25–30 horsepower, and it was to be launched down a ramp to save power. However, it was not these details which immediately impressed themselves on his contemporaries, and won worldwide publication in 1843 through such journals as *The Illustrated London News* and *L'Illustration* in France, and by means of many prints and souvenirs; but that here, for the first time, was a logical, consistent embodiment of what one may call the 'aeroplane idea', for all to see and copy. The Aerial Steam Carriage never lost its popularity and influence throughout the century, and was reproduced in countless articles and books the world over.

Henson, who was in the lace trade at Chard in Somerset, had based the *Ariel* (as it was also called) on the teachings of Cayley, whom he acknowledged as 'the Father of Aerial Navigation'; he had somewhat grandiose dreams of its future as the inaugurator of an international airline – scenes from which fantasy future appear in some of the published prints – and tried to form an Aerial Transit Company, with his friend John Stringfellow (1799–1883, Figure 5.10), also an engineer in the lace trade. All this activity took place before even a model was completed, let alone a full-size machine.

The model, with a span of 20 feet and wing area of 62.9 square feet was fitted with an excellent little steam engine built primarily on Henson's designs, but improved by Stringfellow: the machine was tested at Bala Down, near Chard, from 1845 to 1847. But after descending the ramp, it could not sustain itself. Henson thereupon abandoned his model, married, and emigrated to the USA in 1848.

Stringfellow, however, carried on and built another model in which he fitted a new engine (Figure 5.11) of an improved Henson design which he had built: this little machine was a variation on the Henson theme, and had curved wings of 10.5-feet span and 12-square-feet area, with flexible trailing edges – a feature copied from the bird, which was wrongly believed to act as a gust damper and make for stability – along with a Henson tail; it was launched from an overhead wire in a shed at Chard in 1848, and at Cremorne Gardens. Much controversy has taken place over whether it ever flew in the sense that it overcame the momentum of its launch, and maintained a horizontal or rising flight path. Captain J L Pritchard has shown that there is no contemporary evidence that it ever flew, and good reason to believe that it did not; and even the cautious Octave Chanute said

Figure 5.10 John Stringfellow. (Science & Society Picture Library)

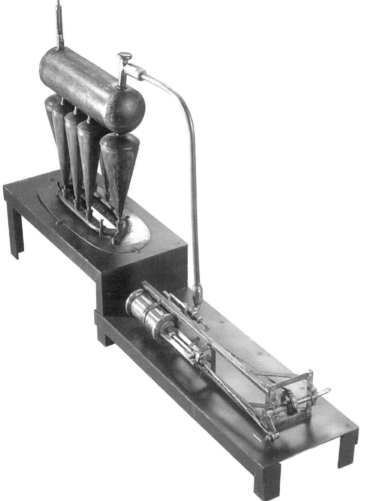

Figure 5.11 The original steam engine and boiler made for the Stringfellow flying machine of 1847/48. (Science & Society Picture Library)

Figure 5.12 (above) André Jacques Garnerin, depicted in an engraving by Edward Hawke-Locker: 1802. (Science & Society Picture Library)

Figure 5.13 (right) Robert Cocking, from a lithograph by Louisa Corbaux, after J B Beech: 1837. (Science & Society Picture Library)

that this 'machine cannot fairly be said to have "demonstrated the practicability of making a steam engine fly"', the quotation within the quotation being by Brearey, Secretary of the Aeronautical Society. In view of this, perhaps one could say that this Stringfellow model showed some evidence of being able to fly; but it does mean that the first authenticated model flight must now be credited to Du Temple in *c.* 1857–58. For some years Stringfellow seems to have abandoned aeronautics; but he took it up again in the mid-1860s with far-reaching results (see next section).

There are two special events in the field of parachutes to record during the first half of the century. Garnerin (Figure 5.12) made the first parachute descent in England over London – his fifth jump – and properly started British parachute history, on 21 September 1802. Cayley, having considered Garnerin's device, suggested in 1809 an inverted (dihedral) parachute to overcome the wild oscillations suffered by Garnerin, owing to the lack of porosity in the canopy.[3] This suggestion of Cayley's was almost certainly the cause of an elderly water-colour painter, Robert Cocking (1777–1837, Figure 5.13) deciding to make and test a Cayley-type parachute in 1837: unbelievably, he did not first test it with a dead weight, and on 24 July of that year ascended in his device, suspended beneath a balloon piloted by Charles Green: at a height of some 5000 feet, Cocking released himself; but the parachute broke up in the air and crashed near Lee Green, in Kent, Cocking dying of his injuries. As a result of this accident, the American balloonist John Wise experimented at Philadelphia, with dropping a dog on a Garnerin type of parachute,

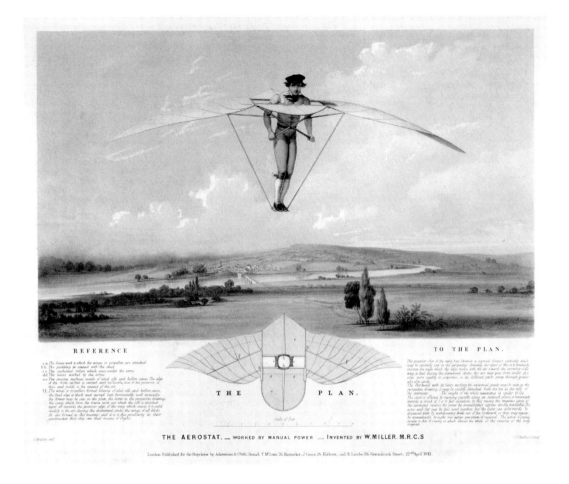

and a cat on a Cocking type: the cat made a steady comfortable descent, whereas the dog oscillated violently, but the Cocking type was not to be used thereafter.

As a tailpiece to this section one ought to mention a splendidly eccentric suggestion put forward by Georg Rebenstein, of Nuremberg, which consisted of a cubiform hot-air balloon which could be collapsed like a concertina in midair, and then used as a glider to descend to earth (1835). There was also Doctor W Miller's frivolous – but beautifully engraved – design for a man-powered ornithopter in 1843 (Figure 5.14); and further fruitless designs for ornithopters by Duchesnay (1845), von Drieberg (1845), Marc Seguin (1846) and others.

Figure 5.14 Miller's design for a man-powered ornithopter, depicted in a coloured lithograph by C F Cheffins, after John Absolon: 1843. (Science & Society Picture Library)

Significant dates in other fields (1800–49)

1801 First practical steamboat in operation (the paddle steamer *Charlotte Dundas* in Britain).

1805 Battle of Trafalgar.

1807 First commercial success of the steam paddle boat (Fulton's *Charlotte Dundas*).

1807 First commercially successful steamboat (Robert Fulton's *Claremont* on the Hudson River, USA).

1812 First commercially successful steamboat in Europe (the paddle steamer *Comet* on the Clyde).

1815 Battle of Waterloo, and final eclipse of Napoleon.

1822 First iron steamship built (in England for France).

1825 Stockton–Darlington railway opened.

1829 Stephenson's *Rocket* service.

1830 Liverpool and Manchester railway opened.

1831 British Association founded.

1833 Emancipation of slaves in the British Empire.

1835 Colt revolver introduced.

1836 British Patent Office established.

1837 Accession of Queen Victoria.

1838 First successful screw steamship (the *Archimedes*, in Britain).

1838 Brunel's ship *Great Western* inaugurates regular transatlantic service.

1838 Cayley founds the Regent Street Polytechnic Institution.

1840 Penny post introduced in Britain.

1840s Railway networks spread throughout Britain and the Continent.

1840s First successes with the electric telegraph.

1840s Daguerreotype and Calotype photography come into limited use (both were patented in 1839), and start the age of photography.

1842 The *Illustrated London News* first published.

1848 Revolutions in Paris, Venice, Parma, Milan, Sicily, Vienna and Berlin.

Notes

1 In 1815, Cayley had designed and sketched the first tandem aeroplane, a monoplane with outer flapping wing panels, but he did not publish it.

2 First tested in 1822.

3 With the early parachutes, it was soon considered that a hole in the crown tended to bring about a stable descent: it was not realised that the main stabilising factor is the porosity of the fabric.

6 The 1850s and 1860s

The 1850s

Heavier-than-air aeronautics at mid-century, and for nearly two decades thereafter, was still shunned by the established and conventional world of science. But a number of technically minded individuals, engineers and other professional men, were beginning to concern themselves with the problems of mechanical flight; and by the mid-sixties these pioneers were to make their work and interests felt by a larger professional audience and at last begin to attract attention in the higher ranks of science.

At the beginning of this period, with Cayley's fundamental groundwork already laid, and the spectacular publicity attending Henson's Aerial Steam Carriage strongly affecting the more adventurous minds, the aeronautical initiative – for reasons difficult to diagnose – passes almost wholly to France. But it should again be noted here that Cayley's remarkable design for a controllable glider was published in 1852 (Figure 5.5), yet passed unnoticed. After an ornithopter-cum-helicopter suggestion from Aubaud (1851), we find the first consistent French design for a powered aeroplane put forward by Michel Loup in 1853: it consisted of a rigid bird-form monoplane with two propellers, one let into each wing, and a tricycle undercarriage (Figure 6.1). About 1853 Cayley designed, but did not publish, a model with propulsive flappers to be driven by rubber cords

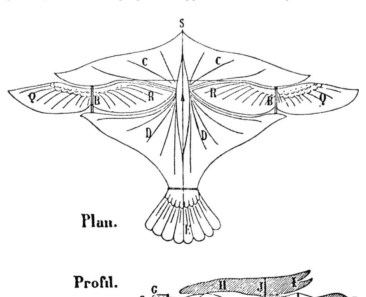

Figure 6.1 *First consistent French design for a powered aeroplane, by Loup: 1853.*

stretched round a spool; and in 1858 Pierre Jullien made an airscrew-driven model with the same type of 'motor' which flew some 40 feet. Bréant then continued the fruitless ornithopter tradition by suggesting a machine in which the pilot pulled down the wings, and elastic raised them (1854). In 1856, Viscount Carlingford had suggested a monoplane somewhat similar to Loup's with a single tractor propeller in the nose; he built a full-size (non-powered) version of his so-called 'aerial chariot' which he seems to have flown as a kite, or attempted to launch unmanned as a glider, in Ireland.

First tested in 1853, and then in 1854, was a parachute-type glider built by Louis Charles Letur which was the first pilot-operated heavier-than-air machine to be tested in the air: it was composed of a canopy wing (which could be pulled down at various points), beneath which sat the pilot operating two large flappers. After some safe descents from a balloon in France and England, Letur was killed in his machine when it was accidentally dragged over trees near Tottenham (London) when trying to land after he had discovered a defect when in the air: he was still attached to the balloon. This crash was on 27 June 1854, and Letur died of his injuries on 5 July.

Then appears an adventurous French sea captain Jean-Marie Le Bris (1808–72), pursuing a courageous aerial career between about 1856 and 1868. He built a full-size glider based on the albatross – a bird he had studied on his voyage to South America – at Trefeuntee in France; and he had this machine placed on a cart, driven along a road and released on the way (1857). In this manner, he made one short glide, but crashed at the second attempt, breaking his leg: the wing area of the machine was said to have been 215 square feet, and the span 23 feet. Later, in 1868, he tested a second machine near Brest, which he seems wisely to have launched on most occasions with ballast on board, but no pilot. It finally crashed and was destroyed; but Le Bris stands as one of the earliest pioneers in practical flying. Evidence about the construction of his gliders is scanty, although a photograph exists of the second machine. They seem to have consisted of a boat-shaped car with wings whose angle of incidence is said to have been adjustable, and a movable tail, the structure and movements being based on the albatross.

With another French seaman, the naval officer Félix Du Temple (1823–1890),[1] one of the first of the new generation of experimenters mentioned above, comes upon the aeronautical scene. Du Temple produced a maturely realised monoplane design after experimenting in the early fifties with an ingenious model which was engined first by clockwork and then by steam: it first took off under its own power, sustained itself and landed safely (c. 1857–58). This model – with the 'demotion' of Stringfellow – now ranks as the first successful powered aeroplane to sustain itself in the air. The design (Figure 6.2) that followed this achievement led Du Temple to another important 'first', the first full-size – albeit unsuccessful – would-be powered aeroplane ever constructed. The design was patented in 1857, and the machine built soon afterwards. It was a machine with swept-forward wings

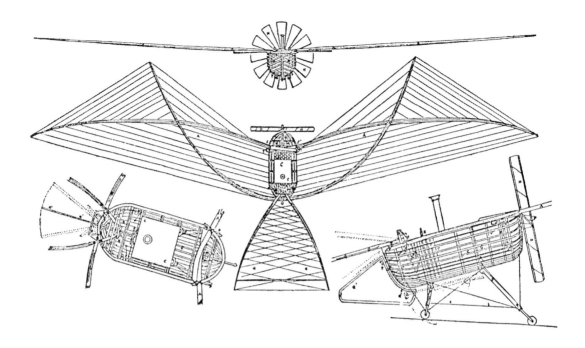

set at a dihedral angle, a tailplane and rudder, a tractor airscrew to be driven by hot air or steam, and retractable undercarriage. Dollfus has established that much later (*c.* 1874) it became the first powered man-carrying aeroplane to leave the ground – just – after a down-ramp takeoff (Figure 7.4). Lack of suitable engines was for long to remain the chronic hindrance to full-scale experiments.

Interesting relief to the main experiments in aeronautics had come in 1852 with the first feasible powered airship, made and flown by Henri Giffard, which was driven at 5 mph by a steam engine; also in 1852 when James Nye proposed propelling airships with rockets; and in 1859 when an Irish priest, E J Cordner, designed, built and even tested a multiple man-carrying kite for ship-to-shore rescue work.

The work of the Frenchman Louis Mouillard, who lived in Algeria and Egypt, and who built his first glider in 1856, is noted on page 66.

Figure 6.2 Du Temple's patent drawings for his tractor monoplane with swept-forward wings: 1857.

Significant dates in other fields (1850s)

1850s First free municipal libraries in Britain.
1851   Singer introduces the first practical sewing machine.
1851   The Great Exhibition is held in Hyde Park, London.
1854   Otis, in the USA, introduces the first safety lift for buildings.
1854   Crimean War (1854–56).
1855   Newspaper tax in Britain is repealed, with consequent increase in number of papers issued.
1856   Bessemer process brings in cheap steel.

The 1860s

The year 1860 marks an important, though indirect, milestone in the history of aviation, for it was then that the French engineer, Lenoir, invented the gas engine: this was to lead, in the 1870s, to the Otto and Daimler petrol engines, and at last to a light but powerful enough motor to propel a heavier-than-air aircraft.

During the decade, there was still a crop of ornithopterists who were 'an unconscionable time a-dying', and who may claim a little attention. Smythies in 1860 proposed a complex machine of fixed and flapping surfaces, the latter operated by a steam engine: he included the interesting notion of a shifting pilot's seat to alter the centre of gravity of the machine, a device resorted to for a short period by Blériot in 1907.

In 1863, an Alsatian industrialist, J J Bourcart built an ornithopter (Figure 6.3) with two pairs of feathering wings, with which he claimed promising results; but it came to nothing, as was inevitable. But it was also Bourcart who, at some time in the 1860s, made a most creditable effort to encourage aviation when he offered a prize of 5000 francs for an airborne duration of 20 minutes, and another of 2000 francs for a duration of 5 minutes at a minimum height of 3 metres.

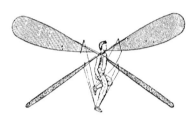

Figure 6.3 Bourcart's man-powered ornithopter: 1863.

Then, in 1864, Struvé and Telescheff suggested a man-powered ornithopter with five pairs of wings, in the belief that they would thus overcome the problems of stability. Also in 1864 Claudel patented a curious machine which consisted of a combination of fixed wings and longitudinally rotating surfaces which were to twist into propellers. In 1867 the great German pioneer Otto Lilienthal was first feeling his way in aviation, and in this year his experimental six-wing ornithopter was tested suspended against a counterweight. Like Cayley, he was never quite to escape from the idea of ornithopter propulsion, even after his epoch-making gliding experiments with fixed-wing gliders, from 1891 to 1896. In 1868, J M Kaufmann, a Glasgow engineer, attracted considerable attention with his model shown at the Crystal Palace exhibition of that year in which a steam engine – with locomotive funnel on the boiler – was to activate two long flappers, and quadruplane wings were to provide lift; the flapping wings were to beat downwards and backwards, and forwards for the upstroke: the model flapped itself to pieces, and the experiments were at an end. Still in 1868, Charles Spencer made a pair of fixed wings of 110 square feet area, attached to which were two outer flappers (with a total area of 15 square feet) which, by manpower, were to propel the machine, which was also equipped with a tail: Spencer seems to have achieved some minor success with this contraption, but did not follow it up. In the same year Spencer patented a delta-wing machine – which he clearly copied from Butler and Edwards the year before (see below) – with both fixed wings and flappers up forward.

One of the more curious developments in aeronautical history took place in France during the early 1860s: this was a sudden rise in enthusiasm for helicopters in France, which manifested itself not only by a number of helicopter designs and models, but by the foundation of an active society to promote them. The helicopter seemed at that time to offer an uncomplicated way of flying, with screws to sustain the machine, and another to propel it. But the enthusiasts soon found their prime movers were inadequate, and so they did not have to face the aerodynamic difficulties which fixed screw blades would lead to. There is an ingenious contra-rotating helicopter design of 1861 to record, by the Vicomte Ponton d'Amécourt; he built this in 1863, in model form, powered by a steam engine; but it was not successful. But his little clockwork-driven models of the same year flew well, and one of them was made to descend by parachute when the engine ran down. The human dynamo who brought the enthusiasts together was one of the great French 'Victorians', the romantic and justly celebrated aeronaut-photographer who called himself simply Nadar; in reality he was Félix Tournachon. In 1863 he founded a society for the promotion of specifically heavier-than-air flying, the Société d'Encouragement pour la Navigation Aérienne au Moyens d'Appareils plus lourds que l'Air: this was soon abbreviated to simply the Société d'Aviation, after La Landelle had coined the word 'aviation' in 1862. In 1864, Nadar founded the journal *L'Aeronaute: Moniteur de la Société générale de Navigation aérienne*. Although only five issues were produced, the journal was revived in 1868 by Abel Hureau de Villeneuve with the modified title *L'Aeronaute: Bulletin mensuel de la Navigation aérienne*. It then ran until 1912, providing the first continuous record of developments in the theory and practice of aviation. Nadar gathered round him a group of talented men, of whom the best known was Gabriel de La Landelle, who became well known for his much-reproduced fantasy helicopter project of 1863, and Ponton d'Amécourt, who has already been noted. La Landelle also created the word 'aviateur' in 1863.

One of the outstanding men of the 1860s was the French Count Ferdinand Charles Honoré Phillipe d'Esterno (1806–83), who in 1864 published his *Du Vol des Oiseaux*; this book was of great importance, as it was the first to draw attention to the soaring – as opposed to the gliding – flight of birds. D'Esterno might also be said to have 'discovered' soaring, and wrote 'in soaring flight, a man can handle an apparatus carrying 10 tons, just as well as one carrying only his own weight'. In his analysis of bird flight, one seeks in vain for any notion of mature lateral control, but finds only the shifting of the centre of gravity laterally for control: his description of the multiple movements of a bird's wings included a torsion of its wings, but only as steering air brakes, and not concerned with control in roll. Incidentally, d'Esterno's passages on the sliding seat for the pilot, to alter the machine's centre of gravity, may well have influenced Lilienthal in his choice of the hang-glider type of machine, in which the pilot hangs in

Figure 6.4 D'Esterno's design for a glider: 1864.

Figure 6.5 First delta-wing aeroplane design, by Butler and Edwards: 1867.

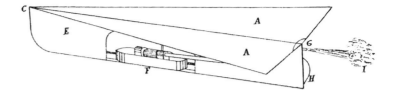

the machine by his arms and swings his hips and legs in any direction he desires. D'Esterno designed and patented in 1864 what must be recorded as the first machine for soaring (Figure 6.4), which was never built, but which included wings whose angle of incidence and dihedral could be changed; which could be swung forwards or backwards in the horizontal plane, and which had large flexible rear portions to act as gust dampers, and a spreading tail fixed to the car by a universal joint, which could swivel and fold up. D'Esterno was the first, and one of the most influential, apostles of man's imitation of the soaring bird, which can, he said, 'sail indefinitely upon the wind without further flapping his wings'. It is also probable that he influenced Ader.

In 1863–68 the French inventor Joseph Pline produced a series of interesting model fixed-wing gliders which incorporated the principle of combining a number of longitudinal barrel-like aerofoils – similar to the barrel vaults of twelfth-century churches – to make up the main wings: although ingenious, the idea led nowhere. In 1865, L P Mouillard, who was to become the second apostle of soaring flight, made the first of his tentative glides. In 1869 there is a strange freak to record, which is said to have been constructed by Frederick Marriott, Henson's publicity agent in his Aerial Transit Co. project of 1842–43: it was a steam-propelled airship-cum-aeroplane, with a wing built out on either side of the envelope for more than halfway along from the nose of the dirigible, and a Cayley-type tail unit at the tail of the envelope: it was said to have been tested over Shell Mound Lake (California) in 1869. This idea is not quite so absurd as some writers have made it, as airships have often been operated in a heavier-than-air condition, developing dynamic lift from the aerodynamic forces on the body and control surfaces.

The jet propulsion of aeroplanes, properly speaking, dates from 1865, when there appeared the world's first mature design for a jet-propelled aeroplane, by the French engineer Charles de Louvrié. His machine, the *Aéronave* was originally designed in 1863 and was then (in 1865) redesigned, but not built, to be propelled by the burning of 'hydrocarbon, or better, vaporised petroleum oil' ejected through two rear jet pipes. There soon followed in 1867 the remarkable and prophetic patent of J W Butler and E Edwards: this was a multiple patent, whose chief interest lies in the delta-wing monoplane configuration – possibly suggested by the schoolboy's dart – which was presented as jet-propelled by steam, compressed air, or inflammable gas and air (Figure 6.5): the inventors also proposed a biplane delta machine, propelled by a pusher propeller rotated by angled jet pipes at the blade ends (Figure 6.6). The single delta version

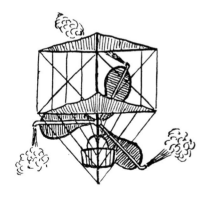

Figure 6.6 Design for a delta biplane with airscrew rotated by tip jets, by Butler and Edwards: 1867.

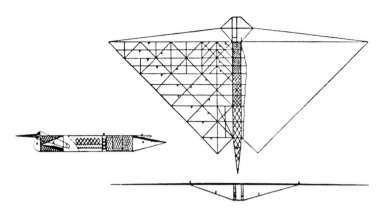

Figure 6.7 Design for a jet-propelled delta-wing monoplane, by de Telescheff: 1867.

was widely publicised. Another remarkable French jet design followed hard on the heels of the *Aéronave* and of the Butler and Edwards delta designs: still in 1867 a Russian officer, Nicholas de Telescheff, also took out a French patent for a delta jet monoplane design (Figure 6.7) with a cylinder where a combustible liquid was to be vaporised, compressed, mixed with air, and ignited to produce the jet efflux.

One of the most important dates in flying history is the year 1866, when there was founded in London the Aeronautical Society (now Royal) of Great Britain. Although not the first society devoted to flying[2] it was by far the most important and influential. Under the Presidency of the Duke of Argyll it soon attracted those men of science and vision who realised that mechanical flight was ultimately possible, and who were determined to study and solve its problems. From now on, the main development of aviation was to lie in the hands of scientifically or technologically trained men. The subject of flying, to which the world had already been acclimatised through ballooning, now took on a new meaning and a new seriousness; and although man-carrying aeroplane flight would continue to be looked upon for many years as visionary, it now became accepted as a proper subject of investigation. Members of the new Society, with their contemporaries on the Continent, now commenced the regular publication in technical journals of their researches and suggestions, and this constant dissemination of knowledge was to become of mounting importance for those engaged in the study of aeronautics.

At the first meeting of the Aeronautical Society on 27 June 1866, a classic paper entitled 'Aerial Locomotion' was read by Francis Herbert Wenham (1824–1908), a marine engineer, and was immediately recognised as another milestone in aviation. Following up Cayley's advocacy of the cambered wing, Wenham pointed out that all birds' wings were cambered and of thicker section at the leading edge: he established that such a wing, at a small angle of incidence, derived most of its lift from the front portion; hence that a long narrow wing (i.e. of high aspect ratio) would be the best type of wing for lifting; and, again following Cayley, that such wings superposed would provide the maximum lift with a manageable structure. Tests were made (*c.* 1858–59) successfully with a model, also tentatively

Figure 6.8 Wenham's multi-wing glider of 1858–59, published in 1866.

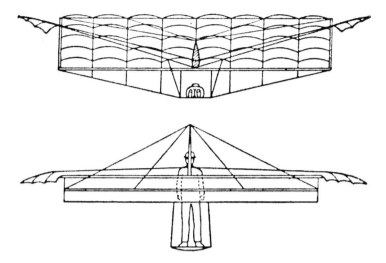

with two full-size five-plane gliders (in which he lay prone), which demonstrated the correctness of his wing-shape theories and marked the practical beginnings of the modern rigid-surface wing, and of the multiplane aircraft (Figure 6.8). Wenham conducted a prolonged study of cambered wings and aspect ratio, and – with John Browning – had the distinction of building the first wind tunnel, in which later tests were made (1871). His influence on the history of the aeroplane was profound: this influence was twofold – through the prominent position he came to take in the newly formed Aeronautical Society, and by the publication of his paper on 'aerial locomotion', in the Society's first annual report (for 1866). Wenham also came later to conduct a fruitful correspondence with Octave Chanute, from 1892 to 1908.

In June 1868 the young Aeronautical Society put on at the Crystal Palace the first aeronautical exhibition to be held in history; it was a curious and not very significant jumble of specimens in the fields of aerostation and aviation, along with 15 ingenious model engines driven by steam, guncotton, gas and oil. But the display was important in its indication of the growing status of ideas and experiments in flying, and of particular interest in its inclusion of a model steam-powered triplane contributed by John Stringfellow, who had temporarily emerged from obscurity (see Figure 6.9). He had evidently been spurred to this effort by reading Wenham's paper, but Cayley must also have been clearly in mind, as the old gentleman had specifically recommended the triplane structure in an article criticising Henson's Aerial Steam Carriage in 1843. The new model, clearly showing its Cayley–Henson ancestry, was somewhat poorly designed and, when tested, proved a failure; but despite its poor performance, it caught the imagination both of contemporary and later inventors. As with Henson's *Ariel*, illustrations of it began appearing the world over, and continued to appear; and there is no doubt that it was the leading influence in persuading Chanute – and through him the Wrights – to adopt a superposed plane configuration. Thus this unsuccessful triplane provided the main 'influence bridge' between

Cayley and the modern biplane.[3] Stringfellow also exhibited another of his little steam engines, and was awarded a £100 prize for it. There is no doubt that Stringfellow was an able engineer, but equally no doubt that he was not very gifted aeronautically. Few other items at the exhibition are now of interest, except the replica of the Phillips helicopter model of 1842, and a fixed-wing glider with ornithopter flappers made by Charles Spencer, which was to remain uncompleted.

Figure 6.9 Stringfellow's model triplane, which led to all future designs with superposed wings: 1868. (Science & Society Picture Library)

The year 1868 also saw the first specific proposal for control of an aircraft in roll, in M P W Boulton's British patent No. 392. The patent is primarily concerned with schemes for jet propulsion, using steam or other gases, but among its numerous proposals are movable surfaces or vanes projecting from the sides of the body of an aircraft. The vanes can be rotated differentially to generate aerodynamic forces to roll the aircraft about its longitudinal axis. Boulton envisaged that the vanes would be operated automatically by a pendulum device to counter any accidental rolling motion of the aircraft, but he also mentioned the possibility of manual control by the pilot. To this extent, he can be said to have foreshadowed the use of ailerons for roll control; but he does not seem to have attempted to put any of his ideas into practice, and there is little evidence that he had any significant influence on later inventors.

Two years later, Richard Harte's British patent No. 1469 of 1870 proposed a monoplane with hinged flaps on the trailing edges of the wings, which look even more like modern ailerons (see Figure 6.10). Harte described these control surfaces acting in three ways: (a) deflected together to act as elevators; (b) deflected oppositely through a small angle to counteract propeller torque; (c) deflected differentially to turn the aircraft. In the latter mode, the effect is to increase the drag of one wing more than the other, and thus to turn the aircraft on to a new heading. To describe this function, I use the term 'steering

Figure 6.10 Harte's design for ailerons to counteract airscrew torque: 1870.

air brakes' suggested by my Farnborough advisors. Such devices have been reinvented several times, and occasionally used on aircraft; although geometrically similar to conventional ailerons, they function quite differently. Downward deflection of an aileron increases the lift on the wing to which it is attached, causing the aircraft to roll about its longitudinal axis, thus inclining the lift force to turn the aircraft on to a new heading.

A word must be said here about one of the greatest of 'aeropropagandists', Jules Verne (1828–1905). With his novel *Five weeks in a Balloon* (1863) and then for more than 30 years, he produced a wealth of aeronautical romance, speculation, fantasy and prophecy, which undoubtedly played a large part in firing the imagination, and acclimatising the minds, of Victorian youth throughout the world. The performance of his fantasy helicopter vessel *Albatros* (1886) foreshadowed that of present-day helicopters. But Verne is now known to have played an even more vital role in history, not in aeronautics, but in rocketry and space travel. For the American Dr Robert Goddard – from whom all modern rocketry directly derives – has recorded that it was the reading of Verne's *From the Earth to the Moon ... and a Trip round It* (English ed. 1873), which alone inspired him to take up the subject of rockets.

Significant dates in other fields (1860s)

1860   Over 1000 newspapers are now published in Britain.

1860s First great spread of photography throughout the world (with the collodion wet-plate process, invented in 1851).

1860s Open-hearth process (1867) further cheapens steel manufacture.

1860s The cycle industry starts in France, then in Coventry, England.

1862   Second International Exhibition held in London.

1866   Britain and USA now permanently linked by telegraph.

1867   Nobel invents dynamite, but its epoch-making role in civil engineering was to come later.

1869   Suez Canal is opened.

Notes

1   There were two brothers involved – Félix and Louis – and the full family name was Du Temple de La Croix: it was Félix who played by far the greater part.

2   The first was the Société Aérostatique et Météorologique de France, founded in Paris in 1852 which, in 1873, was merged with Nadar's society, and then became the Société Française de Navigation Aérienne, which flourished until 1930.

3   It has already been noted that history's first biplane design was Cayley's convertiplane of 1843.

7 The 1870s

The decade of the 1870s was highly productive aeronautically, most of the inventions being French; this was possibly not unconnected with the Prussian invasion of France (July 1870) and the extreme nationalistic feelings and strivings, after the war ended in February 1871. But there was, too, a great expansion of technology throughout Europe, and aeronautics was to benefit from the advances made in many of its branches. In aviation, the ideas came thick and fast; they were good, bad, and indifferent, although even the worst had some touch of ingenuity about them.

The decade was dominated by one great man, Alphonse Pénaud (1850–80), 'doux et modeste, esprit d'une lucidité et d'un bon sens extraordinaires, précurseur en tout ce qu'il a abordé', as Dollfus says. He is one of the aeronautical giants – ranking with Cayley and the Wrights – a sad and brilliant figure who finally committed suicide after losing courage, hope and health; his was a tragedy brought about by mischievous, and probably jealous, criticism and denigration. After a hip disease prevented him following his father (who was an admiral) into the navy, Pénaud devoted himself entirely to aeronautics. In 1870 he introduced a 'motor' of twisted rubber to power models, which incidentally was to do more than anything else to foster air-mindedness amongst the youth of the world.[1] In that year he made the first of his successful model helicopters, and standardised one of the types of contra-rotating helicopter model which still lives on as a toy. The next year (1871) saw his 'planophore', which marked a major milestone in aviation history and provided the modern aeroplane with one of its most important ancestors: as with the Henson and Stringfellow designs, it was constant publication which kept Pénaud's 'planophore' before the later inventors, and built it into the minds of posterity. This model was a stable monoplane of 18 inches span, and wing area of 76 square inches, with its tapering wings bent up at their tips to provide dihedral, and a small diamond-shaped tailplane, also with dihedral tips; it was propelled by a two-bladed pusher propeller at the tail, driven by twisted rubber, with a diameter of 8 inches. This historic machine was the first inherently stable aeroplane to be seen in public: lateral stability was provided by the dihedral wing tips, and longitudinal by setting the tailplane at a negative angle of 8 degrees to the chord line of the main wings: the centre of gravity was placed just in front of the centre of pressure (Figures 7.1 and 7.2). This model was demonstrated in the Tuileries Gardens in Paris on 18 August 1871, before the Société de Navigation Aérienne, and flew 131 feet in 11 seconds. Pénaud thus repeated Cayley's work on stability without at first knowing of it, and further established the character of the modern aeroplane, with main planes in front and a stabilising tail unit. (Later, it was Pénaud who revived interest in Cayley, whom he greatly admired, and re-established him in the minds of inventors.)

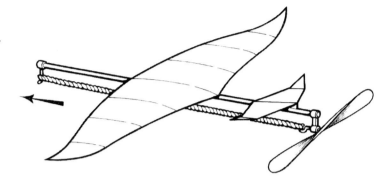

Figure 7.1 One of the most influential machines of history; Pénaud's stable model monoplane: 1871.

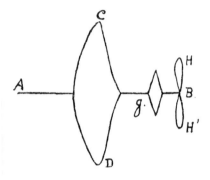

Figure 7.2 Pénaud's own plan-view sketch of his stable model 'planophore' (with tail airscrew: 1871.

Pénaud worked out both the theory and practice of stability, and went on to make and publish many fruitful suggestions and inventions in both aviation and aerostation, as well as the method of instantaneous photography which Marey used soon after for his bird photographs, and which led to the stroboscopic technique. In 1874 Pénaud also made a successful and popular little ornithopter model. But the crowning achievement of his short career was his design – with the assistance of his mechanic Paul Gauchot – for a full-size amphibious tractor two-seat monoplane, which was patented in 1876, but never built (Figure 7.3). It incorporated all his ideas for the practical aeroplane of the future: twin tractor propellers, counter rotating; elliptical wings with curved surfaces, set at a slight dihedral angle and at a 2 degree angle of incidence; twin rear elevators; vertical fixed fin, to which the rear rudder was attached; a glass-domed cockpit; a prophetic single control column to operate the elevators and rudder; a retractable undercarriage with rubber or compressed-air shock absorbers; tail skid; and other ingenious features, including flight instruments such as a compass, a level, a barometer (as altimeter), etc. The movable trailing edges which were also provided were not ailerons, as is so often said, but steering air brakes to act as an auxiliary rudder (see pages 54–5). The estimated weight was to be 2640 lb and the speed 60 mph. It was, as Dollfus says, 'un magistral brevet d'aviation'. Pénaud's work became widely known, and was one of the main formative influences in aviation history: he did, indeed, leave behind him an achievement 'marked entirely by genius (entièrement marquée du génie)'.

From now until the end of the century, the idea of the inherently stable aeroplane – the machine which resists any forces which tend to disturb its equilibrium, and which automatically returns to equilibrium in flight if disturbed – becomes a preoccupation with the European experimenters, equal to their efforts to secure an engine of satisfactory power-weight ratio. Inherent stability is, of course, a relative term covering an infinite variety of degrees of stability – in pitch, yaw and roll – and it was not until Farnborough's B.E.2C of 1913 that satisfactory all-round inherent stability was first attained in a flying machine. As the only feasible flying machines were for long to remain models, it was obvious they would not fly successfully unless

in this rubber-driven model, two tapering pieces of fabric were fixed, one to either side of a pole (with tailplane attached), with rigid spars attached to their leading edges: when these bars beat up and down, an undulating movement was communicated to the fabric, like a skate fish, and the model was propelled forward.

The helicopterists were also active in the 1870s. In 1871 Pomés and De la Pauze suggested a helicopter with a huge adjustable-pitch rotor to be driven by gunpowder. Renoir in 1872 experimented fruitlessly with a screw of 15-feet diameter which he rotated by pedals. And Achenbach, in 1874, designed an outsize helicopter driven by steam, with added propellers for propulsion.[4] In 1877 Emmanuel Dieuaide experimented with a large contra-rotating model, driven by steam, the boiler being on the ground and the steam taken to the machine through a hose. Also in 1877, Melikoff designed a helicopter model shaped like a helical spearhead, which would screw itself up, and parachute down; but his suggested motor and fuel were remarkable, in that he planned for it to 'be rotated by a gas turbine, consisting of eight curved chambers, into each of which charges of the vapour of ether mixed with air were to be successively exploded by an electric spark, and the charge allowed to expand in doing work'. Still in 1877, we find the second – after Phillips – successful steam-driven helicopter model built by the Italian engineer, Enrico Forlanini, later to become well known as an airship designer: Forlanini's machine weighed (loaded) only 7.7 lb, because he hit on the idea of heating up the boiler until the requisite pressure was obtained, then attaching it to the machine and opening the throttle: there were two large contra-rotating two-bladed rotors, the upper one worked by the engine, the lower one fixed to the engine and framework: the machine would rise to some 42 feet, and stay in the air for 20 seconds. In 1878 a French engineer, P Castel, built an elaborate compressed-air-driven helicopter model weighing 49 lb, which had eight rotors arranged in two sets of four and counter-rotating: the compressed-air reservoir was kept on the ground and connected to a hose: but the machine was smashed against a wall, and wrecked, before any successful tests had been made; it was then abandoned. Finally, in 1878 and 1879, Dandrieux made and flew successfully a series of little 'butterfly' helicopter toys worked by rubber; most of these consisted of one or more rotors, with a butterfly-like wing below, or in the middle, or on top: these machines would screw up into the air and glide down (Figure 7.10).

Following Renard's 'decaplane' of 1872–73 an obscure Briton named Linfield made a somewhat similar model to the Renard machine and tested it on a railway truck drawn by a locomotive.

In view of the decisive role in aviation soon to be played by the United States, it should be said here that she was as yet too far from the main stream of endeavour to properly participate. But sporadic inventions had been, and were now being, made there; ornithopter patents were granted to W F Quimby (1869), A P Keith (1870), F X Lamboley (1876), M H Murrell (1877), and I M Wheeler (1887).

Figure 7.10 Rubber-powered helicopter toy in the form of a butterfly, by Dandrieux: 1878–79.

And helicopter designs were put forward by L C Crowell (1862), J Wootton (1866), J B Ward (1876) and others.

Last to be mentioned in this decade is an engine which one day was to make aviation possible, the first four-stroke cycle petrol engine, invented in 1876 by the German engineer N A Otto; it was the world's first practical internal-combustion engine to use liquid fuel, and it marked a great stride forward in engine technology.

The importance to aviation of fuel technology cannot be overemphasised, but it is seldom mentioned. Although petroleum has been known for thousands of years, from the Egyptians onwards, the beginning of the modern petroleum industry, after a tentative start in Britain, is generally considered to be the drilling of the oil well at Titusville (Pennsylvania), USA in 1859, to produce much-needed kerosene for lamps. What today is called petrol (or gasoline) was subsequently a by-product of distillation, and not at first readily marketable.

Significant dates in other fields (1870s)

1870 Franco–Prussian War (1870–1871), and use of photo-microfilms for transmission of letters, etc. by pigeon.
1870s The practical electric motor and dynamo are introduced.
1870s Principal cities of the world are now linked by telegraph.
1871 German Empire is established under the influence of Prussia.
1876 Otto invents the four-stroke cycle gas engine.
1876 Bell invents the practical telephone.

Notes

1 As noted before, he was not the first to introduce rubber; but he was the first to bring it to public attention, and all rubber-driven models derive from Pénaud.
2 It has been a little confusing for historians to find that Brown logically called his tandem monoplane type of model an 'aero-bi-plane'.
3 One of these models was the second (Du Temple's was the first) to take off the ground under its own power.
4 This patented design was also the first in history to include a small vertical rotor to counteract the rotation of the fuselage.

8 The 1880s

The 1880s might appear to provide a lull after the vivid and varied
activity of the previous decade. It seemed as if a saturation of effort
had been achieved amongst inventors – except for Phillips – and that
no vital step was taken, or forward drive made. But this decade now
shows up as a period when the lesser men were indeed abandoning
problems they found too daunting; whereas for the larger figures,
conscious that the epoch of speculation and model-making was almost
played out, it was a time of widespread germination. The latter, some
of them less gifted than others, began acquiring a more mature vision
of what lay ahead, and started to think and plan with the whole
picture of human flight in view rather than isolated lines of research.
These men were aware of a new climate in scientific thought, and were
now passing from romantic speculation to a mood of confidence and
determination.

To usher in the decade, E Dieuaide of Paris published in 1880 one
of the important 'propaganda' items of the century, in the form of a
large wallchart entitled 'Tableau d'Aviation' which illustrated, with
a brief note on each, over 50 heavier-than-air designs from Leonardo
da Vinci to date: it was very popular – as was a companion chart of
aerostation – and showed the would-be pioneers a large variety of
configurations, many of which were constantly republished thereafter.

In 1881 there was published in Paris yet another work on bird
flight, *L'Empire de l'Air* by L P Mouillard (1834–97), which was –
after d'Esterno – the second major source of inspiration to subsequent
pioneers on the subject of soaring and gliding flight: it was later read
by Chanute and the Wrights, in a partial English translation, which
appeared as a publication of the Smithsonian Institution in 1893,
under the title *The Empire of the Air*. Mouillard, isolated in Cairo,
continued to make practical gliding experiments in machines of his
own design and construction, none of which were successful. In 1897
he took out a patent for his last glider type (1896), in which it was
alleged on his behalf that he had introduced control in roll by means
of ailerons: this was untrue, as all he suggested were steering air
brakes, as Pénaud and others had thought of, which had nothing in
common with aileron action (see pages 54–5). Mouillard had been
building ineffectual gliders since 1856.

There are, for the first time in this century, significant items to
record in Russia. First, in 1881, a suggestion was put forward for a
rocket aeroplane, with a swivelling jet for both vertical and horizontal
propulsion: this came from N I Kibalchitch, when he was in prison
and awaiting execution as one of the assassins of Czar Alexander II.
Then, still in Russia, there was the much-advertised alleged flight by a
Captain of the Imperial Russian Navy, Alexander F Mozhaiski, who
had designed an aeroplane based on Henson which was patented in
1881. The actual aeroplane seems to have been completed in 1883,

Figure 8.1 General arrangement drawings of Mozhaiski's steam-powered monoplane, which was tested near St Petersburg: c. 1884.

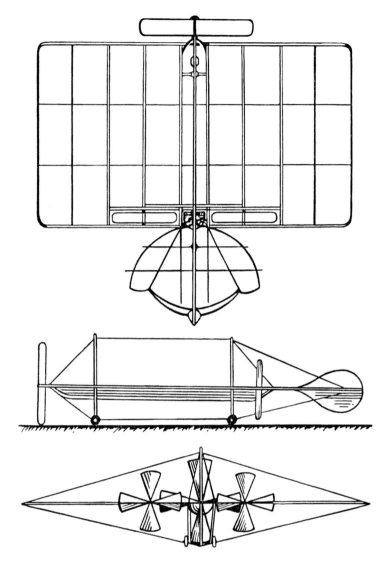

and tested in 1884 (not 1882, as often said), at Krasnoye Selo, near St Petersburg, with an anonymous passive pilot (Figure 8.1). The machine was a steam-powered monoplane – the engine was English[1] – with cruciform tail unit, driven by one large tractor propeller, and two small pusher propellers let into the trailing edges of the wings: it took off down a 'ski jump' ramp, and was said to have been airborne under this impetus for some 20–30 metres (say 65–100 feet): there was no question of a sustained controlled flight. This has been claimed as the first powered flight, which of course it was not; nor was it even the first assisted powered takeoff, which stands to the credit of Du Temple, about 1874. But it can claim to be the second assisted powered takeoff in history. Mozhaiski seems to have abandoned further testing of his machine.

In 1883, a Frenchman M A Goupil designed and constructed a tractor monoplane – minus the engine and propeller – with a bird-shaped fuselage, and deeply cambered bird-shaped wings: he had already designed an engine for this machine, but not built it. He tested the airframe tethered, and obtained very interesting results; in a 13-mph breeze it lifted itself and two men, a total weight of 400 lb. This project was not proceeded with, but he published in 1884 his book, *La Locomotion Aérienne*, in which he set down his theories – including the belief that the stability of a bird was dependent upon the curve of its stomach – and the finished design for his new monoplane, which was never built. Its most interesting feature were the two elevons set on the fuselage just ahead of, and well below the wings; the chief function of these surfaces was to cooperate with the horizontal movable tail to act as elevators; but they were also to be for control in roll, as ailerons: this was the third time an inventor had had a simple idea of control in roll by ailerons; but, without simultaneous rudder action, which was not in Goupil's mind, they would probably have been ineffective if the machine had ever been built and tested. Goupil and his design played a small part in the Wright patent controversy, when Zahm unsuccessfully attempted to show that Goupil had anticipated part of the Wright's control system.

Also in 1883, the first serious but not significant American pioneer, John J Montgomery, built his first monoplane glider which was destroyed just after its first takeoff. In 1885 he built a second machine, with spring-hinged gust dampers, which was unsuccessful; and in 1886, he built his third, with bird-form wings which could be made to rotate about their span-wise axis; but this too was a failure. Montgomery was then to wait until 1905, before starting on the construction of tandem-wing gliders à la Langley.

In 1884 there occurred an event of the utmost importance in aviation, when there first appeared on the scene one of the great men of flying history, Horatio F Phillips (1845–1926); for in this year he was granted his first patent for what became the true foundation of modern aerofoil design, i.e. his two-surface wing sections (Figure 8.2). He had been considering and experimenting with aerofoils, and was concentrating on designing different aerofoil sections and testing them at various angles of attack. He built a wind tunnel in which the airflow was induced by steam injection – the first practical wind tunnel since that made for the Aeronautical Society – and which anticipated the injector drives on supersonic wind tunnels today. Phillips conducted experiments in which curved wings of 'every conceivable form and combination of forms were tried', and took out his first, and most influential, patent in 1884; and his second in 1891. Phillips called his creations 'blades for deflecting air', which were double-surfaced aerofoils of differing thickness and camber; he proved his belief that if a thick cambered wing is used, and if it is curved more on the upper surface than on the lower, then the greater part of the lift generated is due to a reduced pressure (suction) above, and the lesser to the positive pressure underneath. He made a number

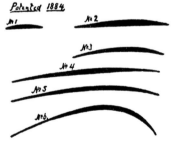

Figure 8.2 Phillips' patent drawing of double-surface aerofoil sections: 1884.

of varying wing sections to demonstrate these forces, and was later to build two large models and two full-size powered machines to show them in actual practice. The presence of an area of low pressure above a cambered wing had been surmised by Cayley; Phillips now properly established the facts, and published them widely; and thereby exerted a powerful influence on aviation thereafter (see also pages 84–5 and Figure 9.7).

It was in the year 1885 that the small world of aeronautics first heard the name of Lawrence Hargrave (1850–1915); but the news came from New South Wales, Australia, and it was the fact of his working so far from the main stream of aviation endeavour, that prevented this remarkable inventor from rising to the heights of men like Lilienthal, Pilcher, and the Wrights; for he was of their calibre. Hargrave's main contributions will be described in the next section but one, but it was in 1882 that he first dedicated himself to aviation, and 1885 when he read his first paper on aeronautics to the Royal Society of New South Wales, of which he had been a member since 1877, and to which he was to contribute no less than 23 papers on subjects which ran from his trochoidal theory of propulsion to the active design and building of aeroplanes. By 1884 he had experimented with some 50 rubber-driven models, and had firmly established his belief in propulsion by flappers. His flappers imitated the action of the primary feathers of a bird, in that each was supported rigidly by a spar on the leading edge, and was unsupported aft: when the spar beat downwards, the flapper surface 'heeled' upwards (as Cayley described it), thus producing a thrust component forwards. Hargrave – somewhat unnecessarily – termed this movement trochoidal: it was, in fact, a simple twisting of the surfaces. One of the most successful of his models is shown here: all his model propulsion until 1888 was by stretched rubber. In 1889 Hargrave built the first rotary engine to be applied to aeronautics, a three-cylinder unit driven by compressed air. His model aeroplanes up to the turn of the decade consisted of elongated dihedrally set flat surfaces of an aspect ratio far less than unity, designed to trochoid inversely to the flappers.

The idea of the 'appareil mixte' – aerostation-cum-aviation – was represented in the 1880s by a number of machines never built, particularly by the Frenchman Olivier, who suggested in 1884 an elongated dirigible with a flat horizontal tail and large dihedrally set wings attached to the top of the envelope. And by a Mr John Beuggar, who patented in 1888 a navigable balloon built in 'the shape of a biconvex lens', and equipped with two propellers in the car slung beneath: 'the lifting power of the balloon alone is not sufficient to cause an ascent, so that it is only when the propellers force the machine ahead, causing the balloon to act as an aëroplane, that flight can be accomplished.'

In 1886 a Monsieur de Sanderval in France experimented with a tail-less glider tethered by a cable.

A little-known machine was completed, also in 1886 by F J Stringfellow – John Stringfellow's son – but apparently not tested successfully: this was a powered model biplane, the first in history, which remained unknown to the other pioneers, and did not influence aviation development.

The great aviation master of the later nineteenth century, Otto Lilienthal, had been maturing his ideas about human flight during this decade; and in 1889 he published one of the classics of aviation history, *Der Vogelflug als Grundlage der Fliegekunst* (*Bird Flight as the Basis of Aviation*), in which he discussed the flight of birds and – of pivotal importance in aviation history – gave tables of air pressures on curved surfaces at different angles of attack. The epoch-making gliding work of Lilienthal will be described in the section after next.

The flappers still persisted with their dreams, paper conceptions, and machines: there was John K Smythies in 1882 with his steam-driven ornithopter; Pompeien Piraud in the same year in France who actually built his bat-formed ornithopter, intended to be attached beneath a balloon appropriately named *L'Espérance*: William Cornelius in England in 1884, with his design for a manually operated ornithopter, with a foot-operated tail; and the Frenchman Pichancourt with his little rubber-driven ornithopter models in 1889. Coming almost within the realm of the flappers was another Frenchman named Hérard, who had built about 1888 a huge machine consisting of five frames of narrow slats which rotated on a horizontal axle, and remained firmly on the ground. In 1888, a curious 'first' in aviation may be noted, when the first photographs were automatically taken from a kite, a device invented in France by Arthur Battut, and operated in this year at Labruguière (Tarn).

The last year of the decade (1889) also saw the beginnings of practical experiments and research in aviation by Sir Hiram Maxim, S P Langley, and – above all – Octave Chanute, all of whose activities were to mature in the 1890s, and will be discussed in the appropriate sections to come. Maxim apart, this represents the true inauguration of aviation in the United States, which will soon gain the final ascendancy.

Among important matters other than aviation, which should be noted during this decade, are the following: the invention (1884) by Charles Parsons of the steam turbine, which was one of the greatest achievements in the history of technology, and was also to lead indirectly to the practical jet propulsion of aeroplanes in the late 1930s and 1940s. Then comes the first near-practical airship, *La France*, built by Charles Renard and A C Krebs in 1884, and propelled by one huge bow propeller driven by a Gramme electric motor delivering 9 hp: she made some six flights in 1884 and 1885, the best of which was a 23-minute circular flight of 5 miles on 9 August 1884, during which a maximum speed of 14.5 mph was attained. Next year (1885), there occurred a much more important event for aviation, when the first practical petrol engines were built independently by Benz and Daimler: the high-speed Daimler engine was by far the most important. Also in that year the first practical motor car built by Benz took to the road: it was automobilisme that alone was to develop the petrol engine, and bring it to a state of sufficiently satisfactory lightness and power as to permit of its application to aviation.

The automobile industry was later to become of vital concern to aviation, both for the engines it provided, and for the engineers who were to be on hand in great numbers by the time aeroplanes had become practical. The internal combustion engine goes back to its origin in the Lenoir gas engine of 1860, which operated on coal gas. Next, in 1876, Otto introduced the four-stroke cycle petrol engine. Although Gottlieb Daimler had in 1884 invented the light, high-speed petrol engine (he first fitted one to a bicycle in 1885) in which year Carl Benz (who had also been developing his petrol engine) built the first successful motor car: the Benz car was not a tricycle, as sometimes claimed, but a robust three-wheel vehicle to seat two. In 1886, Daimler produced his first motor car, which was a four-wheeler.

Significant dates in other fields (1880s)

1880s Dynamite now in general use in civil engineering.

1880s National telephone networks are being developed.

1880s Typewriters now in general office use.

1880s Dry-plate photography (which could record moving objects) now in general use, after its invention in 1871.

1881 House of Commons and Savoy Theatre are lit by electricity.

1882 Marey invents the cinematograph (1882–88).

1884 Parsons invents the steam turbine.

1884 Maxim gun invented.

1885 Benz and Daimler independently introduce the first practical petrol engines and motor cars (1885–86), the first being the Benz (1885).

1885 Rover safety bicycle is introduced, which leads to universal spread of cycling.

1886 Commercial production of aluminium by modern methods introduced.

1886 Linotype printing first used (in the USA).

1888 Dunlop introduces the pneumatic tyre.

1888 Eastman introduces his first Kodak camera, using celluloid roll film.

1889 Eiffel Tower built in Paris.

Notes

1   This engine was published in Engineering for 6 May 1881, where it was entitled, 'Compound engine for aeronautical purposes, constructed by Messrs. Ahrbecker, Son, and Hamkens, Engineers, London'.

9 The powered prelude to practical flying: 1890–1903

In the last decade before men were to fly in powered aeroplanes, three streams of endeavour were being gradually brought to fulfilment; the study of aerodynamics, including propellers – the 'forces acting on bodies moving in air' – pilotage, and engine construction. Slowest came the engine, whose chief problem so far as flying was concerned remained its too great weight for the power produced, whether worked by steam, electricity, gas, oil or petrol. This lack of a suitable engine was keenly felt by all the experimenters, as the wiser of them realised their knowledge of aerodynamics and control depended for further advance on the lessons to be learnt in the air, especially with full-size aircraft manned by a pilot.

Looking back for a moment at the men who have been appearing on the aviation scene since the 1850s to date, they have mostly been of two types; (a) the academic inventors whose creations – sometimes ingenious, but more often wayward or visionary – were realised only on paper, and (b) the model-makers, who were content to experiment only in miniature. Only here and there have there been the descendants of the 'tower jumpers' of old, who have tried to fly, such as Letur, Le Bris, and de Groof.

Now, as the dream of centuries comes near fulfilment, there are to be a growing number of new men – more skilled and sophisticated – who are determined to take to the air: but among such pioneers, who are to be willing to risk life and limb in full-size experiments, two vitally significant streams will appear, whose whole concepts of aviation are distinct from one another; (1) the stream of what may be called 'chauffeurs', and (2) the stream of true 'airmen'. The chauffeur attitude to aviation regards the flying machine as a winged automobile, to be driven into the air by brute force of engine and propeller, so to say, and sedately steered about the sky as if it were a land – or even marine – vehicle which had simply been transferred from a layer of earth to a layer of air.

The true 'airman's' attitude was evident in the pilot's desire to identify himself with his machine – 'je veux faire corps avec la machine', as Françoise Sagan puts it – or ride it like an expert horseman. The 'chauffeurs' came to devote themselves mainly to the pursuit of thrust and lift, and thereby proved singularly unfruitful: they invariably tried to take off in powered machines before they had any true idea of flight control. Whereas the 'airmen' thought primarily in terms of control in the air, and quickly realised that the unpowered glider was the vehicle of choice, in which a man might emulate the technique of gliding birds, and learn to ride the air successfully before having himself precipitated into the atmosphere in a powered flying machine without knowing what would happen, or what he should do, when once airborne. This distinction between chauffeurs and airmen was to prove pivotal in the final conquest of the air.

From now onwards, one can only afford to discuss the more important figures in aviation. Well-meaning and often talented eccentrics had played their part in sustaining interest and helping to create a suitable climate for development; there was to be no lack of them, even into our own [the twentieth] century, but they no longer deserve either space or much credit, although the reader is asked to imagine them perpetually in the background. Also in the background must be left most of the dogged sceptics and disbelievers – some of them able scientists who should have known better – who continued to preach the impossibility of mechanical flight, even after it had been accomplished.

In this section will be discussed the men who concentrated mostly on the powered aeroplane, men who believed that mechanical flight was feasible, and who were determined to bring it about. Oddly enough, each of the three important figures suffered from one serious lack, one serious disability. The lack was the lack of a suitable engine, which led two of them away from the petrol engine (which they should have pursued) and back to the steam engine. The disability in each case was their inability to view the problem of mechanical flight as a whole, a collective problem involving lift, thrust, and – above all – control. They had neither the mentality nor the vision of true airmen, a psychological disability which led them to put the aviation cart before the horse, to neglect the basic problems of control, and to take the chauffeur's point of view. As mentioned above, this distinction is fundamental, as will be seen from the events to come: it is the distinction which was to allow the gliding pioneers to lead the way direct to powered flying, and rob the dogged and ingenious 'power pioneers' of success.

Clément Ader

The first major 'powered' figure of the 1890s was the distinguished French electrical engineer Clément Ader (1841–1925) who became interested in aviation, and might – if he had been less of a chauffeur than an airman – have played a powerful part in aviation history. He made a study of bird and bat flight, had in 1873 experimented with the lift of a 'glider' anchored to the ground by four ropes – he never made a gliding flight – and in 1882 started the construction of his first powered aeroplane, the Éole, which was completed in 1890. He developed a very fine type of powerful but light steam engine, which was his major achievement; but it often appears that his conception of the aeroplane was as romantic and unrealistic as the conception of his engines was practical. The Éole was a bat-formed monoplane with great canopied wings of 15 metres span, and a single steam engine of 18–20 hp driving one tractor propeller (Figure 9.1). In the grounds of a château at Armainvilliers, near Gretz (S et M) on 9 October 1890, the Éole made a takeoff from level ground under

Sir Hiram Maxim

England can almost parallel the story of Ader in the activities of
the expatriate American inventor Sir Hiram S Maxim (1840–1916)
(Figure 9.2), who was already well known as the inventor of the
Maxim gun. But, unlike Ader, Maxim was never truly concerned with
the problem of practical flying; for he set himself only 'to build a flying
machine that would lift itself from the ground', not a flying machine
that would fly. He started in the late 1880s with the testing of aerofoils
in a wind tunnel and on a whirling arm, and also experimented
with propellers. He also developed a remarkably light steam engine.
Then, in 1889 and 1891 he took out somewhat vague patents for his
proposed vehicle.

*Figure 9.2 Sir Hiram Maxim,
depicted in a chromo-
lithograph by Vincent Brooks
Day of a caricature by Leslie
Ward, better known as 'Spy'
of* Vanity Fair *magazine.
(Science & Society Picture
Library)*

In 1893 he built the machine in the grounds of Baldwyns Park, Kent. It was not in any true sense a flying machine, but what one might now call a huge 'lift test rig'. It was basically a biplane, with the outer wing panels set at a pronounced dihedral angle, and two monoplane elevators, one in front and one behind: the total lifting area was no less than 4000 square feet. Maxim equipped this machine with two 180-hp steam engines (Figure 9.3), each driving a pusher propeller of 17.8-feet diameter; there was a four-wheel 'undercarriage' of steel wheels which ran along a straight railway track of 1800 feet; in addition, there were four extra raised wheels on outriggers which, if the machine rose more than about 2 feet, engaged a wooden guard rail on either side directly above them, and restrained the vehicle from rising any higher. The total weight of this monster rig, including its three-man crew, was some 8000 lb, thus giving a wing loading of about 2 lb per square foot.

Figure 9.3 One of the steam engines from Sir Hiram Maxim's flying machine. Maxim donated this and several other items to the Science Museum in 1896, thus helping to form the initial basis of the Museum's aeronautical collection. (Science & Society Picture Library)

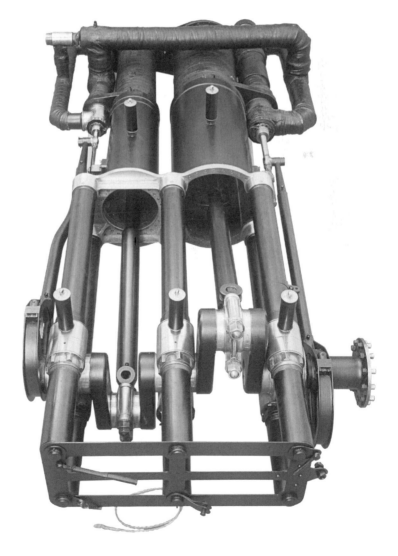

On the third test run, on 31 July 1894, Maxim had the boiler pressure at 320 lb per square inch; and after running along the track for 600 feet, the outrigger wheels were all engaged with their upper rails, and the machine was airborne: but, soon after, a rear outrigger axletree broke, and the machine fouled the guard rails, whereupon Maxim shut off steam and brought it to a stop. Although the machine was rebuilt, and further tests and demonstrations were made during 1894–95, that was virtually the end of Maxim's practical work in aviation until 1910 (which see), when he built a machine which never succeeded in leaving the ground.[2] He had spent, on his own admission, £30,000.

It had all been time and money wasted: Maxim's contribution to aviation was virtually nil, and he influenced nobody. Owing to his reputation as an inventor much attention is still often paid to Maxim's aeronautical work; but even the older and generous-minded aeronautical historians, such as J L Pritchard and M J B Davy, can find little to say for him: the former speaks of Maxim's 'great and expensive and not very useful experiments'; and the latter writes that 'the value of his work in regard to mechanical flight seems to lie mainly in his demonstration that the steam engine complete with boiler, etc., could be lightened to weigh from 8 to 9 lb. per h.p. without fuel and water'. He was not only chauffeur-minded, but was not in the least interested in the practical problems of flying: he was concerned with lift and thrust, and demonstrated their workings; but that was all, and it was in no way original.

In his book *Natural and Artificial Flight*, published late in 1908, he blandly stated that:

> it is very gratifying to me to know that all the successful flying machines of to-day are built on the lines which I had thought out at that time [i.e. 1893–94], and found to be the best. All have superposed aeroplanes of great length from port to starboard, all have fore and aft horizontal rudders,[3] and all are driven with screw propellers.... the fact that practically no essential departure has been made from my original lines, indicates to my mind that I had reasoned out the best type of a machine even before I commenced a stroke of the work.

It is hard to imagine anyone uttering more egregious nonsense, and it is sad to think that these remarks were made by a man who was certainly talented.

S P Langley

We come now to the first major aeronautical figure in the United States, Samuel Pierpont Langley (1834–1906) (Figure 9.4), and he is in many ways a tragic figure: for he was ultimately beaten down by 'contumely and ridicule' for his unsuccessful man-carrying aeroplane of 1903, and died a disappointed and bitter man. Langley was a distinguished mathematician and astronomer, and latterly became Secretary of the Smithsonian Institution, the great National Museum

Figure 9.4 Samuel Pierpont Langley with his chief mechanic and pilot Charles Manly on 11 April 1890. (Science & Society Picture Library)

of the USA. He had had an interest in the problems of human flight for many years, but when he finally had time to indulge it, he emerged as a talented but chauffeur-minded investigator. It was almost entirely his chauffeur attitude to aviation which caused the ruination of his later hopes and ambitions.

He had started his serious investigations of flight in 1887, when he constructed a whirling arm 'of exceptional size, driven by a steam engine', in order to determine 'what amount of mechanical power was requisite to sustain a given weight in the air, and make it advance at a given speed'. He came to the conclusion that 1 hp could sustain over 200 lb in the air, at a horizontal speed of somewhat over 60 feet per second. From 1887 onwards, apart from testing stuffed birds on his whirling arm in 1889, Langley made and tested some 30 to 40 rubber-driven models which, with variations, reached nearly 100 types. In this laborious work he was chiefly inspired by Pénaud. In 1892–93 he built his first four steam-driven models, starting oddly enough with No. 0, then Nos. 1, 2 and 3, which were all failures, and which – with scant regard for etymology (see Glossary) – he called 'Aerodromes'. His No. 4 (1893) and No. 5 (1894), both also steam driven, were also both failures. Langley had endless trouble, particularly with his catapult-launching mechanisms (on a houseboat by Quantico on the Potomac River), also with stability, and with wing distortion in flight. By the end of 1894, he remarked sadly that 'what might be called a real flight had not yet been secured'. In 1895, he rebuilt the No. 5 as a tandem-wing monoplane, to which configuration he now confined himself, and which it is almost certain was suggested by one of the tandem-wing models tested in England by D S Brown in 1873–74 (Figure 7.6), and illustrated in the Aeronautical Society's Annual Report for 1874. Also in 1895, he completely rebuilt the No. 4, which now became No. 6. With these two models Langley at last achieved success next year on 6 May 1896 when No. 5 made a flight of 3300 feet, the first successful flight of any of the large models he had made; and on 28 November 1896, when the No. 6 flew well for ¾ mile.

The No. 5 had a wing area of about 65 square feet, a steam engine of about 1 hp driving two propellers amidships, and a cruciform tail unit: its all-up weight was some 30 lb (Figure 9.5).

Satisfied at last that he had proved the possibility of mechanical flight, and realising that a full-size aircraft would entail much time and expense – although he would have liked to build one – Langley 'made the firm resolution not to undertake the construction of a large man-carrying machine'.

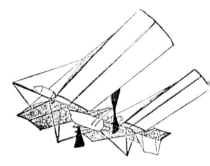

Figure 9.5 Langley's steam-powered model Aerodrome No.5: 1896.

That Langley did ultimately build a man-carrying Aerodrome was due partly to the United States declaring war on Spain in 1898, but mostly to the far-sightedness of President McKinley himself, who was impressed by Langley's models, and appointed a military committee to report on them. The result was that Langley, in December 1898, accepted a bold and enlightened invitation by the War Department to build a man-carrier, with a $50,000 subsidy. The United States thus became the second of the world's governments – following France's commissioning of Ader in 1892 – to officially support the building of aeroplanes.

Langley rightly regarded the engine as the main problem, and he commissioned (in 1898) Stephen M Balzer of New York to build a petrol engine to weigh not more than 100 lb, and the output be not less than 12 hp: it was intended that two such engines should be used in the Aerodrome. In 1899, Balzer delivered a five-cylinder air-cooled rotary engine, which derived from his automobile engine of 1894. But this Balzer engine, although its weight was within the prescribed limit, would not produce more than 8 hp, and that for only a few minutes. The engine side of the Aerodrome was in the hands of Langley's assistant Charles Manly (Figure 9.4), who then tried to purchase a suitable engine from the trade, but without success. Manly, after unsuccessfully modifying Balzer's engine as a radial, took over the whole project, and himself redesigned it to conform with Langley's new demand that a single motor should be produced, to give 24 hp. The redesigned engine (still five cylinders) was completed in

December 1901, and first tested in January 1902, when it gave 521 hp at 950 rpm, with a power/weight ratio of 3–96 lb per horsepower, a remarkable achievement. The name of Balzer was until recently almost unknown to historians, as it had been dishonourably suppressed by Manly in his official contribution to the Langley *Memoir on Mechanical Flight*; and Manly has therefore always received the entire credit for the engine. But credit should be about equally divided between the two men, as Balzer had a remarkable flair for the petrol engine, and certainly provided the basis of Manly's design. However, the Manly-Balzer engine would probably not have provided enough power for the Aerodrome in any case, as Mr Robert Meyer, of the National Air and Space Museum, Washington DC, has shown.

Langley first built – and completed in 1901 – a quarter-size model powered by a small petrol engine, which ultimately gave 3.2 hp at 1800 rpm: this little engine was also supplied by Balzer as a rotary; and after it proved a failure, was also converted by Manly to a radial. This quarter-size model was also a failure: it could not sustain a horizontal flight path when it was tested two or three times in June 1901; and only made a successful flight in August of 1903. But it takes a minor place in history as the first petrol-engined aeroplane to fly tentatively (1903). In May–June 1901, Langley fitted his quarter-size petrol-driven tandem-wing monoplane with another set of wings, transforming it into the world's first tandem-wing biplane. As with the original monoplane – to which configuration it returned – this temporary expedient was a failure. The official photograph of the biplane is dated 11 June 1901.

The full-size Aerodrome – the Aerodrome A as it was called – was completed in 1903, and was a tandem-wing monoplane, with the wings set at a pronounced dihedral angle: the total lifting area was 1040 square feet, and the span 48 feet. The pilot sat in a cockpit between, and below, the trailing edges of the front pair of wings, with the engine and twin propellers just behind him. Aft of the propellers, and set below the connecting boom of the aircraft – and connected with the cockpit by a keel – was a wedge-shaped vertical rudder of 95 square feet; and aft of the second pair of wings was a large cruciform tail unit set at a negative angle of incidence, which was fitted with spring attachments to the boom fuselage to act as a gust damper; this, in addition, was to be used as the elevator, but not rudder. The total weight of the Aerodrome, with pilot was about 730 lb (Figure 9.6).

When the machine was ready for testing, Langley indulged in the folly of perpetuating the catapult-launching technique he had used for his models, except now that it was a catapult below – not above – the machine: this mechanism was placed, as before, on the top of a houseboat on the Potomac. An over-water takeoff was apparently planned to avoid physical injury to the pilot. It was the brave Manly who volunteered as that pilot. The extent of such monumental folly may be truly gauged if one remembers that Manly had never even tried to fly a glider, let alone a completely untried powered machine, and he was now to be precipitated into the air at some 30 mph,

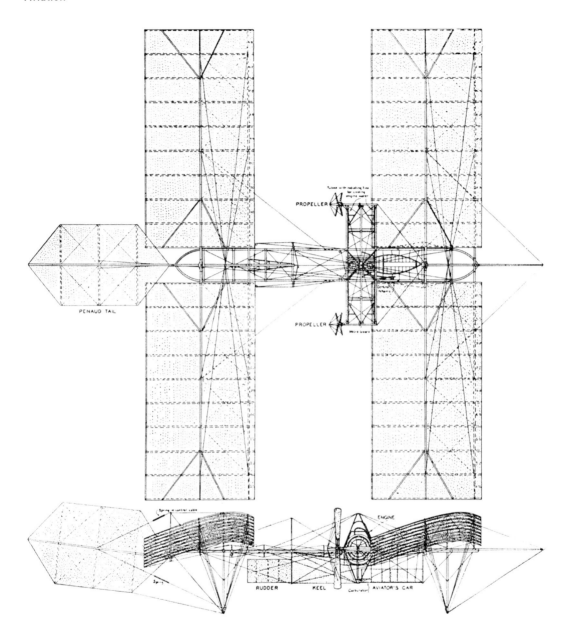

Figure 9.6 General
arrangement drawings of
Langley's full-size petrol-
powered tandem-wing
Aerodrome A: 1903.

without the slightest idea of what would happen when he got going;
he would have a rudder and an elevator, but no experience in the
cockpit working of them, and no idea at all as to how they would
affect the flight of the Aerodrome. Manly did not know that, when
he applied the rudder, the outer wings would start rising as well as
turning. What is almost as bad was that, whether the Aerodrome came
down on land or water, the first part of it which would impact the
surface was Manly's frail cockpit, as it hung well below the rest of the
machine, including the safety floats provided. It seems incredible to us
today that Langley should have been prepared to risk a man's life in

this way. Considering the unlimited flat space available nearby, where Manly could have safely tested the Aerodrome in longer and longer hops, and gained some idea of what effect the controls would have, it is impossible to understand Langley's thought process. This launching madness represented the final *reductio ad absurdum* of the chauffeur's attitude to aviation.

What happened, in the event, must certainly have been a blessing in disguise for Manly; for on both of its only two tests, on 7 October and 8 December 1903, the Aerodrome crashed straight into the Potomac, with Manly struggling out unhurt after each ducking. On both occasions, the machine had apparently fouled the launching mechanism; but some authorities believe that the second crash was due, at least partly, to the aircraft's structural weakness.

From the official War Department report on the tests (written in 1903) two passages may be quoted:

> The claim that an engine-driven, man-carrying Aerodrome has been constructed lacks the proof which actual flight alone can give.... In the meantime, to avoid any possible misunderstanding, it should be stated that even after a successful test of the present great aerodrome, designed to carry a man, we are still far from the ultimate goal, and it would seem as if years of constant work and study by experts, together with the expenditure of thousands of dollars, would still be necessary before we can hope to produce an apparatus of practical utility on these lines.

It is ironic to consider that in December of that very year 1903, the Wrights made the first flights in history; and in 1905 they were to build a fully practical aeroplane which could easily keep flying for half an hour; and the cost of all this was borne by the modest profits of a bicycle business.

Langley abandoned all further work in aviation, primarily owing to the vicious and totally unjustifiable attacks on him by Congressmen and the Press. But in face of such attacks, the War Department also withdrew its support, regretting that they were 'not prepared to make an additional allotment at this time for continuing work'. Langley died, heartbroken, on 27 February 1906.

The tragedy of Langley was the tragedy of a man whose basic attitude to the problem of flight was misconceived. His was the approach of a talented scientist who fervently believed that the aeroplane could be successfully achieved, but achieved from 'outside'; it was almost a spectator's attitude. Instead of approaching aviation through the glider, and realising it was flight control that was the pivotal problem, he believed he could best come to the subject through powered models; and then advance to a full-size powered machine. And he had taken from 1887 to 1903 – 16 years – to fail in his solution of the problem, a failure stemming directly from his chauffeur's attitude of mind. But even allowing for this attitude, it is still impossible to explain his choice of a catapult launch over water for a completely untried powered machine.

Langley's technical influence in aviation was virtually nil; many of his figures turned out to be wrong, and so did some of his most important theories; and his tandem-wing concept did not have any appreciable effect on his successors. But his influence as a well-known scientist, who was prepared to risk ridicule for his belief that man could, and would, fly in the air in powered aeroplanes, was great; it was to be one of the main factors in the Wrights taking up aviation. Perhaps, because of this, Wilbur Wright should speak his epitaph here: 'It is really pathetic', wrote Wilbur to Chanute after Langley's death, 'that he should have missed the honour he cared for above all others, merely because he could not launch his machine successfully. If he could only have started it, the chances are that it would have flown sufficiently to have secured to him the name he coveted, even though a complete wreck attended the landing. I cannot help feeling sorry for him. The fact that the great scientist, Professor Langley, believed in flying machines, was one thing that encouraged us to begin studies.'

The powered machines – model or full size – designed or made by Hargrave, Pilcher and Lilienthal, will be discussed in the next section, as their creators' greatest contributions to aviation came through gliders or kites.

Other inventors

We must now return to Horatio Phillips, and to note first his patent of 1890, in which he suggested a cigar-shaped fuselage topped by a tandem multi-wing structure, each set of wings comprising 13 superposed 'slats'; and then his later patent of 1891, which developed his 1884 patent by providing the double-surface aerofoil with a bi-convex leading edge (Figure 9.7) intended to decrease drag, and preserve the lifting properties of his previous aerofoils; but this type of wing section was to some extent a retrogresion. In 1893, Phillips decided to add practice to theory by building and testing his first 'Venetian blind' multiplane machine which was tested tethered on a circular track at Harrow in May; the span of this large model was 19 feet with a chord of only 1½ inches, the total area being 140 square feet. This test trig was powered by a steam engine driving a 6.5-foot tractor propeller, and ran around a track of 323-feet circumference: with the front wheels always on the ground it rose some 2–3 feet off the circular track when running at about 40 mph. Later – the exact date is as yet unknown – Phillips built another, and similar, machine with a larger track of 628 feet circumference, and it lifted

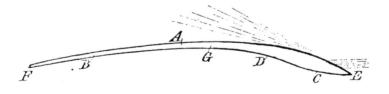

Figure 9.7 Drawing from Phillips' second patent for double-surface aerofoils: 1891.

some 385 lb. After these convincing displays of his high aspect-ratio aerofoils, Phillips abandoned practical testing until 1904 and 1907 (see page 150).

Victor Tatin returned to active aviation in 1890 with the first test of a remarkable steam-driven model aeroplane built in collaboration with Charles Richet. This large machine, with its steam engine enclosed in a nacelle driving two airscrews in tandem, one at either end of the nacelle, had a span of about 21 feet, the wings being given a pronounced dihedral. There was a Henson-type horizontal tail. The first test took place over the sea at La Hève in 1890: it was launched down a ramp and started well, but then the tail became twisted, and the machine crashed into the sea. Rebuilt, it was tested again in 1896 and 1897 over the roadstead at Giens, and made three flights – the best of which covered about 460 feet – before the machine dived into the sea. But events elsewhere were now too advanced for this aeroplane to influence the main stream of aviation, and it must be looked upon as a creditable but isolated achievement.

There was also the 1890 project – realised in unsuccessful model form – of the Frenchman Graffigny, who designed a steam-powered tractor monoplane with three pairs of wings in tandem, and two pairs of propellers, with a tailplane-cum-elevator, but no rudder.

One of the most interesting of the minor pioneers was Gustav Koch of Munich, who unsuccessfully indulged an interest in gliding flight, and also (in 1891) designed a tandem-wing powered machine, also unsuccessful; but he also designed (in the 1890s) a monoplane, whose fuselage was constructed like a Venturi tube, with a turbine inside, using an unspecified fuel.

The important work of F W Lanchester in aerodynamics will be noted later (see Chapter 12): but he must appear here briefly. It was early in 1892 that he first started experiments with model gliders. The first announcement of his circulation theory of sustentation was in a paper entitled *The Soaring of Birds and the Possibilities of Mechanical Flight*, which he read to a meeting of the Birmingham Natural History and Philosophical Society on 19 June 1894. This historic paper was not printed: what is even worse is that Lanchester did not bother to preserve a copy. During 1895 and 1896 he revised and expanded the paper, and it was this revision, containing one of the most vital discoveries in technological history – the circulation theory of sustentation – which was refused for publication by the Physical Society in 1897: this refusal has brought much subsequent ridicule on the Society, but the truth is that Lanchester's language was almost incomprehensible (see page 151).

In 1891 there appeared in Munich a book by a Swiss artist, with a taste for physics and mathematics, named Carl Steiger-Kirchofer (generally known as Carl Steiger), called simply *Vogelflug and Flugmaschine* (*Bird Flight and the Flying Machine*). In it Steiger displayed a remarkable grasp of many fundamentals of the aeroplane, and he included designs of what he proposed, which were many years in advance of his time (Figures 9.8 and 9.9): unfortunately, as so

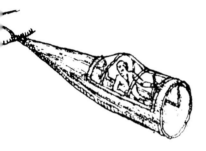

Figure 9.8 Design for fuselage section of a powered monoplane, by Steiger: 1891.

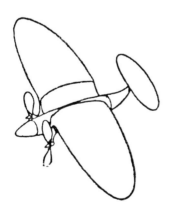

Figure 9.9 Design for a powered monoplane, by Steiger: 1891.

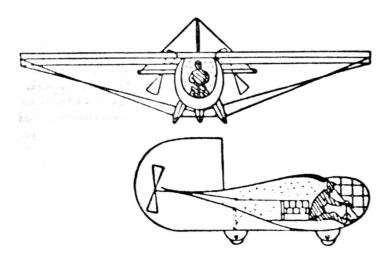

*Figure 9.10 Design for a
monoplane with airscrews aft,
by Steiger: 1892.*

often with men who did not primarily seek for experience in the air
– although Steiger seems to have made a few attempts to glide – his
flight-control concepts were primitive: he intended control in yaw to
be by such methods as rocking the tailplane about its longitudinal axis
(the equivalent to a bird twisting its tail), by differential speeds of two
airscrews, and by the use of steering air brakes. For control in pitch,
by shifting the centre of gravity, swinging the wings fore and aft to
shift the centre of pressure, and faster rotation of the airscrews. He
also provided for oddly modern-looking enclosed cockpits in his 1891
book (Figure 9.8) and in his patent for a flying machine taken out
in 1892 (Figure 9.10). Steiger, whom I have only recently been able
to study, may well repay more attention in the future. Also in 1892,
the Austrian Professor Wellner proposed a rotating-paddle machine,
in which the paddles rotated on longitudinal axes to support the
machine, rather than propel it.

A curious incident in aviation history came in 1893, when the
inventor of the turbine, Charles Parsons, had the passing whim to
make a model helicopter, which he then turned into an aeroplane,
without really being concerned with aviation at all. He used them as
a test-bed for his small ¼-hp steam engine to test the effect of steam
jacketing: with a total area of some 22 square feet, it flew for about
300 feet.[4]

One of the more interesting suggestions of the decade came in
a paper of 1894 by the great Russian 'father' of space travel, K E
Ziolkowski, who in that year published his *Der Aeroplan, oder
die vogelähnliche Flugmaschine*, in which he suggested a powered
monoplane based on the rigid arched wings of the soaring bird, with
a tractor propeller, a streamlined fuselage, a cruciform tail unit, and a
four-wheel undercarriage (Figure 9.11).

A somewhat surprising would-be aviator has recently been
revealed in the person of another Swiss artist, the famous romantic,
Arnold Boecklin, who had a minor passion for flying, and who both

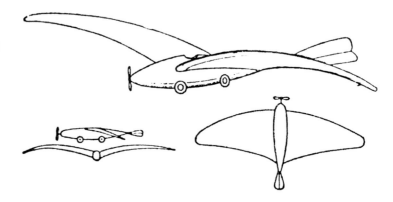

Figure 9.11 Design for a powered monoplane by the Russian space-travel pioneer, Ziolkowski: 1894.

attempted gliding experiments, and – in 1894 – proposed a Henson-derived powered monoplane with braced high aspect-ratio wings, and a tail unit: but nothing came of Boecklin's enthusiasm, or his design.

Strange as it may seem, the ornithopter was still alive in 1890, and an elaborate full-size machine was built by E P Frost in that year; but its steam engine did not produce its estimated power, and the tests came to nothing; no less a man than F W Brearey eulogised this hopeless machine, and described it as a 'beautiful illustration of the winged machine … devised and constructed with perfect imitation and arrangement of every feather in the wing of a crow': the machine weighed about 650 lb, minus pilot.

A special word must be said here about the Aéro-Club de France (founded 1898) and the Aero Club (later Royal) of Great Britain (founded 1901). The French club, apart from initiating a decade of sporting ballooning – as did the British one across the Channel – came to play a unique role in European aviation as the focus for all the aviation pioneers, the disseminator of scientific information, and the inspirer to perpetual effort in the conquest of the air; whereas the British club remained almost exclusively social and sporting.

One of the most important events in the 1890s did not at the time concern aviation, but was later to prove of far-reaching influence in the history of the aeroplane: this was the winning of the legal freedom of the roads for the automobile in Britain in that year 1896, when it became no longer necessary for a man with a flag to precede every motor vehicle on the highway. The result of such mechanical freedom from bondage was a vast expansion in Europe of the automobile industry: this led to a major proliferation of sportsmen and other potential pilots, and – far more important – of mechanics, a large reservoir of whom were thus available when the powered aeroplane came to need them.[5]

Claims of various kinds have been made by, or for, a number of men during this period, i.e. Gilmore, Herring, Pearse, Watson, and Whitehead: these cases are briefly discussed on pages 283–7.

Notes

1   For a detailed survey of the Ader claims, see the present writer's publication entitled *Clément Ader: his Flight-Claims and his Place in History* (1968).

2   Maxim's machine is sometimes seen in photographs, minus its outer wing panels; most of these are of the machine when it was used to run members of the public up and down the track, for a local charity, later in the year, when these panels were purposely removed.

3   Incidentally, no aeroplane of the time – or previously – had both fore and aft elevators: Maxim could not have looked very carefully at the Wright machine (which had no horizontal surfaces aft), nor at the Voisins, which had rigid biplane tailplanes.

4   It is preserved in the Science Museum.

5   An indication of the importance and spread of automobilisme, was the founding of the two great national clubs, the Automobile-Club de France, founded in Paris in 1895, and the Automobile Club (later Royal), founded in London in 1897.

10 The gliding prelude to practical powered flying: 1890–1903

It was through the glider that men came to fly in powered aeroplanes. The philosophy behind this sequence of events was the simple one of flight control. A glider is a slow machine – and can even remain stationary in relation to the ground – and it is a comparatively safe task to learn how to fly it, provided one has the necessary talent, and that one perseveres and learns properly how to control it in pitch, roll and yaw. Having mastered the flight control of gliders, it is then easy to progress to a powered machine, and master the additional problems that it presents.

If the glider approach to flying is not followed, the risks and dangers are immense; and it was foolhardiness or ignorance which prompted those early pioneers who attempted to build powered aeroplanes to start with. To think of being cast into the air – as Langley was willing to cast Manly – in a powered flying machine without the pilot having had a moment in the air previously, is to partake of a nightmare. Even if the tests are made by a progressively longer series of hops, the dangers are still great; as the matter of 'hopping', as such, does not meet the bill of full commitment to the air, which is what the pilot must ultimately contend with. In fact, the better that the pioneer has solved the aerofoil and engine problems, the more dangerous will the tests be, since the aviator will be more quickly at the mercy of such an alien environment.

This was the reason why the Wrights, with their outstanding talent, were able to solve the basic control problems in the three short 'seasons' of gliding (1900–02); and to take confidently to the air in powered machines in three further seasons (1903–06). Whereas a whole 'team' of European pioneers, from Ferber in 1902 onwards – who also had the complete set of flight-control clues from the Wrights in 1902–03 – unwisely abandoned the glider approach to flying and consequently took until November of 1907 before any of them could stay in the air for a single minute; until September of 1908 before they could keep flying for an half an hour at a time; and until 1908–09 before they learnt the Wrights' lessons in flight control, and could properly manoeuvre aeroplanes in the air.

Otto Lilienthal

The key figure in aviation during the last decade of the century, and one of the greatest men in the history of flying, was the German Otto Lilienthal (1848–96). The past culminated in him, and the future was born in him. He was the first man in the world to launch himself into the air and fly. It was his gliding that led directly to the work of Chanute and the Wrights, whom he resembled in his approach to aviation, in his talents, and in his high qualities of integrity and humility. Lilienthal, says Dollfus simply, 'est le père de l'aviation moderne'.

His decisive influence in bringing aviation to its penultimate phase owed a great deal to photography and the printing industry; for in 1871 Maddox invented the dry-plate negative, whose emulsion was rapid enough at last to arrest movement; and by the 1890s the dry-plate camera had become a fine and sophisticated instrument. Also in the 1890s, the methods of printing photographs in journals and books had resulted in the halftone block. The outcome of this combination of technologies – along with the photographic skill of the operators – was a superb series of photographs of Lilienthal gliding, which were reproduced photographically the world over, and brought home the true reality of his flying to the pioneers-to-be: Lilienthal was, indeed, the first man to be photographed in an aeroplane. Most important of the publications in which the Lilienthal photographs and text were published were an issue of *McClure's Magazine* of 1894, which was probably the first serious illustrated description of Lilienthal which the Wrights saw, and Means' *Aeronautical Annuals* for 1896 and 1897.

Lilienthal was born in 1848 at Anklam in Pomerania, and was given an excellent technical education at Potsdam and Berlin. From childhood he had been interested in human flight; and, with his brother Gustav, had been enthusiastically engaged in youthful flying 'experiments' with flapping wings. In 1869 (not 1867 as previously thought) the brothers experimented with a six-wing ornithopter suspended against a counterweight. From 1867 until 1870, Otto studied at the Berlin Technical Academy; he had only just graduated in mechanical engineering when the Franco–Prussian War was upon him, and he volunteered for service and was present at the siege of Paris. He was demobilised in 1871, and went into engineering professionally.

Lilienthal resumed his flying experiments immediately after release from the army, and he was still bent on developing the ornithopter. Curiously enough, he remained devoted to the ornithopter all his life, and only took to fixed-wing gliders as a preparation for powered flight; he also warmly recommended gliding as a worthwhile open-air sport. He later wrote:

> One can get a proper insight into the practice of flying only by actual flying experiments.... The manner in which we have to meet the irregularities of the wind, when soaring in the air, can only be learnt by being in the air itself.... The only way which leads us to a quick development in human flight is a systematic and energetic practice in actual flying experiments. (1896)

Thus spoke a true airman, whose whole ambition and effort were devoted to getting up into the air and flying. But although he became fully convinced that he must first learn to fly a fixed-wing glider, he harboured the curious conviction that it was the ornithopter with which man would ultimately triumph. This is reflected in another typical passage of his:

Natural bird flight utilises the properties of the air in such a perfect manner, and contains such valuable mechanical features, that any departure from these advantages is equivalent to giving up every practical method of flight. (1889)

It must be said unequivocally that it was a blessing for the future of aviation that the fixed-wing gliding prelude to his powered attempts took so long, as it was in this field that his great strength and influence lay. In this he was unlike Pilcher, who was in a hurry to fit an engine, and who spent too little time in gliding to get on 'intimate terms with the wind', in Lilienthal's felicitous phrase.

Lilienthal determined that he must study bird flight much more intimately than it had been studied before; not only the structure and types of bird wings and their aerodynamics, but the application of the data gained – especially that dealing with wing areas and lift – to the problem of human flight. He was among the first, since Cayley discovered the principles, to realise that bird propulsion is brought about by the airscrew action of the outer primary feathers; and he fully described the technique. The results of his researches were published as a book in 1889, entitled *Der Vogelflug als Grundlage der Fliegekunst* (*Bird Flight as the Basis of Aviation*), which is one of the classics of aeronautical literature. Although this book was not available in an English translation until 1911, excellent articles in English both by, and about, Lilienthal were available from 1894 onwards, as has been said; but it is worth noting that, in 1901, Chanute lent the Wrights a copy of the *Vogelflug* with a partial translation in typescript, whilst Lilienthal's table of wing areas and lift had already been published in the *Aeronautical Annual* for 1897.

By 1889, Lilienthal had come to the conclusion that he must now learn the air and its moods in fixed-wing gliders; and in that year he built his first fixed-wing machine, which will be called the No. 1 glider.[1] This was a tail-less bird-form glider and was not successful. Nor was the No. 2 of 1890 successful, although it probably had a tail.

These first experiments were made from a springboard at his home in Berlin-Lichterfelde, and on convenient ground nearby. The first serious tests were made in 1891 at Derwitz, between Werder and Grosskreuz, near the Magdeburg railway. Then in 1892, Lilienthal moved his test location to a gravel pit between Berlin-Steglitz and Südende. Early in 1893 he moved again to a height called the Maihöhe at Steglitz, on which he erected a hangar from whose roof he took off in his gliders, the total height above the level ground below being some 10 metres (say 33 feet). Then still in 1893, he found the ideal places in the Rhinower hills, first between Neustadt a.d. Dosse and Rathenow; and then the slightly higher Gollenberg, near Stölln, not far off. In order also to have a convenient experimental station nearer at hand, Lilienthal had an artificial hill thrown up in the spring of 1894, near a brick works in Lichterfelde, a suburb of Berlin: this hill was – with a hangar built into the conical top – about 15 metres high (say 50 feet), and had a base diameter of 70 metres (say 230 feet), which

Lilienthal used to make the remark, from time to time, that 'Opfer müssen gebracht werden' (sacrifices must be made). It forms a tragically appropriate epitaph for this great man, and the words are carved on his gravestone in Lichtefelde cemetery.

If he had lived, Lilienthal – like Pilcher – would almost certainly have accomplished some degree of powered flight before the Wrights. He had had long experience of the air, and made some 2500 gliding flights; he was arriving at the true concept of flight control; and he would have arrived sooner or later at the propeller aeroplane. Above all, like Pilcher and the Wrights, he was a true airman, and a person of high talents and complete integrity. It is hard to overestimate the vital force which this outstanding pioneer injected into aviation, as much after his tragic death as before. His influence was universal and profound: extracts from his technical writings were translated and read by all who were convinced that mechanical flight would one day be accomplished, and – as said above – the overall effect of his work was greatly increased when his successful flights were well photographed, and published the world over by means of the then new method of halftone reproduction, and other techniques, in books and periodicals; these photographs, and the information which accompanied them, also demonstrated forcibly that it was necessary and possible for a man to be launched into the air, and fly, in order to gain essential experience in design and control, before he embarked on powered flights. Lilienthal was the direct inspirer of Pilcher, the Wrights and Ferber, and may fairly be described as the world's first true aviator; that is to say, he was the first man to fly practical heavier-than-air aircraft consistently and successfully.

Lawrence Hargrave

In some respects the work of Lawrence Hargrave (1850–1915) (Figure 10.4) in the 1890s should have been discussed in the previous section on the powered prelude. But although his ambition lay in the direction of powered aviation, and although his work in this field was excellent and original, it was his invention of the box kite that placed him most firmly in the front rank of history. Hargrave was a remarkable man, of a high talent and integrity, and of great generosity, who refused to patent his inventions, and published his researches for all to see and use, however they liked, 'in order that all might benefit from the results of my labour'. (For his earlier work, see page 69.)

Hargrave invented the box kite – in various forms – in 1893 (Figure 10.5), but it was the simple version which was to play such an important part in aviation history. The result was an admirably stable ensemble, with great lifting power; on one occasion (1894) he himself was lifted 16 feet off the ground in a 21-mph wind by a train of four of these kites. He records that his box kite was a combination of two previous concepts.

But in 1894, when he designed and built his first full-size machine, it was a glider which emerged, which was not of box-kite, but

Figure 10.4 Lawrence Hargrave. (Science & Society Picture Library)

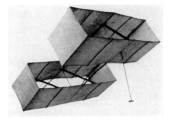

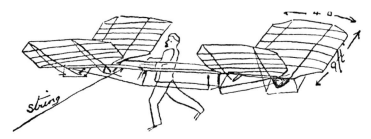

Figure 10.5 (above) The box kite, invented by Hargrave: 1893.

Figure 10.6 (right) Hargrave's sketch of his first full-size machine, a tandem-wing glider: 1894.

of monoplane tandem-wing configuration, with dihedral, and a wing area of 150 square feet; this was inspired by Lilienthal, and represented the latter's inspiration combined with Hargrave's new concept. This machine (Figure 10.6) was caught by a side gust and wrecked in June 1894, either when tethered or flying freely.

But Hargrave returned to the greater stability of the box-kite configuration – where he needed additional lifting surface – for his first powered man-carrier design in 1895 which, with a wing area of 480 square feet, was to be powered by a steam engine; but this machine was not constructed, owing to the poor performance of the engine which was built first. A particular feature of this design was that he intended it should first be tested suspended from a train of box kites, to ensure the safety of the pilot.

In 1896 Hargrave completed the design for his second powered man carrier, which was a box-kite biplane, and was to incorporate a steam engine driving four flappers (within the front box-kite cell), and a small forward cruciform control surface acting as elevator-cum-rudder; with this machine it was intended to make free takeoffs from water, and four wing-tip floats were provided for this purpose. But again, the engine was a failure; and the machine never left the drawing board. Although this design was to remain completely unknown to the world, it bears a striking resemblance to the Voisin-Archdeacon float glider of 1905 (Figure 10.7), which was indirectly descended from the Hargrave box kite, their common ancestor.

Figure 10.7 Hargrave's sketch of his second design for a man-carrying box-kite aeroplane: 1896.

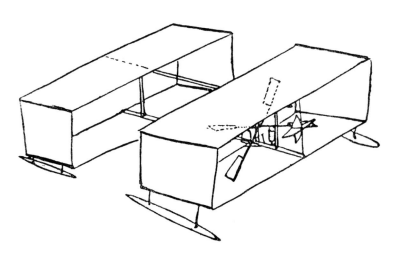

In 1899, Hargrave decided to visit England, with his family, to make the personal contacts he so badly lacked in Australia; and the most important event of his stay in this country was the paper on his kites which he delivered to the Aeronautical Society in London, with Percy Pilcher in the Chair, on 26 May 1899. It was on this occasion that he showed his box kites, the first time they had been seen 'in the flesh', so to speak, in Europe. He also presented some of them to the Society, and these were later borrowed by Pilcher. Incidentally, it is still not clear why information about these box kites, with their promise of inherent stability, was not acted upon sooner: they were published in the 1893 Chicago Conference Proceedings (1894), in Chanute's classic *Progress in Flying Machines* (1894), and in Means' *Aeronautical Annual* (1896). Gabriel Voisin records that he first heard of them in 1898; yet it was not until 1905 that he incorporated the box kite in the float gliders he built for Archdeacon and Blériot.

Hargrave's third and last full-size design came at the beginning of 1902, when he had moved to a new waterfront home at Woollahra Point, on Sydney Harbour. This machine, which was built in a modified form – of tubular tinplate – was interesting (Figure 10.8), with multiple main wings, and a smaller multiplane tail unit, with a steam engine driving a single tractor propeller.[2] The design was subsequently modified to have a single large float placed centrally, with two smaller side floats. But Hargrave's 25th engine proved to be a failure, at the end of 1903. Then, in 1906 – and it is hard indeed to find an explanation for this delay – Hargrave turned again to the petrol engine; it was, however, to power flappers instead of a propeller. But this engine, too, was a failure. In March 1906, Hargrave abandoned his full-time aviation experiments.

The story of Hargrave is one of the most curious in aviation history. His geographical isolation from the only stream of history was previously thought to have been the only stumbling block to his

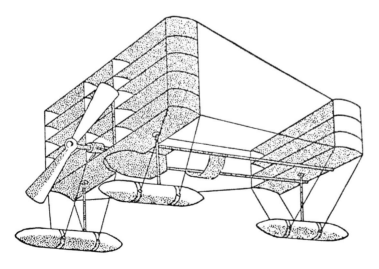

Figure 10.8 Sketch of Hargrave's third design for a man-carrying aeroplane, a multiplane box-kite type: 1902.

becoming a more influential figure in history: but this is now seen to be only a half-truth. For he not only had an excellent aeronautical library, but he was kept *au courant* with what was going on in America and Europe by correspondence with Chanute, Baden-Powell and others. And there was also his visit to England in 1899. But it is Mr Hudson Shaw – the leading authority on Hargrave – who has pointed to a vital lack in Hargrave's life; this was the lack of a technically minded friend within his own environment, with whom he could constantly discuss his work, and through whom he could clarify his own ideas. This diagnosis is surely correct; but I feel that Hargrave also possessed some inherent disabilities – or weaknesses – which were due to the fact that he was basically chauffeur-minded; he was not a true airman in his approach to aviation. The only occasions on which he was ever airborne were a few tests with his 1894 glider, and a few feet off the ground beneath one of his kite trains. He had, after all, been actively experimenting with model aeroplanes since about 1885; and in that year he told the Royal Society of New South Wales that he had already experimented with nearly 50 models. He was then to continue active experiments, including the construction – surely misguided – of no fewer than 26 motors, until 1906. Thus we have a talented man spending some 11 years in researching and testing, apparently without its ever having crossed his mind that he should have built, and properly mastered the glider and its flight control, before proceeding to powered flight.[3] If he had gone from the fully controllable glider to the powered aeroplane, he would in all probability have achieved powered flight long before his financial position became strained. Hargrave was certainly one of the great aviation pioneers of history, but he did not possess enough of the peculiar mixture of talents and characteristics necessary to achieve his end. He was indeed a splendid character, but one cannot help feeling that he was an aeronautical genius *manqué*.

Octave Chanute

Another of the outstanding figures in aviation history was the French-born American civil engineer Octave Chanute (1832–1910), who lived in Chicago. His importance was fourfold: (1) he was the first great historian of aviation, who provided the would-be pioneers with an exhaustive description of all that had been done in the past in aviation, and who provided clearly expressed ideas on what had to be done next; (2) he became the chief go-between, and disseminator of aeronautical information, between America and Europe, keeping each Continent informed about the activities of the other, and also making a vitally important visit to Europe in 1903; (3) he finalised the Lilienthal-type hang-glider in biplane form; and (4) he was the much-valued friend and encourager of the Wright brothers. As a result of these activities, he was universally regarded (from about 1896) as the 'grand old man' of aviation, and rightly accorded the respect due to the elder statesman of flying.

Chanute had first become interested in aeronautics about 1855, not – as previously thought – as a result of having met Wenham in England. At intervals in a very busy and successful career, he collected every piece of information available on the history of heavier-than-air flying; and after sifting and assessing a vast amount of material, he wrote a series of articles for *The Railroad and Engineering Journal*, starting in October 1891, and continuing for 27 issues; these were reprinted, with additions, in book form in 1894, under the title *Progress in Flying Machines*, a volume which soon became – and will always remain – one of the classics of aviation. This work, and Lilienthal's *Vogelflug*, became the two bibles of flying, and were read by every experimenter the world over. Anyone who read and digested Chanute's book would have before him the whole picture of aviation up to date, and then be in a position not only to appreciate what had already been accomplished, but what directions should next be taken to achieve human mechanical flight.

Then, in 1896, inspired by the example of Lilienthal, Chanute publicly exhorted inventors to build full-size gliders, and get into the air and experiment for themselves. Although at this time he was 64, and too old to fly himself, Chanute designed a number of man-carrying gliders, and secured the help of a young engineer, A M Herring, to help him with their design, and to pilot them. Chanute had but one main ambition, and that was to achieve, as he said, 'an apparatus with automatic stability in the wind'; he aimed at 'automatic equilibrium exclusively'. But owing to some curious misstatements and misunderstandings which have arisen over the years, and gained a regrettably wide currency, he has been wrongly credited with various ideas and achievements which he never attained or even claimed. So, for the record, the following should be set down: (1) Chanute never employed hinged control surfaces, either rudders or elevators; (2) he aimed at as high a degree of inherent stability as possible; (3) where pilot control was concerned, he only employed the Lilienthal hang-glider technique of body-swinging control, although Chanute aimed at reducing the necessary movements, and Herring contributed a further technique – to increase the controllability – of the pilot pushing and pulling his whole body backwards or forwards, using smooth horizontal bars under his armpits as 'rails' (Figure 10.9); (4) Chanute introduced the excellent 'Pratt-truss' method of rigging his multiplanes; (5) Chanute considered applying power to his gliders, but did not proceed with the idea.

Chanute selected a location on the south shore of Lake Michigan, near Miller (Indiana) as the most convenient place for testing his machines. His first two machines, both built and tested in 1896, were a multiplane hang-glider, and a biplane glider.

Chanute's multiplane machine was a hang-glider with pivoting multiplane wings – at first eight pairs, then four pairs – with a separate fixed surface placed above all, a tailplane and a fin. The main wings, restrained by rubber 'springs' from a nose bowsprit, could swivel backwards from the roots (in the horizontal plane) under sudden gusts

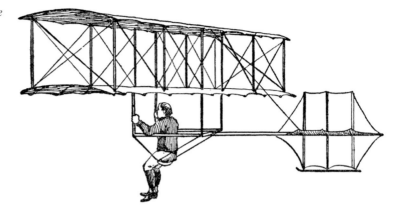

Figure 10.9 Chanute's biplane hang-glider, utilising the Pratt truss system of rigging: 1896.

in order – it was fruitlessly hoped – to shift the centre of pressure. It was first tested in July 1896, and made some 300 short glides, but it was not successful. A second machine of this type was built, and tested again without success by Herring at the Wright's camp at the Kill Devil Hills in October 1902.

Chanute's second machine became the classic biplane hang-glider which helped to determine the Wrights' biplane configuration and rigging, and represented the finalisation of the Lilienthal type of biplane hang-glider: he called it his 'two-surface' machine. It was the direct descendant of the Stringfellow triplane model of 1868, and also owed a debt to the Lilienthal biplanes of 1895. This machine of Chanute's was first designed – and first tested on 29 August 1896 for a few glides – as a triplane; then the lower wing was removed, leaving it a biplane of 12.45 square metres (say 134 square feet) wing area (Figure 10.9). It had an elongated Cayley-type cruciform tail unit on a semi-flexible outrigger, the upward elasticity – secured by rubber 'springs' – being introduced by Herring according to a modified Lilienthal practice, in the hope that it would act as a gust damper. This famous biplane was successfully flown by Herring from August to mid-September 1896, and made flights of up to 109 metres. At least two of these machines were built; one of them was rebuilt for the St Louis Exposition of 1904, and it was there flown by William Avery to test Chanute's new launching device, which consisted of a cable wound over an electrically operated drum. It was this 1904 machine which a French pioneer, Jacques Balsan, bought in St Louis, and later presented to the Musée de l'Air in Paris.

Chanute's last machine was a strange oscillating-wing triplane hang-glider, built in 1902, and tested unsuccessfully by Herring in October of that year at the Wrights' camp at the Kill Devil Hills, near Kitty Hawk. The triplane wings were pivoted span-wise, and their angle of incidence could be collectively reduced by sudden air pressure, as they were restrained by rubber 'springs': it had a Cayley-type cruciform tail unit.

It was in 1900, at the age of 68, that Chanute was contacted by the Wrights, and a close friendship developed. Chanute quickly realised their true merit; he spared no pains, through voluminous correspondence and several meetings, in encouraging them in everything they did, in discussing with them their problems, and even offering them financial assistance – which was gracefully declined. But it should be emphasised, in view of certain partisan books and articles, that the only technical debts the Wrights owed Chanute were his excellent Pratt-trussed biplane structure, and the suggestion of catapult launching: in the all-important spheres of aerodynamics and flight control, they owed him nothing, and Chanute freely admitted this. Their friendship and mutual trust was threatened for some years – as can now be clearly established – by Chanute claiming the Wrights as his pupils, which claim was as absurd as it was untrue. The Wrights were never, in any sense of the word, Chanute's pupils.

To Chanute, as the supreme middleman of aviation, goes the credit of being the unique channel through which information about – and illustrations of – the two first Wright gliders were first presented to Ferber in 1902; and of the vital third glider to the Continental world of aviation in general, in 1903; thus directly precipitating the revival of aviation – and the birth of practical flying – in Europe. Octave Chanute's immense prestige on both sides of the Atlantic ensured the maximum advertence to what he reported; his influence was always for the good, and always exerted in the absolute conviction that mechanical flight was imminent: nothing pleased him more than when the Wrights finally conquered the air during the years 1903, 1904 and 1905. Let us leave the last word to Wilbur Wright: 'In patience and goodness of heart he has rarely been surpassed; few men were more universally respected and loved.'

Augustus Moore Herring, who was Chanute's assistant, is remembered today chiefly as the pilot of Chanute's gliders. But he has also a small place in history as the first American to buy a Lilienthal glider from the master himself: hoping to improve it with alterations – in what particulars it is not yet clear – he tested it in 1896 at Chanute's 'station' on Lake Michigan, but it was not successful. Herring later (1898) built a powered biplane, powered by a compressed-air engine. Herring made hops of 50 and 72 feet with this machine at St Joseph (Michigan) in October 1898. (See note on pages 284–5.)

Percy Pilcher

The most distinguished British pioneer in practical aviation since Cayley was undoubtedly Percy Sinclair Pilcher (1867–99). He and Lilienthal were the only two men in the world whose work – up to the time they were killed – showed that they might well have flown powered aeroplanes before the Wrights, had they lived. He was a man similar to them in antecedents, in approach, in temperament, in outlook, and in his determination to get up in the air and fly: he was a true airman in every respect. His personal characteristics of integrity, modesty and pertinacity were also similar to the Wrights'; he was rightly described by Chanute as 'a most lovable character'.

After six years in the Royal Navy, he retired in 1885 to take up engineering. After going through the shops in Glasgow, he attended lectures at London University. He worked in a Southampton shipyard, then in 1893 he was appointed Assistant Lecturer in Naval Architecture and Marine Engineering at Glasgow University. In 1896 he joined Maxim as an assistant, and in 1897 became a highly valued member of the Aeronautical Society; he was elected to its Council in the same year. He left Maxim in 1897 and soon after he became a partner in the engineering firm of Wilson and Pilcher.

Aviation had for long interested him, and he was first able properly to indulge his interest at Glasgow during the early months of 1895. Pilcher was a direct product of Lilienthal's inspiration, but his independence of spirit showed itself in his remark that he 'had seen photographs of Lilienthal's apparatus, but I purposely made my own [glider] before going over to Berlin to see his, so as to get the greatest advantage from any original ideas I might have'.

In the event, he went to Berlin in April 1895, after he had completed his first glider, the *Bat*, but before testing it. Pilcher refused to believe Lilienthal's assurance that a tailplane, as well as a fin, was essential for flight. This view of Pilcher's indicates not only a certain naivety of approach at this time, but a quite extraordinary ignorance of the literature of aviation, where he would have found abundant evidence of the necessity of a tailplane. Pilcher started to experiment with the *Bat* at Cardross, on the Clyde: it was a Lilienthal-type hang-glider with the wings given a very pronounced dihedral, and only a vertical fin aft: he found he could not fly with it at all. 'I would not believe him,' wrote Pilcher of Lilienthal, 'but found out that he was quite correct.' So he converted his tail unit into a cruciform structure of fixed fin and tailplane, and thus succeeded in making some promising glides; but he found that his over-pronounced dihedral tended to 'capsize me sideways, which always meant a breakage in the machine'. The *Bat* had a wing area of 150 square feet, a weight (empty) of 45 lb; with Pilcher on board, it weighed 190 lb thus giving a wing loading of about 1½ lb per square foot.

Pilcher's second glider, the *Beetle*, was built during the summer of the same year 1895: it was also a hang-glider, but with square-cut wings of 170 square feet area, no dihedral, and a high-set cruciform tail unit composed of two intersecting discs: but the pilot hung with his head below the wings, giving a low centre of gravity and making the machine difficult to handle; the machine was also heavily built and weighed 80 lb. Pilcher soon abandoned the *Beetle*, and went back to using the *Bat*, now with reduced dihedral. With the glider in this form he obtained the best results so far. On 12 September he hovered 12 feet above the ground for half a minute, and flights under tow were made on other occasions.

His third machine was named the *Gull*, built at Glasgow late in 1895 and 'intended for practice only on calm days', and having a wing area of 300 square feet. But he said he had not the patience to wait for such calm days; he twice had the *Gull* broken in stiff breezes, and finally did not bother to repair it.

Late in 1895, Pilcher learned of Lilienthal's new biplane gliders, but he mistrusted them, believing that there was too much surface above the centre of gravity. When he visited the German pioneer for a second time, in June 1896, he flew one of these machines, but still remained sceptical of their stability, especially in squally conditions.

Pilcher's fourth glider, the *Hawk*, was his classic machine. It was built in Glasgow during the winter of 1895–96, and first flown in the following summer at Eynsford in Kent – after he had come south to work for Maxim. It was also a hang-glider; but, for the first time, there was a wheeled undercarriage, each wheel being fitted with a 'very stiff spiral spring'. This, incidentally, was the first sprung undercarriage of history.[4] The slightly arched wings, with a camber of up to 5 inches (situated 2½ feet from the leading edge) had an area of 180 square feet, and a span of 23 feet 4 inches; the tail unit a triangular tailplane to which a triangular fin was later added, which could hinge up *in toto* from near the trailing edge of the wings, but not down. In all his previous machines, Pilcher had varied Lilienthal's practice of hinging only the tailplane. It would appear from Pilcher's writings that he did not fully appreciate Lilienthal's reasons for this device (see later). The weight of the *Hawk* was 50 lb; with pilot, 195 lb; there was thus wing loading of just over 1 lb per square foot. The pilot, supported by his shoulder blades and forearms, had his head, shoulders and most of his chest, above the wings.

Launching gliders was always to present a difficult problem, as winds neither held their direction consistently, nor their strength: so Pilcher, from 1895, employed a towing technique, with a fishing line passed over a pulley on the top of one hill, with he himself in his glider poised for takeoff on the top of a neighbouring hill, and then pulled into the air. This form of assisted takeoff produced many excellent glides, including his record of some 750 feet, which he achieved on 20 June 1897.

Pilcher had for long – if not from the beginning – intended to build a powered machine; and in 1896 he took out a remarkable patent (No. 9144 of 1896), the illustrations to which have been largely forgotten (Figure 10.10). This was the world's first practical design for a powered aeroplane based on glider experience, and capable of being built and flown at least tentatively. Pilcher wrote in 1897:

> It is my intention this winter to make another machine very similar to this [the Hawk], but having small oil [i.e. petrol] engine situated just in front of me on the machine, with a shaft passing over my head, working a screw propeller of about 4 feet diameter, situated behind me. The machine will be started in exactly the same way as the soaring machines, by running down an incline, and when in the air the screw will be started to revolve, and in this way I hope to be able to maintain horizontal flight. From soaring machine experiments, it appears that an expenditure of about two H.P. per minute is necessary; I shall therefore

Figure 10.10 Pilcher's patent drawing for his first powered machine: 1896.

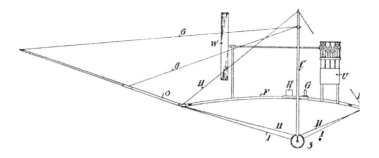

use an engine of about four H.P., because of the inefficiency of the screw and other losses. The flying speed would be about 30 miles per hour.

Here, in 1897, is a formulation of a practical powered aeroplane undreamed of anywhere else in the world at this time: it is the colloquial description of his patent of the year before.

There is only one aspect of Pilcher's work that calls for historical criticism, which may best be dealt with here; that is his neglect of flight control by movable surfaces, and his reliance on the hang-glider configuration with body control; this even applies to his 1896 patent for a powered machine. He often speaks of a 'rudder', but reference to his patent, and to the *Hawk* itself, which is preserved in the Royal Scottish Museum, makes it clear that it was only a fixed fin. The only movable surface he provided for was the upward (only) hinging of his tailplane, at first à la Lilienthal; then, in the *Hawk*, of the whole tail unit: this was to minimise the effect of the tail's possible impact on the ground when landing, to prevent the tail from being pushed up – if the machine was gusted to a halt – and so causing a nose dive, and to make the machine's reaction quicker when the pilot threw his body backwards to raise the nose. Pilcher may not have realised the second of these reasons, which nearly caused Lilienthal's death in 1894, as in his patent he only gives the first and third as reasons for his hinged tail unit. This lack of attention to control surfaces is a very curious feature in a man who looked upon gliders as a means of acquiring flying experience before advancing to powered machines; and in a man trained in marine design, where the control surfaces on submarines must have been well known to him.

Pilcher, like the Wrights, having sought in vain for a commercial engine of suitable power/weight ratio, decided to build one of his own. He reckoned that the *Hawk*, being of a total all-up weight of some 190 lb glided at about 20–25 mph, with a pull on the launching tow-line of 20–30 lb. Pilcher therefore estimated that a powered version of the *Hawk*, once it was launched, and with the weight of the engine included, would require an engine of 4 hp to sustain it in the air, driving a propeller of 5-feet diameter, with a 4-feet pitch: engine and propeller would weigh 40 lb and 3½ lb respectively; i.e. 43½ lb in all.

Pilcher, along with his other work, spent most of the next year (1898) in constructing this engine at the works (in which he was a partner) in Great Peter Street, Westminster. We know from the inquest that the engine was completed and even bench tested, by 1899. Also in 1898, he was trying to form a company to promote his flying machines. He wrote to Professor Fitzgerald, in Dublin, at the end of 1898:

> during the last year [i.e. 1898] I was not able to do anything with the flying work, as we were very busy getting our new business into going order; but the Summer before, when I was able to devote some time to it, the results we obtained were most encouraging, and consequently we are most anxious not to let the experiments drop altogether. In America, experiments are continually being made,[5] and it would be heartrending not to try and keep one's place in the work that is being done.

But 1898 was most notable as the year in which Pilcher's ideas underwent a radical change. This was brought about by an exchange of correspondence with Octave Chanute in the USA. Accounts of the numerous successful and accident-free flights made by the quadruplane and biplane at Indiana in 1896 (see pages 100–1) finally convinced Pilcher that a safe multi-surface glider could be built. After first drafting a design for a quadruplane inspired by the Chanute machines, in 1899 he built a triplane into which he intended to fit his engine, abandoning the powered *Hawk* proposal.

On 26 May 1899 the Australian Lawrence Hargrave gave a talk to the Aeronautical Society in London – at which Pilcher took the chair – in which he demonstrated his box kites (which he had invented in 1893), and soaring kites, several examples of which he presented to the Society. The soaring kites, resembling tethered gliders, greatly intrigued Pilcher. He later borrowed some of these kites and tested them.

It was then that Fate struck. Pilcher had arranged to give a gliding demonstration for Henniker Heaton, MP, on 30 September 1899 at Lord Braye's seat, Stanford Hall, near Market Harborough, in Leicestershire, where he was now making his flight trials. In addition to the tried and tested *Hawk*, Pilcher had his newly completed triplane on show, and some of the Hargrave kites. The weather was miserable, with gusty winds and showers, but it eased a little in the afternoon and Pilcher decided to go ahead with the demonstration of the *Hawk* following trials of the kites.

On its first flight, the *Hawk*, with Pilcher piloting, was successfully launched from level ground: it was towed off by a line which ran over a pulley, and was attached to two horses: all went well, and the machine was rising smoothly, when the towline parted, and the *Hawk* glided gently to earth. The same thing happened next time, and then Pilcher decided on a third attempt. When the *Hawk* was at about 30 feet above the ground, a bamboo rod in the tail assembly suddenly snapped; the tail unit collapsed; and the *Hawk* dived into the ground. Pilcher was alive when released from the wreckage; but, after lingering on through the Sunday, he died early in the morning of Monday, 2 October 1899, without recovering consciousness.[6]

Pilcher was one of the great aviation pioneers of history; and, if he had been spared, he might have attained proper powered, sustained and controlled flight before the Wright brothers. Like Lilienthal, he approached the problem of flight with a balanced and mature attitude, knowing that theory and practice must constantly interplay and develop together. Chanute lists Pilcher's specific achievements as (1) the demonstration that too much dihedral reduces stability in side winds; (2) that an unduly low centre of gravity makes the machine difficult to control; (3) that safe takeoffs can be made by towing; and (4) that a light-wheeled undercarriage is convenient for moving the machine about, and for absorbing shocks in landing. After his death, practical productive work in aviation in Britain became virtually moribund until the arrival of Cody's machine of 1908.

A suitable epitaph for Pilcher – a true airman – might be the following words he himself wrote in 1897:

> The object of experimenting with soaring machines is to enable one to have practice in starting and alighting, and controlling a machine in the air.... They are excellent schooling machines, and that is all they are meant to be, until power, in the shape of an engine working a screw propeller, or an engine working wings to drive the machine forward, is added; then a person who is used to sailing down a hill with a simple soaring machine will be able to fly with comparative safety.

Other inventors

Of less technical stature than Chanute, but of great importance in aviation during the last decade of the century, was another American, James Means (1853–1920).[7] He was an industrialist who was primarily an intellectual, and gave up his business when he amassed enough money for his family to live on, and devoted himself to the promotion of aviation. He had a fine mind, excellent judgment, and high integrity. Although Means productively studied bird flight, then kites and gliders, and designed model gliders in 1893–94 (Figure 10.11), it was in the literary field of information and propaganda that his influence was most strongly felt. For in 1895 he issued the first of the three volumes of his *Aeronautical Annual,* a triple work of far-reaching importance and influence, which appeared in 1895, 1896 and 1897. As Means himself said, later on, he 'thought that if he could gather the best of the world's literature on the subject and publish it, it might bring experimenters together, thus preventing waste of effort'. This, Means proceeded to do, and to great effect. Like Chanute, he was determined to disseminate as much information about flying as possible, being convinced that mechanical flight would one day be achieved. So he collected and edited the most significant papers he could find on past and current developments, including the work of Lilienthal, Chanute, Langley, Hargrave and others; and also performed a valuable service by reprinting some of the classic papers by Cayley and Wenham, besides giving bibliographies and other

useful material. These admirable volumes, which were also published
in London, were read and studied by everyone seriously interested
in heavier-than-air flight, and provided them with valuable data and
encouragement. But it is symptomatic of the general apathy of the
public, and the *fin-de-siècle* doldrums into which aviation had fallen,
that Means was depressed enough to place the following dedication
at the head of his last volume (1897), just six years before the Wrights
flew: 'To the memory of those who, intelligently believing in the
possibility of mechanical flight, have lived derided, and died in sorrow
and obscurity.' He was happily to live – to his great satisfaction – to
discover how much his *Aeronautical Annuals* had meant to the Wright
brothers; and to witness, not only the triumph of the Wrights, but
the general triumph of the aeroplane as a practical vehicle. Means
was always to pursue his interest in, and concern for, aviation, and
himself proved to be an inventor of a high order. In 1909 he patented
a smoke-signal device for signalling from aircraft, and (also in 1909)
an aircraft launcher: then in 1909 and 1911, he patented a simplified
control column for aeroplanes. But his lasting value lay back in the
1890s, where he helped others to make history.

On 27 January 1894 an interesting event occurred at Pirbright
Camp in England when Captain B F S Baden-Powell (brother of the
first Chief Scout) made his first ascent sitting suspended from kites; he
used monoplane kites, and flew first with one kite, then with a train
of them. He should thus be reckoned as the first partially successful
user of man-lifting kites outside the Orient, despite Pocock and
Cordner: he thus started a minor fashion in military aerial observation
techniques, which Cody was later to perfect.

Amongst the aviation pioneers there have been a number for
whom extravagant claims have been made – as has already been noted
– by persons not wholly disinterested. One of the most notorious
– notorious because his very minor talent has been exploited in
campaigns to discredit the Wrights – was the so-called 'Professor'
John J Montgomery of Santa Clara College in California, USA. Oddly
enough the best account – plain and unvarnished – of his work,
appeared in the official court records of an action brought by his heirs
against the United States government (1917–25) which they lost when
seeking to invalidate the Wrights', and other, patents. Montgomery
first constructed models and unsuccessful full-size gliders during the
years 1883–86. He then abandoned his experiments until late in 1903;
then, having been impressed by the form of Langley's Aerodromes,
he designed and built Langley-derived tandem-wing machines, but
unpowered, which he intended should be taken up beneath hot-air
balloons and released. A balloon parachute jumper named D Maloney
agreed to pilot one of these balloon-borne gliders, and on 16 March
1905, he made a perilous descent from about 500 feet. On 29 April
of 1905, a public display was planned, and Maloney again cast off
and 'luckily reached the ground without accident'. On 18 July of the
same year, another glide was made from a balloon and the machine
crashed, killing Maloney. A Mr Wilkie was then persuaded to pilot

Figure 10.11 Model glider built by Means, the Editor of the Aeronautical Annual: *1893–94.*

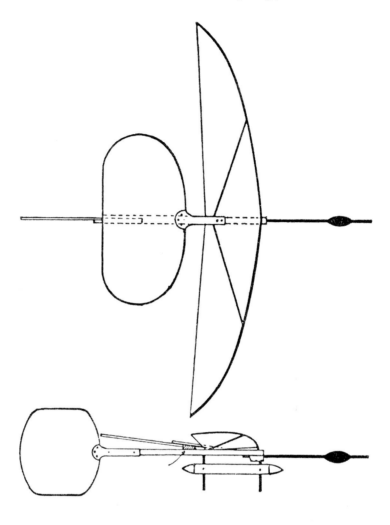

one of these gliders, and he narrowly escaped with his life on 22 February 1906. Finally Montgomery himself was killed in 1911 in an 'improved' glider which he had constructed. Montgomery was not lacking in courage, but he lacked essential knowledge and experience and, despite the ingenious idea of launching a glider from a balloon – which had been proposed by Cayley in 1852 – achieved little but publicity. He made no real contribution to aviation.

* * * * *

Practical aviation in Europe at the turn of the century had reached a regrettable state of moribundity. Lilienthal and Pilcher were dead; Kress had abandoned his work after the crash of his machine in 1901; Jatho was making tests which were to lead nowhere; and only Ferber was enthusiastically but fruitlessly following Lilienthal before he was to be reorientated by news of the Wright gliders. Airships and balloons were occupying most of the aeronautical stage, and as far as the public was concerned the achievement of mechanical flight was still far off. This view was also shared by many serious but discouraged investigators in England, France and Germany. What was worse, the few men who preserved their vision were often ridiculed, and the sceptics could proudly point to such great scientists as Lord Kelvin to support them. Kelvin even went so far as to commit his views to paper in a now notorious letter (it was written in answer to Major Baden-Powell's invitation to him to join the Aeronautical Society).

Dear Baden-Powell, I am afraid I am not in the flight for 'aerial navigation'. I was greatly interested in your work with kites but I have not the smallest molecule of faith in aerial navigation other than ballooning or of expectation of good results from any of the trials we hear of. So you will understand that I would not care to be a member of the Aeronautical Society. Yours truly, Kelvin.

This remarkable letter was dated 8 December 1896; in this year Lilienthal had died, Pilcher was gliding successfully in England, and Langley making powered models in America: just seven years later the Wrights were to fly a powered aeroplane.

Far away in Australia, Lawrence Hargrave laboured at the problem, but he was too far off the beaten track. The initiative in aviation had passed to the United States; but even there only a few men believed in the 'cause' and only one – Langley – was making any satisfactory progress, although Chanute was busy with ideas.

But with the wisdom of hindsight we can now see that this apparently barren field had been richly sown, and was only awaiting the favourable weather conditions to bring up a rich crop. The petrol motor, in the service of both automobiles and motorcycles, had reached a stage when it could be adapted for flying machines; and in 1896 the motor car had finally been given the freedom of the roads in Britain, and the spread of automobilism thereby became fast and furious: apart from the immense technical advance which followed this emancipation, there was rapidly built up a great reservoir of trained mechanics, men who would be ready to serve powered aviation when it should arrive. There was a great deal of technical information on aerodynamics lying in somewhat obscure books and periodicals, and Chanute's *Progress in Flying Machines* (1894) conveniently summed up the historic and contemporary endeavours for anyone who wished to know how the land lay; and there was also to hand a growing number of competent and enthusiastic mechanics and amateurs dedicated to the pursuit of 'automobilisme', but ready and willing to transfer their allegiance to the aeroplane whenever it should arrive. Finally there was a growingly air-minded public and press, thanks to the long tradition of ballooning and the recent developments in practical airship building, especially in Santos-Dumont. There was, therefore, an admirable overall 'climate' awaiting the birth of the new vehicle.

Then, in the last year of the century, all the necessary talents and circumstances conspired finally to favour two modest but determined cycle makers of Dayton in Ohio, who in that year 1899 became seriously determined to conquer the air; and, within the span of four short years, were to succeed brilliantly.

Significant dates in other fields (1890s)

1890s Electric tramways now in general use throughout the world.

1890s Telephones now in general use.

1890s Halftone reproduction of photos now in universal use (after first commercial development in 1882).

1895 Automobile-Club de France founded.

1895 First cinema theatre opened (by Brothers Lumière in Paris).

1896 Freedom of the roads granted to motorcars in Britain, leading to a vast expansion of the motor industry.

1896 Parsons introduces the marine turbine, and puts on a startling and decisive demonstration with his *Turbinia* at the Spithead Review of 1897.

1897 Practical wireless telegraphy introduced by Marconi (first trans-Channel, 1899; first transatlantic, 1901).

1897 Diesel makes first successful compression-ignition engine (which he had patented in 1892).

1897 Automobile Club (later Royal) founded in London.

Notes

1 The numbering system adopted here is taken from the late Gerhard Halle's *Otto Lilienthal und seine Flugzeug-Konstruktionen* (1962), a booklet which Herr Halle kindly wrote at my instigation: it was published by the Deutsches Museum, Munich. All gliders before *No. 13* were monoplanes.

2 A small point has come to light concerning the drawing of Hargrave's third multiplane design for his third man-carrying aeroplane shown in Figure 10.8. This was not actually done by Hargrave himself: it turns out to have been drawn by his friend Sidney Holland, to whom Hargrave sent a rough sketch of his design on 26 September 1901: Hargrave indicated a machine with six main planes forward, and four tailplanes, with three floats, and the pilot lying prone. Holland drew out a tractor machine following these lines, even to the slings for the prone pilot; so the sketch may be taken as a true rendering of what Hargrave had in mind.

3 It is interesting to find even Hargrave believing in the idea of steering air brakes. In a statement to the Royal Society of New South Wales on 3 June 1885, he said: 'In larger machines this (i.e. body movement) would have to be done by making the area of the tail-surface variable for ascending or descending, and tilting one corner up or down for turning to either side.'

4 It is sometimes said this was also the first wheeled undercarriage in history. It was, of course, far from being so. Quite apart from the many designs and models with wheels, the following full-size machines had wheeled undercarriages prior to the *Hawk*: Cayley's gliders of 1849 and 1853; Du

So when the Wrights built their first glider in 1900 it incorporated two ideas which the brothers were to utilise throughout their early work – the intentionally unstable aeroplane which could be kept flying satisfactorily only by the pilot's skill, and the warping of the wings for control in roll. 'We therefore resolved', wrote Wilbur, 'to try a fundamentally different principle. We would arrange the machine so that it would not tend to right itself.' Their technique of wing warping consisted of a helical twisting of the wings, which produced a positive angle of incidence on one side, and a negative angle on the other, thus causing the machine to return to the horizontal, or to bank: they also believed – mistakenly – that they would be able to steer to right or left by warping alone, but no attempts at such steering were made until 1901.

The glider was completed in September of 1900 at Dayton and transported to the lonely sand dunes of Kitty Hawk,[5] on the coast of North Carolina, a place decided upon after receiving from the Washington Weather Bureau a comparative table of locations having strong and constant winds. This No. 1 glider was similar to the kite, but had fixed biplane wings of 17 feet span, with warping control, a movable forward elevator – which they called a 'horizontal rudder' – and a prone pilot position in order to be more comfortable, make landing safer, and to reduce head resistance: the wing area was 165 square feet. It had no tail surfaces. This tentative machine was flown during October, and provided the Wrights with the first confirmation of their basic ideas. It was mostly flown as a kite (the controls worked from the ground); owing to lack of strong winds, only a few manned pilot-controlled kite flights were made, and only a few free piloted glides: it showed good response to the elevator and to the wing-warping device. The forward positioning of the elevator, on this and on all Wright aircraft until 1910, was dictated by their belief that it provided the safest fore and aft control, especially when the centre of pressure on the wings travelled backwards and caused the machine to nose-dive. This glider also confirmed their disbelief in any automatic stability: they had at first rigged it with a dihedral angle and found it flew badly in gusty winds; so they abandoned dihedral, and temporarily rigged their wings level.

They returned to Dayton well pleased with their short stay at Kitty Hawk. They were now all the more determined to fly; but also to proceed carefully and logically, concentrating particularly on control in the air: 'When once a machine is under proper control under all conditions, the motor problem will be quickly solved', wrote Wilbur when building this first glider.

Next year (1901) they constructed their biplane glider No. 2, with the wing area increased to 290 square feet, a span of 22 feet, an anhedral 'droop' of 4 inches, and the warping wires worked by a hip cradle. The Wrights had been working on figures for wing area and camber compiled by Lilienthal – which they read in translated articles – and other experimenters, and they decided on a camber of 1 in 12 for the new machine. In July they transported it to the

Kill Devil sand hills near Kitty Hawk, and made the first glide on the 27th of the month. The flights continued through the first half of August, and many were witnessed there by Chanute on the first visit which he paid to the camp. The glider was launched by two men – one of the brothers and a 'local' – who grasped the wing tips and ran the machine the short distance necessary for it to become airborne. They soon found that their wing camber was too deep, and was producing an excessive movement of the centre of pressure as the angle of incidence changed. So they reduced the curvature to 1 in 19, and the performance and control were greatly improved. Glides of up to 389 feet were made, and control maintained in winds of up to about 27 mph.

The Wrights returned to Dayton with mixed feelings. They had achieved a certain measure of success, but they realised that their results were far from satisfactory. They now began to suspect the accuracy of Lilienthal's calculations, upon which they had relied until now. The aircraft also showed an alarming tendency – when being warped – for the positively warped wings to swing *back*, and for the whole machine to slew round as it side-slipped, and crash. 'Having set out with absolute faith in the existing scientific data', wrote Wilbur, 'we were driven to doubt one thing after another, till finally, after two years of experiment, we cast it all aside, and decided to rely entirely upon our own investigations.'

It was this dissatisfaction with the whole situation that then led them, between September 1901 and August 1902, to undertake a vigorous and intensive programme of research, including the testing of aerofoil sections in a wind tunnel and on a bicycle, as well as thoroughly reworking all their aerodynamic problems. In this way they laid the secure foundations for later success, and then set about building their new glider (No. 3) with confidence.

It is interesting to note that Wilbur, at Chanute's request, gave a lecture in Chicago (18 September 1901) on the two short 'seasons' of gliding, in which he not only gave a description of the machines but also of the wing-warping technique. 'A devilish good paper', was how Chanute described it, 'which will be extensively quoted.' It is also interesting to remember that Langley, in 1901, had made his unsuccessful petrol-powered model Aerodrome which was to precede the full-size machine tested in 1903.

The new glider (No. 3), built of spruce and cloth and 'to withstand hard usage', was constructed during August and September of 1902, and first flown on 20 September. Between that date and the end of October nearly a thousand glides were made; they met and surmounted their last major control problem; and by the end of the season possessed a fully practical machine which had only to be copied and slightly modified before they were ready to fit an engine. This new biplane glider had a wing area of 305 square feet, a span of 32 feet 1 inch, a camber of 1 in 24 to 1 in 30, the same anhedral 'droop' or 'arch' as the No. 2, and the same warping system: but there was added to the rear a double fixed fin to counteract (by its weathervane action) the swing-back of the wings on the positively warped side, in the case either of regaining lateral balance after being gusted out of the horizontal, or of the pilot initiating a bank. The machine, which was launched by two men, like its predecessor, behaved well in some of the glides; but severe trouble arose with deliberate warped banks or gust-produced (non-warped) banks, when the pilot – in trying to limit the bank or in trying to return to the horizontal – applied positive warp to the dropped wings in order to raise them: instead of coming up, these dropped wings would sink or swing back, and the machine would spin and crash.

The Wrights diagnosed the basic trouble as warp drag (aileron drag today) where the positive warp increased the resistance of the wings on one side, and the negative warp decreased it on the other, causing them not only to bank, but to turn about their vertical axis in the opposite direction to that originally anticipated. The addition of the fixed rear fin caused them much more trouble than it cured. For, in the acts of banking noted above, the resulting side slip caused the fin to act as a lever, and rotate the wings about their vertical axis, thus increasing the speed (and thus the lift and height) of the raised wings, whilst retarding and lowering the dropped wings. When the pilot applied positive warp to the dropped wings, it simply aggravated the situation, and produced a spin, by swinging back the dropped wings through warp drag, thus increasing their incidence beyond the stalling angle.

This problem was solved by converting the fixed double fin into a single movable rudder, which – with its cables fastened to the warp cradle – was always turned towards the direction of bank, thus counteracting the warp drag. As the rudder was also (but unintentionally) adjusted to more than compensate for the warp drag, the machine could also be made to perform a smooth banked turn. Experience with this glider also convinced them that all their machines should continue to be made inherently unstable to allow of sensitive and immediate response to the controls.

After this vital step, the Wrights had a practical and highly success-ful glider, with which they made nearly a thousand perfectly controlled glides often in winds of up to 35 mph; they set a distance record of 622½ feet, and a duration record of 26 seconds. 'The flights of 1902', wrote Orville, 'demonstrated the efficiency of our system of control for both longitudinal and lateral stability. They also demonstrated that our tables of air pressure which we made in our wind-tunnel would enable us to calculate in advance the performance of a machine.'

Both brothers became experienced and skilful pilots; and with so much flying behind them both, and so many theoretical and practical problems solved, they felt fully justified in their fundamental idea of constructing an unstable machine whose stability and control in the air depended solely upon the pilot's skill. They realised that if such a machine could be suitably engined they would have in their hands not only a machine that would fly, but a practical aeroplane that would be almost as sensitive and manoeuvrable as a bird.

Figure 11.3 Principal drawing of the Wright patent of 1903 (granted in 1906), showing the wing-warping, rudder and elevator system.

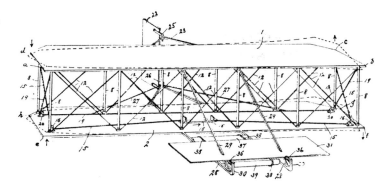

The combination of warp and rudder, rather than the warping idea itself, was the most essential feature of the patent applied for by the Wrights in 1902, and granted in 1906 (Figure 11.3). This feature of the Wrights' work is consistently misunderstood – and hence misrepresented – by many writers.

They returned to Dayton justly elated and fully confident of success. But there were still two major problems facing them – the engine and the propeller. The engine was not at first seen as a serious question since they thought one of the numerous automobile engines on sale at that time would be suitable: but on enquiry, they found that none of them were light enough for their power. And so these remarkable men set to, and not only designed their own motor, but built it: it was of 12 hp, was water-cooled, and weighed (with all accessories, plus water and fuel) about 200 lb. When it came to the question of propellers, the Wrights realised that the problem was indeed formidable, as the small amount of published material was useless to them: so they conducted their own basic research, developed a satisfactory airscrew and so finally surmounted their last major obstacle.

It was in 1902 and 1903 that news and illustrations of the Wrights' gliders became available in France; and, first through Ferber, then through Chanute's lecture in Paris (on 2 April 1903), the Europeans were directly influenced to revive aviation on the Continent.

The Wrights' first powered machine, the Flyer – a name they applied to all their powered machines – was constructed during the summer of 1903; it was transported to the Kill Devil Hills on 23–25 September, where the brothers found their camp in bad repair, and the 1902 glider damaged. They repaired the glider to practise on, giving it a new double rear rudder like the one on the new Flyer. Then came weeks of careful preparation, practice gliding, and many minor but exasperating setbacks. Mechanical breakages, repairs, replacements, and adjustments of one kind and another delayed having the Flyer ready for tests until 12 December, when all was in good order. But unfavourable weather postponed the first test until 14 December. The brothers summoned as witnesses their friends from the nearby Kill Devil Life Saving Station, and carried their machine to the end of the starting rail.

The powered Flyer,[6] which stood there ready for its first trial, was a biplane of 40 feet 4 inches span, a wing area of 510 square feet, and camber of about 1 in 20, supported on two long skids; the 12-hp engine drove two pusher propellers by means of cycle chains, one of which was crossed to produce counter-rotation (Figure 11.4). In appearance and control it was similar to the No. 3 glider of 1902, except that both the vertical rear rudder, and the front elevator were now double structures.

On this day, 14 December, it was placed on the 60-foot launching rail which had been laid downhill and into wind. The Wrights tossed a coin to decide who should be the first pilot, and Wilbur won. But the test was a failure: the Flyer ran down the rail, rose from the carrying truck, climbed steeply, stalled and ploughed into the sand, causing minor damage to the structure. Wilbur admitted that the failure was due to his error in putting on too much elevator, and thus bringing the nose up too high. The damage was soon repaired and they again waited for a suitable day. Incidentally, even if this first trial had succeeded, it would not have counted as a true flight, as the takeoff was downhill and so assisted by gravity.

On Thursday 17 December conditions were again suitable, with a wind of some 20–27 mph, and the takeoff rail was laid down on level ground. Local witnesses were again summoned, who now numbered five, and a camera was set up and trained on the end of the takeoff track. With Orville at the controls – it was now his turn – the engine of the Flyer was run up, and at 10.35 am the holding rope was released and the machine was off.[7] It rose from the truck after a run of about 40 feet and made an undulating flight of some 12 seconds, covering 120 feet before it landed. The rise and fall was due to inexperience with the elevator, which was too evenly balanced, and to consequent overcorrection; airspeed was about 30 mph. Although of only 12 seconds' duration, this flight was, in Orville's words, 'the

Figure 11.4 Replica of the Wrights' 12-hp engine. (Science & Society Picture Library)

first in the history of the world in which a machine carrying a man had raised itself by its own power into the air in full flight, had sailed forward without reduction of speed, and had finally landed at a point as high as that from which it started' (Figure 11.5).

After a minor repair, three more flights were made that morning, the brothers alternating as pilot (Figure 11.6): the second flight covered about 175 feet; the third some 200 feet; and the fourth, which lasted 59 seconds, covered 852 feet; but the true distance through the air was just over half a mile, owing to the head wind.[8] On landing after this last flight the elevator was damaged, and it was decided to end the trials. The machine was carried back to the camp and there, a few minutes later, it was overturned by a gust of wind and wrecked. 'As winter was already well set in, we should have postponed our trials to a more favourable season, but for the fact that we were determined, before returning home, to know whether the machine possessed sufficient power to fly, sufficient strength to withstand the shocks of landing, and sufficient capacity of control to make flight safe in boisterous winds, as well as in calm air. When these points had been definitely established, we at once packed our goods and returned home, knowing that the age of the flying machine had come at last.'

The Wright brothers had tentatively conquered the air four-and-a-half years after they had written to the Smithsonian Institution asking for books on flying. Now, in 1903, Wilbur was 36 years old, Orville 32. They had made the first powered, sustained and controlled flights, and possessed the first potentially practical flying machine. No aeroplanes other than the Wrights could remain in the air for

more than 20 seconds until November of 1906; and it was not until November of 1907 that a full minute's duration was achieved by a European machine. The Wrights' task now was to produce a properly practical machine, which they evolved successfully in 1904 and 1905.

Owing to a curious chain of circumstances the world was only given a garbled description of the flights of 17 December, and they were therefore treated as the wayward efforts of two eccentric brothers. But even more astonishing was the fact that the Wrights flew in public continually in 1904 and 1905 without attracting worldwide attention.

Back in Dayton the brothers began designing their powered Flyer II and a new motor. Construction was finished in May, and a new 'aerodrome' established eight miles east of Dayton, near Simms Station: it was a 90-acre field called the Huffman Prairie (or Pasture) lent to the brothers by a Dayton banker, Torrence Huffman. This, the world's first aerodrome for aviation, saw the first tests of Flyer II on 23 or 26 May. The new machine, basically similar to the No. 1, had the camber decreased from 1 in 20 to 1 in 25, a much more efficient engine of 15–16 hp, and lower gearing to new propellers. During the summer, autumn and winter, 105 trials and some 80 brief flights were made, the Wrights concentrating on becoming familiar with the controls, the care of the engine, and the use of the assisted takeoff device which they first employed on 7 September. The latter consisted of a weight hung from a rope inside a tall derrick: the rope travelled to the top of the derrick, down to the starting end of the

Figure 11.6 Wilbur Wright piloting Flyer I on 17 December 1903. (Science & Society Picture Library)

launching track, along the track to the takeoff end, then back to the starting end, where it was attached to a hinged rod on the lower wing. When the weight was released, the rope – working over pulley wheels – drew the aircraft on its truck fast along the length of the launching track. This assisted takeoff device was used by the Wrights – and by all Wright aircraft – until 1910, although a few owners of Wright machines were attaching wheels to the skids in 1909. Although the majority of flights in the 1904 season were short, they were of great importance; were often witnessed by friends, including Chanute; and were photographed. The first circular flight was made by Wilbur on 20 September – after which the manoeuvre became commonplace – and the first flight of over 5 minutes took place on 9 November, when Wilbur made almost four circles of the pasture, a distance of about 2¾ miles.

The flights in 1904 were all made at very low heights, so that in learning both the particular characteristics of the aircraft and the craft of pilotage in general, they had a good chance of survival in a crash. This low-flying policy was also retained for a further reason: there was still one flying problem they could not understand or solve, and that was the Flyer's tendency not to respond to the controls, then stall and go out of control, when making a tight turn. This trouble was not mastered until September of 1905.

As their patent was pending in America and other countries, the Wrights allowed witnesses close up to the machine, but no photographs were allowed to be taken other than their own. Groups of pressmen had visited them by invitation on two days at the start of the season, but weather and mechanical failure had prevented flights on both occasions, and the disillusioned Press had refused to take notice of them thereafter until late in 1905, despite constant reports from the local farmers and others, who through 1904 and 1905 came to take the sight of a flying aeroplane for granted at a time when many authorities were asserting that mechanical flight was impossible.

In 1905 the Wrights designed their Flyer III and completed it in June. It proved a thoroughly successful vehicle, and ranks as the first all-round practical aeroplane in history. Wing area was slightly reduced, to 503 square feet; the span was 40 feet 6 inches; the camber was put back to 1 in 20; the wings were rigged horizontally flat with no anhedral droop; the biplane elevator was enlarged and placed farther out in front of the wings; the double rear rudder was also enlarged and placed farther back; and the whole machine was mounted higher on its skids and made more robust. New propellers were fitted, but the excellent 1904 engine was retained. This new machine made its first flight at the Huffman Prairie on 23 June and its trials went on until 16 October. They made over 40 flights this season, and were airborne for just over three hours; this time they were out for reliability and endurance. In September, the trouble they were having in tight turns was diagnosed as a tendency of the lowered wings to slow up and stall; and the cure seen to be in putting down the nose to gain speed when turning. On 26 September 26th they flew

11⅛ miles in 18 minutes 9 seconds; on 29 September, 12 miles in 19 minutes 55 seconds; on 3 October, 15¼ miles in 25 minutes 5 seconds; on 4 October, 20¾ miles in 33 minutes 17 seconds; and on 5 October, 24⅕ miles in 38 minutes 3 seconds, at an average speed of 38 mph, a flight, as with others of this series, which only stopped because the fuel was exhausted. The last flight of the season was made on 16 October. Apart from the achievement of a practical aeroplane, the Wrights had made a final and important change in their flying control system during the latter part of this season. In the course of seeking a cure for the stalling on turns, they had disconnected the warping and rudder wires. This allowed of any desired degree of warp or rudder movement being made, either together or separately; and, amongst other things, made re-establishment of lateral equilibrium in gusts, etc. possible without any turning movement being brought about by the rear rudder. This freeing of the controls, and their proper coordination in the air, contributed still further to the mastery of mechanical flying. The final step was to seat the pilot upright, which was done when the 1905 Flyer was modified for practice flying in 1908, when upright seating for two was fitted. It was not to be until 16 October 1908 that a European pilot was to equal the Wrights' 1905 performances, when Henri Farman (who was then British) flew for 41 minutes 32 seconds.

With the Flyer III of 1905 the Wrights had now for all practical purposes 'conquered the air': in the words of Charles Dollfus, speaking of the brothers' work, 'ils ont changé la face du Monde'.

As the year 1905 had progressed, and as the Wrights' flights had become ever more impressive, word of their success had been reaching various commercial and military quarters, and even the Press was slowly awakening to what was going on. However, the Wrights, who had decided that they would not reveal their invention to the world without legal protection and some financial reward for their work, grew worried about the preservation of secrecy. As their patent was still pending – it was not to be granted until 1906 – they were not anxious to have shrewd spectators come close up to the machine. They had tried to interest the United States government on three occasions, but, to their anger and astonishment, they were stupidly rebuffed on the grounds that the Board of Ordnance was not interested in aircraft that did not exist! The Board could not understand that the Wrights were offering it a completed practical machine. Thereafter they began looking overseas for recognition, starting first with an offer to the British government. By the end of 1905 and the start of 1906, informed quarters in France were convinced that the Wrights had had a triumphant and successful season in 1905, and had produced a practical aeroplane: this view was put forward unequivocally in the January (1906) issue of *L'Aérophile*, and caused widespread consternation in Europe, and a confused determination to rival the Wrights' achievements (see pages 141–4). In England, where public, and even technical, opinion was moribund in the extreme, only a few men realised the true significance of what was happening: chief of these was Colonel J E Capper, Superintendent of the Government

Balloon Factory (to become later the Royal Aircraft Establishment), who had met the Wrights[9] and privately written to the War Office on 30 January 1905:

> I wish to invite very special attention to the wonderful advance made in aviation by the brothers Wright. I have every confidence in their uprightness, and in the correctness of their statements.... It is a fact that they have flown and operated personally a flying machine for a distance of over three miles, at a speed of 35 m.p.h.

Negotiations with the United States government broke down when the US Army completely refused to accept the fact that the Wrights were offering them a finished aeroplane, and not – as the Army thought – asking for financial assistance in building one: this was despite the most explicit statements and explanations by the Wrights. Disillusioned and rightly resentful of the treatment they had received from their own government, they then (in 1905) decided to offer their Flyer to the British government. Negotiations with Britain dragged on for some years, and foundered chiefly on the Wrights' demand – understandable but short-sighted – that no-one should be allowed to view the machine until after the purchase had been completed; such purchase depending on an agreed performance having been carried out by the machine. They did not want the Flyer examined, then some excuse made for not purchasing it, despite its ability to perform as stated.

There was also some question of the French purchasing the Flyer; but that, too, fell through for the time being.

So they decided to stop all flying, and thus provide no opportunity for commercial or military spying, or other unwelcome visitations; then to continue negotiations with anyone who was interested in the idea of buying the Flyer.

And so it came about that for two-and-a-half years, from 16 October 1905 until 6 May 1908, they never once left the ground, nor allowed any stranger to see their aeroplanes. And so the first great phase of the Wright brothers' career came to an end, to be followed in 1908 by a second and no less triumphant one.

It is perhaps appropriate to close this section with Sir Walter Raleigh's words: 'It is not extravagant to say that the 17th of December 1903, when the Wright brothers made the first free flight through the air in a power-driven machine, marks the beginning of a new era in the history of the world.'

Notes

1   There is now evidence to show that it was an article on Lilienthal in an issue of *McClure's Magazine* in 1894 (pp. 322–31) which first aroused Wilbur's interest: it was excellently illustrated by dramatic photographs of Lilienthal gliding, and this magazine is known to have been subscribed to by the Wright family. Lilienthal's death in 1896 probably finally focused Wilbur's active attention.

2   *The Papers of Wilbur and Orville Wright*. Edited by Marvin W McFarland, 2 vols, New York, 1953.

3   Other forms of truss could have been used.

4   It has been suggested that such 'chauffeurs' as Maxim and Langley were comparatively old men, whereas the 'airmen' were young; but many young men were also 'chauffeurs' and the aged Chanute was a true 'airman'.

5   From 1901 onwards, they flew from the Kill Devil sand hills, 4 miles south of Kitty Hawk, where they set up a hutted camp.

6   In later years the machine became known by the historically incorrect and inappropriate name of *Kitty Hawk*, a name which has now unfortunately 'stuck' to it.

7   It has sometimes been stated that the Wrights used an accelerated takeoff device for their first flights. This is not so. In 1904, as described later, they invented the weight-and-derrick method of assisted takeoff in order to operate from the confined space of the Huffman Prairie near Dayton, and to make them less dependent upon the weather.

8   This was the Wrights' own estimate.

9   Capper was sent by the War Office to report on the aeronautical aspects of the St Louis Exposition of 1904. When he was in the USA he went to see Chanute, Langley and the Wright brothers. He visited the Wrights on 23 October 1904. He was one of the few people to whom the Wrights showed photographs of their machines in the air. Capper was deeply impressed by the brothers, and was high in their praise long before he wrote the memorandum quoted here from the RE Committee; and much of the inspiration for Cody's first powered aeroplane of 1908 came from the Wrights via Capper.

12 The beginnings of practical aviation in Europe, and elsewhere: 1902–1908[1]

Figure 12.1 Count Ferdinand von Zeppelin: c. 1900. Photograph from the official album of the Zeppelin Naval Airship Company, published in 1924. (Science & Society Picture Library)

During the opening years of this century in Europe the prospect of achieving a practical powered aeroplane seemed very remote. Aeronautical attention was fixed on the balloon and the dirigible airship, the latter coming rapidly into prominence. In 1900 Count von Zeppelin (Figure 12.1) flew his first giant airship over Lake Constance: in 1901 Santos-Dumont piloted his dirigible No. 6 round the Eiffel Tower, thereby winning both a prize and the acclaim of Europe. In 1903 the Lebaudy brothers achieved the really practical dirigible when they saw their ship piloted on the first properly controlled aerial voyage in history; on 12 November it flew 38 miles from Moisson to the Champ-de-Mars, inside Paris. With these, and an ever-growing series of flights, the practical airship 'arrived' (Figure 12.2) in the world of transport after its birth with Giffard in 1852.

Figure 12.2 Maiden flight of the Clement-Bayard airship in London, c. 1908, depicted in a coloured print. (Science & Society Picture Library)

1902 and 1903

The true revival of aviation, and the birth of practical flying, in Europe was due directly to the Wright brothers, as is clear both from the configurations adopted and from the numerous contemporary statements by the pioneers themselves. The revival was effected through the work of four Frenchmen in 1902–04, and resulted in two parallel streams of development of the biplane; and later in the revival and development of the monoplane.

The Wrights precipitated the European revival in two phases, the one reinforcing the other. First to be influenced was Captain Ferdinand Ferber, of the French artillery, the only European disciple of Lilienthal still seriously pursuing aviation in 1901: he was experimenting with a hang-glider derived from the great German pioneer. He had begun by making and testing gliders in 1899, influenced by Lilienthal, and from that year until the end of 1901 made four machines, starting with kite forms and ending with a Lilienthal-type glider; all, however, were pursued without success. Then, about October 1901, he happened to read a magazine article on gliding: this led to a correspondence with Chanute in America and, in January 1902, to Ferber receiving from him a reprint of Wilbur Wright's first Chicago lecture (given on 18 September 1901) describing and illustrating the Nos. 1 and 2 Wright gliders of 1900 and 1901 and their wing warping; neither had rear fin or rudder. This event proved decisive for Ferber and thus for European aviation.

Ferber promptly abandoned the Lilienthal tradition and, as he said of himself, took 'solely to the Wright type in 1902', the first of which he tested at Beuil in June 1902. This was Europe's first Wright-type glider, but it was crudely constructed and did not even incorporate wing warping. In *L'Aérophile* for February 1903, this machine was well described and illustrated. It was the first piloted Wright-type glider to be properly 'seen' by the Europeans. The Ferber machines had non-rigid surfaces, the most primitive elevator control, and no warping: later he placed a triangular vertical rudder at each wing tip. The results, as might be expected, were poor; and Ferber had at that time neither the knowledge nor experience to make much improvement. Thus the form of the Wright aeroplane first came to Europe in 1902 without its substance. Meanwhile Ferber, who was dogged and ambitious, had also built a powered twin-propeller Wright-type glider without an elevator, which he hung and tested on a giant whirling arm at Nice in December 1902: this machine was also a primitive affair, with totally inadequate lifting surfaces and controls, and was a complete failure. But Ferber was later to have a powerful influence on European flying.

There were four other European pioneers who deserve mention during these barren early years. The first, isolated in Austria, was Wilhelm Kress who had been experimenting with rubber-driven models since 1877, and in 1880 published a remarkable design for a powered flying boat.[2] In 1898–99 – curiously paralleling Langley's models – he constructed a full-size man-carrying flying boat: it was a tandem-wing machine with rear elevator and rudder, powered by an over-heavy 30 hp Daimler petrol engine driving two propellers. Kress had to wait until October 1901 to test it: then unfortunately the machine was capsized and wrecked by too sharp a turn while taxiing on the Tullnerbach Reservoir, before any flight test could be made. Although ingenious, and the first full-size petrol-driven aeroplane to be built, it did not influence the course of aviation.

In Germany, Karl Jatho briefly emerged to take a small place in the early history of the aeroplane, but he did not influence aviation.

Jatho was a civil servant in Hanover, and in 1903 completed what was little more than a large powered kite: it had a 9-hp petrol engine and a primitive pusher propeller, but there were neither tail unit, nor control surfaces forward of the 'planes', and only rudimentary rudder and elevator devices. On 18 August he made a 'running jump' claimed to be 18 metres; then in November, with the structure modified to biplane form, the machine made another hop of 60 metres (say 200 ft). These tests took place on the Vahrenwalder Heide, north of Hanover with takeoffs, probably downhill; they are not claimed as true flights, even in Germany, where the word *Flugsprung* (leap into the air) has been used for them: he therefore may make the minor claim to be the first German to leave the ground in a powered aeroplane, somewhat like Ader in France.[3]

In England, S F Cody (who will appear more importantly later) was following Baden-Powell in experiments with man-lifting kites. Cody patented his man-lifting kite in 1901, and it consisted of a train of kites supporting a cable, up which ran another kite – the actual man-lifter – with a seat hanging beneath, the rise and fall of this big kite being controlled by the pilot altering its angle of attack. The kites had an excellent form, being basically a Hargrave box kite with wings built out from the top – the large aerofoils being on the front cells and the small on the back. These kites were tested by the British War Office in 1904–05, and officially adopted in 1906.

1903 and 1904

In March 1903 Octave Chanute arrived on a visit to Europe, and on 2 April gave an illustrated talk in Paris at a *diner-conférence* of the Aéro-Club de France, describing in detail his own and the Wrights' gliders; but this time it was the sophisticated No. 3 Wright glider in its final form that received most attention, along with the information – but not raison d'être – of the simultaneous use of warping and rudder. This pivotal lecture was followed by illustrated published reports of it, and fuller articles written by Chanute and others, including (in August) scale drawings of the Wright machine. It was these new revelations of the Wrights' successful gliding – Chanute's own gliders were largely disregarded – and the excellent accompanying photographs and drawings of the Wrights' No. 3 machine, which precipitated the chief revival of aviation in Europe. This revival had as its mainspring and leader the rich lawyer-sportsman, Ernest Archdeacon, who now (1903) created an Aviation Committee in the Aéro-Club de France to promote heavier-than-air flying; the avowed intent was to beat the Wrights in the race to achieve the powered aeroplane.

The Comte de La Vaulx – who was to found the Fédération Aéronautique Internationale in 1905 – wrote later (1911) of Chanute's lecture:

For most of his [Chanute's] listeners, except Ferber and his friends, it was a revelation, a revelation even a little disagreeable; when we spoke at times in France rather vaguely about the flights of the Wright brothers, we were far from doubting their remarkable progress; but Chanute was now admirably explicit about them and indicated their full significance. The French aviators at last felt that, despite their own enlightened views, they had been resting on the laurels of their elders a little too long, and that it was time for them to get seriously to work if they did not wish to be left behind. These facts particularly impressed themselves on the mind of one man, who was to play a great role in the evolution of French aviation – Ernest Archdeacon.... Anxious to keep for his country the glory of seeing born the first man-carrying aeroplane which would raise itself from the ground by its own power ... Ernest Archdeacon decided to shake our aviators out of their torpor (de secouer le torpeur de nos aviateurs), and put a stop to the indifference of French opinion concerning flying machines.

Although feeling was running high, as contemporary documents make very clear, Archdeacon, Ferber and their friends seemed strangely complacent, and were content to make haste slowly. Archdeacon was a wealthy Paris lawyer, automobilist, balloonist and patron of flying, and it was not until next year (1904) that he had made at Chalais-Meudon 'une reproduction de l'appareil Wright', which was flown briefly with only minor success at Berck-sur-Mer (Merlimont) in early April 1904: the pilots were Captain Ferber and a newcomer from Lyons, a young architectural-student-turned-engineer named Gabriel Voisin, who had for some years been interested in heavier-than-air flight. Surprisingly enough, the machine had no wing warping or other control in roll.

Inspired by Archdeacon to emulate the Wrights, an able engineer named Robert Esnault-Pelterie (Figure 12.3) also built and tested in May 1904 what he falsely claimed was an exact copy ('absolument semblable') of the 1902 Wright glider, except for details; he found it was unsatisfactory and decided to improve it. He clearly could not make the warping work properly, and – like the other Europeans – did not understand the significance of Chanute's description of the simultaneous use of warping and rudder. Esnault-Pelterie then asserted that warping was structurally dangerous. In October 1904 he tested a rebuilt version, using – for the first time in history – ailerons, or rather primitive elevons, instead of the warping and front elevator: this machine, despite its ingenuity, was a crude affair and a failure, and Esnault-Pelterie – like his friends – would not take the trouble to experiment, modify and improve. The deplorable influence of Esnault-Pelterie on French aviation did not take effect until 1905, when his lecture was given, and published later in the year.

But having recorded both the new inspiration and the tradition-inspired modification – as well as the overt imitation of the Wrights by Archdeacon and Esnault-Pelterie – the historian can only view the general situation in Europe with amazement. Contemporary statements show clearly that the impact of Chanute's talk, and

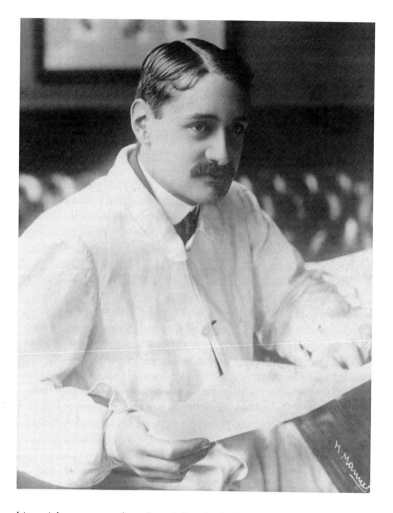

Figure 12.3 Signed photograph of Robert Esnault-Pelterie by Henri Manuel. (Science & Society Picture Library)

his articles, were profound; and that Archdeacon and his friends were at first genuinely determined to press ahead with gliding, and then powered flight. As already mentioned, Chanute described and illustrated his own 1896 glider, but gave greatest prominence to the key machine of the Wrights, their successful modified glider of 1902. The French pioneers of the time made it abundantly clear that it was the gliding successes of the Wrights that directly inspired them to emulation; not one of these men turned even briefly to the Chanute type of hang-glider, although a handful went off on quite different tacks (see below). It was the 1902 modified Wright machine which, by its success, now came to dominate the French mind, and was to directly inspire and precipitate the main stream of French – and European – aviation, despite the lack of understanding of its control system.

Next there is the question of what Chanute said, and what he subsequently published. It has often been assumed that he gave only a sketchy idea of the vital machine, the Wrights' modified No. 3 glider; this assumption is quite incorrect. Chanute not only published

1904, 'protested against the tendency we seem to have in France of slavishly copying (à copier rigoureusement) the gliding machines of the Americans…. Shall we some day have to read in history that aviation, born in France, was successful only because of the labours of the Americans, and that only by slavishly (servilement) copying them, did the French thereafter obtain any results?'

Fourthly, there is no doubt that the Europeans, to a man, greatly underestimated the complexities of learning to design, build and fly an aeroplane: they had simplified the whole subject in their minds to such a degree that they felt, now that the Americans were getting up in the air in gliders, they would do the same in no time at all, and then progress easily to the triumph of powered flight.

There was not one pioneer at that time – and they all revealingly spoke, wrote, or tried to build flying machines – who had more than a faint conception of the difficulties involved. Their attitude was well summed up by the editor of *L'Aérophile* (January 1904), when he wrote: 'gliding flight, so vigorously launched by Monsieur Archdeacon, will not be long in bearing its own fruit. What do we lack? A few specialists trained in the tricks of the trade.'

Fifthly, arising out of the last, was the strange state of mind which seemed collectively to possess the Europeans. This prevented them from arriving at a clear idea of what they were about; from formulating the basic problems to be solved, and from methodically going about the solution of them. This state of mind seems to have been an amalgam of overconfidence, inertia and a certain distrait dilatoriness, coupled – incredibly – with an inability to appreciate the essentials of the subject: I say 'incredibly' in view of the fact that we are considering Frenchmen of undoubted talent; not only one or two individuals, but a whole group of them ostensibly dedicated to the pursuit of aviation. This extraordinary state of mind among the members of the French Aéro-Club, and those few outside it, resulted in a persistent but leisurely kind of 'slapdashery', despite the aims and protestations of Archdeacon's Aviation Committee.[4] A particular feature of this attitude was the refusal by all the French pioneers to persist in their efforts, to 'go at' a problem until it was solved, and to make more than a few glides in any of their machines before abandoning them, or radically changing their configuration. It was this attitude, and its outcome, which was later to lead to bitter self-criticism by the officials of the Aéro-Club for 'notre inexcusable torpeur'. Perhaps there was not a deep enough will to fly.[5]

The first three leading French pioneers, Ferber, Archdeacon and Esnault-Pelterie, all started by copying (as they thought) one or other of the Wright gliders, and went on to modify them: yet, it must be repeated, by the end of 1904 there had only been some four primitive gliders built and tested, and not one of them came anywhere near to being a properly flyable machine.

There can be little doubt that if the Europeans had possessed the necessary devotion, humility and pertinacity, they could – with all the information and clues Chanute provided – have speedily duplicated the Wrights' gliding achievements, and added far-reaching improvements in stability, by the middle of 1904; successful powered flight on the Continent would have followed rapidly thereafter. With the variety of engineering talent available in Europe, the year 1906 (at the latest) should have witnessed there the full conquest of the air, with adequate inherent stability added to the Wrights' control philosophy. The military and political influence of such a development would have proved of prime importance in the history of Europe, and of the world.

There was one fundamental concept which the European school arrived at and clung to, after failing to understand the construction, operation or significance of the Wright glider. This was the concept of inherent stability, which they came to find had been dominant in their almost forgotten traditions. Inherent stability they could understand and pursue, while control still meant little to them beyond rising from the ground and steering automobile fashion. It is interesting to note that the type of stable, tailed, machine they were slowly groping towards was basically a more practical type of vehicle, with a greater development potential, than the Wright type; but the considerations noted above drastically retarded its growth. It was Ferber who took the next step towards this cherished ideal of stability, at the end of 1904.

Ferber, who had abandoned the front elevator on his glider (having inexplicably failed to make the surfaces rigid), again fitted one and made some tentative glides. He also used an ingenious testing device before launching out in free flight, consisting of an inclined rope between wooden towers with a trolley running down it, from which the machine was hung. Then (1904) he made a vitally important and influential move. He completely rebuilt his glider and created a new type, with both forward elevator and fixed horizontal tailplane, as well as the two triangular wing-tip rudders. This machine marks the beginnings of the full-size stable aeroplane. With this novel glider Ferber now established a new configuration, a new dogma, which was to dominate European aviation for nearly a decade – the dogma of the longitudinally and laterally stable aeroplane consisting of Wright-type main wings set at a dihedral angle, and forward elevator, with a fixed horizontal rear tailplane: the rudder was later to retreat to the rear and become part of the tail unit. Ferber, also in this year 1904, made the first tentative flight with a passenger in a heavier-than-air machine, when he took his mechanic Marius Burdin for a short glide at Chalais Meudon.

Ferber's debt to the Wrights was put on record in his own book *L'Aviation* (1909) in which he headed one of his chapters 'Ferber in pursuit of the Wrights, from 1902 to 1906.' He was also to say (in 1908) of Wilbur Wright, 'without this man I would be nothing … without him my experiments would not have taken place.' And, without Ferber, France's progress would have been even more delayed.

Also worthy of mention is the first machine designed by Leon Levavasseur, who also designed the engine, the first of what were to

Figure 12.4 An example of an Antoinette engine. This one was originally fitted to the airship Nulli Secundus. *(Science & Society Picture Library)*

be the famous line of Antoinette engines (Figure 12.4), named for Mlle Antoinette Gastambide. This huge bird-form monoplane (not a canard type) had curved dihedral on the wings: it was powered by one Antoinette engine driving two four-bladed airscrews, and ran on rollers down two tracks. It was tested without success in 1903 at Villotran, near Chantilly. This machine has the odd distinction of being the first French aeroplane to be powered by an internal combustion engine.

In 1904, two scientific papers were published which would later be recognised as fundamental contributions to aerodynamic theory. Ludwig Prandtl, of Göttingen University, demonstrated that the effects of viscosity in air flow could be neglected except in a thin 'boundary layer' close to the surface of a body. This discovery made it possible to calculate the drag due to skin friction; and it also provided the key to understanding how the flow over a wing changes as the angle of incidence increases.

At the University College of North Wales, G H Bryan produced a mathematical theory of aircraft stability and control, which was to be used by E T Busk and others at Farnborough from 1912 as a design method to develop a practical stable aircraft. Modern methods of calculating aeroplane stability characteristics are still essentially founded on Bryan's analysis.

In October of 1904 various prizes were announced by the Aéro-Club de France, to stimulate aviation in Europe, among which were the: Coupe Ernest Archdeacon for (a) the first powered machine to cover 25 metres, for which the pilot would win a trophy (this was won in 1906 by Santos-Dumont), and (b) for the first powered machine to cover 100 metres, for which the pilot would receive a prize of 1500 francs; and the Grand Prix d'Aviation Deutsch-Archdeacon for the first man to fly 1 kilometre in a circle, the prize for this being 50,000 francs (this was won by Henri Farman on 13 January 1908).

The roster of the significant aircraft produced as a result of the new drive to emulate the Wrights was as follows, only the last named showing any sign of practicability:

1903   Ferber Wright-type glider; and powered machine;
1903   Ferber Wright-type glider (modified); Levavasseur powered monoplane;
1904   Wright-type gliders by Archdeacon, Esnault-Pelterie, and Ferber.

1905

The Europeans continued their slow and confused progression. The only significant feature of Continental aviation – which in practice still meant French aviation – was in conception, not execution: this was the crystallising of their determination to pursue the inherently stable tailed aeroplane, rather than the inherently unstable machine espoused by the Wrights. In this they were maturing the stability concept laid down by Cayley in 1809, publicised by Henson in 1843, popularised by Pénaud in the 1870s, and perpetuated by most of the model makers and full-size designers in Europe thereafter. In more detail, the European situation that matured in 1905 may be itemised as follows:

(a)   the complete abandonment by the Europeans of the Wrights' doctrine of inherent instability;
(b)   the consequent settled pursuit of inherent stability;
(c)   the consequent abandonment of the pure Wright glider configuration of forward elevator, wings, rear rudder and no rear horizontal surfaces;
(d)   the development – following Ferber's inherent stability idea – of the Wright glider-plus-tailplane configuration;
(e)   the inauguration of the second type of European biplane configuration, i.e. the Wright-glider-cum-Hargrave-box-kite;
(f)   the final, but still tentative, European attempts to fly gliders; then the abandonment of this basic flight philosophy of Lilienthal and the Wrights (which postulated that mastery of glider flight should precede attempts at powered flight);
(g)   the tentative application of power to the first European biplane configuration.

The core of the European situation in 1905 was the final failure of her pioneers to comprehend the Wrights' philosophy and technique of aeroplane flight, which prevented the successful building and flying of Wright-type – or any other type – of gliders, despite the descriptions, photographs, and explanations published in 1903. It represented the strengthening of the 'chauffeur' attitude of winged automobilism, as opposed to the attitude of the true airman. This situation was worsened in 1905 by Robert Esnault-Pelterie lecturing to the Aéro-Club de France in January about his 1904 tests with Wright-type gliders, and the publication of his misleading lecture, with illustrations, in *L'Aérophile* for June 1905. This published lecture did much harm, both short and long term, and was one of the chief factors in the further retarding of aviation in Europe. Its one beneficial result was, by virtue of its large and clear illustrations, to put the visual idea of ailerons firmly in the minds of the pioneers, ready for such time – still far ahead – when they would come to realise the true nature of control in roll. All ailerons used in aviation thereafter can readily be traced back to Esnault-Pelterie's two surfaces as illustrated in that issue of *L'Aérophile* of June 1905. 'It seems almost ridiculous', Wilbur Wright was, with justice, to say to Chanute in 1906, 'that the French have never made any success at gliding in all these years.'

In February an added, but minor, stimulus to aviation took place in Paris when the Aéro-Club de France staged an exhibition and demonstration of model aeroplanes, where many unfamiliar shapes appeared along with familiar echoes of Pénaud, Langley, Chanute and the Wrights. Also early in the year, Archdeacon had his second glider built – with a view to an engine being added later – and it was seen that he had followed Ferber into the stability idiom by adding a fixed tail unit of tailplane and fins, but retaining the Wright-type front elevator: on 26 March, this machine – luckily pilotless – was towed down a wooden slipway and off into the air by an automobile at Issy,[6] but it soon suffered a breakage in the tail unit, and crashed.

Ferber, encouraged by the performance of this new stable glider, built a similar but slightly larger glider, in which he installed a 12-hp Peugeot motor driving two coaxial tractor propellers between the outriggers of the front elevator. He attempted to fly this machine on 25 May at Chalais-Meudon and, although it could not sustain itself in horizontal flight, it made a creditable shallow 'power glide'; it was launched from an overhead cable. This aircraft therefore ranks as the first rationally conceived and constructed aeroplane to become airborne in Europe, and the first full-size petrol-powered machine to become properly airborne. Although Ferber was to make two more powered machines, the second of which made flights in 1908,[7] he was not to exert any further considerable influence on aviation: but he deserves great credit for establishing the idea of the stable tractor biplane, which emerged out of a failure to build a proper Wright-type glider, coupled with a strong feeling for the traditional European aircraft consisting of a stable tailed aeroplane, a type which was laid down by Cayley and firmly established by Pénaud in 1871: but the Wright forward elevator was still present. Furthermore, and also very much to Ferber's credit, was his preservation of the true airman's attitude to his machine (see below); and although he wished to incorporate inherent stability, he never conceived of the aeroplane as an airborne land machine, or a semi-inanimate kite. It was clearly Ferber's example that led de Pischof to carry on the tractor biplane

*Figure 12.5 The Voisin-
Archdeacon float glider,
combining Wright and
Hargrave features: 1905.
(Science & Society Picture
Library)*

tradition in 1907, and thence to the main European stream of that
type.

The most significant aircraft of 1905 were the two float gliders
designed and built by Gabriel Voisin in cooperation with Archdeacon
and Louis Blériot (Figure 12.5). Gabriel, with his brother Charles,
later in this year set up the first aircraft factory (at Billancourt) and
there produced many of the successful – and unsuccessful – early
aeroplanes. The Voisin-Archdeacon float glider became the prototype
of the 'classic' European biplane: having absorbed some of the lessons
of 1904, the designers decided to adhere to the Wright idiom of
biplane wings and forward elevator, but to follow the old European
tradition in having a stabilising tail unit: in this they did not follow
Ferber, but turned to Hargrave's box kite (which had become well-
known in Europe) both for the main wings and the tail unit. This
decision had a far-reaching effect on aviation; it was a retrogressive
step, a step away from considering the aeroplane as a true flying
machine, which Ferber – along with his wish for inherent stability
– recognised was the right attitude of mind. The Voisin machines
represented the idea of the aeroplane as a flying land vehicle, to be
steered like an automobile rather than being flown like a bird; or, to
look at it in a slightly different way, as a giant kite (with or without an
engine) to be dragged through the air with a pilot on board to guide
it, rather than a flying machine with the pilot as an integral part of the
whole aeroplane. It was largely the Voisin machines which encouraged
and perpetuated this mistaken attitude. In the Voisin-Blériot glider a
dihedral angle was formed by canting the terminal side curtains: there
was a pronounced camber on all the lifting surfaces, a shorter span,
and a single-cell tail unit. It is not known how much this variation was
due to the views of their new client, Louis Blériot, an engineer who
now came into aviation from the profitable business of manufacturing
automobile lamps. Voisin was entirely preoccupied by inherent
stability about the three axes, and was unaware of the need for any
control in roll: this is why the box kite appealed to him so strongly,

and why he was to preserve as many of its features as possible in his later machines (Figure 12.6).

Both of the Voisin gliders were mounted on floats and towed off the River Seine (between Sèvres and Billancourt) by an Antoinette-powered motorboat, and piloted by Gabriel Voisin. The Voisin-Archdeacon made two tests, on 8 June when it was airborne for 150 metres, and on 18 June when it 'flew' for 300 metres. This machine was later tested without success on the Lake of Geneva; it was finally sold to a Frenchman named Bellamy, who brought it to England in 1906, and put an engine and propellers in it, but without success. The Voisin-Blériot float glider was tested on 18 June 1905, when it crashed, giving Voisin an unpleasant ducking. The Blériot later underwent extensive and not very profitable modifications, which will be noted later. However, the experience with the Archdeacon glider decided Voisin to standardise this basic configuration of the biplane, and although the powered Voisins were not to be fitted with 'side curtains' on the main wings until the summer of 1908, this machine was the prototype of the first generation of European biplanes.

It was also in 1905 (on 18 July) that Maloney was killed on a Montgomery tandem glider, released from a hot-air balloon at Santa Clara, California.

In England an almost unknown, and now authenticated, event took place in 1905 when S F Cody (Figure 12.7) built, and flew at Farnborough, a biplane kite glider with Esnault-Pelterie-type ailerons. Cody was an attractive and flamboyant expatriate American (naturalised here in 1909), an expert cowboy, marksman, theatre showman, and friend – but not relative – of Buffalo Bill Cody. He was one of the valuable 'curiosities' of aviation, with no technical training but great energy, common sense, and considerable originality, who contributed to aviation history more by his courage and enthusiasm

Figure 12.6 A Voisin biplane taking part in the Paris–Bordeaux race on 3 September 1910. Coloured lithograph by Marguerite Montaut. (Science & Society Picture Library)

Figure 12.7 Signed photograph of Samuel Franklin Cody: 1912. (Science & Society Picture Library)

than by any real innovation, except in the realm of the kite. Having tired of confining himself to man-lifting kites, he made this large manned machine which was flown as a kite and then released to glide down. Its two below-wing elevons were supplemented (in a revised version) by a rear elevator; but despite its brave showing, it was a primitive affair with non-rigid wing surfaces and inadequate flight control – the elevons were too small and placed too far inboard – and did not advance aviation technically.[8]

Despite the vociferous appeals and urges to emulate the Wrights which were being uttered in France all through 1903 and 1904, the Continental pioneers – as seen above – took things in very leisurely fashion; the impetus seems to have died down, and during the whole of 1905 the only aeroplanes tested in Europe were the following, none of which were successful:

- Archdeacon glider No. 2;
- Voisin-Archdeacon float glider;
- Ferber powered biplane;
- Voisin-Blériot float glider;
- Cody glider-kite.

The Wright brothers had, in 1905, produced their Flyer III, the first practical powered aeroplane of history, which could bank, turn, circle and make figures of eight, all with ease, and could fly for over half an hour at a time. This machine was flown from 23 June to 16 October 1905, and when the season was ended, with some 40 flights accomplished, the Wrights knew that they had well and truly conquered the air. News of this spectacularly successful season of flying reached France in successive accounts during that autumn, the first to hear of it being Ferber in a letter from the Wrights of 9 October 1905, just before they closed their series of flights: but the French public first read it in a letter from the Wrights published in *L'Auto* on 30 November. It was an admirably lucid and matter-of-fact letter, describing some of their flights, and giving details of such matters as their troubles with lubrication: they referred to their half-hour flights as matters of interest between technicians, and what must have immediately affected Besançon – to whom it was addressed – was the obvious ring of truth in every word. After the news of their 1903 success had died away, with many pioneers in Europe not really believing it (and nothing much happening for nearly two years) this fresh news – with the long flight durations – came as a veritable bombshell to the Continent. 'One may imagine the stupefaction of most of the French aviators', wrote the Comte de La Vaulx, 'when they read the letter.' From the vociferous and mixed chorus of belief and disbelief, there emerged the confirmation of Chanute and other witnesses, and of a French journalist sent over to the USA to investigate. So in January 1906 the Editor of *L'Aérophile*, followed by Victor Tatin (in the same issue), admitted publicly that the Wrights had done what they claimed. Here is the Editor (Georges Besançon):

Thus we have the definitive proof that aerial navigation by purely mechanical means, has just made the decisive step. We can only regret that it was not to be *chez nous*.

And here is the venerable and venerated Victor Tatin:

The glory of having obtained the first results is therefore for ever lost to France, ... Unfortunately, for some years, in spite of that all it was possible to have in the way of stimulation from the news reaching us of the partial success and the well-founded hopes of the Americans, we have remained in a regrettable state of expectancy, when we had here 'chez nous' all that was necessary to resolve – better and more rapidly – the problem of which the solution abroad has today aroused us; – but aroused us a little too late, alas.

On 14 October, 1905, there was born in Paris the Fédération Aéronautique Internationale, the prime mover being the Comte Henri de la Vaulx. Its aim may be expressed in the words used at the Olympic Congress in Brussels in June of that year:

This Congress, recognising the special importance of aeronautics, expresses the desire that, in every country, there be created an Association for regulating the sport of flying, and that thereafter there be formed a universal aeronautical federation to regulate the various aviation meetings, and advance the science and sport of aeronautics.

This great Federation – known everywhere as the 'FAI' – has brought incalculable benefit to world aviation and aerostation over the years.

1906

Although the Wrights did not fly in the year 1906, it was their unseen presence which pervaded the whole European scene, and underlay every move the Continental pioneers made during the year. This was primarily due to the shattering impact of the news of the Wrights' successful 1905 season.

In the midst of this mood of despondency and self-criticism, we are faced with yet one more inexplicable problem: for in the January issue of *L'Aérophile* there was published the basic text of the Wright patent (with illustrations), which had been applied for by the brothers in 1903, and was now granted. The version in *L'Aérophile* was not complete, but it took care to include the Wrights' lucid description both of the means of lateral control – by warping-cum-rudder – and, for the very first time, its aerodynamic *raison d'être*: in other words, here, in January of 1906 was published for all to see, the chief 'secret' of the Wrights, and the principal key to their mastery of flight control. Yet no one in Europe took the slightest notice! I can find no informed discussion, let alone appreciation, of the Wrights' flight philosophy in the European writings of the time. We can only surmise that the Continental pioneers were so set in their 'chauffeur' attitude of mind, that the passages in the Wright patent describing warp drag, and its counteraction by the rudder, meant nothing to them: they were simply not thinking along the lines of dynamic flight control at all, and had had so little experience with their gliders that they had never experienced warp or aileron drag (Figure 11.3).

To make this whole situation even more extraordinary, we find Archdeacon – in his manifesto of August this year (see below) – saying that the second and greater difficulty about aeroplane flight, after the problem of the light engine which he said had now been solved, was 'that of equilibrium and the actual control of the machine', which was 'unfortunately far from being solved'. One wonders just what he and his friends thought the Wrights were talking about in their patent specification. It is almost inconceivable to us today that such obtuseness should have prevailed among these men, with all the talent and resources they had at their disposal.

Modern readers may wonder why so much surprise is expressed at this European attitude, and the consequent delays. Apart from the same surprise – and indeed exasperation – being shown by the pioneers themselves, one need only consult the periodicals of the day to realise the prodigious amount of time and effort being put into fruitless aviation projects. The technical basis of proper aeroplane flight and control was readily available to all; but a general paralysing malaise seems to have overspread the European pioneers which, as said above, was basically associated with the 'chauffeur' attitude. It was this attitude which kept them preoccupied with the machine on the ground, rather than control in the air, and resulted in so much wasted effort. There was also, strange to say, no single pioneer who would adopt a given configuration, as the Wrights had done, and then – regardless of whether it was the best one – pursue it methodically and relentlessly to the stages of workability and success.

The manifesto by Archdeacon just referred to, was published in *L'Aérophile* for August 1906, and was preceded by a revealing statement from the President of the Aéro-Club de France, L-P Cailletet, in which he said that the purpose of the manifesto was to shake the members out of their inexcusable torpor ('pour secouer notre inexcusable torpeur'), Archdeacon, who refused to admit the Wrights' flights, exhorted his friends to overtake the 'slight advance (légère avance) which the Americans have made'. He then reminded them of the existence of the famous 'Prix Deutsch-Archdeacon' for the first kilometre circle (on offer since 1904, and not to be won until 13 January 1908!); but he said nothing of the two other prizes, also offered in 1904, for the even more modest distances of 25 and 100 metres respectively, which were at last to be won this year by Santos-Dumont. Archdeacon concluded his manifesto by declaring, with italicised emphasis: 'the discovery of aerial navigation is imminent, and there is just time for us in France to make the first public demonstration'.

It is surprising that it was not until August 1906 that the Aéro-Club made this appeal: it was still, as it had been since 1903, a case of making haste slowly. No wonder that the more enlightened members of the Club were becoming ever more fretful and frustrated. It was now the late summer of 1906: no European powered aeroplane had yet flown, and no powered machine seemed within sight or hope of flying. The only hope was that a few hops might be achieved with the Vuia monoplane or the new Santos-Dumont biplane (see below). Ferber had been launched into the air last year in his tentative powered machine, and had reduced the angle of glide by the action of his engine and propeller; but that was all. The more honest Europeans realised that the position was well-nigh ridiculous, and as the President of the Aéro-Club said, 'inexcusable'.

The most important achievement of the year was the perfecting by Leon Levavasseur of his two Antoinette aero engines (named after Antoinette Gastambide, daughter of the firm's chief), of 24 hp and of 50 hp. His first engine was fitted to his abortive bird-form monoplane of 1903; then, with outstanding success, his motors powered motorboats from 1904 onwards. Now, from this year 1906, Antoinette motors were to become the chief power standby of European aviation until 1909: Antoinette motors might even be said to have made early European flying practicable. There was no comparable advance in European propellers, which remained primitive devices until Chauvière's sophisticated airscrew of 1909.

In March appeared a prophetic and influential machine by a Paris-domiciled Transylvanian, Trajan Vuia, a tractor monoplane on a four-wheeled undercarriage powered by a Serpollet carbonic acid motor, with a rear rudder, and later a long spreading rear elevator. It was not successful, but made some 11 hops between March of 1906 and March of 1907, the best being of 24 metres in August 1906. But it was probably this Vuia monoplane – which ranks as the first full-size conventionally shaped monoplane in history[9] – which influenced Blériot to abandon biplanes and take to monoplanes.

It was virtually a misspent year for Blériot, who again collaborated with Voisin and built a powered biplane (his No. III/IV) derived from the 1905 float glider; but it was a failure. He altered it drastically during the year, and it appeared with – in varying combinations – elliptical tail unit, elliptical wings, conventional wings; with one 24-hp Antoinette motor driving two airscrews, then with two such motors. The machine was tested on floats on the Lake d'Enghien, and finally on wheels at Bagatelle in November, where it crashed without having flown: it was in this last form that it bore two small between-wing ailerons, the third machine in history to be fitted with these surfaces. But it was time wasted for all concerned.

The Man of the Year in the eyes of all air-minded Europeans was undoubtedly the rich Paris-domiciled Brazilian, Alberto Santos-Dumont (Figure 12.8), who had done more than anyone to make Europe air-minded since 1898, with his series of odd-shaped little airships which sometimes flew excellently, but were apt to crash gracefully and safely on Parisian rooftops or trees. Then, when he visited the United States for the St Louis Exposition in 1904, he heard from Octave Chanute – whom he met there – about the Wrights'

Figure 12.8 Alberto Santos-Dumont, shown in a chromolithograph by Vincent Brooks Day and Son Ltd from a caricature by George Hum of Vanity Fair. *(Science & Society Picture Library)*

success with their first two powered Flyers of 1903 and 1904: it was evidently this which turned Santos toward powered aviation, tentatively in 1905 with a helicopter (which could not fly), then in 1906 with an aeroplane proper. The latter was his 14-bis – so called because it was at one time flight-tested beneath his airship No. 14 – which became one of the most famous aeroplanes of history. The 14-bis was a sterile creature that led nowhere: it had cellular box-kite wings of 52 square metres area, set at a pronounced dihedral angle, which derived from the Wrights and Hargrave via Voisin: but instead of longitudinal stability being obtained by a tail unit, he transferred the front elevator outrigger into a long covered fuselage with a single large box-kite cell on the end (front) which acted as a combined elevator and rudder, later only as an elevator. There was no tail, and the first engine was a 24-hp Antoinette which lay on the lower planes and drove a crude pusher propeller. In July it was tested suspended beneath Santos' airship No. 14, after being tried out suspended from a trolley running on an overhead wire. Then, on 13 September, at Bagatelle (where all subsequent tests were made) it made its first free takeoff,

145

but covered only 7 metres, and made a bad landing. Repairs were accompanied by the fitting of a 50-hp Antoinette. On 23 October, it made one hop flight of 60 metres and won the Archdeacon prize for a 'flight' of 25 metres. Then Santos fitted octagonal ailerons – one in each outer box-kite cell – and on 12 November flew it (on one of several hops) 220 metres in 21⅕ seconds: he thereby won the Club's 1500 francs prize for the first flight of 100 metres; being officially observed and approved, the 14-bis was accredited as having made the first powered flights in Europe. This event, which was indeed modest enough, caused a sensation in Europe, and was even taken by some to herald the 'arrival' of the powered aeroplane: 'une ère nouvelle commence!' exclaimed Ferber. But the machine was a freak by any standards; was nowhere near being a practical aeroplane; and although it added *éclat* to aeronautics, it did nothing to promote or influence aviation, except perhaps to draw fleeting attention to dihedral at a time when European investigation of control in roll was virtually non-existent. The 14-bis was abandoned after one more brief hop (4 April 1907). One of the more interesting results of Santos' first European hops was the offer, by the Reims champagne firm of Ruinart, of a prize of 12,500 francs for the first aviator to fly the English Channel.[10]

On 12 September, a Danish engineer, J C H Ellehammer, had made a 'hop flight' of some 42 metres in an odd biplane on the island of Lindholm, which is sometimes claimed as the first European flight: but this claim is quite invalid, as this Ellehammer II 'flew' tethered to a central post, and it had a fixed rudder and automatic (pendulum) longitudinal control, thus making the pilot a passive passenger. It made no free flights. The engine was an excellent three-cylinder air-cooled radial of 18 hp designed by Ellehammer.

Finally, it is the historian's duty – and a melancholy duty indeed if he is an Englishman – to record the continuing neglect of practical aviation in Britain, a neglect as deplorable and inexcusable as it is still inexplicable, in view of the wealth of technological talent then present in the country. Here is a serious statement from a well-known authority of those days, Patrick Alexander (quoted in the *Daily Mail* of 24 November 1906):

> Great Britain and the British Empire stand easily in the van of progress. We know more about the science of aeronautics than any other country in the world. As yet, we have not attempted to apply our knowledge, but silently and quietly we have been studying the subject, exhausting every possible theory and fact, until today our scientists may lay claim to have conquered the air on paper. To achieve the victory in practice will not be a difficult matter.

Comment on such an incredible *obiter dictum* would be superfluous.

The list of powered aircraft that took off the ground, or attempted to, in 1906 was as follows:

- Vuia I and I-bis. Best distance was 24 metres (say 80 ft);
- Blériot III/IV. Never left the water, or the ground;
- Ellehammer II. No free flights; but best of tethered 'hops' was 42 metres (say 140 ft);
- Santos-Dumont 14-bis. Best distance and time was 220 metres in 21⅕ seconds (say 720 ft).

1907

The year 1907 witnessed the true, but still tentative, beginnings of practical powered flight in Europe, following the 'false dawn' of 1906. Three important configurations, all confirming the European inherent stability idiom, became well defined during the year; but only one machine achieved significant flights. These configurations were as follows:

(a) The pusher biplane, Wright-cum-Hargrave-derived, with forward elevator, 'open' biplane wings, and box-kite tail unit, but with no control in roll. This type was represented by the first two successful Voisin machines, the Voisin-Delagrange I and the Voisin-Farman I; the latter, after important modifications by Henri Farman, was the first European aeroplane – and the only one in 1907 – to achieve productive flying (October 1907 onwards), and the first to stay in the air for a single minute (9 November).

(b) The tractor biplane, derived from Ferber, but with no surfaces forward of the propeller: this was first seen in December in the de Pischof machine which, although itself not successful, was to exert much influence later.

(c) The tractor monoplane with main wings, fuselage and tail unit, developing from the Vuia (which itself made some hops in 1907), seen in the promising Blériot VII and the diminutive Santos-Dumont 19, both of November, but both only tentative.

Starting with the monoplane, we find Blériot – having abandoned the biplane – attacking the problem of practical aviation with extraordinary energy and intrepidity: but he dissipated his energy by changing from one configuration to another. He first built his No. V 'tail-first' canard monoplane, in which he only managed some four takeoffs in April before it crashed and was abandoned. Then came his No. VI, a Langley-type tandem monoplane named *Libellule* (*Dragonfly*), fitted with wing-tip elevons and a 24-hp Antoinette: he made a number of short hop flights in this during July and August at Issy before it, too, crashed and he narrowly escaped death. He had modified it en route, and in September exchanged the 24-hp for a 50-hp 16-cylinder Antoinette;[11] his best hop was 184 metres.[12] Then 'avec infatigable ténacité', he built a third monoplane which was of vital importance. For, at one stroke, Blériot established the 'modern' tractor monoplane configuration with long enclosed fuselage (also enclosing a 50-hp Antoinette engine) with the main wings forward and a rear tail unit, the machine resting on a two-wheeled undercarriage with a third wheel near the tail. Long to remain indecisive about his control systems, Blériot curiously decided to make this No. VII inherently unstable, with only the rudder and elevons forming the tail unit. He made some six flights in all at Issy during November and December; on the last hop flight he crashed the machine and abandoned it: the best flights were two each of about 500 metres (say 1640 feet), one including some tentative turns.[13]

Also new in the monoplane field was Esnault-Pelterie, who built the first of his tapered-wing bird-like tractor monoplanes, powered by his own excellently designed 25-hp seven-cylinder fan-type engine. This REP No. I (REP were his initials) was particularly interesting for its designer's return to a primitive version of the Wrights' wing warping which he had done so much to discourage. The machine made short flights at Buc in November and December, the best being 600 metres, but it had little influence on contemporary design, its very short fuselage providing poor longitudinal stability. But his later machines were to fly well in 1908 and 1909.

Vuia made further short hops with his No. I monoplane in March, and tested his No. II briefly and unsuccessfully in June–July at Bagatelle, when he abandoned it, and ceased to play an important part in aviation.

Santos-Dumont, after his new biplane had failed to fly in March (see below), also abandoned the biplane and next built a combined aeroplane and airship (his No. 16); but this curiosity was destroyed on the ground during its first test in June. Then, in the winter, he turned his attention seriously to the monoplane and built the first of his remarkable miniature machines which in 1909 were to become famous by the strange name of Demoiselle. The new machine, the No. 19 was tested in only three 'hops' (November) before being abandoned: it was a tractor monoplane built of bamboo poles, with a wing span of only 5 metres; a supporting area of 9 square metres, and a 20 hp two-cylinder Dutheil-Chalmers engine lying on the jointure of the wings: the pilot sat under the wings and controlled the machine by means of a combined rudder and elevator at the rear, two rudders at the side, and a forward elevator: it had a pronounced dihedral angle on the wings, but no control system for control in roll except leaning his body from side to side. It was damaged on 21 November at Buc, and not revived as a type until the end of 1908. It had made only three takeoffs, the best covering 200 metres.

Turning now to the biplane, one must again mention Santos-Dumont, who completed a small biplane based on the 14-bis, his No. 15, but working the other way round, as a tractor biplane. Its wings were covered in plywood, but the most interesting feature should have been the pair of small rectangular ailerons mounted ahead of the wings on short outriggers.[14] It was intended to fit a 16-cylinder 100-hp Antoinette, but that was not yet available, and a 50-hp was installed. This machine was damaged when taxiing on 27 March.

Figure 12.9 Hop flight being made by the Voisin-Delagrange I: 1907. (Science & Society Picture Library)

After repairing it, and fitting the 16-cylinder engine, he still could not make it fly. Santos now turned to the monoplane, as we have seen.

Meanwhile the most important practical steps in aviation were being taken by the Voisin brothers at their Billancourt factory. As a result of the experience with their two 1905 float gliders, and having briefly flown (in May this year) a modified type of Chanute hang-glider with box-kite tail, they came to standardise a type of machine which was to persist until the year 1910. This was a stable pusher biplane with forward elevator, and tail unit containing the rudder, but with no form of control in roll.[15] In its first form, it showed its origins clearly in the Wright biplane wings and forward biplane elevator (the latter soon reduced to monoplane form), and the Hargrave box-kite tail unit. The Voisins built two similar machines, one of which was for Henry Kapferer: this never flew. The other – with a 50-hp Antoinette motor – was for Delagrange: it made six hops in March (Figure 12.9): it was then tried on floats on Lake d'Enghien, without success; and finally, fitted with wheels again, it made two takeoffs at Issy in November 1907, and crash-landed on the second.

Neither of these first two Voisins was a success; but in the summer a third machine was built for a newcomer to aviation, the English-born – but not English speaking – Henri Farman (Figure 12.10). Farman, who was the son of a prominent English journalist domiciled in France, was an artist turned motor racer, and came to exert a far-reaching influence on the whole sphere of aviation. He first flew his new Voisin – the Voisin-Farman I – also with a 50-hp Antoinette in September; and thereafter pursued his new profession with a vigour and pertinacity only matched by Blériot. He proceeded to modify and improve his Voisin; he went on altering it right to the end of 1908, and by the end of that year had become the most successful and famous of the European pilots. On 26 October (1907) he had won the Archdeacon Cup with a flight of 771 metres in 52⅗ seconds. In November he made turns, and on the 9th an unofficial circle of some 1030 metres in 1 minute 14 seconds. This was the first European flight longer than the Wrights' 59 seconds in 1903. It was obvious now that he would soon win the Deutsch-Archdeacon prize of 50,000

Figure 12.10 Henri Farman, depicted in a lithograph by Lucien-Henri Weiluc: 1910. (Science & Society Picture Library)

Figure 12.11 De Pischof's trend-setting tractor biplane: 1907. (Science & Society Picture Library)

francs offered for the first man to fly a kilometre circuit, i.e. to round a post placed 500 metres away from the start, and return (see later). By the end of the year he had already made important alterations to his Voisin, especially the exchange of the huge box-kite tail unit for a similar but much smaller unit, the fitting of a monoplane elevator, and the rigging of his wings at a slight dihedral angle.

A de Pischof built a biplane which he tested without much success at Issy (1907–08) (Figure 12.11) its chief role being further to consolidate the tractor biplane tradition started by Ferber in 1905; it was, in fact, de Pischof who was the first to dispense with all forward control surfaces, and so crystallise the modern tradition, although in a somewhat primitive form, with a cruciform tail unit 'sprouting' from the rear of the centre section: de Pischof used a three-cylinder 25-hp Anzani fan-type engine, driving the first sophisticated propeller in Europe, a Chauvière. In England, where interest in aviation was beginning to grow, an important exhibition of model aeroplanes was held at Alexandra Palace in April: no first prize was awarded, but the second was given to A V Roe for his 8-foot span Wright-type model.

It was also in this year that the ageing Horatio Phillips made the first tentative hop flight in Britain in a strange and quite impractical machine incorporating a large number of his high-aspect-ratio aerofoils in four tandem frames, and powered with a 20–22 hp engine driving one tractor propeller. Phillips succeeded in becoming airborne for about 500 feet. It was his last appearance in aviation.

At Farnborough, S F Cody took the intermediate step between kites and aeroplanes by fitting a 12-hp Buchet motor to one of his modified man-lifting kites, and 'flying' it suspended from a wire at Farnborough, without anyone on board. Cody then commenced construction of his British Army Aeroplane No. 1 (see under 1908). Meanwhile, J W Dunne, working in great secrecy for the British government, had built his first swept-wing biplane (the D.1) in search of inherent stability, inspired by the form of the winged seed of the Zanonia plant: it was tested only once – when it was damaged – this year as a glider at Blair Atholl (Scotland). It was next fitted with two 12-hp Buchet motors, but was damaged on the ground at its first takeoff attempt, and abandoned.

One of the important events of the year in aeronautics took place with the publication of an erudite book, *Aerodynamics*, by Frederick W Lanchester, well known as an automobile engineer, who next year issued his second book, *Aerodonetics*. Lanchester is recognised as one of the great figures of aeronautical history (Figure 12.12). Although the profundity of Lanchester's theory of sustentation is universally recognised, his books were very difficult to understand, even by specialists; consequently his theory was not applied by anybody and his books made no impact on practical aviation. The German engineer Ludwig Prandtl (1875–1953) had evolved an essentially similar theory, expressed in a much clearer mathematical form, and, largely through translations and expositions of Prandtl's work, the theory of lifting wings was made known to the scientific world, and thence made its impact on aeroplane design and construction. It was not until 1915, in a paper which he read to the Institution of Automobile Engineers, that Lanchester recast his theory in a form more capable of application to practical aircraft design. The circulation theory of wings is today referred to as the 'Lanchester–Prandtl Theory'; but as communication is the key to technological influence, one must pay primary tribute to Ludwig Prandtl and to the school of aeronautical research workers which he established at Göttingen.

The Wright brothers had been continuing their complex negotiations for the sale of their aeroplanes on both sides of the Atlantic; and although both Wilbur and Orville visited Europe this year, a satisfactory conclusion of their affairs was not to be reached until early in 1908. But during 1906 and 1907 they had been building some half-dozen improved engines, and two or three improved and 'finalised' aircraft, one of which was to make aviation history. This finalised type of Wright biplane, which we will call the type A, was a two-seater, basically similar to the Flyer III, and with a Wright 30-hp engine. In expectation of a French manufacturing agreement, the new Wright was shipped to France in July 1907, and remained in store at Le Havre until the summer of 1908. The brothers had also taken stock of European aviation and found it so backward that they felt they had nothing to fear from Continental progress; which indeed proved correct.

Figure 12.12 Diagram of a wing-tip vortex, from Lanchester's Aeronautics: *1907.*

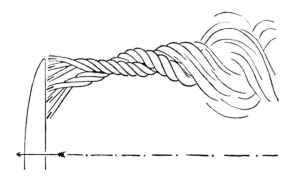

Also, in 1907, there appeared the first tentative man-carrying helicopters. After some six centuries of experiments with models, this type of machine arrived at the stage of lifting a man for the first time in history. There are two claimants for this 'first', Paul Cornu and the Breguet brothers, but the French authorities have established that the Breguet-Richet machine – Richet collaborated – was the first to take off with a man (29 September at Douai); but it was not a free flight, in that four men steadied it, and although not helping to lift the machine, they certainly aided its stability in the air. The Cornu helicopter, on the other hand – a much more compact two-rotor machine – was the first to fly freely with a man without any connection with, or help from, the ground (13 November, near Lisieux). So, although the matter is somewhat academic, the proper 'first' should go to Paul Cornu. Both machines had Antoinette engines, the Breguet a 50-hp and the Cornu a 24-hp, but the flights – although genuine enough – can only be regarded as extremely tentative, the practical helicopter not appearing until the 1930s.

Machines off the main lines of influence which merit inclusion here were the following: 1. The Tatin-de La Vaulx monoplane built by Mallet with a 50-hp Antoinette driving two pusher propellers: it took off twice at St Cyr in November 1907, but was abandoned when it crash-landed after the second takeoff; 2. The tail-less monoplane by I Etrich and F Wels, with swept-back wings, intended to be powered by a 24-hp Antoinette, but tested at Oberalstadt (Bohemia) only as a glider: this machine ultimately led to the famous Taube monoplanes of 1909–13. The first man-carrying triplane of history, which Ellehammer introduced – his No. III – this year, with an excellent five-cylinder 30-hp Ellehammer radial: the machine made many hops, but was not successful.

To sum up for 1907, it may be said that, despite the talented men who were now growing up in European aviation – many of them attracted away from automobilism – the same basic attitudes and habits of mind possessed them now as had possessed them in 1903. The 'chauffeur' philosophy was still dominant, and still no-one realised that mastery of glider construction and control – which they could easily have accomplished within a year of Chanute's revelations in 1903 – would have led rapidly to mastery of powered flight. The main reason for this neglect was their basic mistake of regarding flight control as only passive and corrective – as an extension of inherent stability – and not as both corrective and as a positive dynamic means of manoeuvre (see pages 167–8). They also failed to realise that even the corrective function of flight control needed a control system which would be instantly effective about all three axes: hence their neglect of proper control in roll. In view of Chanute's partial revelations of 1903, and the explicit revelations in the Wright patent published in 1906, it is well-nigh incredible that this dual function of flight control was not properly comprehended, let alone appreciated and utilised, by the Europeans until they saw Wilbur Wright's display of mastery in France, from August to December of 1908.

Nor had the Europeans progressed beyond the most primitive of ungeared propellers, revolving at engine speed, despite the modest presence of the Chauvière propeller on the de Pischof biplane. No-one came forward, in this important but neglected sphere, to initiate proper research and development. Yet again we meet this incomprehensible stagnation.

Continental pioneers were understandably unwilling to risk any effective catapult, or other launching methods, with their embryo machines: they would certainly not have known how to control them if they found themselves suddenly committed to the air, and would assuredly have suffered many a casualty. Not having had to face the problems of flight control in gliders, they underestimated or neglected flight control in general – especially control in roll – in their powered machines; they therefore concentrated on forcing them into the air in small straight-line hops. Henri Farman alone had begun to acquire the 'airman's' attitude by the end of 1907; Blériot was to embrace this attitude next year.

The only strong suit of the Europeans was their traditional pursuit of inherent stability, and their correct insistence on the adoption of a tailplane to bring it about longitudinally, and wing dihedral for lateral stability. But this persistent pursuit of stability was largely nullified by their equally persistent refusal to appreciate the vital role of flight control. This neglect of control – one of the two chronic European diseases – was worse confounded by the second disease, the refusal by the European pioneers to think out and adopt any definite configuration and pursue it through test and modification, until success was reached. Blériot's production of no fewer than three basic configurations in this one year, 1907, with no proper testing and development of any of them, was typical of the Continental attitude. It was again a question of time-wasting 'slapdashery'. Blériot had been working at the problem of flight since mid-1905; but only at the end of 1907 had he even arrived at a promising configuration: he was to labour until mid-1909 – two more years – before he could achieve a practical aeroplane. Here we have a typical, and incomprehensible, case history of European pioneering. Equipped with all the information and clues that anyone could wish for, and with ample funds, a talented and fearless man took no less than four years – 48 months, 208 weeks – to progress from an unsuccessful (but feasible) float glider to a practical powered machine; and, even then, he had others to aid him in the designing of his aircraft.

The case history of the Voisin machines is equally extraordinary. Gabriel Voisin was tentatively piloting Archdeacon's Wright-type No. 1 glider in the spring of 1904; but it was not until November of this year, 1907, that the powered machine he built for Henri Farman (and modified by him), could remain in the air for 60 consecutive seconds; and not until November 1907 and January 1908 that this same machine could make its first two wavering circles, yawing round on rudder alone. The standard Voisins were indeed never to have any control in roll, right to the end of their days in 1910.

There was, therefore, only one European aeroplane – the Voisin-Farman 1 – which, by the end of 1907, could remain airborne for a single minute. But at least it was a beginning, and Europe had to be content with small mercies.

1908

January to July

The year 1908 was an *annus mirabilis* in aviation history, for the Wright brothers first flew in public – Wilbur in France in August, and Orville in the United States in September – and revealed in dramatic fashion the true nature of the aeroplane and its control in the air. They revealed a type of flying machine whose every part and feature had grown out of masterly design and experimentation, a machine inspired by a clear vision of the nature of mechanical flight, and of the proper kind of vehicle to accomplish it. This vision and this experimentation were seen to have conditioned and unified the whole aircraft, its aerodynamic qualities, its construction, motor, propellers and – above all – its flight control system.

The Wrights also revealed themselves, not only in their consummate skill as pilots, but in their personal modesty and integrity in the midst of their triumphs. Where the Europeans chauffeured their machines cautiously and doggedly, as if they were steering winged automobiles through the alien air, the Wrights rode their aircraft as if man and machine were one; rode them with perfect ease and assurance; rode them with the mastery of born airmen. They were, indeed, the mythical 'hommes oiseaux' come to life, as François Peyrey described them.

In Europe, little realising that one of the machines which was to bring about this revolution was lying in a crate some 100 miles away, the French aviators acclaimed 'la mémorable victoire' of Farman when he won the Grand Prix d'Aviation for the first circle at Issy on 13 January (Figure 12.13): the prize was donated by Henry Deutsch de la Meurthe and Ernest Archdeacon, two of the most generous and far-sighted benefactors of early aviation. Farman flew the prescribed kilometre circle and, owing to his having to make such a wide turn (on rudder alone), he probably covered 1500 metres (nearly a mile). He was airborne for 1 minute 28 seconds. This was by far the longest and most impressive flight yet made in Europe; last year – 1907 – it was also Farman who had been the first European to fly for over a minute.

The period from January to August saw only modest technical advance in European flying, but some interesting achievements. The Voisin biplane remained throughout these months the only near-practical European aeroplane, and Farman and Léon Delagrange shared the duration honours between them, the former renaming his machine Henri Farman No. 1-bis in March, after having the wings covered with rubberised fabric and the engine changed temporarily to the new 50-hp Renault, but changed back rapidly to the 50-hp

Figure 12.13 Henri Farman flying the first European full circle at Issy: 13 January 1908. (Science & Society Picture Library)

Antoinette. Delagrange, who had taken delivery of his new Voisin – the Voisin-Delagrange II, soon modified to become the III, with two side curtains – started to make some good flights, and on 23 June had flown over 14 kilometres (8¾ miles) in 18 minutes 30 seconds at Milan. Farman on 6 July had flown for 20 minutes 20 seconds at Ghent. The first passenger flight had been made on 14 May by Wilbur Wright, taking C W Furnas; and the first passenger flight in Europe was then made by Farman, taking Archdeacon, on 29 May. The first woman to fly in an aeroplane was Madame Thérèse Peltier, when Delagrange took her up at Turin on 8 July: the same lady became the first of her sex to fly solo soon after, but she did not become a qualified pilot.

Captain Ferber reappeared briefly with a promising stable 50-hp tractor biplane, the Ferber IX (also called Antoinette III, as Ferber had joined the firm) which made a number of hops and short flights from July to September at Issy, the best covering 500 metres: it had a front elevator, wing warping, fixed rear tailplane and fin, and wing-tip rudders (later exchanged for a single tail rudder): this machine certainly added to Ferber's influence in leading Europe towards the practical tractor biplane type, but was not itself a success. This was Ferber's last machine. He next bought a standard Voisin.

In the European monoplane field there was much activity and promise of things to come. First tests were made in February with the new Gastambide-Mengin I designed by Levavasseur from which – after making important alterations to it – he was to develop his famous Antoinette monoplane at the end of the year. Blériot built his No. VIII on the lines of the enclosed monoplane of 1907, then modified it radically until it emerged as the No. VIII-bis and flew in June: this Blériot had a 50-hp Antoinette engine and was the first of his machines to have the typical 'Blériot look', with open trellis fuselage supporting the tail unit: Blériot had also given serious but inadequate attention to control in roll by equipping it with two flap-type ailerons – the first in the world – but unwisely abandoning them later in the summer for still inadequate pivoting wing-tip ailerons on the same machine – a reversion to the practice on his Langley-type *Libellule* of 1907: this final revision of No. VIII was numbered the VIII-ter, which flew well in the latter months of the year (see later). Meanwhile Esnault-Pelterie made a number of flights in his REP No. 2, still using his simplified wing warping, but with greater fin area.

Amongst other projects and attempts of this period should be mentioned three curious failures, each bearing a well-known name in aviation, and each proving stillborn when completed. In 1907 Levavasseur had made a model of a pusher monoplane, with deep wing curvature, a long tapering fuselage with rudder, tailplane, fin and tail propeller, and – forward of the wings – a horizontal stabiliser flanked by elevators (or elevons): he built a full-size version of this (the Antoinette I), and then abandoned it. The Voisins built for Henri Farman the English-titled *Flying Fish* with a long fuselage, four sets of small wings in tandem (three at the front and one at the back), fixed tailplane and rudder, and Renault engine driving a tractor propeller; this – called also the Henri Farman II – was also abandoned. And Henry Kapferer built another tractor tandem-wing monoplane with two sets of wings, a forward elevator and fixed tailplane, powered by an REP engine; this, too, was abandoned. It is hard to say why the last two men temporarily neglected the promising types of aircraft under development for what were aeronautical freaks, fruitlessly derived from Langley.

In England S F Cody had, in the spring, completed his British Army Aeroplane No. 1 at Farnborough, with the assistance of Colonel Capper, which had been commenced in the winter of last year. It was a Wright-derived biplane with forward elevator and rear rudder, with another rudder on top of the wings, and small between-wing ailerons (which were abandoned before the machine finally flew): it was powered by a 50-hp Antoinette engine driving two propellers between the wings: but it was not to be tested until September (see later).

Incidentally there also occurred at Farnborough that May an event of considerable aeronautical importance when successful ground-to-air wireless transmissions were made to the free balloon *Pegasus*, 20 miles away.

Also in England, A V Roe built a full-size aeroplane based on his prize-winning Wright-type model of 1907: tests were made at Brooklands in June, a few flights were made towed by a motor car, and a few hops were made, almost certainly after downhill runs (Figure 12.14). In later years it was alleged that free powered hops were also made, but Roe's claim to be the first Briton to fly a powered machine in Britain – the American Cody was not yet naturalised – has been disallowed in favour of J T C Moore-Brabazon. (See pages 179–80).

In the United States, aviation – apart from the Wrights – may be said to have revived with the work of the Aerial Experiment Association based on Hammondsport (NY), Lake Keuka, an organisation founded by Mrs and Dr Graham Bell, Glenn Hammond Curtiss, and others. They completed the first of their series of biplanes – they referred to them as 'aerodromes' following Langley – in March: this was the *Red Wing*, designed by Lieut. T Selfridge (who in September was to be the first to die in an aeroplane); it made

Figure 12.14 A V Roe (seated) with the biplane in which he made his first flights at Brooklands: 1908. (Science & Society Picture Library)

only two short hops (on 12 and 17 March) before crashing. The first four machines from this 'stable' had a general family resemblance – derived from both Wright and European forms – and were to lead to an important and influential stream of aviation design, especially in America. The biplane wings were curved toward one another in a slight double bow; there was a forward elevator, and a tail unit comprising tailplane and vertical rudder: the first three machines had Curtiss-designed 30-hp engines. As the Association came thus late into the aviation field, their machines could take full advantage of the lessons learnt in Europe, and were growingly successful with each new aircraft. The *Red Wing* had no control in roll; but the second machine, the *White Wing* (designed by F W Baldwin), was fitted with four small ailerons outboard of the wing tips, the first ailerons to be used outside Europe:[16] *White Wing* made five takeoffs in May, the best being for 1017 feet. The third, the *June Bug*, was designed by Glenn Curtiss – it also had the wing-tip ailerons – first flew in June, and won the *Scientific American* magazine's prize for the first official public flight in the United States of more than a kilometre (4 July): this covered 5090 feet at 39 mph in 1 minute 42½ seconds. The last machine of the year (No. 4), called the *Silver Dart*, was designed by J A D McCurdy and followed the same lines as the others, including ailerons: it first flew at Hammondsport in December 1908. The considerable success of these aircraft led direct to the excellent Curtiss machines of 1909, which will be noted later.

Meanwhile the Wrights had secured agreement to have their machines built in France, and an official acceptance test was also at last to be made before the US Army authorities. In April the Wrights took their 1905 Flyer III to the Kill Devil Hills in order to regain their skill as pilots:[17] it was modified to take the pilot and one passenger sitting upright on the wing; on 6 May they flew for the first time since 1905, and from 6 to 14 May made 22 flights for practice. On 14 May Wilbur and Orville made the world's first two passenger flights, each taking C Furnas, the second covering about 2½ miles in 3 minutes 40 seconds.

By the end of May, Wilbur had arrived in France to remove the new Wright A from store and prepare it for its first public flights. At the invitation of Léon Bollée he assembled the machine in Bollée's factory near Le Mans. Interest in France mounted high as Wilbur

flown, smoothly, expertly and with complete mastery of manoeuvre. Climbing, banking, turning – with rapid and graceful circles and figures of eight – and even glides with the engine off, displayed both an aircraft and a flying technique undreamt of in Europe. There was no limit to the astonishment, no end to the praise and adulation. An English authority wrote that the machine described circles 'in a manner that was altogether unknown to Europe'. As the flights continued, the repentant French aviation writers could scarcely find words adequate to express their amazement: 'au Camp d'Auvours, Wilbur Wright continue la série de ses merveilleuses performances'; 'les glorieuses performances'; 'les performances sensationnelles'; and so on. Nor was praise wanting for Wilbur himself, whose quiet charm and modesty became a legend. 'I know of only one bird, the parrot, that talks,' he said at a dinner, 'and it can't fly very high.'

As the first excitement died down, and as the world of aviation treated the Camp d'Auvours as a new Mecca, the European designers and engineers made some wise and rueful assessments of their own efforts since 1903. One of the earliest realisations that dawned upon them was that the Wrights could never have attained such perfection without years of prodigious labour and experimentation: they thereupon investigated the previous history of the Wrights' machines, and publicly accepted the facts of the early flights as we know them.

Wilbur's flying at Auvours drew every serious aeronautical investigator to examine the aircraft and watch its performance; to discuss aviation with him; and to fly with him when possible.[19] Wilbur divided his flights between taking passengers – on some 60 of the 104 flights – and performing endurance and height tests for record and prize-winning purposes. He made his first major endurance flight on 21 September, when he was in the air for over an hour and a half, and covered 41 miles. Of the seven flights in 1908 lasting over an hour, three lasted for over 1½ hours, and one lasted 2 hours 20 minutes, in which he covered 77 miles (31 December), which broke all his own records and won the Michelin prize of 20,000 francs. On 10 October he had taken a passenger for the record 'two-up' flight of 1 hour 9

Figure 12.15 Wright biplane above the Camp d'Auvours, Belgium, 1908, depicted in a chromolithograph by Ernest Montaut. (Science & Society Picture Library)

Figure 12.16 Wright type A being flown by C S Rolls: 1909. (Science & Society Picture Library)

minutes, and covered about 45 miles. On 18 December, he broke all altitude records – his own, Orville's and Henri Farman's (see below) – by reaching 360 feet.

It is fitting that a French historian (Charles Dollfus) should sum up: 'The first flight [by Wilbur Wright] took place on August 8th 1908. Numerous flights followed, which revolutionised aviation by the quality of the pilotage, and by the manageability and versatility of the machine. The mechanism of wing-warping was also a revelation. Finally, the "haute personalité" of Wilbur Wright, his reserve and his sureness, the nobility of his character, culminated in conquering the world of aviation and the general public.'

Meanwhile triumph and tragedy attended Orville Wright's US Army acceptance trials at Fort Myer. He made ten flights, starting on 3 September, which included four of over an hour, and two which created altitude records of 200 and 310 feet. The flight of 1 hour 2 minutes 15 seconds, on 9 September, was the world's first flight of an hour, a duration not to be achieved by a European until Paul Tissandier flew for 1 hour 2 minutes 13 seconds on his Wright biplane on 20 May 1909. On 17 September Orville was making his third flight with a passenger – this time with Lieutenant T E Selfridge – when the machine crashed from a height of 75 feet, and was wrecked. Lieutenant Selfridge was killed and Orville injured: it was the first fatality in powered aviation.[20]

The robust and sophisticated aircraft which thus brought the first period of powered flying to a close were of what is now known as the Wright type A (Figure 12.16): it had a span of 41 feet and a wing area of 510 square feet. They were efficient two-seaters which, despite the low-powered 30-hp engine, had an ample power margin, thanks to the overall excellence of design of both airframe and propellers, and to satisfactory gearing. The records show that at least seven of these machines were built, all similar except for small details. These seven machines – reduced to six after the Fort Myer crash – were the Wrights' 'ambassadors' and brought about a proper understanding of their technique and achievements, as well as the disadvantage, for general use, of their inherent instability. Wilbur's machine, as assembled and flown in August 1908, was also the first aeroplane to be fitted with dual control; it was designed with an eye to instruction.

Although completely overshadowed by the Wrights' performances, the Europeans – and Curtiss in America – were making steady headway in endurance flights. Delagrange, Blériot and Farman set the pace. Delagrange covered 247 kilometres (15 miles) at Issy on 6 September; Farman flew for 40 kilometres (nearly 25 miles) at the Camp de Châlons, on 2 October. It was Farman who made the first true cross-country flight in history on 30 October, when he flew from Bony to Reims, 27 km (16¾ miles) in 20 minutes. On 31 October Farman also won temporarily the official height record at 80 feet, although Wilbur Wright had already flown higher and was soon officially to beat all records by a large margin. Blériot made a celebrated cross-country flight – using his VIII-ter with pivoting wing-tip ailerons – from Toury, around Artenay, and back on 31 October (with two landings en route), a distance of about 28 km (some 17 miles) in about 22 minutes flying time. Delagrange continued successfully flying his Voisin at Issy and at Port Aviation (Juvisy), and both he and Farman had now the full quota of four 'side curtains' on the main wings of their Voisin.

Farman had been first to follow the Wrights' lead on control in roll, and had taken a great step forward by fitting four large flap-type ailerons in time for his cross-country flight of 30 October. This started the European tradition of large effective ailerons, which he was to establish fully and successfully on his own self-designed 1909 biplane. In November of this year he added another small wing on top of his well-tried and much modified Voisin, thus converting it uselessly into a triplane (Figure 12.17): he sold this famous machine in spring 1909, and thereafter designed his own machines.

Figure 12.17 Henri Farman flying his Voisin when converted to a triplane: c. 1908. (Science & Society Picture Library)

Amongst a growing amount of experimentation – much of it naive and fruitless – there are a number of important aircraft to note. The leading pioneers had been building new machines, some with the intention of exhibiting them at the first Salon de l'Aéronautique,[21] which was held in Paris for a few days at the end of December. Some of the machines shown had not flown at all, some only waveringly.

Among the aeroplanes which had been completed and flown promisingly by the end of the year, the most important were the first two of Levavasseur's true Antoinette monoplanes, the Antoinettes IV and V. They were the first members of an outstanding aircraft family which flourished in 1909 and 1910, and grew out of the Antoinette I and the Gastambide-Mengin of early 1908. Both the new Antoinettes had flap-type ailerons, a form of control in roll which was abandoned on all subsequent Antoinettes in favour of the Wrights' wing warping.

Also tested in only four short hop flights from September to December (before being abandoned) were the Goupy and de Caters triplanes built by the Voisin brothers. The Goupy was illustrated in the aeronautical press earlier in the year when under construction: in the tractor tradition, it was to lead directly – in 1909 – to another and more famous triplane made and flown by A V Roe in England.

Santos-Dumont now returned briefly to aviation with another version – the Santos-Dumont 19-bis – of the small Demoiselle with the engine now below on the undercarriage driving an outside propeller by a long belt; but this machine was a failure and never left the ground. But the idea of the Demoiselle was sound and was to flourish later.

Esnault-Pelterie had been making flights on his REP 2 and had by the year's end built and flown an improved machine, the REP 2-bis, one of the machines to adopt the Wrights' wing warping, although inadequately. Various and somewhat vague claims have been made for the REP machines, but although they possessed some degree of streamlining, a semi-metal construction, a practical control column, and an excellent engine, there was nothing either particularly outstanding or original about them; the same qualities – and better – had been developing elsewhere and, despite considerable later success, these aircraft stood to one side of the main productive stream of aviation.

In England the main event of this period was the first official aeroplane flight by Cody: he put his machine through a number of tests at Farnborough starting properly on 19 September; its ailerons were removed after the tests of 29 September; and on 16 October – having already made some hops – it achieved its first proper flight (1390 feet) at the end of which it crashed: this is now recognised as the first official powered aeroplane flight in Great Britain. Cody was a colourful, ingenious and intrepid pioneer, who helped materially to make Britain air-minded, but technically he did not influence aviation.

In November–December, the new swept-wing Dunne D.4 powered biplane was tested in Scotland; but the 30-hp REP motor (giving only 21–23 hp) was not strong enough to fly it. In December, England saw her first resident to become a qualified aeroplane pilot, in the person of J T C Moore-Brabazon (later Lord Brabazon), who learnt to fly in France on a standard Voisin, two of which he was to purchase, and one of which he was to bring back to England in the new year.

Aviation in countries other than America, France and Britain, got off to a slow start, despite the presence of so much activity nearby. The first hop flights in Germany took place on 28 June at Kiel, when J C H Ellehammer, made two – of some 11 seconds each – in his No. IV, a biplane. But Germany herself was at last awakening to a science she had once done so much to promote, and her first true aviator, Hans Grade – Karl Jatho can scarcely qualify – was making preliminary ground tests with his triplane à la Ellehammer at Magdeburg in October. Delagrange had made the first aeroplane flights in Italy in May, at Rome.

Away from the main stream of aeronautics, but of importance, was a suggestion this year by a French artillery officer and engineer named René Lorin, which was published in *L'Aérophile* (1 September) in Paris and was followed by other articles which continued up to the period of the First World War. It concerned a new method of jet propulsion which, although not itself practicable, was to exert considerable influence on workers to come. Lorin suggested a slender streamlined aeroplane to be propelled by two in-line petrol engines – one on either side of the fuselage – which were to be fitted with special exhaust nozzles on each cylinder, and thus form two intermittent reaction propulsion units. An interesting feature of the design was the provision of a hinged mounting to direct the jets downward for a near

the pilot), and did not appear fully fledged (four in all) until July–August 1908. These standard Voisins disappeared in 1910 after ailerons or warping had become universal.

16 It is now known that Lawrence J Lesh fitted ailerons to his Chanute-inspired biplane hang-glider and flew it near Montreal in September 1907: see paper by K M Molson in *Journal of the Canadian Aviation Historical Society*, Vol. 12 No. 2, 1974.

17 They first 'warmed up' on their 1902 glider, now fitted with a double rudder.

18 In recent years a somewhat novel myth has been put about on both sides of the Atlantic concerning the Wrights. As one French writer put it, 'The Wright aircraft was never able to leave the ground under its own power until the 1908 period, when it was fitted with a French engine, built in France by the firm of Bariquand and Marre of Paris.' For the record, it should be said that, (a) the outstanding flights made in the USA by Orville Wright in 1908 were made with a Dayton-built Wright engine; (b) Wilbur Wright flew brilliantly in France from 8 August to 30 October, also with a Dayton-built Wright engine; (c) after that date he used a standard Wright engine built under licence by the Paris firm named above. At no time did the Wrights use any engines other than those they designed themselves; in fact, they were not at all satisfied with the work done for them by Bariquand and Marre in the early days.

19 The first British pilot was, of course, Farman. The first 'resident' Briton to fly as a passenger was Griffith Brewer, who first flew with Wilbur on 8 October, followed during the same day by the Hon. C S Rolls, Frank Hedges Butler and Major Baden-Powell, who were already well-known balloonists. Wilbur had considerable trouble with his three women passengers owing to the aerodynamic (and moral) hazards of their skirts, which had to be tied round with string below the knees; the first was Mrs Hart O Berg who was taken up on 7 October.

20 A blade of the starboard propeller developed a longitudinal crack which caused it to flatten and lose its thrust, thereby setting up an imbalance with the good blade: the consequent violent vibration loosened the supports of the propeller's long shaft, causing the latter to 'wave' to and fro, and thus enlarge the propeller disc: the good blade then hit, and tore loose, one of the four wires bracing the rudder outriggers to the wings, the wire winding itself round the blade and breaking it (the blade) off. Orville cut the motor and tried to land; but the rudder canted over and sent the machine out of control, despite Orville's near-successful effort to right it.

21 Strictly speaking it was the aeronautical section of the Salon de l'Automobile and, apart from balloons, airships, and Ader's historic Avion III, comprised 16 aeroplanes including the Blériot monoplanes (Nos. IX and XI), the Blériot biplane (No. X), the incomplete Antoinette VI, the REP 2, Santos-Dumont's Demoiselle (No. 20), two standard Voisins and a standard type A Wright: the rest were mostly unflown or unflyable machines of some interest but little importance.

13 The aeroplane as an accepted vehicle: 1909

During 1909 the aeroplane came of age, and became accepted as the world's new practical vehicle. This acceptance was particularly signalised by two events, Louis Blériot's Channel crossing on 25 July, and the first great air meeting at Reims in August. The former was a splendid feat of daring, aided by good luck, performed in an unsuitable machine; it fired the public's admiration – and imagination: it shook the confidence of governments in the invincibility of navies; and it cast a long and ominous shadow across the minds of many sober men, filling them with dread and apprehension for the future of mankind.

The Reims meeting, with its prizes for distance, speed, altitude and passenger-carrying, was an outstanding success – socially, officially, and above all, technically. It reinforced the message of the Channel crossing by bringing together the best in machines and pilots in an effective concentration, and exhibiting the variety and possibilities of the new vehicle: the impact on public and governments alike was formidable.

It was inevitable that the eyes of the world would remain fixed on the Wrights for much of 1909; for the brothers continued to make spectacular flights in France (at Pau), Italy, Germany and the United States, and at last received the universal honour and acclaim they deserved. But significant developments in Europe were soon attracting attention. Having been put firmly on the right 'control' road by the Wrights' example, European aviation – and Curtiss in America – developed and blossomed into mature success during 1909.

Two general achievements soon emerged as dominant in aviation, and came to condition all future flying. The first was effective control in the air, control in three dimensions – in pitch, yaw and roll. This stemmed direct from the Wrights, and involved the understanding of control in roll and its coordination with both directional and longitudinal control, not only to preserve equilibrium, but, equally important, the dynamic employment of this coordinated control to *initiate* manoeuvres. Until Wilbur Wright flew in France in 1908, the Europeans had looked upon flight control in a spirit of passivity; as a technique of simply remaining intact in the air by corrective action.[1] It had been the chauffeur's attitude, so often noted before, in which the pilots saw themselves as driving their winged automobiles off the ground and keeping them in equilibrium on the aerial highway; and only steering them cautiously to right or left when necessary. Then, in 1908, the Europeans saw Wilbur using his flying controls actively and dynamically as an airman. Translated into the sphere of equitation – an analogy which Wilbur himself had favoured – it meant the difference between a rider whose whole effort is devoted passively to staying on the horse's back, and one who actively rides and commands the horse, and bends it to his will.

The second achievement was the successful marriage of control and manoeuvrability with the inherent stability which had been a concept fostered by the Europeans (in models and full-size attempts) ever since Cayley advocated it in 1809: with this union, having now matched their mentors in control, the Europeans were henceforth to make their own major contribution to aeronautical history.

Deliberate inherent instability, which the Wrights had seen as an essential factor in their development and mastery of flight control, meant that the aircraft had to be actively pilot-controlled during every second in the air: hence Wright pupils had to acquire considerable skill before they felt confident to fly successfully. The training time was not long by our standards, but it was rather discouraging to the average would-be pilot, who rightly demanded a reasonable amount of repose and security when airborne. The stable aeroplane – not to appear in its fully-fledged form until the British B.E.2C of 1913 – increased safety, and reduced the measure of skill necessary to fly an aeroplane, thus increasing the number of potential pilots, and allowing the less skilful a wider margin in their pilotage; and all this without sacrificing controllability.

The next important feature of the first half of the year was the rise of the monoplane, a class of flying machine till then regarded as a tentative and doubtful proposition. It was the successful emergence, with steadily improving performances, of Levavasseur's two graceful Antoinettes (the IV and V), and of Blériot's small No. XI, that put the monoplane squarely in the public eye, a position of prominence greatly enhanced by these aircraft being the only protagonists in the 'battle of the Channel'.

Despite the growing success of the monoplane, it was the biplane which in the eyes of professional and amateur alike, still represented the only fully tried and reliable species of aeroplane during the first six months of the year; but even here, only two makes were fully established, the manoeuvrable two-seat Wright, with its rightful aura of fame; and the limited but reliable single-seat Voisin, already obsolescent, on which almost anyone in their right mind could become safely airborne in straight hop flights in calm weather, after the briefest of briefings on the ground (Figure 12.6).

But, by the close of the Reims meeting, a newcomer, the Henry Farman biplane (basically the Henry Farman III), had blazed its way into acceptance as the leading biplane of the day – and the morrow – with a highly attractive compromise between Wright-like manoeuvrability and Voisin-like stability, and an overall look of flyability and reliability. Close runner-up in this class of biplane, and superior in speed, was the Glenn Curtiss 'Reims machine', which was soon to become, so to say, the Farman of the USA.

There also appeared two tentative tractor biplanes, which were later to condition the form of the modern biplane: these were the Goupy II, with its staggered wings, and the Breguet I, both of which had sensibly eschewed the Wright-derived forward elevator.

A passing tribute – perhaps coupled with a retrospective sigh – should be paid to the many inventors on both sides of the Atlantic who designed a multitude of aircraft during 1909. Few of them ever left the ground, few possessed true originality, and fewer still combined originality with any degree of practicality. In short, there was in 1909 – along with the few successful aeroplanes – a prodigious amount of wasted aeronautical energy.

In the sphere of propellers, the year saw at last one European product, the Chauvière, to rival the Wrights; it appropriately came to propel the Farman and Blériot machines. In the matter of engines, the aviators of the day had little difficulty in agreeing that it was in these prime movers that the chief weakness of aviation lay: it was now not the heaviness, but the unreliability of the engines, which was the bugbear of early flying, despite the many excellent qualities of the ubiquitous Antoinette, the Vivinus, the Anzam, the REP and the revolutionary rotary Gnome. But still the most reliable of all was the 30-hp Wright motor, soon to be rivalled by the Gnome.

The collective identity of the aeroplane as revealed at Reims showed the world's new vehicle as capable of conveying two men through the air in comparative safety at some 40 mph; of being kept in satisfactory aerial equilibrium; of being adequately controlled and manoeuvred; and of being able to fly reliably for two or more hours at a time. It was now evident to the world that the flying machine had truly 'arrived', and that the way was open to rapid progress.

* * * * *

Public attention was still focussed on the Wright brothers. In January Wilbur moved to Pau in southwest France, where he set up the first 'powered' flying school, and taught the three Frenchmen who his contract with the French manufacturers called for.[2] Orville, now fully recovered, had come over from the United States and, together, the brothers were honoured and fêted throughout Europe. Wilbur – using a new type A machine built in Dayton and assembled at Pau – then gave demonstrations and lessons (to Lieutenant Calderera and another Italian lieutenant) at Centocelle, near Rome, from 15 to 25 April, to great acclaim. While at Centocelle, Wilbur took up the first aerial cinematographer (on 24 April).[3] Then Wilbur and Orville returned to America in May to make further demonstration flights, and receive the acclaim of their own countrymen. In August, Orville returned to Europe and made spectacular flights in Germany during September and October. Meanwhile Wright machines were being built under licence in France and England (by Shorts) and proved successful, popular and robust, despite their inherent instability (which made piloting them quite an accomplishment), and their takeoff technique. The first Short-built Wright – made for the Hon. C S Rolls (Figure 13.1) – flew in October 1909. Incidentally, it was on a standard Wright A machine that the first flight of an hour was made by a European (Paul Tissandier) on 20 May in France.

Figure 13.1 C S Rolls: c. 1900. (Science & Society Picture Library)

The European airmen, with the Wrights' achievements and technique to emulate, now started to come into their own. They unreservedly acclaimed the Wrights' superiority in flying, but did not trust their inherently unstable machines for general use. But they had at last learnt from the Wrights the lesson of proper control in roll, Farman taking to ailerons, Blériot to warping; and Levavasseur at first fitting ailerons to his Antoinettes, and then taking to warping. Only the Voisins remained stubbornly unaffected, with no form of control in roll. The Wrights, on the other hand, clung to their instability and – somewhat irrationally – to their weight, derrick and rail launching, although during the year some owners of Wright machines added wheels to the skids,[4] the first Wright machine with wheels being the Wright A (*Schreck*) which made its first wheeled takeoff on 20 September 1909 at Port Aviation (Juvisy).

During the first half of this year, there arose a growing number of aviators, designers and amateurs, and the forms of their aircraft began to multiply. There was still also much wasted effort and wasted construction by a surprisingly large eccentric 'fringe'. However, the dominant types of aeroplane became more efficient and reliable, and now set the general style for some years to come. The 'message' of powered flying began spreading over the world, and the beginnings of national aircraft industries, as well as government concern with aviation, were now to be seen throughout Europe.

In France, which naturally remained the aeronautical centre of affairs in Europe, the five more important producers of aircraft were Farman, Blériot (Figure 13.2), Levavasseur, the Voisins and the Wrights (by proxy). Whereas the Wright biplane remained basically

Figure 13.2 Louis Blériot: 1909. (NMPFT/Daily Herald Archive/Science & Society Picture Library)

Figure 13.3 Fighting the
Storm; *Hubert Latham flying
an Antoinette at Blackpool,
c. 1910s. (Science & Society
Picture Library)*

the type A, the Europeans pressed ahead. Blériot developed his small
No. XI monoplane, on which he exchanged his first engine, a 30-hp
REP, for the new 25-hp three-cylinder Anzani: the machine was fitted
with efficient Wright-type wing warping, with his patented control
column ending below in the *cloche*, to which warping and elevator
cables were attached. With the success of the XI, he soon abandoned
his two other new types shown in the Salon, the No. IX which was a
long-fuselage variation of the VII-ter, designed to take the 16-cylinder
100-hp Antoinette; and also his biplane (No. X), a type which he now
eschewed; but he also persevered with his two-seat No. XII.

A new and popular aviator appeared in the handsome person
of Hubert Latham – half French, half English – who always flew
Antoinettes, and whose skilful pilotage did much to advertise the type
(Figure 13.3). The Antoinettes were in many ways the finest of the
early monoplanes, with advanced construction, and the fine 50-hp
Antoinette engine; they were also by far the most elegant machines of
this period. By mid-year, the Antoinettes IV (Latham's machine), V,
and VI were all flying successfully, the IV and V fitted with ailerons,
the VI and VII (nearing completion) with wing warping, with which
all subsequent Antoinettes were to be fitted.

Santos-Dumont introduced in March the world's first successful
light aeroplane, his new (No. 20) machine which became the standard
Demoiselle, with one of various engines placed again on the wings;

*Figure 13.4 Santos-Dumont
light monoplane, Demoiselle:
1909.*

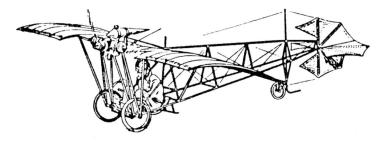

171

there was a robust three-boom bamboo fuselage – in place of the single boom – a combined rudder-cum-elevator, and body-operated wing warping (Figure 13.4). It found a small but enthusiastic market on into the year 1910.

With Esnault-Pelterie improving his REP monoplanes, but not making significant advances, and the Voisin brothers continuing to produce their stereotyped box-kite machines (Figure 12.6), we come to the next – and very important – innovation, the self-designed and constructed biplane of Henri Farman's, which was named the Henry Farman III (Figure 13.5).[5]

This Henry Farman biplane was to become even more popular as a safe sporting machine than that of the Wrights, as he gladly learned from them, but not they from him – in the matter of stability. This first true Farman showed its Wright, Hargrave and Voisin parentage plainly enough; but Farman had transformed his modified Voisin type into a light, robust and handsome machine with a single front elevator carried on a slender outrigger, four ailerons instead of the sterile non-aileroned and side-curtained wings of the Voisin, and an open biplane tail unit sporting twin rudders; he also fitted a light four-wheeled undercarriage, with turned-up skids added for safety in nose-down landings. It was first fitted with a 50-hp Vivinus motor, and then with a completely new power plant, the 50-hp seven-cylinder rotary Gnome[6] which had been developed by the end of 1908; with its descendants, this machine was to become one of the classic aeroplanes of history. The Henry Farman III first flew in April of 1909.[7]

In America, Curtiss had meanwhile produced an outstanding aeroplane in his Golden Flier, the second of which (un-named) was soon to be seen at Reims: these started the main rival tradition to the Wrights in the USA. Developed from his *June Bug*, with his 30–40-hp engine, these biplanes had a forward biplane elevator, large between-wing ailerons, fixed rear fin and tailplane, and tricycle undercarriage.

Figure 13.5 Farman's Henry Farman III, one of history's classic aeroplanes, shown here in a coloured lithograph by Marguerite Montaut: 1909. (Science & Society Picture Library)

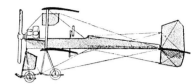

Figure 13.6 Breguet tractor biplane: 1910.

Figure 13.7 The first machine to attempt the Channel crossing (and to fail) was Levavasseur's aileroned Antoinette IV, Latham piloting: 19 July 1909. (Science & Society Picture Library)

They represented, with the Farman, the new and successful compromise between stability and controllability. Curtiss fitted one of his new 50-hp engines in the Reims machine.

Back in Europe, as I have said, are two other machines of note, which – although not at first outstandingly successful – established once and for all the basic tractor biplane form of the future. First was the Goupy biplane – the Goupy II – which was designed by Ambroise Goupy and the Italian naval Lieut. A Calderera, Wilbur Wright's first pupil at Centocelle in 1909: it was built in the Blériot factory, and was the world's first tractor biplane with fuselage and tail unit: it first 'hopped' in March: the Goupy had staggered biplane wings with elevons (first at mid-wing position then pivoting on the wing tips), a long fuselage and a biplane tail unit: it already possessed the familiar modern 'biplane look' and clearly influenced A V Roe in his successful biplanes of 1911 and after. The second of these influential machines was Louis Breguet's biplane, which first flew in June; in this first of his long line of biplanes he was feeling his way with a somewhat maladroit design, and it was not until next year (1910) that he produced a clean 'modern' type machine (see Figure 13.6).

The outstanding aeronautical event of the year was Louis Blériot's flight across the Channel on 25 July, thereby winning the *Daily Mail* £1000 prize. By rights he should not have won it: for Latham, in his aileroned Antoinette IV – a robust aircraft with a suitable engine – set off from Sangatte (near Calais) on 19 July; but he had engine failure when seven or eight miles out and had to 'ditch' in the Channel, being rescued by the escorting French destroyer (Figure 13.7). Others also had it in mind to attempt the Channel crossing, including the Comte de Lambert (Wilbur Wright's first pupil) and even Wilbur himself. But success was to attend Blériot, who – feeling none too fit after a recent

accident – took off from Les Baraques (near Calais) at 4.41 a.m. and landed in the Northfall Meadow by Dover Castle at 5.17½ a.m. on 25 July after a devious and perilous flight of about 23½ miles in his frail and quite unsuitable No. XI monoplane (Figure 13.8), with its three-cylinder 25-hp Anzani motor (Figure 13.9).[8] 'No pilot of today,' says Dollfus, 'no matter how great, could repeat this exploit in such an aircraft and with such an engine.' But luck was with him, and he triumphed: it was a fitting climax to a courageous career. This flight had as vivid and profound an effect on kings and governments as it had on the general public. 'The day that Blériot flew the Channel,' wrote Sir Alan Cobham, 'marked the end of our insular safety, and the beginning of the time when Britain must seek another form of defence besides ships.' Although the writing on the wall was clear enough to most of those who controlled the destinies of Europe, there were still many military commanders who could not stomach the idea of an aero-plane being of any more service in war than a flying observation post.

Two days after Blériot's Channel crossing – on 27 July – Latham again started from Sangatte in the Antoinette VII (with wing warping) and again suffered the ill fortune of engine failure, this time only a mile from England: this was the first occasion on which the 16-cylinder 100-hp Antoinette engine was used in a sustained flight.

The fame which attended Blériot's flight had an immediate effect on the embryo aviation industry; for Blériot, it resulted in orders for over 100 aircraft, and the type XI – in various modifications – became known the world over, and remained in service even into the First World War.

If the Channel crossing made the greatest impact on the public, it was the Reims aviation week which provided the greatest technical

Figure 13.8 Blériot crossing the Channel in his No. XI monoplane: 25 July 1909. This chromolithograph by W d'Ertahial shows the aircraft over the Channel near Calais. (Science & Society Picture Library)

Figure 13.9 Three-cylinder Anzani engine, similar to the one fitted to Blériot's No. XI. (Science & Society Picture Library)

and governmental stimulus to aviation, and proved to officialdom and the public alike that the aeroplane had indeed 'arrived'. The first great aviation meeting of history was held from Sunday 22 August to Sunday 29 August in the year 1909, on the plain of Bétheny, three miles north of Reims, the scene (in 1901) of the military review in honour of the Tsar. The full official title of the meeting was 'La Grande Semaine d'Aviation de la Champagne', and was under the patronage of the President of the Republic; the whole event was initiated, promoted and financed by the Champagne industry, and managed by a 'comité d'organisation' under the presidency of the Marquis de Polignac. As an added inducement to the world of aviation, the Champagne industry offered a number of highly generous prizes which resulted in highly creditable performances. The aeroplane was thus finally ushered into civilisation by courtesy of the most civilised, urbane and sophisticated industry of France. The meeting was an unqualified success, both technically and officially (in the way of its later influence), financially, and even socially. Many military and political chiefs, including Lloyd-George – who was then Chancellor of the Exchequer – attended and were deeply impressed. 'Flying machines are no longer toys and dreams,' said Lloyd-George, 'they are an established fact. The possibilities of this new system of locomotion are infinite. I feel, as a Britisher, rather ashamed that we are so completely out of it.'

The final list of entries numbered 38 machines, but only 23 took off during the eight days – some only briefly – with 22 pilots flying them, some sharing aircraft and some flying more than one. There were over 120 takeoffs, which resulted in 87 flights of over 5 km (3 miles), and some seven of 100 km (62 miles) or more, the longest being 180 km (112 miles). The best speed obtained was nearly

48 mph, and the best height 155 metres (508½ feet). The types of machine (with numbers of each which flew) were:

Biplanes		Monoplanes	
Breguet	1	Antoinette	3
Curtiss	1	Blériot type *XI*	2
Henry Farman	3	Blériot *XII*	1
Voisin	7	Blériot *XIII*	1
Wright	3	REP	1

The figures may be summarised as follows:

Machines finally entered	38
Machines which were airborne (15 biplanes and 8 monoplanes)	23
Aircraft types which were airborne (5 biplanes and 4 monoplanes)	9
Engine types used	12
Pilots who were airborne	22
Takeoffs made	Over 120
Flights made of more than 5 km (3 miles)	87
Greatest timed distance flown (Farman)	180 km in 3 hours 4 minutes 56⅖ seconds
Highest speed over a 30-km course (Curtiss)	75 km/h (46⅗ mph)
Highest speed over a 20-km course (Curtiss)	75.7 km/h (47 mph)
Highest speed over a 10-km course (Blériot *XII*)	76.95 km/h (47⅘ mph)
Greatest altitude (Antoinette *VII*)	155 m (508½ ft)

There were some excellent performances, with the distance Grand Prix being won by Farman – having just previously exchanged his Vivinus engine for a rotary Gnome – with 180 km (112 miles) in 3 hours 4 minutes 56⅖ seconds; the 30-km and 20-km speed contests were won by Curtiss with 46⅗ and 47 mph respectively, and the 10-km by Blériot at 48 mph. Latham won the height prize with 155 metres (508½ feet). There were some crashes – including the burning of Blériot's XII – but no serious injuries; but what struck observers as strongly as the fine performances was the general unreliability of the engines. The Reims meeting was an unqualified success, and its influence was profound and far-reaching over the whole field of aviation. It led to a great expansion of aircraft and aero-engine design and construction, and was to set the fashion for many future meetings of the kind in Europe and America. Reims marked the true acceptance of the aeroplane as a practical vehicle, and as such was a major milestone in the world's history.

Shortly after, on 7 September, aviation saw its first pilot killed when Eugène Lefebvre crashed at Port Aviation Juvisy) when test-flying a new type *A* Wright. And on 22 September the veteran pioneer Captain

Ferber was killed at Boulogne, when his Voisin hit a ditch when taxiing at speed.

* * * * *

The practical powered aeroplane had taken exactly 110 years to emerge from idea to reality. The process started when Sir George Cayley first formulated its basic nature in 1799, and came to fruition in 1909 at Reims, when the aeroplane was finally exhibited as a practical and accepted vehicle. Before 1799 there had been an age-old desire to fly; bold but misguided attempts to fly by means of wings attached to the body; speculation at all levels of intellect; some few fine flashes of reason or intuition; and – in 1783 – the achievement of air voyaging by balloon.

The 110 years from 1799 to 1909 may accurately and conveniently be divided into two periods; there was first a century-full of forerunners (1799 to 1899), who laboured to bring powered aviation to the threshold of accomplishment; and then ten years in which the practical machine was finally achieved, primarily by the achievement of flight control on gliders, prior to the introduction of power.

Although a considerable variety of configurations had appeared since 1903, including triplane, tandem, canard and even annular, aeroplanes, only two basic types of practical aircraft had crystallised: these were the pusher biplane with forward elevator, represented by the Wright, Voisin, Farman and Curtiss machines; and the tractor monoplane, represented by the Antoinettes and two types of Blériot. All these machines flew at Reims.

Waiting in the wings, so to speak, and still not matured enough to succeed when it appeared at Reims, was the prophetic tractor biplane, with all control surfaces aft of the propeller, represented by the Breguet; and the still tentative Goupy which was not seen at the meeting.

Each of the successful aircraft types at Reims, except the Voisin, possessed the following characteristics:

(a) a pair of cambered biplane or monoplane wings as its main lifting surfaces;

(b) a horizontal elevator for control in pitch, placed forward of the wings on the biplanes, aft on the monoplanes;

(c) a vertical rudder (aft) for control in yaw, which also provided one component in satisfactory directional steering;

(d) a helical twisting ('warping') of the wing tips, or hinged ailerons, to provide control in roll in combination with the rudder, either for preserving lateral balance or to effect banked turns;

(e) a light petrol engine driving one or two propellers – pusher on the biplanes, tractor on the monoplanes – to provide the necessary thrust for forward propulsion;

(f) a robust but light construction, including a strong wheeled undercarriage on all but the Wright machines, which had skids;

(g) an airspeed of between 35 and 45 mph;

(h) a flight duration of between one and two hours;

(i) the ability to maintain satisfactory flight – except as yet in strong winds – and to bank, turn and circle safely in the air.

All these types, including the Voisin, but excluding the Wright – which was designed as inherently unstable – had a considerable amount of inherent stability built into them, including fixed tail surfaces, and were thus comparatively simple to fly in favourable weather. The Voisin – safe, slow, but sterile – was alone in possessing no form of control in roll.[9] The prevailing weakness in all the aircraft was the unreliability of the engines, and it was to be many years before this menace to aerial safety and efficiency was remedied.

One other important characteristic to be noted was the ability of the aircraft to carry passengers; among the machines at Reims which showed themselves capable of carrying passengers, the Wright and the Blériot XII were the only machines specifically designed for, and capable of, carrying a passenger in comfort as a regular part of their duties.

* * * * *

Aviation, in this year 1909, was now seriously embarked upon in other countries of Europe. But it is curious and unhappy to note how backward Britain still was in practical aviation, despite her important contributions made by former generations, and the technical leadership she now held in other branches of applied science. A particular blow was the Report of the Sub-Committee of the Committee of Imperial Defence on 'Aerial Navigation', which was approved in February 1909. This Sub-Committee had to report on the dangers to which Britain could be exposed from the air; the naval or military advantages to be gained from the use of airships or aeroplanes; and the amount of money to be allocated to aerial experiments. It was perhaps the most deplorable Committee ever to sit on aeronautical matters: it was appointed in October 1908, when Wilbur Wright was at the height of his triumphant demonstrations; and when Farman, Blériot, Delagrange and others, were forging ahead. It did not take evidence from a single pilot; and it was mesmerised by airships. Where aeroplanes were concerned, the Report stated that 'The Committee have not been able to obtain any trustworthy evidence to show whether great improvements may be expected in the immediate future, or whether the limit of practical utility may have already been nearly attained.' It was therefore decided to help airship-building, to which private enterprise would not be attracted, by allocating £45,000 for their construction; and to stop all the money at Farnborough which was being spent on aeroplanes – which was £2000! – and put all responsibility for aeroplanes on to private manufacturers. Can one wonder, in the face of such monumental ineptitude, that Mr Winston Churchill 'thought that there was a danger of these proposals being considered too amateurish. The problem of the use of aeroplanes was a most important one, and we should place ourselves in communication with Mr. Wright himself, and avail ourselves of his knowledge.' Mr Churchill was then President of the Board of Trade.

It was no wonder that, after Blériot's crossing of the Channel, H G Wells let fly in the *Daily Mail* in these words:

> What does it mean for us? One meaning, I think, stands out plainly enough, unpalatable enough to our national pride. This thing from first to last was made abroad.... Gliding began abroad when our young men of muscle and courage were braving the dangers of the cricket ball. The motor-car and its engine was being worked out 'over there', ... Over there, where the prosperous classes have some regard for education, ... where people discuss all sorts of things fearlessly and have a respect for science, this has been achieved.... It means, I take it, first and foremost for us, that the world cannot wait for the English. It is not the first warning we have had. It has been raining warnings on us – never was a slacking, dull people so liberally served with warnings of what was in store for them.... In the men of means and leisure in this island there was neither enterprise enough, imagination enough, knowledge, nor skill enough, to lead to this matter.... Either we are a people essentially and incurably inferior, or there is something wrong in our training, something benumbing in our atmosphere and circumstances. That is the first and gravest intimation in M. Blériot's feat. The second is that, in spite of our fleet, this is no longer, from the military point of view, an inaccessible island.

However, despite the general malaise, in 1909 the country was becoming slowly more air-minded. The indefatigable Cody – still not naturalised and therefore deprived of various British 'firsts' – flew a mile in May, made a cross-country flight of nearly 6 miles in August, and flew 40 miles in September on his No. III. A V Roe, abandoning his unsuccessful type of 1908 biplane, and following the Goupy triplane of 1908, built two triplanes this year; on the first he could 'hop' for 900 feet by July, and by December he could fly half a mile on the second. Dunne was improving his stable V-wing biplane; the first 'full-size' British exhibition had been held at Olympia in March; the first aviation meetings in Britain were held at Doncaster and Blackpool (in October). The firm of Short Brothers had an order to build six standard type A Wrights, and the first flew in October piloted by its owner, the Hon. C S Rolls, who was to buy a second – French-built – Wright next year. Frank McClean was another who bought a Short-built Wright. Other British citizens were favouring – or about to favour – Farmans, Voisins and Blériots.

It has already been noted that J T C Moore-Brabazon had (late in 1908) learnt to fly in France on a Voisin, and later brought a second one to England. On this Voisin which he called *The Bird of Passage*, Moore-Brabazon had made the first flights in Britain by a British-born Briton, during the last days of April and the first of May, at Shellbeach (Leysdown). He now went on to win the *Daily Mail* £1000 prize for the first circular mile on an all-British-built machine (30 October): this flight was made on the second machine which the Short brothers constructed to their modified Wright design at their new works at Shellbeach. This hybrid machine did not really quite merit the fame it won: it was constructed basically on the Wrights' ideas but with Cody–Curtiss between-wing ailerons. It was not a success; but the Shorts were later to produce admirable machines of their own design.

Although there were many experimenters in this country during the year, little of basic importance took place; the few new aircraft were mainly variations on French or Wright themes, and almost all of the practical flying in England was done on foreign-designed aircraft. But a word should be said about the Alsatian painter José Weiss, French educated and English domiciled, who for many years had been experimenting with stable model gliders based on bird forms; in 1909 he built, and G England flew, an interesting full-size glider designed on the same principles. The Weiss glider gave rise directly to the first aeroplane of a newcomer to aviation, Frederick Handley Page, who in this year built his Blue Bird with Weiss-type swept-back wings; it was not successful, but was to lead thereafter to a famous line of British machines.

British tardiness in aviation had been more than matched elsewhere on the Continent of Europe. Germany at last saw her first native pilot, Hans Grade, briefly fly his triplane – derived from Ellehammer – at Magdeburg in January; then Grade built a Demoiselle-like machine which flew well at Borck in September. Austria saw her first flight in April at Vienna (the French Legagneux on a Voisin); and the Austrian Igo Etrich – who had made and flown an interesting glider in 1907 – first flew his powered aeroplane *Taube* in November at Wiener-Neustadt. Legagneux on his Voisin made the first flight in Sweden at Stockholm in July. Blériot made the first flight in Romania, at Bucharest, in October. In Russia, Van den Schkrouff flew a Voisin at Odessa in July, followed by Cattaneo, Legagneux and others at Moscow and St Petersburg. De Caters, Blériot and Zipfel flew in Turkey: and Mamet in Portugal.

A word must be said here about the Comte Charles de Lambert, Wilbur Wright's first pupil, who was not only the first man to fly in the Netherlands (this year) but performed one of the memorable feats of early aviation when he was the first to fly over a city. On 18 October (still in this year) he took off from Port Aviation at Juvisy on the Wright A (*Brancsy*) – his own Wright had been damaged – and made straight for Paris where he flew directly over the top of the Eiffel Tower; then returned to Juvisy after a flight of about 50 minutes. This event caused almost as great a sensation as Blériot's channel crossing in July.

The flying of powered aeroplanes had become an established and popular activity in 1909, although passenger carrying – an everyday practice of the Wrights – was only slowly making headway on the Farmans, Antoinettes and Blériots. Aviation, having been transformed by the example of the Wrights in 1908, had now reached its first maturity and was settling into well-defined moulds. Having learnt the basic lessons of flight control, the Europeans and Curtiss had rejected the Wrights' concept of inherent instability and had aimed at, and were attaining, excellent manoeuvrability with an increasing degree of inherent stability, thus making their machines comparatively safe and easy to fly. The biplane was for the present standardised as a machine with forward elevator, pusher propeller, aileron control, fixed horizontal tailplane(s) and one or more rear rudders, as in the new Farmans. But already, in this year 1909, there were embryo biplanes of great future importance which had already – and rightly – eschewed the Wrights' forward elevator idiom, and transferred this means of control in pitch to the rear: notable among such machines were the Breguet and Goupy biplanes. The monoplanes had, of course, adopted the age-old rear elevator by 1908.

The removal of the front elevator, and the idiom of the tractor airscrew and long fuselage, had been accomplished by Goupy and Breguet, but was not to exert its full influence until 1911. Produced from time to time, but never to prove a strong favourite, was the triplane, which – descended from Stringfellow – had emerged with the Goupy I of 1908 and the A V Roe of this year 1909. The monoplane form, however, was firmly and finally established in Europe as a type with tractor propeller, main wings with ailerons or warping, and a fuselage and tail unit, as seen in the Antoinettes and Blériots.

The direct influence of the Wright brothers was now virtually at an end. Having created the practical aeroplane, having successfully first germinated and then rejuvenated – or rather recreated – European aviation, their designs from now onwards were not to influence the coming aeroplanes: rather were the Wrights to follow European trends and influences. Interestingly enough, the brothers were never to experiment with the monoplane.

Propellers and engines had also been slowly developing into practical forms, and by the end of 1909 the engines were divided mainly into the single bank in-lines (such as the Wrights), the Vees (such as the Antoinettes), the fan types (Anzani, etc.), and the rotary (the Gnome). Horsepower ranged from 25 hp (the Anzani) to the 100 hp (the Antoinette); this last motor – with 16 cylinders – was powering the two-seater Antoinettes being built in the latter half of the year.

In view of the dangers of flying, it is interesting to note the casualties which were sustained in heavier-than-air flying up to the end of this important year 1909. Since the beginning of the nineteenth century there had been five men and one woman killed on parachutes; and Letur (1854) and de Groof (1874) killed in their curious and miscellaneous craft, one of which might be called a parachute-type glider, the other an ornithopter. But since the proper inauguration of fixed-wing flying with Lilienthal, there had only been seven fatalities, six of them pilots, as follows:

- 1896 Lilienthal: glider.
- 1899 Pitcher: glider.

- 1905 Maloney: Montgomery glider.
- 1908 Selfridge: passenger on a type A Wright.
- 1909 Lefebvre: type A Wright.
- 1909 Ferber: Voisin.
- 1909 Fernandez: biplane of his own design.

By the end of 1909 the aviation records stood at: 47.85 mph for speed (Blériot, on a Blériot XII, at Reims); 145.59 miles for distance (Henry Farman on a Farman at the Camp de Châlons); and 1486 feet for height (Latham on an Antoinette at the Camp de Châlons).

Notes

1 Dollfus agrees with this view: in *Les Avions* (1962) he says of the Wright machine of 1908, 'The ease of its flight came from the fact that its lateral control – wing warping – was utilised not, as were the primitive ailerons of the French machines, to right the aircraft, but as a means of control for turning.'

2 The machine which Wilbur used in France in 1908–09 – the Wright A (*France*) – was the first in history to be fitted with dual controls.

3 This year also saw the first still photographs taken from aeroplanes. After one or two tentative shots by unknown operators, M. Meurisse, flying in an Antoinette piloted by Latham, took a series of photos in December of Mourmelon airfield and its surroundings. There is now some evidence that Wilbur Wright may have taken up a cinematographer at Auvours in early September 1908.

4 The Wright machines were manhandled about the aerodromes on two single-wheel dollies, one under each wing. They sometimes took off from the rail without the derrick and weight, but not often, owing to the short length of the rail.

5 The Farman brothers, Henri and Maurice, were now in business as constructors; but each brother designed his own distinctive machines. Maurice also tested during this year his modification of the Voisin type, but it was not successful: it was later that he became a powerful rival to his brother with the famous 'Longhorns' and 'Shorthorns'.

6 The Gnome was designed by the brothers Seguin, and first 'flew' when it powered Paulhan's Voisin in June 1909.

7 Farman himself – 'Monsieur Henri' as he was always called – was Europe's outstanding pilot from the autumn of 1907 to well into 1910, and one of the most prominent manufacturers in France from 1909 to 1937. Son of British parents living in France, he retained British nationality until 1937, although he could scarcely speak any English. He was an art student who became successively a champion cycle racer and champion automobile racer, before he turned to aviation. He was a delightful man, of 'un courage tranquille' as Dollfus put it, who developed a remarkable mastery of both pilotage and the technical problems of aviation.

8 The times of takeoff and landing are those given by the official observers.

9 The Voisins could only be flown in dead calm weather.

14 Practical powered flying: 1910–1914

1910

This year saw the wide popularisation of flying, with exploits, meetings, races, competitions and demonstrations staged to meet the new public demand to see aeroplanes, and even to fly in them. This great popular interest led to a rapid expansion of aviation, and to a proliferation of aeroplane types. But, despite a growing reliability of aircraft and engines, basic technical progress was slow. The increase in joy-riding directed attention to the aeroplane as a possible passenger vehicle, and its ability thus to carry 'cargo' also drew attention to potential uses in war. In both these respects it is interesting to note the contemporary state of the dirigible airship, particularly the Zeppelins – the first of which flew in 1900 – which this year started their remarkable passenger flights between various German cities, a service in which – between 1910 and 1914 – five of these craft carried over 35,000 passengers some 170,000 miles without a single fatality or injury. As for the airship's military possibilities, the world had recently been made unpleasantly aware of the German army's interest in Zeppelins, and all which that implied.

Despite the large number of newly designed aircraft, most of the popular and productive flying was performed on the well-tried Wrights, Blériots, Antoinettes, Henry Farmans and Curtiss machines which were being produced in quantity, and steadily improving in construction and performance.

Taking the monoplane first, it was on a Blériot that the first night flights were made by a Frenchman Emil Aubrun, when on 10 March he made two flights of about 20 km each from – and back to – Villalugano, a suburb of Buenos Aires (Argentine). In Europe there was Louis Blériot producing mostly improved type XI machines, but also a new two-seat version. Blériot machines won particular successes when de Lesseps made the second Channel crossing in May,[1] and the Franco-American J B Moisant made on 17 August the first Channel crossing (Calais to Dover) with his mechanic as passenger, in a two-seater Blériot (Figure 14.1).[2] More spectacular was the Peruvian Georges Chavez' flight from Brig over the Simplon Pass on 23 September, but it ended in tragedy when he crashed fatally on coming in to land at Domodossola.

It was also Moisant who built, this year, the first aeroplane entirely of metal: it was a monoplane, mostly of aluminium; but it could not fly.

Blériot's 1909 Channel crossing not only led to many orders for his own machines, but to many imitators. The year saw directly Blériot-derived monoplanes in the Humber, Lane, Nicholson, Lascelles *Ornis*, Neale, Avis, Deperdussin and Nieuport. This first Nieuport must be singled out because, although it was derived from the Blériot, it also

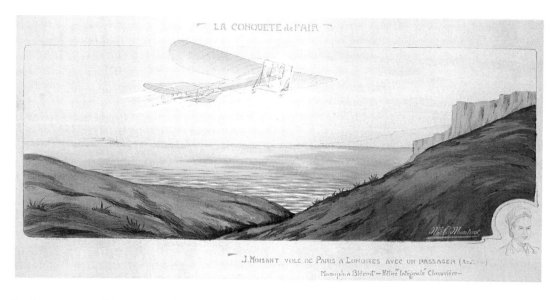

LA CONQUETE de l'AIR

J. MOISANT VOLE DE PARIS A LONDRES AVEC UN PASSAGER (Août 1910)
Monoplan Blériot — Hélice Intégrale Chauvière—

broke new ground: it was a single-seater, with fully enclosed and streamlined fuselage, and could be fitted with a number of engines: with a 20-hp Darracq it could fly at about 45 mph.

Also standing somewhat by itself, and derived from the Etrich-Wels glider of 1907, with a touch of Blériot added, was the Etrich Taube (pigeon) in Austria which, under the licensed maker's name of the Rumpler Taube, was later to develop into a famous First World War reconnaissance aircraft: it had large rearwards extending wing tips – for warping – and gave the machine its bird-like appearance. It should be said here that the name Taube became applied to various types of monoplane similar to the original Etrich machine with its swept-back wing tips.

The Antoinette inspired the Star and – combined with Blériot influence – the Hanriot, which became one of the more popular machines. The Avis grew out of the Blériot and the Santos-Dumont Demoiselle; then the latter, on its own, gave rise to an enlarged offspring in the first of the long line of Blackburn aircraft; and Blériot-influence also helped Handley Page in the production of his new monoplane. Two canard-type monoplane types, with more complex ancestry, were the Valkyries A, etc. (Figure 14.2), and the ambitious Gnome-powered float plane of Henri Fabre, which made the first seaplane flight in history (28 March) at Martigues, near Marseilles followed by flights of up to nearly 2 miles by September. Levavasseur

Figure 14.1 J B Moisant piloting the first cross-Channel passenger flight: 17 August 1910. Coloured lithograph by Marguerite Montaut. (Science & Society Picture Library)

Figure 14.2 Valkyrie canard-type monoplane: 1910.

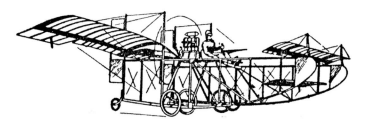

continued to produce his excellent Antoinettes at Mourmelon, all
now being fitted with his distinctive pivot-twist type of warping.
The majority of monoplanes were now equipped with normal
'twist' warping. As a class, the monoplane also did particularly well
competitively at many of the meetings, especially the second Reims
meeting in July.

Amongst the biplanes, the most successful and popular was
undoubtedly the Henry Farman; it now flew in two forms, the
standard '1909' (No. III) type, and a new version with extended upper
main planes which bore the only two large ailerons: these machines
were to be seen at every aviation meeting, and they too inspired close
imitators in such makes as the Sommer, Zodiac, Neale, Howard
Wright (no relation to the Wright brothers), Euler, Bristol and the
new Short. It was the multiplication of Henry Farman-type biplanes
that led to the common appellation 'box kite', such as the Bristol
'box kite', a popular and persistent, but incomprehensible, misnomer,
since it was the Farman machines and their progeny that deliberately
abandoned the box-kite structure of wings and tail units.[3] A famous
Farman occasion was when two Henry Farmans fought out a chance
duel for the *Daily Mail*'s £10,000 prize for the first flight, with or
without stops, from London to Manchester in April; the Frenchman
Louis Paulhan (Figure 14.3) won against Claude Grahame-White
(Figure 14.4), but the latter had the distinction of making a short
night flight – the first in Europe – between two stops (28 March).
Grahame-White later won the Gordon Bennett speed contest at the
Belmont Park meeting in the USA with an average speed of 61 mph.
The Maurice Farman (Figure 14.5) biplane, with its characteristic
swept-up skid-cum-outrigger support for the front elevator, was flying
successfully, but was not yet widely used.

Both in Europe and the United States the Wrights were still
popular; but their popularity, like their influence, was now slowly
on the wane. This year the Wrights made important changes in their
control system: first of all they equipped their modified standard type
with a fixed tailplane aft of the double rudder; and then, soon after,

converted it into a rear elevator working in concert with the front elevator. Then appeared the Wright Model B, which for the first time showed the Wrights abandoning the front elevator (Figure 14.6), with a proper wheeled undercarriage. But the brothers also produced in this year their fine little racing biplane, the Model R, which appeared in two forms – both without a forward elevator – the *Baby Wright* (with a span of 26 feet 6 inches), and the *Baby Grand* (with a span of 21 feet) which flew at over 70 mph at the Belmont Park meeting in October.[4] The most noteworthy flight by the old Wright A type was the Hon. C S Rolls' double crossing of the English Channel, without landing in France, on 2 June. All the Wright types were still pusher biplanes with warping.

One of the most influential biplanes flying successfully in 1910 was the Goupy III of 1909, which was demonstrated at meetings both in France and England, and so reinforced its design 'message' to the more far-sighted constructors. Breguet had also cleaned up his biplane design, and now produced an excellent machine which became even more important than the Goupy in establishing the tractor biplane type in rivalry to the pusher (Figure 13.6).

The familiar side-curtained Voisin biplanes soon became outmoded, and they disappeared from serious flying early in the year; the Voisin company, after trying a type with no front elevator, then commenced the construction of aileroned types, but did not achieve success during the year. They also showed an interesting military machine at the Salon in October, in which the familiar nacelle supported a large machine gun: it was not successful.

It was during this year that Sir Hiram Maxim returned to aviation, driven on, it would seem, by his experience in the Sub-Committee of 1908–09, with a curious biplane showing Wright and Curtiss-derived forward and rear elevators, three pusher propellers, an arched dihedral on the wings, and Wright warping: it was greeted with much acclaim by the press – one technical journal devoting to it 8 pages and 21 illustrations – but it never left the ground. This was the last that was heard from Maxim in practical aviation.

Another unsuccessful, but prophetic, machine was the Coanda biplane (strictly speaking a sesquiplane) exhibited at the Paris Salon in October. It was of all-wood construction, with fully cantilevered wings – which, however, did not look very robust – and an Antoinette-like fuselage with obliquely cruciform tail unit; it was equipped with a reaction propulsion unit consisting of a 50-hp Clerget engine driving a large ducted fan in front of it, the latter enclosed in a cowling which covered the nose of the machine and part of the engine: the fan was a simple air fan driving back the air to form the propulsive 'jet'. Although inevitably earthbound, this aircraft stands as the first full-size attempt at a jet-propelled aeroplane.

In the United States, the now standardised Curtiss biplane – closely similar to the 1909 type – was earning as high a reputation as the Wright machines (Figure 14.7) and was establishing itself successfully in the popular and official mind with such flights as that from Albany

Figure 14.5 Maurice Farman; lithograph by Henri-Lucien Weiluc: 1910. (Science & Society Picture Library)

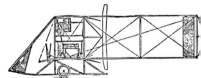

Figure 14.6 Wright Model B biplane, with wheeled undercarriage: 1910.

Figure 14.7 Standard Curtiss biplane: 1910.

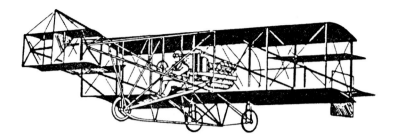

to New York city on 31 May (by Curtiss himself), and that from New York to Philadelphia and back on 13 June (by C K Hamilton). Even more remarkable was the flight, on 14 November, by Eugene Ely when he safely took off from the American cruiser *Birmingham* in Hampton Roads: the warship had had an 83-foot platform built over the foredeck for the takeoff. Two months later, on 18 January 1911, Ely bettered this performance by flying 13 miles out to sea from San Francisco, and landing on the cruiser *Pennsylvania*; then taking off and returning to the city. Curtiss himself was the first man to carry out bombing tests, when he dropped dummy bombs on the shape of a battleship marked out by flagged buoys on Lake Keuka on 30 June.

Some other biplanes remain to be mentioned: Cody was making some excellent flights, and in December won the British Empire Michelin Cup with a flight at Farnborough of 185.5 miles in 4 hours 47 minutes; but he was always to keep somewhat doggedly apart from the main and advancing stream of the biplane, and – despite his long flights – did not contribute technically to aviation. The Dunne tailless No. 5 was flying well at Eastchurch, and the type was to develop even more successfully later. Two biplanes were built and tested by a newcomer to aviation, Geoffrey de Havilland, who had, as he said, been attracted away from the motorcar industry to aviation by Wilbur Wright's flying at Auvours in 1908: the first 'D.H.' was a curious machine with a long fuselage reaching out fore and aft of the aileroned wings, with elevator on the front and rudder at the back: this No. 1 crashed on the first takeoff. Then came his second machine, of the Henry Farman type, which flew well and was acquired – along with its creator – by the government factory at Farnborough,[5] which now by ingenious subterfuge began unofficially to renew aviation research. Thus, in December, de Havilland became both the first Farnborough designer and test pilot under the new aeroplane 'regime', and started one of the most distinguished careers of aviation history.

To the many famous names of flying was also now added that of T O M Sopwith, who took his pilot's licence in November at Brooklands.

First flights were made in Spain and Switzerland,[6] the latter also producing her own first aeroplane in the Dufaux biplane, which flew across Lake Geneva on 28 August. Aviation also reached both South America and Asia: first flights were made in the Argentine (on a Voisin), and Brazil (on a Henry Farman), and the first flight in Asia took place at Saigon, in Indo-China, on a Henry Farman, followed soon after by a flight in China.

Public enthusiasm for flying was well reflected in the large number of aviation meetings held during the year, and the static exhibitions such as the Paris Salon and the show at Olympia in London. On the Continent there took place over 20 flying meetings, including those at Barcelona, Berlin, Bologna, Brussels, Budapest, Cannes, Copenhagen, Florence, Geneva, Le Havre, Lyons, Milan (Figure 14.8), Munich, Nice, Reims, Rouen and St Petersburg. In Britain there were meetings at Blackpool, Bournemouth, Burton, Cardiff, Dublin, Doncaster and Lanark. There was also a meeting at Heliopolis in Egypt. Three important meetings took place in the USA; at Los Angeles in January; the Harvard-Boston meet at Boston Harbour, in September; and the Belmont Park meet at Long Island, New York, in October. The Belmont Park meeting merits special attention, as its quality and venue attracted influential attention from American financial, military and social spheres: it was also an international occasion, with overseas teams from England and France, and helped – more than any other occasion – to popularise flying in the country, as well as stimulating technical development. It was just before the Belmont Park meeting that Grahame-White, already having flown at the Harvard-Boston meeting, made his spectacular landing on the roadway near the Capitol in Washington when he paid a flying visit from the Benning Race Track, on 14 October 1910.

Often passing unnoticed, but of great historical importance, was a patent granted in February to a then obscure German engineer named Hugo Junkers: it was for 'an aeroplane consisting of one wing, which would house all components, engines, crew, passengers, fuel and framework'. Although the 'flying wing' aircraft envisaged here by Junkers was never to be fully exploited, this patent marked the origin of the deep cantilever wing which was to be made and first used by Junkers in 1915, and then widely employed in aircraft construction.

With the spread of flying, the toll of accidents and deaths inevitably rose. The first mid-air collision took place on 2 October at Milan, when an Antoinette collided with a Henry Farman, both pilots luckily surviving the resulting double crash.[7] Chavez, as already noted, was killed after flying over the Simplon Pass; Delagrange was killed flying a Blériot (4 January); and the Hon. C S Rolls was killed at the Bournemouth meeting on 12 July, after fitting wheels, and an outrigger surrounding his tail unit bearing an auxiliary elevator, to his standard French-built Wright A: this elevator was torsionally unstable, and, under stress when diving, gave way and wrecked the machine. This was England's first loss of a powered pilot. Twenty-seven other pilots and two passengers were also killed in 1910, making a total of 32 aviation fatalities for the year.

On 27 August, radio was used for the first time between the ground and an aeroplane in flight when McCurdy both sent and received messages from a Curtiss at Sheepshead Bay (New York State), using an H M Horton wireless set. Late in the year, the first practical airspeed indicator was invented by the French Captain A Étevé, which was

Figure 14.8 Poster advertising the flying meeting held at Milan between 24 September and 3 October 1910. (Science & Society Picture Library)

tested in January 1911: this was a plate, blown back against a spring by air pressure.

Another 'first' of the year was the first woman to become a qualified pilot: she was the French *soi-disant* Baroness de Laroche, who received her 'brevet de pilote d'aéroplane' on 8 March.

Aerodromes were now becoming established in Europe, apart from the many open spaces that lent themselves informally to flying. By the end of the year the best-known in France was still the historic military ground at Issy-les-Moulineaux, a suburb of Paris, where flying inconveniently shared the space with the army; then there was the Camp de Châlons (Mourmelon, etc.), near Reims, where the Antoinette works had been set up; Pau, which was monopolised by the Wright and Blériot schools; Nice; Port Aviation (Juvisy), near Paris; and Croix d'Hins, near Bordeaux. In England the most popular aerodromes were at Brooklands and Hendon, with other flying fields at Wembley, Park Royal, Hounslow Heath, Wormwood Scrubs, Fambridge (Essex), Maplin Sands (Essex), Dagenham, Camber Sands (near Rye in Sussex), as well as the Royal Aero Club grounds at Shellbeach (Leysdown) on the Isle of Sheppey, and at Eastchurch.

The year 1910 stands out as the last well-defined period of early flying history, in which one can say that the aeroplane, having matured technically in 1909, achieved an international popularity. With that in mind, it must still be wondered at that the whole sphere of aviation – after so many years – was still moving in such a haphazard manner, with virtually no organised and systematic research, planning and development, and no adequate financial or scientific support. Perhaps the reason for this strange state of affairs, even as late as 1910, lay in the intransigent attitude of those ultraconservative army and navy circles which, despite the prophecies of many enlightened men, conditioned the view of politicians and financiers.

Records for 1910 stood at 68.2 mph for speed (A Leblanc of France on a 100-hp Blériot at New York); 10,476 feet for height (G Legagneux of France on a 50-hp Blériot at Pau); and 363.34 miles for distance in a closed circuit (Tabuteau of France on a 60-hp Maurice Farman at Buc).

1911

Basic progress was again slow in 1911. But this year saw the first long-distance flights, the growing popularity of joy-riding, an added apprehension and concern about aerial warfare, the first actual use of the aeroplane in war, and a number of innovations in practical flying.

Long-distance flying came into its own when Pierre Prier flew non-stop from London (Hendon) to Paris (Issy) on a Blériot (12 April) 250 miles in under 4 hours; and continued in the form of races (with stops), such as those from Paris to Madrid (won by Védrines on a Morane, Figure 14.9); Paris to Rome (won by Conneau – whose pseudonym was André Beaumont – on a Blériot) which should have

Paris-Madrid à vol d'oiseau

Védrines sur monoplan Morane

Figure 14.9 Jules Védrines flying the monoplane, designed by Leon Morane, in which he won the 1911 Paris–Madrid air race. Coloured lithograph by Marguerite Montaut. c. 1911. (Science & Society Picture Library)

continued to Turin; the first European Circuit Race of some 1000 miles from Paris back to Paris, via Brussels, London and Amiens (also won by Conneau); the German national circuit race (won by Koenig); and the *Daily Mail* British national 1000-mile circuit race (again won by Conneau). In America McCurdy flew a Curtiss go miles over water from Key West to Havana, in January; H N Atwood flew a Wright biplane from St Louis to New York via Chicago in August (1266 miles in 28 hours 53 minutes); and in September–November C P Rodgers made a remarkable and adventurous flight in a Wright EX biplane across the USA from Long Island to Long Beach (California), via Chicago and San Antonio (Texas), covering some 4000 miles in 82 flying hours and in 82 stages: it took him 49 days – he was followed by a special train with spares and also his wife and mother – and as the machine crashed nineteen times, it was virtually rebuilt by the time it reached California. Other notable flights were Latham's crossing of the Golden Gate at San Francisco on his Antoinette on 7 January; and Lincoln Beachey's hazardous flight on a Curtiss over Niagara Falls and under the nearby suspension bridge on 28 June.

The aircraft in use during the year included ever-improving versions of tried machines, with new machines also coming from both famous and unknown makers. The manufacture of aircraft was also steadily expanding despite a lack of large-scale investment in the industry. The three basic types of aeroplane – pusher biplanes, tractor biplanes and tractor monoplanes – were becoming more specialised and efficient, and benefiting from a steadily increasing volume of aerodynamic research. Aero engines, too, were undergoing a similar improvement in power, lightness and efficiency.

Metal was entering more frequently into aircraft structures, and it is fruitless to pursue too far the question of priorities in this

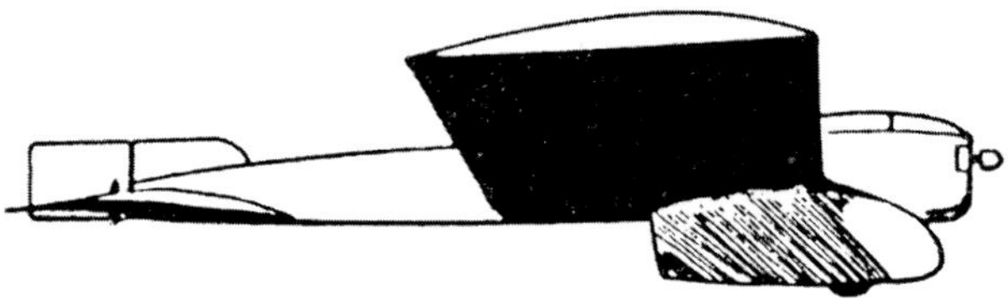

Figure 14.10 Levavasseur's Monobloc Antoinette: 1911.

controversial field of 'firsts', except to repeat here that the full-size Langley Aerodrome of 1903 had a main structure of steel, but did not fly, and various aeroplanes thereafter incorporated metal parts. Most aeroplanes were still made substantially of wood, generally spruce, and were braced with wire: coverings were of silk or linen. But another feature of aircraft construction, cantilevered wings,[8] comes into special prominence this year with Levavasseur's revolutionary monoplane the Latham (also called the Monobloc Antoinette) shown at the Reims 'Concours Militaire' (Figure 14.10). This remarkable three-seater had fully cantilevered wings, completely enclosed and streamlined fuselage, and 'spatted' undercarriage: two engines were tried at different times – the engine was also enclosed – the 50-hp and 100-hp Antoinette. Owing to hasty construction, lack of power and other faults, it only succeeded in flying a few yards, and was a failure: but it exerted a powerful influence on later designers. Streamlining, which had already been carried out in some measure by a number of builders, was taken a step further in the Tatin-Paulhan torpedo-shaped monoplane – it was called the Aéro-Torpille – with a pusher propeller at the tail-tip of its long fuselage, driven by a shaft from the 50-hp Gnome enclosed amidships. As tailpieces to these remarks on construction, it should be recorded here that the second retractable undercarriage[9] appeared this year on the otherwise unimportant German Wiencziers monoplane: it was a primitive affair consisting simply of fitting each 'leg' with a hinge so that the wheels came up rearwards to lie flush beside the fuselage. Secondly, the first oleo-undercarriage appeared, fitted by the Frenchman Esnault-Pelterie (to be followed next year by that fitted to the Farnborough B.E.2). Farnborough also fitted an airspeed indicator to an aeroplane; this was the first to utilise the differential pressure in a pitot-static tube.

In the monoplane sphere there were developments of the standard types, as well as new machines, by such makers as Bristol, Handley Page (the so-called Yellow Peril), Blackburn, Vickers, Blériot, Nieuport, Morane, Deperdussin, Esnault-Pelterie (who now had a conventional fuselage on his new machine) and Hanriot; but no basically new departures were made except in those aircraft already noted.

Amongst biplanes there was more real progress, especially in England, where two important machines set the style for many tractor biplanes to come. First the Avro biplane (Figure 14.11) with a 35-hp Green engine, which was to lead to the famous line of type 504 trainers: the 1911 machine had an interesting feature in its wing warping, which next year was to give way to ailerons. Second, the

Figure 14.11 (above) First Avro biplane (type D), with wing warping: 1911.

Figure 14.12 (right) First practical seaplane, by Curtiss: 1911.

B.E.1 biplane produced in the government factory at Farnborough to the designs of F M Green and Geoffrey de Havilland: this famous type, with its sharply slimming fuselage, was to grow into a successful reconnaissance machine of the First World War. Amongst the other British biplanes it may be said that Shorts produced what has been claimed as the first twin-engined aeroplane in history in their Triple-Twin biplane with an independent engine at either end of the nacelle,[10] one driving a single airscrew, the other driving two: the Tandem Twin soon followed, with each motor driving a single airscrew.

On the Continent a number of successful biplanes were produced, such as the new Maurice Farman (the precursor of the so-called Longhorn with its skid-outrigger support for the front elevator), the three-seat military Breguet with various engines, and the Albatros in Germany. The Voisin firm curiously reverted to a 'canard'-type biplane, which was then fitted with additional floats by Fabre and became the world's second amphibian: it was flown by Colliex from Issy and landed on the Seine, and then made the return journey (in August): but it cannot be classed as a practical machine.

One of the outstanding achievements of the year was the introduction by Curtiss (in January) of the first practical seaplane of history: it was basically a standard Curtiss land plane with a large single float beneath the centre section, and small auxiliary floats beneath the wings (Figure 14.12): it first flew at San Diego (California) on 26 January. But there is little doubt that he was strongly influenced by a development of the seaplane which Fabre had tentatively introduced after his pioneering machine of 1910. On 25 February Curtiss took up the first passenger to fly in a seaplane. And also in that February of 1911, Curtiss fitted wheels to this machine, and thus created the first amphibian. Curtiss soon became the world's leading pioneer and promoter of seaplanes.

The role of the aeroplane in warfare came in for much attention during the year, probably as a result of Germany's Zeppelin programme. The concern of governments became reflected in various ways. Although some prophetic statements were voiced about the aggressive role of the aeroplane, it was not considered by most authorities to extend much further than observation and a little light bombing or incendiary dropping. In England, money was at last voted in some quantity for aviation – when wiser heads reversed the absurdities of the 1909 Report – and official interest in the aeroplane was also shown at the Hendon meeting in May which was attended by leading military and political figures, including Mr Winston Churchill, who had long been convinced of aviation's important future. In France, the first 'Concours Militaire' took place at Reims (October–November) for the display of aircraft that could be utilised in war. In America, as noted before, Ely both landed and took off from a warship at sea in January: then, also in January, the first live bomb test was made by the US Army from a Wright biplane at San Francisco, shortly followed by the first bombsight, made by the United States Lieutenant Riley Scott (who next year won the Michelin prize for bomb-dropping). Rifles and machine guns were being carried experimentally in various aircraft, and it is impossible to say which machine was the first to be designed or adapted for warlike use, although the two-seater Nieuport of this year, with its machine gun, was one of the earliest. Some of the most interesting machines for which the makers had a military use in mind are noted later. Needless to say, the armies of Europe were paying their compliment to the aeroplane by equipping troops and transport with machine guns for anti-aircraft use.

It was in October that the aeroplane first saw service in war, when the Italian Captain Piazza, in a Blériot, made a reconnaissance flight of about an hour from Tripoli to observe the Turkish positions near Azizia (22 October). After this, the aeroplane was used in various campaigns prior to the First World War, primarily for reconnaissance.

Somewhat trivial in themselves, but popular indications of what an aeroplane could perform, were the three 'mass' passenger flights in France in February and March when a special Blériot (a freak machine which was not repeated) lifted 10, a Breguet 11, and an outsize Sommer 13: this impressive progression of numbers became less impressive when close examination of the photographs revealed a number of boys among the passengers! But these flights served to direct attention to the prospect of multi-place and transport aircraft.

Another small sign of things to come was seen in the first air-mail flights – they were little more than stunts – which took place at Allahabad in February (by the Frenchman Pequet); between Hendon and Windsor in September by Gustav Hamel, C H Greswell and E F Driver; and at various places in the United States in September and October.

Gliding and soaring, which had been practised experimentally since the Wrights' flights of 1900–02, was put on a new and sounder basis by Orville Wright, who in October set up a world soaring record of 9¾ minutes at the Kill Devil Hills, a record that stood for a decade: the flights were made on a new biplane glider, based on the powered Wright Model B, with rear rudder and elevator, and the addition of a forward fixed vertical fin and an 8-lb bag of sand placed 7 feet out in front on a pole.[11] One of the main and significant reasons for this short Wright gliding 'season' – the last ever to be held at the Kill Devil Hills – was to test an automatic stabiliser; but the tests were not carried out.

It was the Swiss inventor Ruchonnet, domiciled in France, who first introduced 'monocoque' construction in 1911; but it was not until next year that it was successfully applied in the Deperdussin (see page 196).

Miscellaneous but interesting happenings in aviation during the year which deserve mention are the following: the Assistant Superintendent at Farnborough (Lieutenant T Ridge) was killed on the factory's S.E.1 (in August) in one of the first clear cases of spinning (the first recovery from an unintentional spin was F P Raynham's on 11 September):[12] a sign of the times at Farnborough was the change of its title, in April, from the Balloon Factory to the Army Aircraft Factory; this followed the Balloon School of the Royal Engineers being retitled the Air Battalion: the first aeroplane-to-ground radio transmissions in England were made by Dorrington Bangay from a Flanders monoplane at Brooklands: the French pilot R Grandseigne, on a Caudron, made a successful night flight over Paris in February; the Dutchman Anthony Fokker, at the age of 18, built his first aeroplane which made tentative flights: the first air-sea rescue took place when Hugh Robinson in a Curtiss seaplane landed on Lake Michigan in August and rescued another pilot who had crashed in the lake: the United States saw as her first qualified woman pilot the dramatic critic Harriet Quimby (also the first woman to fly the English Channel, in 1912), although Miss Blanche Scott and a Dr Bessica Raiche had made some informal flights before her. Montgomery was killed this year when testing one of his gliders.

World records for 1911 stood at 82.73 mph for speed (E Nieuport of France on a Nieuport monoplane at Châlons); 449.2 miles for distance over a closed circuit (A Gobé of France on a Nieuport monoplane at Pau); and 12,828 feet for height (R Garros of France on a Blériot XI at St Malo).

1912

This year was marked by a large-scale, and official, concern with the aeroplane's role in warfare; and by several important technical advances, including the introduction of monocoque construction, the first flying boat, the first flight at over 100 mph, and the extended use of metal in aircraft structures.

The year also saw the growing ascendancy of the biplane – especially the tractor biplane – and the beginnings of the monoplane eclipse. This eclipse, despite some notable exceptions, was due partly to the obvious advantages in lift, strength, compactness and lightness possessed by the biplane as opposed to the weakness and inefficiency of large braced monoplane surfaces at a time when thin wing sections were regarded as obligatory; although Junkers, Levavasseur and others had proposed thicker, and internally strong enough, monoplane wings. Aerodynamics and structure research was still proceeding only slowly, and without any proper coordination.

The standard type of tractor biplane was even more firmly established by the improved, aileron-equipped, Avro, and the Farnborough B.E.2 of this year; the B.E.1 of last year was also still flying productively. But it was the arrival of the Farnborough B.S.1

which was of paramount importance. Designed chiefly by Geoffrey de Havilland, it was the first single-seat scout of history, and ancestor of every scout and fighter thereafter.[13] One of its more immediate progeny was the excellent S.E.5 of the First World War. The B.S.1 was a single-bay biplane of 27.5 feet span, powered by a 100-hp Gnome: this remarkable and handsome little aeroplane, with excellent streamlining, had a speed of 92 mph. In April, the Army Aircraft Factory became the Royal Aircraft Factory.

The most important structural innovation was the monocoque[14] fuselage, in which the skin (or shell) carried all or most of the loads, as opposed to a framework fuselage left open, or covered in with wood or textile material. This first wood monocoque structure was designed by the Swiss Ruchonnet and applied by Béchereau in the Deperdussin monoplane called the Monocoque Deperdussin (Figure 14.13), an admirable streamlined machine, powered by a partially enclosed 140-hp Gnome, on which Jules Védrines won the Gordon Bennett Cup and the world's speed record of 108.18 mph at Chicago on 9 September. This invention of monocoque construction stands as one of the milestones in aviation, but although certain other makers soon followed – even with experiments in metal monocoque – the practice did not become widespread; and even by the end of the First World War only a handful of Allied and German machines were built with monocoque fuselages, the latter being the most original and advanced. Another structural experiment was the adoption, by H Reissner, of corrugated aluminium wings (without fabric covering) in his canard-type monoplane, thus anticipating the practice of Junkers. Still more ambitious were the first tentative flights by an all-metal aeroplane in history, the French Tubavion monoplane of Ponche and Primard; but a fatal accident put an end to its tests.

The seaplane came properly into its own this year, and it was Curtiss who figured as its most important pioneer and exponent. Having established the float plane last year, he had turned to the flying boat, and (still in 1911) had built an unsuccessful machine, virtually a modification of the float plane, with an enlarged float to house the pilot. Now (1912) he built the first successful flying boat, a further modification of his 1911 float plane. This machine led to a curious chain of events, as it prompted the French designer Denhaut to build his Donnet-Lévêque pusher flying boat with a nacelle-type hull (which was stepped), with the tail unit on booms, and with no front elevator: he thus set the basic style for future flying boats and was soon paid the

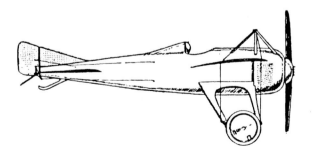

Figure 14.13 Béchereau Monocoque Deperdussin: 1912.

Figure 14.14 (above) First cabin biplane, an Avro: 1912.

Figure 14.15 (right) Maurice Farman Longhorn; first built in 1912.

compliment of partial imitation by Curtiss himself who – still in this year – produced a long-hull type with no front elevator, a flying boat which was the first of a long line of successful Curtiss boats. On 12 November, at the Washington Navy Yard, the US Navy's Curtiss float seaplane A-1 was the first aeroplane to be successfully launched from a powered catapult. The catapult, driven by compressed air and mounted on an anchored barge, was invented by Captain W I Chambers, and the pilot was Lieut. T G Ellyson. An earlier attempt to devise a method of launching an aeroplane from the limited space available on a ship was tested at Hammondsport in September 1911, when Ellyson successfully took off in a Curtiss float plane, suspended from a trolley running on an inclined wire cable rigged from high up on the beach down to the shore.

The first seaplane meeting was held at Monaco in March, at which seven machines competed: all were biplanes, and all at this time were, of course, float planes, including one or two amphibians. The first prize was won by Fischer who flew a Henry Farman.

Both old and new biplanes and monoplanes were appearing in 'cleaned up' and sophisticated forms, and the ideals of streamlining were slowly gaining acceptance, though impeded by the still ubiquitous struts and wiring on most machines. Amongst the many new machines of the year was the Bristol monoplane (designed by Coanda); and the world's first enclosed cabin aeroplanes, the Avro cabin monoplane and the Avro cabin biplane:[15] the latter established another small title to fame when Lieut. Parke successfully pulled it out of a spin, the second earliest example of such survival (Figure 14.14). Also, a robust machine developed out of the already familiar Maurice Farman types, powered by a 70-hp Renault engine, and having the characteristic swept-up skids supporting the front elevator – hence Longhorn (Figure 14.15): this type became famous among First World War pilots, many of whom were trained on them.

Military aviation now became the serious concern of the leading European nations. In Britain the Royal Flying Corps was founded in April, with both a Military and Naval wing, and a Central Flying School was later established at Upavon. The first Military Aeroplane Competition was held at Larkhill, Salisbury Plain (in August), in which some 30 British and French machines took part. Marking was for a variety of characteristics and abilities – including landing in a ploughed field – and S F Cody won with his new biplane, powered by a 120-hp Austro-Daimler engine. But this success was not truly deserved, as the Farnborough B.E.2 piloted by de Havilland, won the highest marks; but it was obliged to fly *hors concours*, as it was a government aircraft and the Farnborough Superintendent (Mervyn O'Gorman, Figure 14.16) was one of the judges. In September a Military and Naval review of aircraft took place at Hendon, and a similar heightened interest in the aeroplane's role in warfare – without much advanced thinking on the subject – was witnessed on the Continent and in the United States. Despite the traditional army view that the main use of aircraft was observation, limited tests were continued with airborne machine guns and light bombs, as well as the more enthusiastically encouraged experiments with radio, including the first successful artillery spotting carried out by the B.E.1 over Salisbury Plain. Naval flying added shipboard aircraft to its armoury when, after a takeoff on 10 January 1912 (not in December 1911) by Lieutenant C R Samson in a Short biplane[16] from a trackway on the forecastle of HMS *Africa* (at anchor). Takeoffs were also made in this year 1912 from HMS *Hibernia* and HMS *London* when under way, flights which led the way to many similar achievements, and later to the aircraft carrier proper.

Figure 14.16 Mervyn O'Gorman; charcoal drawing: 1930. (Science & Society Picture Library)

On the Continent, the year saw the same rising official concern with aviation. Germany, impressed and bemused for some years by her Zeppelins and other airships, suddenly awoke to the importance of the aeroplane, and a public campaign led the way to governmental action and the setting up of a military flying school. France, already alarmed by the German airships, and aware of the potential usefulness of the aeroplane, increased her production of aircraft, experimented with new bombing gear, and sent aircraft to take part in the great military manoeuvres of September, at Poitou.

A curious situation concerning military monoplanes should be mentioned here. Owing to two crashes in England, and a report by Blériot in France on the structural weakness of certain monoplanes, a temporary ban on all monoplanes was foolishly imposed by the army authorities in both countries, which undoubtedly aided the eclipse of the monoplane and retarded research into the aerodynamic and structural problems which would have promoted the type.[17]

Two more important technical 'firsts' during the year were the first parachute drop from an aeroplane, using a static line, made (1 March) by Captain Albert Berry at St Louis in the USA; and the first automatic pilot built by Lawrence Sperry and successfully demonstrated on a Curtiss float plane at Hammondsport on Lake Keuka, in New York state.

Among the exploits of the year should be mentioned the first cross-Channel flight by a woman, the American Harriet Quimby in a Blériot from Deal to Cape Gris-Nez (in April) (Figure 14.17); and Frank McClean's flight through Tower Bridge on his Short float plane, and his landing on the Thames at Westminster (in August), a double feat for which he was rightly reprimanded by the police and – just as rightly – acclaimed by the public.

Finally must be recorded the tragic death from typhoid fever of Wilbur Wright on 20 May: 'This morning at 3.15', wrote Bishop

Figure 14.17 Caricature of an Edwardian lady aviator, possibly Harriet Quimby, on a Blériot-type monoplane; coloured lithograph by René Prejelan: c. 1912. (Science & Society Picture Library)

Wright, 'Wilbur passed away, aged 45 years, 1 month and 14 days. A short life, full of consequences. An unfailing intellect, imperturbable temper, great self-reliance and as great modesty; seeing the right clearly, pursuing it steadily, he lived and died', a fitting epitaph for the greatest man in aviation.

Records of 1912 stood at: 108.18 mph for speed (by J Védrines of France on a Deperdussin[18] at Chicago, after first passing the 100 mph mark in February at Pau); 628.15 miles for distance over a closed circuit (A Fourny of France on a Maurice Farman at Étampes); and 18,405 feet for height (by R Garros of France on a Morane-Saulnier at Tunis).

1913

French historians refer to 1913 as 'La Glorieuse Année' and indeed it was a memorable year in various departments of aviation. Most spectacular perhaps were the first intentional aerobatics – including loops and upside-down flying – by the Frenchman Adolphe Pégoud on his Blériot in September, which formed an unconscious prelude to the necessary manoeuvres of wartime flying.[19] Although Pégoud was the first true exponent of these new 'stunts', he was not the first to loop the loop, this distinction belonging to the Russian Nesterov who performed the feat in a Nieuport monoplane on 20 August, at Kiev. Looping now became a popular feat and soon passed into the normal

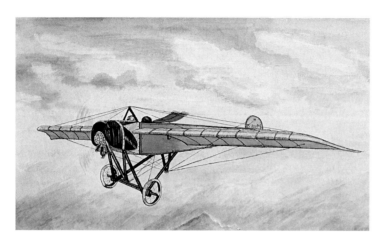

Figure 14.18 Morane-Saulnier monoplane flying over the Alps; watercolour by K J B Munro: c. 1910. (Science & Society Picture Library)

repertoire of flying. Pégoud also made the first parachute jump from an aeroplane in Europe, on 19 August.

A number of impresive long-distance flights were also made, including those by Védrines on a Blériot (November–December) from Nancy to Cairo via Prague, Vienna, Belgrade, Sofia, Constantinople and Tripoli, with a number of stops, a distance of some 2500 miles; by Bonnier and Barnier on a Nieuport (November–December) from Paris to Cairo over a similar course, but more to the east and via Bucharest; and by Garros on a Morane-Saulnier (September) in the first non-stop flight across the Mediterranean, from St Raphael in the South of France to Bizerta in Tunisia. Such performances, especially the long-stage flights, said much of the growing reliability of engines and airframes. A Morane-Saulnier monoplane is shown in Figure 14.18.

One of the lasting achievements of the year was the first true and proper inherently stable aeroplane – i.e. a practical manoeuvrable and 'all-round' stable machine – at Farnborough. It was the B.E.2, now modified according to the research work of E T Busk who had come to the factory in 1912 and was tragically killed in a crash in 1914: designated the B.E.2C, it became one of the most successful and early reconnaissance machines, of which nearly 2000 were subsequently built. Another pioneer product of the Farnborough factory was the prototype F.E.2A pusher biplane fighter, which can perhaps be claimed as the first aeroplane designed specifically to fight in the air, that is to say to attack other aircraft: it was based on the Maurice Farman tradition and subsequent Farnborough variations, but the design was not to be produced – in the shape of the Vickers Gunbus and Farnborough F.E.2B – until 1915–16. Farnborough was now rapidly becoming the foremost of the world's aeronautical research establishments; it was developing both aircraft and aero engines, methods of inspection and testing, and aircraft accessories, as well as conducting basic aerodynamic research.

Two outstanding fast machines were built and flown during the year. The Sopwith Tabloid (Figure 14.19) – designed by Harry Hawker and F Sigrist – was a small two-seat biplane with a single

Figure 14.19 Sopwith Tabloid designed by Hawker and Sigrist: 1913.

wing bay, inspired by the Farnborough B.S.1; it was powered by an 80-hp Gnome, had a top speed of 92 mph, and could climb to 15,000 feet in 10 minutes. The Tabloid was spectacularly flown and publicised by Harry Hawker, and showed officialdom and public alike what extraordinary manoeuvrability a well-designed small biplane could achieve; it undoubtedly helped, with the S.E.2 (B.S.2) and its successors, to revolutionise the concept and design of biplanes in general, and scouts and fighters in particular: it also played a large part in finally killing the monoplane, as no monoplane of the period – or of the foreseeable future – could hope to match the Tabloid's powers of climb and manoeuvrability.

The second of the fast aeroplanes worthy of special mention was the improved Monocoque Deperdussin, with a completely enclosed 160-hp Gnome on which Prévost broke the world's speed record three times during the year at Reims, the final figure being 126.67 mph. This Deperdussin is one of the 'classic' forward-looking aircraft of history, and had it not been for the virtual disappearance of the monoplane within a year or two, might well have led to a rapid development of monoplane fighters. Curiously enough, both the Tabloid and the Deperdussin employed wing warping, although the Tabloid changed to ailerons on the later production machines.

A number of other important aircraft were produced during this year. A V Roe built his first Avro type 504 biplane, with staggered wings, developed from his 1911–12 biplanes – with a large debt to Goupy – which became one of the most famous and widely used aeroplanes in history, especially as a two-seater trainer (Figure 14.20). It was first powered by an 80-hp Gnome and had a speed range of 35–82 mph: in slightly modified forms and with a number of engines, it continued in service, after many thousands had been built, until the early 1930s. The Dunne No. 8 swept-wing tail-less biplane, built in 1912, and now powered by an 80-hp Gnome, made a notable flight in August from Eastchurch to Paris: the aerodynamic research

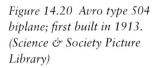

Figure 14.20 Avro type 504 biplane; first built in 1913. (Science & Society Picture Library)

embodied in this remarkable aircraft was to inspire many followers: one of the machines directly inspired by Dunne was Hill's Pterodactyl of 1926. Russia now entered aeronautical history with the precursor of all large multi-engined aircraft, the four-engined Bolshoi (Russian for 'The Great'), a cabin biplane designed by Igor Sikorsky who had earlier been concerned with helicopter experiments which he had temporarily abandoned for conventional type aircraft: he was afterwards to leave Russia and become the leading helicopter pioneer in the USA. The huge Bolshoi (the span was 28.2 m, say 92½ ft) when its nature and performance became understood, struck the world of aviation as a highly remarkable aerial phenomenon, without rival or precedent. Powered by four 100 hp Argus engines – at first arranged in two tandem tractor-pusher groups, then four separate tractors – made its first flight on 13 May 1913 at St Petersburg, piloted by Sikorsky himself. Among its achievements was a flight (with eight on board) of 1 hour 54 minutes. The Bolshoi included a large cabin, fully glazed, in which there were four armchairs, a sofa and a table, with the pilot and copilot's seat up front fitted with dual control (Figure 14.21). The subsequent history of this outstanding aircraft is noted in the next section.

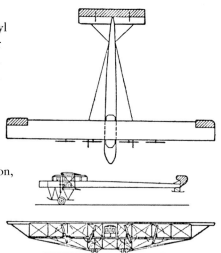

Figure 14.21 Sikorsky four-engine Bolshoi: 1913.

The second seaplane meeting at Monaco drew a selection of float monoplanes, float biplanes, and biplane flying boats, all of which were established as successful types: the main event was the first race for the new Schneider Trophy (Figure 14.22) in April, which was won by Prévost on a Deperdussin float monoplane at an average speed of 45.75 mph.

Night flying, after its tentative beginnings in 1910, was carried a stage further at Hendon when a Henry Farman biplane was fitted with two rows of electric lamps (on the leading edges of upper and lower wings), and was taken off, flown, and landed successfully in a series of tests.

On 7 August, when testing his new biplane carrying W H B Evans the cricketer as a passenger, S F Cody and Evans were killed when the machine broke up in the air and crashed over Laffan's Plain, Aldershot. Overrated by some, underrated by others, Cody had played a human, rather than a technical, role in aviation history: the Farnborough authorities, where he had done so much of his work, wrote his epitaph in the words: 'History accords him the prime virtues of courage and perseverance.' Perhaps Cody's most valuable contribution, when viewed in the historical perspective of today, was in creating much valuable air-mindedness in Britain at a time when both the government and the public were lamentably apathetic about flying in general, when the land of Cayley, Wenham and Pilcher was all but aeronautically asleep.

Records for 1913 stood at: 126.67 mph for speed (M Prévost of France on a Deperdussin at Reims); 634.54 miles for distance over a closed circuit (A Seguin of France on a Henry Farman at Buc); and 20,079 feet for height (G Legagneux of France on a Nieuport at St Raphael).

1914

Figure 14.22 The Schneider Trophy, designed by E Gabard: 1913. The trophy became the outright property of the Royal Aero Club after a third British victory in 1931, and was donated to the Science Museum in 1977. (Science & Society Picture Library)

The traditional lull before the storm found only a few important events in aviation to record, with the major powers actively preparing for war, but only secondary attention being paid to military aeroplanes. Sikorsky in Russia started productive flying with the second of his great four-engined cabin machines: this was the Ilia Mouriametz, a development of the Bolshoi which was powered by four 100 hp Mercedes engines and was fitted successfully at different times with skis, wheels and floats. It first flew in January 1914; on 11 February it flew well with 16 on board; and in June made a record flight – partly at night – from St Petersburg to Kiev and back, with several stops, a distance of some 2560 km (say 1590 miles).[20] Some 75 machines of this type were produced in Russia during the war. But perhaps the most important point about these Sikorsky giants was that they directly inspired Count von Zeppelin to play a leading role in the design and limited production of large aeroplanes. An American, P E Fansler, opened the first scheduled airline in history in Florida, between St Petersburg and Tampa (22 miles) employing A Jannus to pilot a Benoist flying boat, and carrying both passengers and freight; this airline continued successfully for some weeks, but Fansler's enterprising example was not followed up at the time. Also in America, Curtiss was testing successfully his twin-engined flying boat America for a projected transatlantic flight to be undertaken by the Englishman Lieutenant J C Porte; but the war put a stop to it. In France, Lawrence Sperry of the USA demonstrated his new gyroscopic stabiliser for aeroplanes (installed in a Curtiss flying boat) and with it won the Concours de la Sécurité en Aéroplane at Buc.[21] Sperry later invented the turn and bank indicator, and did more than any other inventor to bring about safety in flying, and automatic piloting of aircraft. A converted Sopwith Tabloid on floats, piloted by C H Pixton, won for Britain the second Schneider Trophy speed contest at an average speed of 86.78 mph, and raised the speed record for seaplanes to 92 mph.

The speed and other records noted on previous pages give a somewhat misleading idea of the performances of work-a-day production aircraft carrying a productive load. The position in mid-1914, regarding aircraft performance in Britain, France, Germany and the United States, was that one or two machines such as the Tabloid and Deperdussin had a maximum speed of about 90 mph, but most of the available aeroplanes had a maximum speed of some 65–75 mph. Individual aircraft, engines and performances will be noted in the next section.

The aeroplane was now to enter its first major war, in which it would benefit greatly from the intensive research and experience expended by the combatant nations, all of which would later benefit the whole field of flying. Also for the first time the name of the aeroplane was to be unjustly darkened by its association with warfare.

Gnome engines driving one airscrew. This Short machine may perhaps stand as the first to fly, having two independent engines and two or more propellers.

11 Photographs of this aircraft are sometimes published by mistake for the 1900–02 gliders: the difference is easily detected in the lack of a forward elevator and the presence of a rear elevator in this 1911 glider.

12 For early spins, see *The Aeroplane*, 30 January 1953, and *Aeronautics*, July 1960.

13 This distinction is often, but wrongly, claimed for another excellent machine, the Sopwith Tabloid, which did not make its first real trial flight until November 1913. It is highly probable, if not inevitable, that it was the B.S.1 which directly inspired the Tabloid. The comparative neglect of the B.S.1, and the fame of the Tabloid at its expense, poses an important problem of aviation history: the answer, as we see it today, lies chiefly in the deplorable attitude adopted by certain early writers – and others – who sought to denigrate the Farnborough products, coupled with the lack of channels available to Farnborough to 'blow its own trumpet'.

14 Monocoque: from the Greek *monos* (single) and the French *coque* (eggshell). Considerable confusion has arisen in historical studies over the meaning of 'monocoque' and 'stressed-skin' construction: these words are discussed in the Appendix on page 204.

15 Later this year, Etrich's high-wing cabin monoplane – the Taube-Limousine – flew successfully in Austria.

16 The modified to 1910–11 Short S.38. See *Sheerness Guardian*, 13 January 1912.

17 It is said that Mr Churchill, then First Lord of the Admiralty, wisely refused to allow the ban to apply to the Naval wing; but I have been unable to confirm this.

18 His mascot was a reproduction of Leonardo da Vinci's *Mona Lisa* on the fuselage.

19 At Brooklands, at the end of September, Pégoud performed a vertical S (a bunt followed by a half loop), an inverted loop, a bunt-and-roll-out, and a tail slide. He had made his first loop at Buc on 21 September.

20 Culinary history here combined with aeronautical, as there was served aboard the Ilia Mouriametz the first full meal to be eaten in the air.

21 The judges decided not to award the Grand Prix to any of the competitors, but Sperry was given the next highest award and so won the 'Concours'.

15 The First World War: 1914–1918

War was declared in July and August, and the opening of hostilities found the Allies with a combined total of some 208 aircraft on the Western Front (48 British,[1] 24 Belgian and 136 French are the approximate figures), with the Germans possessing about 180 machines. In addition a considerable number of training and other miscellaneous aircraft remained at home bases on both sides.

The general pattern of aircraft development in the war followed naturally upon the duties expected of the machines. The aeroplane started the war as an aerial intelligence agent or scout, for visual and then photographic reconnaissance – it was soon fitted with radio – and then added spotting for the artillery as another of its tasks. This was taken at first to demand a slow and stable two-seater, although one or two types of fast single-seat scout were available from the start. As anti-aircraft fire improved, speed and climb became growingly important, qualities which became even more vital when the machines had to defend themselves from attack by other aircraft. This in turn led to specially fast and highly manoeuvrable aircraft to defend the reconnaissance machines, the vulnerable observation balloons, and later the bombers; and, of course, to shoot down those same types – along with airships – when flown by the enemy, as well as the enemy fighters. And so, out of the fast single-seat scout there was born the single-seat fighting scout, or simply the 'fighter'. When bombing was introduced, it was at first carried out by the slow reconnaissance machines and later by the specialised medium and long-range bombers. But in-between these categories, and superseding the old two-seat reconnaissance type, arose the general-purpose machine, which grew out of the two-seat reconnaissance type – often known as a fighter-reconnaissance aircraft – which could spot, spy, fight, 'strafe' targets on the ground and, in a small way, bomb. In addition, certain more specialised types were produced for special duties (see below).

Typical of the early operational two-seat reconnaissance machines was the British B.E.2C (Figure 15.1), with an RAF (Royal Aircraft Factory) eight-cylinder, 90-hp V-type engine: it had staggered wings – giving a good view up and down – a span of 37 feet, and a maximum speed of 75 mph,[2] it could climb to 10,000 feet in 45 minutes, and stay up for about 3¼ hours. Armament was at first a revolver or rifle, and later, a sideways-firing machine-gun: as one RFC officer put it, 'the early war pilot went into battle armed more as a sportsman than as a soldier'. Other British reconnaissance types were the B.E.2, 2A and 2B, and the famous Avro 504. Analogous types were the French Henry and Maurice Farmans, and the German Albatros, LVG, and Rumpler Taube, the last being a monoplane with swept-back bird-like wings.

The early fast single-seat scouts were typified by the Sopwith Tabloid and the Bristol Scout of 1913 and 1914. The latter was powered with various rotary engines, including the 80-hp Gnome

Figure 15.1 Farnborough-designed reconnaissance biplane, B.E.2C: 1914–15.

and the 100-hp Monosoupape, with a speed range of 40–105 mph. French equivalents were the Nieuport and Morane scouts, the latter a monoplane; and the German Fokker monoplane (Eindecker). This type of aircraft was revolutionised as soon as a fixed forward-firing gun was devised, thus converting it into a piece of flying artillery aimed at the enemy, a development which is described below.

Figure 15.2 Vickers F.B.5 Gunbus pusher biplane: 1914.

It was soon realised that the reconnaissance aeroplanes, both fast and slow, must be able to defend themselves from, and destroy, the enemy's similar machines; but as the propeller was revolving at the front of the fuselage, this feat was almost impossible for the tractor machines, except for 'pot shots' from the side with small arms. The available single-seat scouts were admirable in performance but helpless without a forward-firing gun. So the two-seat pusher biplane was revived, and in 1914 and early 1915, the two-seat Vickers F.B.5 Gunbus (Figure 15.2) went into action, the observer seated right in the front of the nacelle and wielding a machine gun on a pedestal. Although slow (70–80 mph) and somewhat cumbersome, they dealt severely with the German reconnaissance machines, such as the Rumpler and other Taube types, when they could reach them. Similar types were the D.H.1 and 2, and later the F.E.2B and 6: the D.H.2 and the F.E.8 were single-seaters.

Then, on 1 April 1915, the famous French ace Roland Garros, in J M Bruce's words, 'opened the era of true fighter aircraft', when he first shot down a German Albatros by firing a machine gun through the propeller disc of his Morane-Saulnier L (Figure 15.3) which was fitted with metal deflector plates. Unfortunately, after five such victories in less than three weeks, Garros was himself shot down by ground fire and captured, along with his machine, which he tried to destroy, but failed: the secret was now out. A team of three German designers examined this device, then rapidly improved on it: they produced a gun properly synchronised to fire past the blades when they were not in line with the muzzle.[3] Fokker was commissioned to produce this interrupter gear, and he seems later to have taken credit for its invention. By July 1915, some Fokker (Eindecker) E.1 scouts (Figure 15.4) were operational with the new gun, and the first Allied machine was shot down with it on 1 August. Thus developed the so-called 'Fokker scourge', which continued until Allied aircraft could be similarly equipped. The Fokkers were by no means as efficient as they should have been, but the lack of effective opposition lent them fame. The first Allied machine to rival the Fokker was the French Nieuport with a machine gun fixed on the top wing; it soon incorporated a synchronised gun, and with this it went into action in January of 1916. By April 1916, when the British F.E.2B became fully effective, the Fokker ascendency was neutralised, and was soon in eclipse. From then onwards, there was to be a constantly alternating superiority of fighters, as new designs were produced in quick succession by the Allies and by Germany.

The British single-seat fighting scout, developed from the Farnborough B.S.1, the Sopwith Tabloid, and another remarkable

Figure 15.3 Morane-Saulnier L, with forward-firing gun utilising airscrew deflector plates: 1915.

Figure 15.4 Fokker E.1 (Eindecker) scout, with interrupter gun gear: 1915.

Farnborough prototype the S.E.4 (of 1914), produced a line of formidable and famous aircraft. The Tabloid grew into the Sopwith Pup (1816), the Sopwith triplane (1916) and the Sopwith Camel (1917), all with rotary engines. The Pup, with a 100-hp Monosoupape motor, had a top speed of 110 mph, a ceiling of 18,500 feet, and an endurance of 1¾ hours: the Camel, with a 130-hp Clerget, had a top speed of 120 mph, a ceiling of 19,000 feet and an endurance of 2½ hours. The outstanding in-line motored fighter was Farnborough's S.E.5A (1917) which was powered by a 200-hp Hispano-Suiza, had a top speed of 130 mph, a ceiling of 22,000 feet and an endurance of 3 hours (Figure 15.5). These, and most fighters, were fitted with progressively more powerful motors, of which the latest type is given here. The most notable French fighter was the S.P.A.D. (1916) which many American, and some British, pilots flew. The German single-seat fighters, which were equally successful, included the Albatros D.III (1917), the Pfalz D.III (1917), the Fokker triplane (1917) and the Fokker D.VII (1918): the last was perhaps the finest all-round fighter of the war: it incorporated a type of semi-cantilever wing system, a 160-hp Mercedes engine (amongst others), a speed of 125 mph and a ceiling of 21,000 feet: its superiority lay in a combination of qualities, especially its rate of climb and its manoeuvrability. Performance figures for the various contemporary versions of these machines were similar; and by the end of the war the best fighters on either side had a service ceiling of some 25,000 feet, a top speed (low down) of 155 mph and of 140 mph at 10,000 feet, to which they could climb in about 10 minutes.

Meanwhile the two-seat reconnaissance machine was developed to defend itself and also fight, thus becoming the so-called fighter-reconnaissance type, the first successful example of which was the Sopwith 1½-Strutter of 1916 (named for its centre-section strut arrangement), with a fixed forward-firing synchronised gun and a movable rear gun mounted on a Scarff ring for the observer:[4] this machine, which had a top speed of 100 mph, was also fitted with ingenious air brakes,[5] one of the earliest uses of them in production aircraft. Later in 1916 came the R.E.8, and (in 1917) the famous and formidable Bristol Fighter with a speed of 115 mph at 10,000 feet, and a service ceiling of 20,000 feet: it was fitted with various in-line engines including the 250-hp Rolls-Royce Falcon, and could scout, fight and defend itself with success. Analogous German machines were the L.V.G. (1916), Aviatik (1916), Hanoveraner (1917) and Halberstadt (1917).

The bomber developed from the slow reconnaissance aircraft – three Avro 504s raided the Zeppelin works at Friedrichshafen in November 1914 – and the two-seat reconnaissance fighter became the first light bomber. Then specialised light bombers were produced, the most effective of which were the De Havilland D.H.4 (1917), the D.H.9 (1917) and the D.H.9A (1918), the latter carrying a bomb load – under the wings – of 450 lb at over 100 mph, and remaining airborne for 4 hours.

The heavy bomber, developed for both tactical bombing and assault on cities, was typified by the twin-engine Handley Page O/400 and the similar German Gotha, which were both in active operation from 1917 onwards. The O/400 flew at 60–80 mph for 8 hours with a bomb load of 1800 lb carried internally.[6] The Gotha, on which the Germans relied for long-range bombing after the Zeppelins had proved too vulnerable, had a slightly lower performance and bomb load, but was an excellent machine: perhaps the best – and certainly the widest used of the German 'giant' bombers – was the four-engine Staaken R VI and its developments, the R XIV being shown in Figure 15.6. By the end of the war Handley Page had built a number of four-engined V/1500 bombers which were prevented by the Armistice from bombing Berlin: these had a speed of 70–90 mph, a radius of action of 1300 miles, and a bomb load of 7500 lb.

The seaplane quickly came into its own for reconnaissance, bombing and torpedo-dropping, and particularly successful were the Short float planes and the Felixstowe F.2 flying boats, the latter being the excellent creations of John Porte. Airships were quite extensively used during the war (Figure 15.7): the British, French and Italian Navies used mainly small non-rigid airships (colloquially called 'blimps') for antisubmarine patrols; but the Germans concentrated on the development of the rigid airship. The majority of these were built by the Zeppelin company, and they were used both for long-range bombing and for naval scouting. Countering the German airships was a major task of the Royal Naval Air Service, and one result of this was the development of an entirely new type of warship, the aircraft carrier, by a process of evolution. Initially, seaplane tenders were in use, from which the aircraft were off-loaded by crane to take off from the sea, alongside the ship. In 1915, one of these ships, HMS *Vindex*, was fitted with a small flight deck forward; and, on

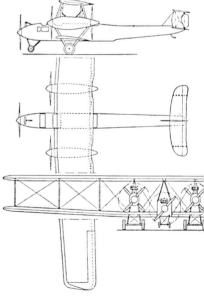

Figure 15.6 Zeppelin-Staaken R XIV five-engine bomber: 1918.

Figure 15.7 HMA Delta *airship: 1913. (Science & Society Picture Library)*

3 November, Flight-Lieutenant H F Towler took off in a Bristol Scout from the moving ship. Several seaplane tenders were thus equipped, and at least one attack on a Zeppelin was launched from HMS *Vindex*. In another attempt to develop a Zeppelin interceptor, one of *Vindex*'s Bristol Scouts, flown by Flight-Lieutenant M J Day, was carried aloft on the large Porte Baby flying boat on 17 May 1916, and successfully launched in midair.

To avoid the delays associated with launching flying boats by crane, HMS *Campania* was fitted with a longer flight deck, and specially built Fairey float planes mounted on a detachable wheeled trolley were flown off this from mid-1916. The first landing on a moving ship was made by Squadron-Commander E H Dunning on 2 August 1917 in a Sopwith Pup on the 228-foot long foredeck of HMS *Furious*: he was killed repeating the exercise a few days later, and the experiments ceased until HMS *Furious* had been fitted with a 284-foot long afterdeck, equipped with a primitive arresting gear, in March 1918. From this, it was a short step – though a revolution in warship design – to HMS *Argus*, which appeared in September 1918 with a completely unobstructed full-length flight deck. An operational squadron of torpedo carriers was embarked in October, but saw no active service.

Short flying-off decks were also provided on a considerable number of British cruisers and battleships from June 1917 onwards. Although the US Navy had continued its prewar experiments with catapults, and a British version was tested on HMS *Slinger* from September 1917, this technique was not regularly used until after 1922. Successful experiments were also conducted with single-seat fighters launched from flat-topped lighters towed behind destroyers: on 11 August 1918, Lieutenant S D Culley, flying a Sopwith Camel from one of these lighters, shot down the Zeppelin L.53 off the Belgian coast.

In many departments of aviation and its accessories, important advances and experiments were made. Radio communication with aircraft became universal: aerial photography, many instruments, and armament all made great strides. Even glider bombs, as well as powered radio-controlled aerial bombs – virtually small pilotless bombers – were pioneered during the war. On 12 September 1916 the first demonstration of a pilotless radio-guided bomb was made – the Hewitt-Sperry biplane[7] – which had a 40 hp motor and was capable of carrying an explosive charge of about 140 kg over a distance of some 80 km. A similar machine was produced in England at Farnborough, called the Aerial Target, which was tested in 1917. In Europe the first was the Siemens glider bomb which was tested in October 1916, with an improved design of the same machine (not exploited) in 1917. There was also a biplane glider bomb which made a test flight from Zeppelin LZ.12 on 27 April 1917. This type of weapon remained relatively neglected and undeveloped until the Second World War. A variety of other special developments were also encouraged including, for example, the fitting of Le Prieur rockets to Allied fighters for dealing with enemy observation balloons, although incendiary bullets were satisfactory enough for bringing down these balloons, which at first were widely used for artillery spotting until superseded by aeroplanes. The Royal Aircraft Factory at Farnborough played a leading part in other inventions, and developed the following, most of which were not to be properly exploited for years to come: the first flaps, giving a variation of 5 mph, fitted to the experimental S.E.4 (1914), bubble cockpit covers (1914), corrected bombsights (1915), the application of superchargers to aero engines (1916), tail trimming (1917), a two-pitch airscrew (1918), as well as complete design and prototype construction of various aircraft, including the outstanding S.E.5 fighter (designed by H P Folland) in 1917, which were mass-produced by numerous firms outside the aircraft industry.

One invention, however, was conspicuous by its absence, and that absence reflects great discredit on both enemy and Allies alike, especially, one regrets to record, on the British: the invention was, of course, the free pack-type parachute for escape from aeroplanes.[8]

Basic aerodynamic research and development centred chiefly on the production of improved wing sections of high lift and low drag, most of the productive work being carried out at the National Physical Laboratory and at Farnborough in England, and the Aeronautical Laboratory at Göttingen in Germany under Professor Prandtl. Apart from the all-important military aircraft (see below), surprisingly little attention was paid to improving aircraft structures. The traditional fabric-covered framework of wood or metal persisted, and only in Germany was monocoque construction developed in a progressive way, the Albatros, Roland and Pfalz scouts having excellent monocoque fuselages of wood.

Aero engines advanced from the small in-line and rotary types of 1914–15, such as the 80-hp Gnome, Le Rhône and Oberursel rotaries, and the 90-hp V-type RAF and 100-hp Daimler, to the large in-line motors of 1917–18, which included the 12-cylinder 360-hp Rolls-Royce Eagle VIII, 12-cylinder 400-hp American Liberty, and the eight-cylinder 240-hp Mercedes.

Flying techniques naturally depended on the strength and manoeuvrability of the aircraft available, and, where fighters were in question, designers were also concerned with the necessity of varying the degree and nature of inherent stability to allow of greater sensitivity to the controls. Both the exigencies of aerial combat and the ever-improving effectiveness of anti-aircraft gunnery forced the aeroplane to climb quicker and higher, and to manoeuvre with extreme agility: what had once been thought of as dangerous stunt aerobatics became normal flying tactics, and part of the everyday training of the pilot.

It was in Germany that one of the most vital and far-reaching aeronautical innovations took place during the war years. It has already been noted that Hugo Junkers had in 1910 patented his thick-section cantilever wing, without external bracing with struts or wires. It was not until 1915 that this epoch-making invention was successfully applied in aviation, and then in conjunction with metal construction. With his J.1 Junkers produced an all-metal (iron and steel) fully cantilever-wing monoplane, which made its first successful flights in December 1915, powered by a 120-hp Mercedes motor: it attained a speed of 105 mph. The German authorities, however, were sceptical of such a revolutionary step,[9] and proved obstructionist in face of both Junkers' achievements and proposals. But although progress was slow, he pressed on: in 1917 the improved J.2 appeared, still constructed of iron and steel, and in the same year he produced the remarkable J.4. The latter was an all-metal cantilever sesquiplane for ground attack, chiefly constructed of duralumin, and heavily armed and armoured: it was a two-seater, powered by a 200-hp Benz motor, with a top speed of 95 mph, and was produced in quantity. Then came the first low-wing cantilever monoplane fighters; the first was the J.7/9 of 1917, the second the J.10 of 1918 (Figure 15.8), which was later to lead to the successful small passenger machine, the F.13 (J.13) of 1919. These first of the world's low-wing cantilever monoplanes represented a complete innovation, and were at first looked upon with suspicion, owing chiefly to the high centre of gravity and its possibly adverse effect on lateral stability: but the fears were

Figure 15.8 Junkers low-wing cantilever monoplane fighter: 1918.

proved groundless. It is interesting to note that one of Junkers' main reasons for adopting the low wing position was to minimise injury to the crew in a crash, as the wings would be the first to hit the ground and thus absorb a large part of the initial shock.

The influence of Junkers was to affect the whole course of aircraft evolution. He may be fully and fairly credited with the design and construction of (a) the first practical cantilever wing aeroplanes, (b) the first practical all-metal aeroplanes, and (c) the first practical low-wing monoplanes, all of which he continued to develop successfully over the years.

The aircraft industry in Europe and America had, of course, expanded enormously. To take Britain as an example; from the handful of machines available in 1914, through all the losses of the intervening years, the number in service in 1918 was some 3300; and the number built reached the huge total of 55,000. The few hundreds of men employed in the industry in 1914 had been swelled by 1918 to nearly 350,000 men and women.

War in the air had been envisaged for centuries, and had even been prophetically described by Francesco de Lana in 1670. When the balloon was invented in 1783, there was a new outburst of aggressive prognostications, and balloons were in fact used passively for military observation from the eighteenth century onwards, with one balloon bombing raid (by the Austrians against Venice) in 1849. As the powered aeroplane came nearer to achievement, two camps of speculators arose; those who prophesied and advocated the use of the aeroplane in war, such as Maxim and Ader, and those who felt that the aeroplane's power would neutralise itself when both sides possessed this destructive potential, such as the Wrights, who were proved wrong. The aeroplane has, of course, transformed the whole conduct of warfare; and one unfortunate but understandable result of the early successes in this field became its role – in the eyes of many – as a symbol of destruction. It took the rise of the light aeroplane and the development of air transport in the 'between wars' period to mitigate the flying machine's evil reputation in the world's mind, and establish its parallel but peaceful role as a productive and often life-saving carrier of passengers and cargo. As Cayley prophesied, 'We shall be able to transport ourselves and our families, and their goods and chattels, more securely by air than by water.'

Notes

1   The British types available at the outbreak of war included the B.E.2, 2A, 2B, Avro 504, Sopwith Tabloid scout, and Bristol scout. Trainers included various Farmans, as well as Blériot monoplanes.

2   From now onwards, aircraft speeds will be given to the nearest 5 mph, or in approximate ranges, where machines have a top speed below about 250 mph. Where speeds above that figure enter history, the figure will be given to the nearest 10 mph or even more approximately, according to

circumstances. Aircraft speeds are governed by so many factors, and are listed differently by so many apparently reliable sources, that published figures can seldom be considered accurate except in highly specialised cases where complete data is available, and provided for a given aircraft operating under a given set of conditions.

3   Ideas for firing a synchronised machine gun between the propeller blades had been developed by Schneider in Germany (1913–14), and by Saulnier and Peyret in France (1913–14): the two latter proceeded to an advanced test stage, but tests were abandoned because of hang-fire troubles with the ammunition. Saulnier then simply fitted metal deflector plates to the propeller; the first exponent of this technique was Garros, as narrated above.

4   The first practical two-seater was the Caudron G-4 (1915).

5   These air brakes were placed at the rear of the lower centre section, close to the fuselage: they hinged upwards and could be moved to stand vertically, at right angles to the airflow.

6   It has often been stated that it was the capture by the Germans of an intact O/400 – it had the misfortune to land by mistake on a German aerodrome – which inspired the Germans to build the Gotha: this is, of course, quite untrue, as the Gotha was already in production when this event occurred.

7   Built by Curtiss.

8   The parachute, which had been in use since 1797, was inadequately developed in the war for the use of observation balloon and airship crews – the canopy being pulled out of a fixed case – and used on a few German aeroplanes in the war. But no British or French aeroplane crews were allowed parachutes in 1914–18 (although tests were permitted at the end of the war), for the disgraceful reasons (a) that the balloon type was not reliable enough, and (b) that pilots would be encouraged to abandon their machines. There was no excuse whatever for not having produced a satisfactory pack parachute, the problem being relatively simple and already having been tentatively solved and published by an American showman, Leo Stevens: as early as 1908 he had dropped from a balloon with his free-type pack parachute, opened at will by a ripcord when falling. In October 1912, F R Law made a similar safe descent from a Wright biplane, using Stevens' improved 'Life-Pack' parachute: this parachute was described and illustrated in the American magazine *Aeronautics* (October 1912), and could easily have been located by the Allied authorities.

9   The main criticism was that the steel structure was impractically heavy.

16 Between the wars: the first period 1919–1929

This period was one of spectacular and prophetic flying achievements, as well as steady technical progress in aviation. Acceptance of the importance of flying was also being gradually extended in the public mind, and air transport began to establish itself as a means of public transport.

The tone of high adventure was set in 1919 by the first flights across the Atlantic. In May, Harry Hawker and Mackenzie-Grieve had attempted a direct crossing in a single-engined Sopwith biplane, but they had to force-land in the Atlantic, and were given up for lost until they arrived a week later on a Danish steamer which had no radio to announce their rescue. The first completed crossing was accomplished (16–27 May) in stages by the US Lieut.-Commander A C Read and his crew in the Curtiss NC-4 flying boat (Figure 16.1), the only one of three similar aircraft to stay the course: it flew from Newfoundland to Lisbon with two landings in the Azores. The first direct non-stop crossing of the Atlantic was by the British Captain J Alcock and Lieutenant A Whitten-Brown (Figure 16.2) in a converted twin-engine Vickers Vimy bomber (Figure 16.3): they left St John's, Newfoundland on 14 June and crash-landed safely in a Galway bog near Clifden the next day (Figure 16.4), after flying the 1890 miles non-stop from coast to coast in 15 hours 57 minutes at an average speed of 118 mph: the total flying time, from takeoff to landing (some 1950 miles) was 16 hours 27 minutes.

Figure 16.1 Curtiss NC-4 flying boat, which made the first Atlantic crossing, by stages: 1919.

Also in 1919, and of far-reaching importance, was the almost unnoticed publication of a now classic work entitled *A Method of Reaching Extreme Altitudes* by an obscure American scientist named Dr R H Goddard: this book marked the birth of modern rocketry, as it dealt with the liquid fuel rocket, the first of which was successfully launched by Goddard in 1926. It is historically important to note that Goddard specifically stated that it was a reading of Jules Verne's *From the Earth to the Moon* that inspired him to take to rocketry. Significantly enough, the end of the decade saw the first flights by rocket-propelled aeroplanes in 1928–29 (see page 226).

Leaving for a moment the record of great exploits, of which these years saw so many, it is important to trace briefly the trends in aircraft construction. From the functional and structural point of view these ten years saw the monoplane enter into full rivalry with the biplane in the field of transport aircraft, and to a lesser degree in the small light aeroplane class, and amongst racing machines, where its low drag characteristics were vital. This development was due almost entirely to the cantilever wing policy of Junkers, and its successful application by him, and by the German Reinhold Platz, who designed the Fokker-type wing. The cantilever wing grew more efficient as the strength and lightness of materials increased, but continued for

Figure 16.2 Captain John Alcock and Lieutenant Arthur Whitten-Brown: 1919. (Science & Society Picture Library)

Figure 16.3 *Fuelling the aircraft at the start of the first direct transatlantic flight, from Newfoundland to Ireland (Alcock and Brown in their Vickers Vimy): 1919. (Science & Society Picture Library)*

some years in the familiar Junkers and Fokker-type wings, which were thick-sectioned and of large chord at the roots, tapering in thickness and chord towards the tips. Junkers mostly favoured the metal low-wing application, which necessitated a pronounced dihedral angle to provide lateral stability; and Platz the high-wing of wooden construction, which he laid horizontally across the top of the fuselage, lateral stability being aided by the pendulum action of the fuselage and undercarriage. The Junkers practice was to pay handsome aerodynamic dividends in the future, when retractable undercarriages became the rule, as the low-wing arrangement allowed of a much shorter, and therefore lighter, undercarriage which could be retracted into the wings or engine nacelles.

Of particular long-term importance was another German designer, Dr Adolph Rohrbach. He realised that the Junkers corrugated metal surfaces produced high drag, and that they could not bear sufficient of the stresses involved, especially where the wings were concerned. So, in 1919, he started building smooth-skinned metal surfaces, with metal box-spar construction in the wings, thus allowing the primary

Figure 16.4 *Alcock and Brown's Vimy after it crash-landed safely at Clifden, Co. Galway, Ireland: 1919. (Science & Society Picture Library)*

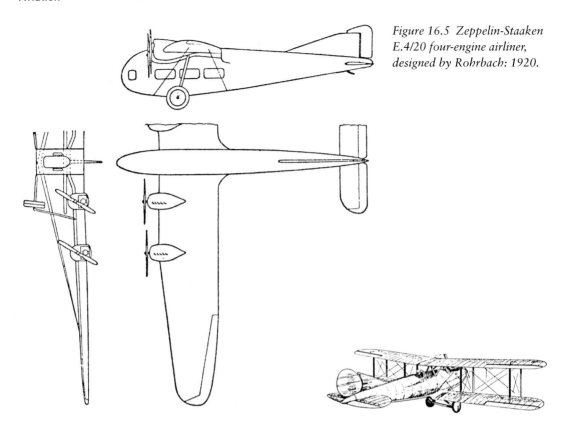

Figure 16.5 Zeppelin-Staaken E.4/20 four-engine airliner, designed by Rohrbach: 1920.

Figure 16.6 Short Silver Streak, of monocoque construction: 1920.

loads to be borne by the surfaces (Figure 16.5). This was the beginning of the modern stressed-skin concept – Rohrbach was probably the first to use the term 'stressed skin', in 1924 – which was further evolved and improved by H A Wagner, who worked with Rohrbach. It was also Rohrbach, in a lecture in the USA in 1926, who helped materially to inspire the first, and revolutionary, American transport machines of the 1930s (see page 204).

The monoplane was not yet to make much headway in the military field, even as a bomber, where it could have been employed with advantage. For fighters, the high-drag but extremely manoeuvrable biplane was still preferred to the low-drag monoplane, a state of affairs which was to be transformed in the next decade.

The ever-growing use of metal – steel and aluminium alloys – in all parts of the aircraft structure, was another vital development, with the gradual adoption – not to become general until the 1930s – of monocoque construction carried out in both wood and metal, or the two combined. A particularly ambitious machine with duralumin monocoque fuselage was the all-metal Short Silver Streak (at first called the Swallow) of 1920, but its example was not to be followed in this country for some years (Figure 16.6).

It should, perhaps, be said here that British construction, both of civil and military aircraft, was strangely conservative and unprogressive compared with the Continent, and later the United

Figure 16.7 Lockheed Vega passenger transport, fist built in 1927.

States. This lack of progress was worsened by the British practice of 'redesigning biplanes of the wood era in high strength alloy steel', as Professor N J Hoff put it: this basic idea, he goes on to say, 'was incorrect from the structural standpoint. It did not utilise the inherent lighter strength of the metals which makes them suitable for the construction of cantilever wings.' This particularly applied to the rebirth of British military aircraft construction about 1924, when the Air Ministry – with Britain's scant supply of suitable woods in mind – ruled that the vital parts of the structures of all new service aircraft were to be made of metal. Even so, some remarkable machines, particularly fighters, were produced during this period.

A major innovation in aircraft construction in the mid-1920s was the high-wing single-engined transport monoplane, to carry a pilot and some six to eight passengers, with a cruising speed of 100 mph upwards, and a range of 500 miles and up. This type derived originally from the Fokker high-wing monoplane of the immediate postwar years, such as the F.II, but it was both revolutionised and crystallised in the United States by the Lockheed Vega of 1927 (Figure 16.7). With a radial engine of either 220 hp or 425 hp the Vega could cruise with a pilot and six passengers at 100 to 135 mph and had a range of 550 or 900 miles: it had fully cantilevered wooden wings, and a wooden monocoque fuselage of an advanced streamlined shape built in two moulded sections. Of particular importance was its practical demonstration that a stressed-skin structure allows the same interior height and breadth of fuselage as that of a framework structure, at a saving of 35 per cent of the cross-sectional area, thus greatly reducing drag and saving much weight and material. The Vega set the fashion and the pace for this general-purpose type of aircraft, and inspired a worldwide development, and its influence spread also to the design of larger transport aircraft.

The military aeroplanes of the decade kept, with some notable exceptions, to the biplane form which, as already mentioned, offered a good performance at a time when speeds were not high enough to encourage designers to exploit the cleaner lines of the monoplane. The English biplane fighters, paralleled by similar machines in other countries, included many successful types, such as the Fairey Flycatcher and Firefly, Gloster Grebe and Gamecock, Armstrong-Whitworth Siskin, and Bristol Bulldog, and reached their zenith at the end of the decade in the Hawker Fury (1929), which had a top speed of over 200 mph, the first military aircraft to exceed this figure (Figure 16.8). Exceptions to the biplane fighter tradition included

Figure 16.8 (below) Hawker Fury biplane fighter: 1929.

Figure 16.9 (right) Bristol monoplane racer, with retractable undercarriage: 1922.

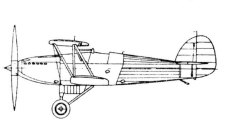

the remarkable Bristol monoplane racer (1922), an experimental mid-wing machine with retractable undercarriage (Figure 16.9); the Dewoitine D-27; and the Junkers K-47 two-seat fighter which was built in Sweden and became the ancestor of the firm's Stuka dive bomber. Comparatively few bombers were built during this period, but fast single-engine types such as the Fairey Fox were made in England, with Fairey and Blackburn machines being built for torpedo carrying. The Americans kept alive the large biplane bomber such as the twin-engined Martin NBS-1 and the Curtiss B-2; and their courageous Colonel 'Billy' Mitchell strove – at the expense of his career – to focus attention on the bomber as the future's most powerful weapon of war over both land and water: his successful sinking of a so-called unsinkable ex-German battleship in 1921, and his outspoken criticisms of American air policy in 1925, had a decisive influence on the future of United States military aviation. In 1928 Britain produced two interesting machines, one an experimental aircraft – the Beardmore-Rohrbach Inflexible, an all-metal three-engined cantilever monoplane – and the large Fairey monoplane, with one 500-hp Napier engine, which was not specifically designed as a bomber but as a long-range record-breaker aircraft. After the first of the latter had crashed, the second (in 1933) flew non-stop for 5309 miles in 57½ hours.

An interesting military 'sideline' was experimenting with airships in the role of aircraft carriers. There had been unsuccessful tests during the war, but in 1918 a Sopwith Camel was successfully released from the British airship R.23. Later in the decade other successful tests, both of releasing and taking on fighters, were made both in Britain and America: but all such work ceased when both countries abandoned large airship construction after the succession of disasters to these lighter-than-air aircraft in the 1930s.

The development of the small fast aeroplane, which was to lead directly to the modern fighter, was a prominent feature of the 1920s, and was mostly due to the encouragement of air racing, especially the Pulitzer Trophy races in the USA, and the international Schneider Trophy races for seaplanes. One of the most important of these early racers was the Dayton-Wright R.B. high-wing monoplane which

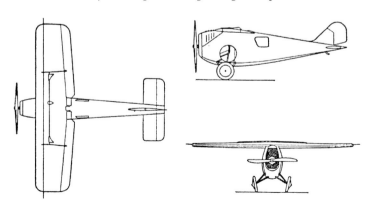

Figure 16.10 Dayton-Wright R.B. racer, with retractable undercarriage: 1920.

Figure 16.11 Curtiss R3C-2 racing float plane: 1925.

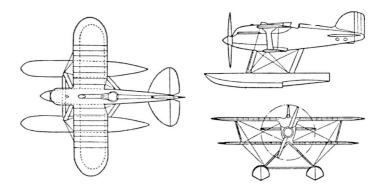

competed for the Gordon-Bennett trophy in France in 1920; for this machine was the first to incorporate a modern-type fully retractable undercarriage[1] (Figure 16.10), a device which was to see much slowness of development, since retractable undercarriages were not to be widely used until the 1930s. At first the more advanced disciplines of streamlining were applied to the biplane, and the 1925 Schneider race was won by the American, J Doolittle, on his little Curtiss R3C-2 at 232.5 mph (Figure 16.11). But a monoplane – an Italian Macchi – won the next year's race, and monoplanes won all subsequent contests. The 1927 Schneider race was especially significant for Britain, for it was won by the Supermarine S.5 at 281.65 mph (Figure 16.12): the S.5 was a low-wing float monoplane designed by R J Mitchell (Figure 16.13) and powered by an 800-hp Napier Lion engine, and was the ancestor of Mitchell's Spitfire. In 1929, Mitchell's Supermarine S.6, with a Rolls-Royce engine, won the Schneider contest at 328.63 mph and later raised the world's speed record to

Figure 16.12 Supermarine S.5, depicted in the Schneider Trophy contest programme for 1929. Illustration by Coombe Richards: 1927. (Science & Society Picture Library)

357.7 mph. These high-speed float planes – chiefly British, American and Italian – laid the foundations for the fighters of the future, and provided ideal opportunities for developing strong and light metal structures, streamlining, and powerful engines.

The non-military sphere of flying saw the most dramatic developments during the decade. European air transport, in the form of properly scheduled airlines, started in 1919, after an interlude of military transport flying which grew out of the immediate needs of official travel after hostilities had ceased.[2] The first civil airline for passengers started on 5 February 1919, when the German Deutsche Luftreederei opened a service between Berlin, Leipzig and Weimar. On 8 February, the French Farman Company opened a tentative Paris–London service with converted Goliath bombers (Figure 16.14).

After some pioneering passenger flights from May to August, the world's first daily commercial scheduled air service opened on 25 August with the first flight – in an Airco D.H.4A – from London (Hounslow) to Paris (Le Bourget), making it in 2½ hours (Figure 16.15). The line was operated for passenger and light freight by the short-lived Aircraft Transport and Travel Ltd: the single fare to Paris was £21. Also on 25 August, the Handley Page Co. opened an ad hoc service to Paris from Cricklewood, using a converted O/400 bomber.

In France, England and America the first transports, both small and large, were adaptations of wartime bombers: all such machines were biplanes. In the smaller class, they were conversions of such single-engined bombers as the D.H.4 and D.H.9, to carry three or four passengers. By about 1922 the British airlines had specially designed single-engined aircraft such as the D.H.34, with a 500-hp Napier Lion engine, which carried eight passengers.

The larger transports – soon called 'airliners' – were adapted twin- or four-engined bombers like the Handley-Page O/400, V/1500, the Vickers Vimy (converted into the Vimy Commercial), or the Farman Goliath bomber, which became the first French airliner (Figure 16.5).

Air transport then spread erratically and sporadically throughout Europe, and a number of other airlines were opened in 1919, including the Dutch KLM. The British company, Imperial Airways Ltd, in which various companies were merged, was formed in 1924 (Figure 16.16). Strangely enough, the United States were slow to open airlines, and it was not until 1927 that a passenger service was inaugurated over one of the various contract mail routes which had been operating since the war: this first passenger service was started in

Figure 16.13 R J Mitchell: c. 1933. (Science & Society Picture Library)

Figure 16.14 (left) First French airliner, a modified Goliath bomber: 1919.

Figure 16.15 (below) Airco D.H.4A passenger transport: 1919.

Figure 16.16 Poster advertising Imperial Airways' Cairo–Baghdad–Karachi service; lithograph by Charles C Dickson: c. 1927. The aircarft depicted is a De Havilland Hercules. (Science & Society Picture Library)

April between New York and Boston, and was operated by Colonial Air Transport.

In the early days of the airliners, there appeared two broad categories of transport aircraft, the single-engined machine taking some three to five passengers, and the larger multi-engined airliner for bigger loads and longer routes.

In both types of machine, Junkers and Fokker made themselves pre-eminent, both favouring monoplanes. They soon came to represent the most influential trends in world design, a position they held until the late 1920s, when the United States began taking the initiative, especially with smaller machines such as the Lockheed Vega already described. In 1919 Junkers had produced his single-engine F-13 transport which carried two crew and four passengers: with its low-set cantilever wings it derived directly from the J.7/9 and J.10, and was in many respects the miniature prototype of the modern airliner. Following the F-13 – which could, like its successors, be fitted with floats – Junkers went on to build an ever-improving series of low-wing cantilever machines culminating in one of the most successful of the larger European transports, the three-engined G-31 (1926), the precursor of the Ju 52 3m transport: the G-31, with three 450-hp radial engines, carried a crew of two and 16 passengers at a cruising speed of 90 mph. This development was paralleled by Fokker – he had set up a factory in the USA as well as in Holland – who during this period produced excellent single-, twin- and three-engine high-wing transports (Figure 16.17). Directly competitive with the three-engine Fokker came, in June 1926, the first successful American transport, the all-metal Ford 4-AT, designed by William B Stout; with three 220 hp engines, it carried ten passengers at a cruising speed of 105 mph.

Then, in 1920, came the first successful large British transport, the twin-engined Handley Page W.8 (derived from the O/400 bomber) which carried a crew of two and 12 passengers (Figure 16.18).

With the developments of the long Empire air routes, Britain was soon building larger machines for such services, and the De Havilland Hercules and Armstrong-Whitworth Argosy – both biplanes with three engines – appeared in 1925–26. The Argosy was powered by three 420-hp Jaguar radial engines, and carried 20 passengers and their luggage at a cruising speed of 95 mph for over 5 hours.

By the end of this decade, the larger three-engined airliners – biplanes and monoplanes – could carry some 15 to 20 passengers, a crew of two or three, and a small amount of freight, at cruising speeds of 90–110 mph over stages of about 500 miles.

A measure of the growth of air transport over the years were the world totals of miles flown on scheduled airlines, China and Soviet Russia excluded: in 1919 the figure was approximately a million; in 1929, 57 million. World passenger figures are also available for the period, and show 5000 for 1919, rising to 434,000 in 1929.

The flying boat also became a popular type of airliner, and after much research into hull shapes, and methods and materials of construction, such excellent machines as the three-engined Short Calcutta biplane boat were available for the Empire routes; this carried 15 passengers at a cruising speed of 90 mph. Similar machines, such

Figure 16.17 (left) Fokker F.VII-3m three-engine airliner: 1925.

Figure 16.18 (below) Handley Page W.8B airliner: 1921.

as the Short Singapore, were produced for the RAF. In Germany, the Dornier Company was producing successful monoplane flying boats, with one or more engines set above the fuselage-hull; and the same firm, in 1929, completed a giant monoplane flying boat, the Do X, with a span of 157 feet 5 inches, 12 525-hp engines and a cruising speed of 110 mph: three of these were built, and one of them once took up 169 passengers. But the Do X can only be called an ambitious freak; all other seaplanes were of much more modest capacity, with passenger accommodation for up to 20. Most countries were building flying boats and float planes in a variety of forms, for both civil and military use, the biplane still holding its own in both these classes of seaplanes.

This decade also saw the rebirth and growth of the glider as a sporting aircraft, and the rise of the light aeroplane. The Germans were responsible for the revival of gliding owing to the Peace Treaty restrictions on military flying, and used the glider both for sport and for undercover training of their future air force. This revival also paid aerodynamic dividends, as much valuable work on reducing drag resulted from it.

The light aeroplane movement started in the mid-1920s, principally in England and Germany, where it was officially encouraged, before spreading to the USA, and both biplane and monoplane types became popular for club and private flying. Symbol of the whole movement, which offered powered flying for pleasure even to the man and woman of modest means, was the admirable, ubiquitous little two-seat biplane named the Moth, first produced by Geoffrey de Havilland in 1925, with a 65-hp Cirrus engine and a speed of 90 mph. It was light but robust, cheap and easy to fly, and – in various subsequent versions – was to remain in universal use for private flying and service training for over 30 years. De Havilland's light D.H.71 Tiger Moth monoplane of 1927 (not to be confused with the Tiger Moth biplane) was another remarkable little machine built for racing, which set up a record of 186.4 mph, over 100 kilometres.

The helicopter, a dream of engineers since the eighteenth century, began to approach practical form in the 1920s. Many inventors had been at work since Cornu and the Breguet brothers had first risen from the ground in 1907. Productive suggestions had been made by such men as C Renard, who suggested flapping rotor blades, but for the wrong reasons (1904); G A Crocco, who first suggested cyclic pitch control (1906); and Ellehammer, the Dane, who demonstrated the latter in a tentative machine (1912). Between 1919 and 1925 the Argentinian Marquis de P Pescara built a number of helicopters in France and Spain which, although unstable and unsatisfactory in other ways, incorporated cyclic pitch control for the first time, and also provided for autorotation in case of engine failure. On 4 May 1924 the French Oehmichen No. 2 made the world's first helicopter flight of a closed kilometre circle.

Back in 1923, the Spanish Juan de la Cierva made his first successful flights in a gyroplane, the C.4, called an Autogiro (Figure 16.19), at Getafe (Spain) then at Madrid. In 1925 he came to

 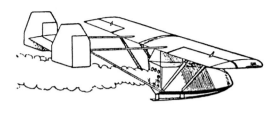

continue his work in England. The Autogiro was halfway towards the helicopter: it consisted of a conventional aeroplane fuselage and tail unit, with a tractor airscrew, above which was a freely turning rotor which provided the machine's lift. The Autogiro could take off with a very short run, and could land almost vertically. Cierva's most important invention and improvement, however, was (in 1922) to cure the machine's tendency to roll over in flight – due to unequal lift between the retreating and advancing rotor blades – by providing a flapping hinge for each blade: the advancing blade automatically moved up as its increased airspeed gave it more lift, but the movement of the air relative to the blade was changed, the angle of attack reduced, and the lift decreased: meanwhile, the opposite process was at work on the retreating blade; whereupon the lift forces on all the blades were balanced and the system rendered stable. In 1933 Cierva first achieved successful 'jump-starts' by gearing the engine to the rotor for takeoff. It was the growing success of the Autogiro during the 1920s and 1930s that undoubtedly spurred on research into the helicopter proper, and Cierva's introduction of flapping blades was to prove a major contribution to the success of the practical helicopter.

Isolated from other programmes of development, but ingenious and prophetic, were the first true aeroplane flights in history in which man-carrying aeroplanes were propelled and sustained in the air by reaction propulsion. On 11 June 1928, F Stamer piloted a canard-type glider propelled by rockets from the Wasserkuppe, one of the Rhön mountains in Western Germany: the venture was promoted by Max Valier, and financed (in part) by Fritz von Opel, the rockets made by F W Sander, and the experiments were directed by the well-known German aerodynamicist A Lippisch. After model tests, the full-size aeroplane made only one – but a successful – flight of about a mile after a ground-towed launch, the aircraft being damaged after landing. On 30 September 1928, von Opel himself flew a specially built glider powered by rockets (Figure 16.20): it was launched from a rocket-propelled cradle, and a successful flight of some ten minutes was made, in which the speed at one point reached 100 mph. These experiments were not continued, but – loosely speaking – they mark the first successful aeroplane flights in history by reaction propulsion (see Glossary).

In 1924, Burnelli pioneered a biplane in which the fuselage was aerofoil-shaped (with engines buried in it) to augment the wing lift, a move toward the flying-wing ideal of Junkers; Burnelli later built a number of monoplanes on the same principles (1928, etc.), but little came of these machines.

Figure 16.19 (left) Cierva Autogiro C.6C: 1926.

Figure 16.20 (above) Glider fitted with rockets, flown by von Opel: 1929.

Figure 16.21 Hill swept-wing tail-less Pterodactyl: 1926.

In 1926, the British Professor G T R Hill produced the first of his swept-wing tail-less Pterodactyls (Figure 16.21) to secure, like Dunne, a machine which would be easily controllable and which would not stall: but the Pterodactyls – and Dunne – did not contribute significantly to the swept-back and delta configurations of today.

After the first transatlantic flights there was a continuous succession of notable flying exploits throughout the decade, many of them acting as 'prospecting' flights for future airline routes. Amongst the more important flights were the following: in November–December 1919, Ross Smith and his crew flew in a Vickers Vimy from London to Australia, over 11,000 miles in 27 days 20 hours; in May 1923, Lieutenants Kelly and Macready made the first non-stop flight across the USA in a single-engined Fokker, 2516 miles in 26 hours 50 minutes; in April–September 1924, two US Army Douglas biplanes (fitted alternatively with floats or wheels) made the first round-the-world flight, 27,500 miles in about 15½ days' flying time; and in July 1924, the first US transcontinental air mail service was started. In November 1925, Alan Cobham made the first of his fine pioneering flights when he flew in a D.H.50 from London to Cairo: in 1926, he flew the same machine to India, Australia and South Africa, thus helping to lay the foundations for the British Empire air routes. On 9 May 1926, Lieutenant-Commander Richard Byrd, in a Fokker trimotor, was the first to fly over the North Pole, from Spitzbergen; and in 1929, on 28 November, he was the first to fly over the South Pole, a double success for America.

One exploit might be said to have transformed the entire picture of American air transport and private flying: this was, of course, Charles Lindbergh's solo flight (Figure 16.22) direct from New York to Paris, on 20–21 May 1927 – 3600 miles in 33 hours 39 minutes – at an average speed of 107.5 mph in his single-engined Ryan monoplane *Spirit of St. Louis*. The United States was already well advanced in service and racing aircraft, and in the operation of mail routes; but it took the romantic impact of Lindbergh – similar in its tremendous impact to Blériot's Channel crossing of 1909 – to make the nation truly air-minded, and so create the financial and technical climate necessary for the large-scale development of aviation.

In April 1928, the first east to west crossing of the Atlantic was made by a Junkers monoplane, the *Bremen* (H Koehl and others), from Ireland to Newfoundland; in May–June 1928, a Fokker monoplane the *Southern Cross* (Sir C Kingsford Smith and C Ulm) flew the Pacific from California to Australia via Hawaii and Fiji; also in 1928, a Savoia flying boat (A Ferrarin and C P Del Prete) flew non-stop from near Rome to Brazil, 4500 miles. As a tailpiece it should be said that in 1929 the German Zeppelin (Figure 16.23) *Graf Zeppelin* flew round the world, 21,500 miles in 21 days, including 7000 miles non-stop from Friedrichshafen to Tokyo – an outstanding achievement.[3]

In research laboratories and workshops, the science of aerodynamics was being extended and deepened by workers in many

Figure 16.22 Charles Lindbergh: 1927. (NASA/ Science & Society Picture Library)

LZ LUFTSCHIFFBAU ZEPPELIN
HAMBURG-AMERIKA LINIE

Figure 16.23 Cover of a Zeppelin company brochure, advertising flights between Hamburg and South America: early twentieth century. (Science & Society Picture Library)

Figure 16.24 Theodore von Kármán: c. 1930–50. (Science & Society Picture Library)

countries. Much of the basic research on lift and drag, which would be incorporated in new wing shapes and sections, appropriate aspect ratios, etc., in the aeroplanes of the thirties, was being mathematically formulated and developed in this period 1919–29. Of particular importance now was the development and fuller understanding of the theory of circulatory motion, and the problems of drag, by the Germans Ludwig Prandtl and M W Kutta, the Russian-born N E Joukowski, and the Hungarian-born American, Theodore von Kármán (Figure 16.24): their work had been in progress since before the war, but formulation and availability for practical application date chiefly from the immediate postwar decade. Another worker who profoundly influenced subsequent aircraft design was the British Professor B Melvill Jones, with the publication of his paper *The Streamline*

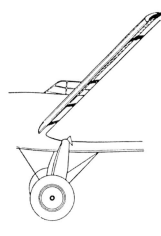

Figure 16.25 Handley Page patent slotted wing: 1920.

Aeroplane (1929). From now on, the science of aerodynamics was to play a major role in the world's scientific institutions.

Also the subject of basic formulation and experiment at this time was propulsion by means of the gas turbine, and it was at the Royal Aircraft Establishment at Farnborough in 1926–28 that Dr A A Griffith made the first practical proposals and experiments. After further research and experimentation, the project was unfortunately shelved and not revived until the mid-1930s, when the RAE at Farnborough and Frank Whittle were working on parallel lines. It is important to note that Dr Griffith did not envisage propulsion by 'pure jet', but by propeller-turbine (turboprop). It was Whittle who pioneered the turbojet engine in this country (see later).

Of particular inventions and improvements, one of the most important was the slotted wing, matured in 1919, with the patenting of the device by Handley Page Ltd. It was a device consisting of a curved slat (at first manually operated and then automatic) which was made to project from the leading edge of the wing and thus force air through the resulting slot and over the upper surface of the wing: the effect was to smooth out the air flow over the wing and reduce turbulence at large angles of attack, and so postpone stalling: it therefore increased the speed range of the aircraft and all but eliminated the stall-and-spin type of crash. In 1928, the Air Ministry ordered slots to be fitted to all British service machines, and the adoption of the device for both large transports and light aircraft materially decreased the accident rate, and increased the general confidence in flying (Figure 16.25).

Instrument flying began to be practical by the end of the war, but it was during the years 1919–29 that blind flying became successful and practical, chiefly as a result of Sperry's work in the United States; Sperry perfected the gyro horizon[4] and directional gyro, and on 24 September 1929, Lieutenant James Doolittle, in a Sperry-equipped Consolidated NY-2 biplane, was able 'to take off, fly a specific course, and land without reference to the earth'. During the next decade, instrument flying was to become a routine accomplishment for all commercial and military pilots.

Many other inventions, improvements and adaptations occurred during the years 1919–29: the flap, which had first been used tentatively in the war, was being experimented with; the retractable undercarriage was successfully pioneered on a few machines;[5] the metal propeller came into its own – but not with variable pitch – together with electric and other powered engine starters; superchargers for aero engines came into use; wing-folding – already in use during the war – became standard practice on certain types of aircraft, especially carrier-borne machines and on light aeroplanes, for ease of transport and storage; the aircraft carrier was further developed as well as catapult launching from warships; and the refuelling of aeroplanes in flight was pioneered in America (1923). The aeroplane became used for an ever-growing variety of purposes, including ambulance work, crop dusting and freight carrying.

In the sphere of aero engines the most far-reaching development was the perfecting of the air-cooled radial engine and its all-important low-drag cowling. This type of engine, light and powerful, soon rivalled the liquid-cooled in-line motors, and shared with them the power-unit market until the arrival of jet propulsion. The radial engine came to power the majority of the world's medium and large transport aircraft, and continued to do so until the jet age started. There were also a few compression ignition (heavy oil) engines now being developed, the only one of significance being the Junkers Jumo, which was first built in 1926, and first fitted to an aircraft in 1929; but the main task of propulsion fell to the conventional four-stroke petrol motor. By 1929 there was a large range of aero engines available for the many types of aircraft: there were in-line engines, from the small type suitable for light aeroplanes, such as the four-cylinder 120-hp De Havilland Gipsy III, to the 12-cylinder, 450-hp Napier Lion, and the 12-cylinder 525-hp Rolls-Royce Kestrel.[6] Radial engines included such types as the seven-cylinder 215-hp Armstrong-Siddeley Lynx in the lowest power range, and the nine-cylinder 550-hp Bristol Jupiter in the larger class.

Performance records for 1929 were 357.74 mph for speed (British Supermarine S-6); 41,794 feet for height (German Junkers W.34 with a Bristol Jupiter engine); and 4912 miles for distance in a straight line (French Breguet 19).

Notes

1 It was also the first to have variable camber.

2 A remarkable transport service for official passengers and mail was carried on, amongst others, by the RAF between Hendon (later Kenley) and Buc near Paris, from January to September 1919, with a regularity of 91 per cent. (See Peter Masefield's now famous paper *Some Economic Factors in Air Transport Operation*, to which I am indebted for these and other details of British air transport.)

3 This journey included the first flight over the Pacific Ocean.

4 Mr Brooks tells me that, although seldom recorded in history, artificial horizons were fitted in the giant German bombers of the First World War.

5 The first primitive, retractable undercarriages were used by Sellers (1908) and Wiencziers (1911). The first modern-type fully retractable undercarriage, as previously noted, appeared in 1920 on the American Dayton-Wright R.B. high-wing racing monoplane which competed in the Gordon-Bennett race of that year: the wheels retracted into the fuselage (Figure 16.10). The year 1922 saw the first machine with undercarriage retracting into the wings, the American Verville-Sperry Racer, a low-wing monoplane sometimes designated the R-3.

6 The term 'in line' is here loosely – but quite usefully – taken to include not only the single bank types, but those with cylinders in V or W arrangements.

17 Between the wars: the second period 1930–1939

This second between-wars decade saw the full maturing of the propeller-driven aircraft, the virtual eclipse of the biplane, and the beginnings of practical jet propulsion. It also saw the aeroplane established as a universal and accepted means of transport, as well as its renaissance as a weapon of war – a prelude to its becoming the decisive military weapon – and then in our own day slowly giving way in face of the rocket missile.

Research over the whole field of fluid mechanics, of which aerodynamics is a part, progressed rapidly in Europe and America. One of the most significant events was the flight (in 1931) of the first practical near-delta-wing aeroplane designed by the German Dr Alexander Lippisch: it was a small machine powered by a 32-hp Bristol Cherub engine (Figure 17.1) incorporating trailing-edge ailerons and elevators – not elevons – as well as wing-tip fins and rudders. He had been experimenting in the 1920s with swept-wing tail-less designs on parallel lines with Dr Hill's researches, which resulted in the Pterodactyls, but more with a view to high-speed flight. Lippisch was the chief pioneer of the delta-wing aeroplane, although many other scientists in related fields were contributing important theoretical research; but the true flourishing of Lippisch's conceptions had to wait for the practical je engine. The delta, or near-delta, forms – if made large enough – ould produce the ideal of many designers to have a 'flying wing', a machine which would have no drag beyond that of the wing itself, in which all the engines, crew and payload would be enclosed: the Northrop N1M of 1940 came near to this ideal but was not altogether successful. In smaller high-speed aircraft, the delta form provides a strong and low thickness-to-chord ratio wing, which helps delay the effects of compressibility set up at transonic speeds, especially by curbing the displacement of the centre of pressure: the delta wing can also be made longitudinally stable, thus avoiding the addition of a separate tailplane, the combined 'elevons' being hinged to the wings. But the ideal of the all-enclosing flying wing will later be paralleled by the choice of a conventional fuselage and very thin wings for supersonic flying.

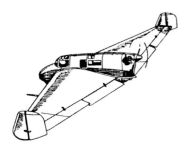

Figure 17.1 Lippisch tail-less research monoplane: 1931.

The science of aerodynamics was strongly augmented by ever-improving methods and processes of manufacture, and the strides taken in metallurgy, especially the production of better steels and light aluminium and magnesium alloys. By the late 1930s the all-metal stressed-skin aeroplane became the rule rather than the exception.

Engine development kept in step with the other technical advances in aviation and took advantage both of aerodynamic and metallurgical research, as well as progressing in mechanical design and efficiency. The air-cooled radial engine grew in popularity, and in America almost ousted the liquid-cooled in-line types; and the adoption of more

Figure 17.2 Rolls-Royce Merlin engine, sectioned. (Science & Society Picture Library)

successful low-drag cowling, and the twin-row cylinder arrangement, helped to bring the radial to a high state of efficiency. By 1939 there were such radials in service as the British nine-cylinder, 1000-hp Bristol Pegasus and the American 14-cylinder Pratt and Whitney Twin-Wasp of 1200 hp. The in-line engine, cooled for so many years by water, exchanged this early system for high-temperature cooling by ethylene glycol, which, with its low freezing and high boiling points – and only needing a small radiator – proved more efficient and economical. By 1939 there were in-line engines of 1000 hp such as the 12-cylinder Rolls-Royce Merlin (Figure 17.2), and similar types in Germany. Most of the smaller in-line engines – made by several European firms – for light aircraft were air-cooled. Although small air-cooled in-line engines continued in production in Europe to power a wide variety of light aircraft, there developed in the United States during the 1930s the flat horizontally opposed configuration of light air-cooled aero engine. These proved highly successful and eventually displaced the older in-line type almost completely for powers up to about 300 hp.

As aircraft speeds mounted by virtue of this multiple progress, the aerodynamic problems were met and dealt with in various ways: streamlining was aided not only by improved airframe design, but by better layout of engines, low-drag engine cowlings, and retractable undercarriages; the latter came into general use in the mid-1930s.

In single-engine types, the wheels were retracted into the wings, and in multi-engine machines into the engine nacelles. To allow of slower landing speeds, the trailing-edge flap in its various forms was universally adopted to preserve maximum lift at minimum speeds.[1]

One of the most important inventions rendered practical in this period, and one of the most important developments in the whole history of aviation, was the introduction of the practical variable-pitch propeller (1932) and, developing out of it, the constant-speed propeller (1935), inventions which allowed the airscrew to give the optimum thrust for all conditions of flying, from takeoff to landing, by variations in the pitch of the blades. The former had been achieved in a tentative way during the First World War, and at various times since; and the latter had even been patented in England in 1924 by Dr H S Hele-Shaw and T E Beacham, and test flown in 1926–27. Both types were ultimately put into practical production in the USA, and were in service in the years noted above. The sequence of events leading to this production followed a complex international pattern.

Amongst other special developments during this period were the pressurisation of aircraft cabins[2] for flying beyond the 'comfortable' height for breathing (about 8000 feet), the first machine to be fully equipped for this being the Lockheed XC-35 in 1937; the use of tricycle undercarriages, which began to appear in the late 1930s; the further development and perfecting of refuelling in flight; the perfection of the automatic pilot to keep aircraft on a predetermined course; instrument flying and approach; and various radio aids to flying.

Our solution to the problem of getting a heavily loaded aircraft into the air was the Short–Mayo Composite, tested by Imperial Airways in 1938; the small four-engined float plane *Mercury* was launched in midair from the flying boat *Maia*. On 8 October, Captain D C T Bennett flew *Mercury* non-stop from Scotland to South Africa, a distance of 5997.3 miles. The air launching of a small aircraft from a larger had been pioneered at Felixstowe in 1916 (see page 211), and taken further by the Russians in 1931–4. In their experiments, as many as four small fighters were carried on a TB-3 bomber.

The helicopter, which had been a popular toy since the fourteenth century, as we have seen, and already showing signs of feasibility in this century, at last arrived in a practical form, although it was to remain undeveloped for some years more. In 1935, Louis Breguet flew his twin-coaxial-rotor machine successfully, but it was neither a practical helicopter nor a properly controllable one. Then, in 1936, after other inventors had also made tentative experiments, came the German Focke-Achgelis FW-61, which may be described as the first practical helicopter of history: it was a twin-rotor machine which could stay up for 1 hour 20 minutes, attain a speed of 76 mph and reach an altitude of 11,243 feet. The success of the FW-61 was not to be fully exploited, although a development of the machine, the Fa 223, was to fly in 1940 and go into production: the Fa 223 was therefore the world's first production helicopter. The design and construction of helicopters in general was to remain in abeyance until the 1940s, when the greatest progress was to take place in the United States (see next section).

Reaction (jet) propulsion, which had been a favourite dream since the eighteenth century, also now became a reality; and despite the pioneer work of Frank Whittle (Figure 17.3)[3] and his successful engine of 1937 – his first patents were taken out in 1930 – it was the Germans who produced the first tentative turbojet of history, the

Figure 17.3 Frank Whittle: 1942. (NMPFT/Daily Herald Archive/Science & Society Picture Library)

Heinkel He 178, which flew on 27 August 1939 (Figure 17.4): it was powered by a centrifugal-flow turbojet engine designed by Dr Hans von Ohain.[4] It has often been assumed, since Whittle's early patents were published, that it was his invention which led the German engineers to develop their jets. This view is not borne out by the facts. Schlaifer, in his detailed study, *Development of Aircraft Engines*, etc. (1950), showed that von Ohain was also absorbed by the challenge of jet propulsion in the early 1930s, and was 'completely unaware of Whittle's patent of 1930, and his engine was different in almost all its details'.

A special tribute should be paid to the high-speed flying of the time. In 1931, Britain won her third successive victory in the Schneider Trophy contest (Figure 17.5) and thus secured the Trophy permanently: the winning aircraft was the Supermarine S.6B (Figure 17.6) which won at 340.6 mph, a machine which led

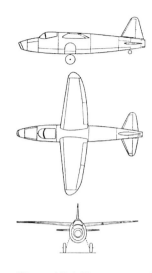

Figure 17.4 First jet aeroplane to fly, the Heinkel He 178: 1939.

Figure 17.5 Front cover of the Schneider Trophy contest programme for 1931. (Science & Society Picture Library)

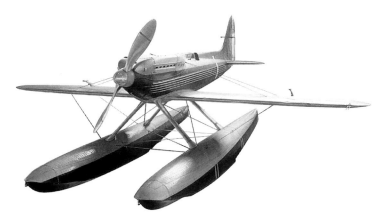

Figure 17.6 Outright winner of the Schneider Trophy, the Supermarine S.6B: 1931. (Science & Society Picture Library)

Figure 17.7 Gee-Bee 7-11 Super Sportster racing monoplane: 1932.

to Mitchell's single-seat land monoplane built to an Air Ministry specification, which was not successful, and then to his own individual design of the Spitfire of 1936. In America, one of the world's best racing aircraft, the Gee-Bee 7-11 Super Sportster (Figure 17.7), set up a record for land planes in 1932 of 294.4 mph and also won the Thompson Trophy. In 1934 came the MacRobertson Air Race from Mildenhall, England, to Melbourne, Australia, which was won by a specially designed twin-engine De Havilland machine named the Comet, which flew the distance in 2 days 23 hours (time in the air 2 days 15 hours 52 minutes) at an average speed of 180 mph: the Comet was the direct ancestor of the Mosquito of the Second World War.

The transport aeroplane in Europe was led by Fokker and Junkers during this period, until the sudden flourishing of American civil aviation in the mid- and late 1930s. The three-engine monoplane transports of Germany and Holland provided the backbone of the Continental airlines, and after the three-engine Junkers G-31 of 1926 there came another distinguished machine, the Junkers Ju 52/3m, a three-engine transport which appeared in 1931–33 and was later mass-produced to provide the Germans with their standard military transport and invasion workhorse for freight and troop carrying, and for parachute dropping: it could carry up to 17 passengers at a cruising speed of 130 mph (Figure 17.8). The Fokker tri-motors of this period can be typified by the F.XVIII of 1932 which took 14 passengers at a cruising speed of about 155 mph. In 1931 the Junkers firm had put into service for the Berlin–London Lufthansa route their giant four-engine G-38, with its deep-section wings in which the engines were buried, carrying a crew of seven and 34 passengers at 115 mph (Figure 17.9). This machine was the precursor in Europe of such four-engine airliners as the Junkers Ju 90 and the Focke-Wulf Fw 200 Condor, which were usefully converted to military purposes soon after.

England kept a very conservative tradition of biplanes in her air transport during most of this period, and Imperial Airways seem to have adopted the slogan 'slow but sure'. Most famous of British airliners were the four-engine Handley Page H.P. 42 and 45 biplanes[5] which went into service in 1931 and became some of the most dignified and reliable aircraft in our flying history: they carried

40 passengers in comparatively quiet comfort at 100 mph. Eight of these aircraft were built, including the well-known *Hannibal* and *Heracles*: they flew more than 10 million miles and were in the air for over 100,000 hours without a fatality. But the H.P. 42/45 was a somewhat backward-looking design, as was another large Imperial Airways machine the Short Scylla, with its four engines, 40 passengers and cruising speed of just over 100 mph. The Armstrong Whitworth Atalanta of 1932 was the first four-engine transport monoplane to go into regular service as a British airliner; like its biplane companions it was particularly useful for the long-haul Empire routes: it carried up to 20 passengers, and cruised at 125 mph: this, however, fell a good deal short of contemporary Dutch, German and American machines.

Smaller commercial machines in Britain included the De Havilland biplane D.H. 84 Dragon (Figure 17.10) of 1932, which grew into the famous Rapide of 1934, carrying eight passengers at a cruising speed of 130 mph for 550 miles.

But it was in the United States that the modern airliner was born, and many of the basic features arrived at in the first years of design and operation are still in force today.[6] The first 'modern'-type airliner was the Boeing 247, which first flew in February of 1933 (Figure 17.11); and the second was the Douglas DC-1 which first flew in July of 1933. In February 1934 there flew for the first time the Lockheed Electra which, although not as important as the others, nevertheless had a considerable influence on subsequent aircraft. These three machines, and their immediate progeny, revolutionised the whole sphere of air transport. The dominating features of these first machines were: (a) low-wing, all-metal, monocoque monoplane construction; (b) two powerful, well-cooled, and supercharged air-cooled radial engines mounted in the wings, allowing level flight on either engine alone in an emergency; (c) variable-pitch propellers; (d) retractable undercarriage; and (e) wing flaps, which allowed of increased wing loading with a slow stalling speed. The Boeing 247 was the only one of the trio without flaps.

The Boeing 247 was developed out of the Boeing B-9 bomber of 1931, which in turn developed from the Boeing Monomail of 1930, the basic ideas for which owed much to a lecture given in America by Adolph Rohrbach in 1926 (published January 1927), which seems to have originally 'sparked' the Boeing engineers. The 247 carried ten passengers, was powered by two 550-hp Pratt and Whitney Wasp

Figure 17.8 (left) Junkers Ju 52/3m airliner: first built in 1931.

Figure 17.9 (above) Junkers G-38 airliner: 1929 (in service 1931).

Figure 17.10 De Havilland D.H.84 Dragon: 1933. (Science & Society Picture Library)

Figure 17.11 First modern airliner, the Boeing 247: 1933. (Science & Society Picture Library)

radials, and had a cruising speed of 155 mph. Although the 247 had fixed-pitch propellers, the 247 D (in service in 1934) had variable-pitch propellers, more powerful engines and a stage length of 750 miles: it was also the first transport to have wing and tail-unit de-icing (inflatable rubber 'overshoes').

The Douglas Company, alive to possible airline demands, rapidly designed their 12-passenger DC-1, and the one and only machine flew in July of 1933, some six months after the 247. It was so promising that a slightly longer version (the DC-2), to take 14 passengers, was immediately put into production, and the first of them flew in May 1934. The DC-2 was an outstanding machine, with two 710-hp Wright Cyclones, a cruising speed of 170 mph and a stage length of 1350 miles: thus it was faster, and had a longer range than the 247. The incorporation of flaps (split), allowing a higher wing loading, and the long enduring multi-spar wing construction, did much to give it a commercial advantage, which led to worldwide sales.

In February of 1934 the Lockheed Electra first flew, and started another but smaller line of successful transports (Figure 17.12). The Electra carried eight passengers, had two 450-hp Pratt and Whitney Wasps, and a cruising speed of 160 mph. Its configuration differed from the others in that it had twin fins and rudders in place of their single units. In 1937 appeared the Electra's offspring, the Lockheed 14, which not only introduced the Fowler-type flap (which increased the wing area), but was the first airliner in service to have two-speed superchargers and constant-speed-cum-feathering propellers.

Figure 17.12 The Lockheed Electra airliner: 1934. (Science & Society Picture Library)

In December 1935 there had flown for the first time the Douglas DC-3, by far the most famous and successful airliner in history (Figure 17.13). The DC-3 was similar to, but slightly larger than, the DC-2, with greater wing area, span and length, and of course, different engines. It carried 21 passengers, was powered by two 1000–1200-hp Cyclones or Twin-Wasps, had a cruising speed of 170 mph, and a stage length of 500 miles. Known also by the name Dakota (or the designation C-47 among others) the DC-3 achieved success so rapidly that by 1938 it was carrying the bulk of American domestic air traffic. It came to fly in the service of virtually every nation and airline, and to perform Herculean tasks under the most varying and exacting of conditions in wartime. When production ceased in 1945, some 13,000 of this unrivalled machine and its derivatives had been built.

Soon after the details of the Boeing 247 had been published, other nations began designing similar machines, but without much commercial success in the face of the highly competitive and rapidly expanding American aircraft industry. Inspired by the 247 was the British Bristol 142 (the Britain First) of 1935, which was the prototype of the Bristol Blenheim bomber; and the German Junkers Ju 86 and the Heinkel He 111, both of which flew in 1935 and were soon developed as bombers. Various other nations constructed machines directly or indirectly inspired by the Boeing 247.

Two large British airliners merit inclusion here, although few were produced, and the types were not developed. One was the Armstrong

Figure 17.13 The most famous transport of history, the twin-engine Douglas DC-3 of 1935; some 13,000 of these machines were built. (Science & Society Picture Library)

Whitworth Ensign of 1938, a large four-engine all-metal high-wing monoplane carrying 40 passengers. The other was the remarkable and aerodynamically advanced De Havilland Albatross of 1937, a four-engine low-wing monoplane of wooden construction seating 20 to 30 passengers.

Although Europe had pioneered the four-engine low-wing transport, the preparations for war, and then war itself, put an end to projects and construction which might well have led to machines which could keep abreast of the USA. It was, therefore, in America that the modern large four-engine airliner for long-haul service saw its beginnings. In June 1938 there flew the one and only Douglas DC-4E, to carry some 40 passengers: but it was a failure: it had triple fins and rudders, and incidentally, was the first large transport to have a tricycle undercarriage, and the first to have power-boosted controls. The 'classic' DC-4, with single fin and rudder, which has given its name to the so-called 'DC-4 generation', was an entirely different design and did not fly until 1942 (see in next section).

The second important aircraft, which was the most influential of the four-engine transport era to go into airline service, was the Boeing 307 Stratoliner (Figure 17.14), derived from the Boeing B-17 bomber, which first flew on the last day of 1938. An improved version, the 307B, was the first to go into airline service (with Trans-Continental and Western Air) in April of 1940: it flew on long-haul internal American routes, carried 33 passengers, and was also the first airliner to go into service with a pressurised cabin.

Of vital importance to the success of transport aircraft in general during this period was the inclusion as standard equipment of such instruments and equipment as the artificial horizon and directional gyro (both of which were being fitted to airliners in the early 1930s), the vertical speed indicator, the barometer scale-setting sensitive altimeter, efficient radio communication, de-icing devices, and – in the mid-1930s – variable pitch propellers. These, and other improvements, allowed of reliable all-weather flying, and created, as Mr Brooks says, 'a complete revolution in operating techniques'.

Seaplane development progressed steadily through the years, in what was to become its last successful phase before the near eclipse of boat and float planes in our time. The most important arrivals in the field were the four-engine flying boats – dates are prototypes – the Martin Model 130 and Sikorsky S-42 (both of 1934), the Boeing 314 Clipper of 1938 (Figure 17.15), and the Short Empire boat of 1936;

Figure 17.14 (below) First four-engine transport, the Boeing 307 Stratoliner: 1938.

Figure 17.15 (right) Boeing 314 Clipper flying boat: 1938.

this was an all-metal four-engine monoplane boat (four Bristol Pegasus 815-hp radials) with a cruising speed of 165 mph, accommodation for 24 passengers and a considerable load of luggage and mail, and a range of 800 miles. In 1937 two of these boats, with extra fuel tanks, made five successful experimental crossings of the north Atlantic. The Short Sunderland RAF patrol flying boat of 1937, which served right through the Second World War and beyond, was the military adaptation of the Empire boat. The successful American Boeing 314 Clipper flying boat of 1938–39, which flew on a regular transatlantic air route during the Second World War, was of a similar type to the Short boats. In Germany the monoplane was well established, and the Dornier boats, and Blohm and Voss float planes, performed valuable pioneer services to aviation: these machines were often catapulted from ships and made many mail-carrying flights across the north and south Atlantic between 1937 and 1939.

Float planes were produced in large numbers during the decade, and were often simple adaptations of land aircraft: they were widely used in naval air services and in countries like Canada – where lakes abound – for communications, air charter, forest patrol and other purposes.

The single-engine light aeroplane, both biplane and monoplane, was produced in great numbers in nearly every country to serve the private airman of business concern, as well as flying clubs and the training branches of the air forces. The DH Moth remained typical for biplanes, and for monoplanes the American Taylor Cub, Model E.2 (the ancestor of the British-built Auster of later on) may be singled out; the Taylor Cub was a two-seat high-wing machine produced in 1931–32, with a 37-hp engine, with a cruising speed of 74 mph, and a range of 210 miles. The light aeroplane was also to become the army observation machine and light ambulance of the Second World War. Some formidable achievements stand to the credit of the light aeroplane during this period, including Miss Amy Johnson's (Figure 17.16) solo flight from England to Australia in 19 days (1930) and James Mollison's from England to Australia (1931), both in De Havilland Moths, and Mollison's crossing of the Atlantic – the first solo east–west crossing – in a De Havilland Puss Moth monoplane (August 1932), this last a remarkable achievement.

There was naturally a great variety of 'in-between' types of aeroplane being produced for special uses; one such type may be described, the single-engine American Stinson Reliant of 1937 (Figure 17.17), a high-wing monoplane, descended from the Vega, Ryan and other types of the 1920s, with a 285-hp radial engine, seats for a pilot and four passengers, a cruising speed of 100 mph and a range of 300 miles: such aircraft were admirable for general business, charter, or feeder-airline operations.

The coming to power in Germany of Adolf Hitler in 1933, and his obviously aggressive intentions, resulted in other governments preparing a large design programme of aircraft intended solely for warfare. So intense and efficient was this sudden drive, that during

Figure 17.16 Amy Johnson: 1930. (NMPFT/Daily Herald Archive/Science & Society Picture Library)

Figure 17.17 Stinson Reliant, small passenger transport: 1937.

Figure 17.18 A group of British Vickers Supermarine Spitfire single-engine, single-seat all-metal fighters, ready for action in 1939. (NMPFT/ Daily Herald Archive/Science & Society Picture Library)

Figure 17.19 Junkers Ju 87A Stuka dive bomber: 1935.

the years 1935 and 1936 the prototypes of many of the world's finest fighting aeroplanes were first flying. Amongst the fighters were the Hawker Hurricane (1935), Supermarine Spitfire (1936) (Figure 17.18), and Messerschmitt Me 109 (1936): amongst the bombers were the Bristol Blenheim (1936) – which grew out of the Bristol 142 – the Vickers-Armstrong Wellington (1936), Armstrong Whitworth Whitley (1936), the Handley Page Hampden (1936), Heinkel He 111 (1936), and Junkers Ju 86 (1936): in 1935 came the Junkers Ju 87 Stuka dive bomber (Figure 17.19).

The advent of such outstanding military aircraft, and the experience of actual warfare in Abyssinia (1935) and Spain (1938) which became testing grounds for our future enemies, gave a great impetus to aircraft design and production in general, along with subsidiary equipment and instruments. By the time these aircraft had passed into the production stage in the late 1930s, a new epoch of flying and fighting was inaugurated. By 1940 the monoplane single-seat fighter was fully established, and the Spitfire II of that year may be taken as a criterion: it was of all-metal stressed-skin construction, had a 1250-hp Rolls-Royce Merlin engine (Figure 17.20), a top speed of about 350 mph at 18,000 feet, a cruising speed of 250 mph and armament of eight .303 machine guns in the wings firing outside the airscrew disc. It is interesting to compare this great early monoplane fighter with the last of our biplane fighters, the Gloster Gladiator, which first flew a year before the Spitfire. The Gladiator had a 840-hp Bristol Mercury radial motor, a top speed of 250 mph, a service ceiling of 33,000 feet, and six machine guns (two in the fuselage, four in the wings): it performed excellent service in the early part of the war. Another notable biplane was the Fairey Swordfish (first flown in 1934) which continued as a bomber, torpedo carrier and rocket attacker throughout the war.

The twin-engined Wellington IA may be taken to represent the heavy bombers of the day: it had two 1000-hp Bristol Pegasus radials, a cruising speed of about 200–250 mph, a radius of action of some 1000 miles, a crew of five, defensive armament of six .303 machine guns, and a bomb load of 4500 lb: the Wellington also incorporated the interesting geodetic structure.

Although several four-engine monoplane bombers were produced in the 1930s, such as the French Bordelaise A.B.20 and the Russian ANT-6, the modern conception of the long-range heavy bomber was first crystallised in the American Boeing Model 299 of 1935 (Figure 17.21); again in 1930, a De Havilland Moth (Figure 17.22) flew from England to Australia in 19 days (Amy Johnson, solo); in 1931 a Lockheed Vega encircled the world, 15,500 miles in 8 days 16 hours (Wiley Post and H Gatty); in April 1933 two Westland biplanes flew over Mount Everest (the Marquess of Clydesdale and others); also in 1933 24 Italian Savoia-Marchetti SM-55 flying boats flew from Italy to Chicago and back (General Balbo and others); still in 1933 (July) the first solo flight round the world, 15,600 miles, was made in a Lockheed Vega in 7 days 19 hours (Wiley Post); in 1934 the MacRobertson race to Australia took place (see earlier in this section); in 1937 a Russian ANT-25 monoplane flew from Moscow to Seattle over the North Pole (V Chkalov and others); in 1938 a Focke-Wulf Condor flew non-stop from Berlin to New York, 3950 miles, and from New York back to Berlin (Captains Henke and von Moreau).

Figure 17.20 Rolls-Royce Merlin III engine: c. 1940. (Science & Society Picture Library)

Figure 17.21 Boeing Model 299 four-engine heavy bomber: 1935.

Figure 17.22 Amy Johnson's De Havilland Moth, named Jason. (Science & Society Picture Library)

Civil air transport figures for miles flown (excluding China and Soviet Russia) were 57 million in 1929 and 185 million in 1939.

The speed record for 1939 was 469.142 mph (German Messerschmitt Bf 109R);[7] there were no height and straight-line distance records for 1939, but the figures for 1938 were 56,046 feet (Italian Caproni 161) and 7158 miles (British Vickers Wellesley).

Notes

1   It was the ageing Orville Wright who, with J M Jacobs, invented the important split flap in 1920, a form of flap which came into general use in the mid-1930s.

2   There were a few machines prior to the Lockheed XC-35 which were fitted with experimental pressure cabins, but none was successful. The earliest was a D.H.4 which was flown at Wright Field (USA) about 1922. This was followed by a Farman machine which was test flown on 21 July 1932, but later suffered a fatal crash.

3   The difficulties, thwartings and disappointments faced by Frank Whittle are detailed in his book *Jet* (1953); and in this connection it is interesting to find the British Under Secretary of State for Air, writing to the British Interplanetary Society as late as 1934: 'We follow with interest any work that is being done in other countries on jet propulsion, but scientific investigation into the possibilities has given no indication that this method can be a serious competitor to the airscrew-engine combination. We do not consider that we should be justified in spending any time or money on it ourselves.'

4   This engine, the He S3b, had an axial inductor, a centrifugal compressor, reverse-flow combustion chambers, and a one-stage inflow turbine.
    The He 178, which only made a few flights, was, however, a successful test vehicle.

5   All eight of these aircraft are generally described as of the H.P. 42 type.
    In fact, although structurally they were basically the same, the H.P. 42 Hannibal class was fitted for the Empire routes, and the H.P. 45 Heracles class for the European service. The Heracles itself had 'carried well over 100,000 passengers by the outbreak of war. This was nearly a fifth of the total number of passengers carried by Imperial Airways during 16 years of operation' (Peter Masefield in the paper already cited).

6   The following information is taken, with kind permission, from articles in *Flight* (April–May 1958) by Mr Peter W Brooks, entitled 'Origins of the Modern Airliner'. These articles have now been revised and enlarged, and published under the title *The Modern Airliner*: this book is already a classic of aeronautical history.

7   The commoner usage would be Me 109R, but it appears that the use of 'Bf' (Bayerische Flugzeugwerke) is technically correct.

18 The Second World War: 1939–1945

The Second World War witnessed an enormous development in aviation, in aero engines, and in every type of equipment used in connection with flying, as well as the arrival of the practical jet-propelled aeroplane, the production helicopter, the winged pilotless missile, and the long-range rocket. In addition, the glider took on a new function as troop carrier, being towed by powered aeroplanes. Although the world's aviation industries were almost wholly turned over to war production, the great variety of aircraft required by the fighting services included many machines which were not built for actual combat; hence the transport and the light plane in all their forms were developed intensively for troop and other transport, and for training, army spotting and ambulance work; and so were ready by the end of the war to provide highly developed peacetime airliners and smaller private and commercial machines. This transport production – under an Allied agreement – fell almost entirely to the United States.

Military aircraft in the war came to be resolved into a number of basic types, but each took over or exchanged a variety of functions as time went on, and strategic and tactical considerations dictated: thus fighters became light bombers, ground attack and reconnaissance machines; and light bombers became long-range fighters, and so on. The main types of manned aircraft may be classified as heavy bombers, medium bombers, light bombers, fighters, night fighters, fighter bombers (including ground attack), transports, liaison aircraft, reconnaissance and photo-reconnaissance aircraft, light observation aircraft, primary trainers, basic trainers, advanced trainers, training gliders, transport gliders, seaplanes (boat, float and amphibian), target towers and helicopters. In addition there were a number of winged pilotless missiles, as well as long-range wingless rocket missiles, the last being exploited only by the Germans; also small wingless 'artillery' rockets.

Some idea of the immense labour extended during this period on the production of aircraft may be had from the approximate combined total of aeroplanes of all kinds manufactured by Britain and America during the years they were at war: the figure stands at over 380,000.

The versatility of a given aeroplane type may be gauged by such a machine as the De Havilland Mosquito – of wooden construction – which was used for bombing, photographic reconnaissance, long-range day fighting, night fighting, and ground attack. In the following notes the progress achieved in various aircraft types during the war will be suggested by comparing the speeds and other factors at the beginning and end of the period: the figures given can only be approximate.

The single-seat, single-engine fighter had a top speed of some 350 mph in 1939–40, and in this class were the Supermarine

Figure 18.1 Hawker Hurricane fighter. (Science & Society Picture Library)

Spitfire and the Messerschmitt Me 109, with the Hawker Hurricane (Figure 18.1) a little behind. By the end of the war the fighter could make 450 mph, and this speed was shared by such machines as the later varieties of Spitfire, the Hawker Tempest, the Me 109 (Figure 18.2), the Focke-Wulf FW 190 and the North American Mustang with a Rolls-Royce engine. (The jet fighters, although operational by the end of hostilities, had no appreciable effect on the war effort, and will be noted later.) Ceiling heights for fighters rose to between 35,000 and 40,000 feet, with a rate of climb of up to 5000 feet a minute. The fighter was soon being made also to bomb and to photograph, and the variety of armament was considerable. The fighter of 1939 with eight .303 machine guns had, by 1945, two 20-mm cannons and four machine guns; or it carried both guns and rockets; or guns and up to 500 lb of bombs.

The twin-engine long-range fighter, or night fighter, such as the Bristol Beaufighter and Messerschmitt Me 110 in 1939–40, had a top speed of around 330 mph and a radius of 650 miles: they, too, became light bombers, ground attack aircraft or photographers, and could carry 750 lb of bombs or the equivalent in rockets. By 1945 the latest De Havilland Mosquito and the Messerschmitt Me 410 were flying at 400 mph: if bombing, the Mosquito could carry 4000 lb of bombs for a radius of action of 750 miles; or unarmed, with cameras, make 1000 miles and back.

The twin-engine medium bomber at the outset of the war was capable of a speed of 200–270 mph, and a radius of up to 1000 miles with a bomb load of 1000–1500 lb. The Bristol Blenheim and Bristol Beaufort were in this class, with the Junkers Ju 88 halfway towards what one might call then the 'medium heavy' (Figure 18.3), with a speed and radius comparable with the first two, but with a larger bomb load. The typical medium heavy bomber that bridged the peace-war period was the twin-engine Armstrong-Whitworth Whitley, with a speed of 190–220 mph, a normal bomb load of 3500 lb and a radius

Figure 18.2 (below) Messerschmitt Me 109 (Bf 109) fighter.

Figure 18.3 (right) Junkers Ju 88 bomber.

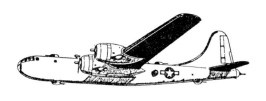

of 1000 miles. The classic heavy bombers of the early war years were the Heinkel He 111 and Vickers-Armstrong Wellington (Figure 18.4): their performances were similar, with speed of 200–250 mph, bomb load of 4500 lb and radius of up to 1250 miles, the Wellington having the greater range. Each machine had a crew of five with defensive armament of some six machine guns. At the end of the war the latest North American B-25 Mitchell was typical of the medium bomber class, and could carry 2000 lb of bombs at above 300 mph over a 500-mile radius; whereas the final light bomber version of the Mosquito – unarmed – could carry a bomb load of 4000 lb at 400 mph for 750 miles and return. The heavier medium bomber had disappeared in favour of the four-engine heavy bomber.

The concept of the four-engine night bomber had been maturing long before the war, both in Britain and the USA, and in 1939 there flew for the first time the Short Stirling, the first – but not entirely successful – heavy bomber of this war: it went into service in 1940, and into action in 1941. Also first flown in 1939, it was also in 1941 that the successful Handley Page Halifax went into action, followed by the Avro Lancaster in 1942. These two machines were designed for night bombing without escort, and the Lancaster became, perhaps, the 'classic' in this field: with a crew of seven, and four 1280-hp Rolls-Royce Merlins, this famous machine could carry a bomb load of 12,750 lb at about 160 mph for 1200 miles and return, and up to 22,000 lb for shorter distances: defensive armament was ten machine guns, and the ceiling was 20,000 feet. The 'classic' four-engine day bomber was the American Boeing B-17E Flying Fortress which, although previously flown on other duties by the RAF, came into its own in the American mass daylight raids of 1942; it had a crew of six to ten, four 1200-hp Wright Cyclone engines, a speed of 225–300 mph, a ceiling of 35,000 feet and a bomb load of 6000 lb for long sorties, 12,800 for medium raids, and 20,800 for very short trips, with a normal radius of some 2500 miles: defensive armament was up to 13 machine guns. The B-17 was followed by the B-29 Superfortress (Figure 18.5) which first saw action in 1944, in the Far East: it dropped the first atomic bombs on Japan in 1945;[1] it had a speed of 300–350 mph and a radius of over 2000 miles, with a maximum bomb load of 20,000 lb. The Germans did not need long-range heavy bombers until it was too late to produce them in quantity, but they had a number of large aircraft under development, such as the Me 264 and He 177, which, if they had been properly exploited, could have been formidable attackers. The same was true of Russia and Japan,

Figure 18.4 (left) Vickers-Armstrong Wellington bomber.

Figure 18.5 (above) Boeing B-29 Superfortress heavy bomber.

Figure 18.6 Short Sunderland reconnaissance flying boat.

the former building one large bomber, the TB-7, and the latter the Nakajima G5N (Liz 2).

A large variety of other military aircraft were developed during the war for use both from land bases and from aircraft carriers, the only type which remained relatively neglected being the seaplane. The only large flying boat in full service by the British was the four-engine Short Sunderland which did excellent reconnaissance work, with its radius of 1500 miles and speed of 150–210 mph (Figure 18.6). Other nations had comparable flying boats, and the Americans in particular an outstanding medium-sized amphibian flying boat, the Consolidated PBY Catalina, with two engines and a radius of 1800 miles. Limited use was made of small float planes for reconnaissance.

The glider experienced a surprising revival, and many large troop-transport types were produced, and played an important part in the invasion of Europe: they were towed by bombers or large transport aircraft. Typical of these were the British Airspeed Horsa which carried two pilots and 15–20 fully-armed troops (or their equivalent in freight), and the American Waco CG-4A, which took 15 troops. An interesting transport glider which was experimented with by the Germans – before appearing in a six-engine version – was the huge Messerschmitt Me 321 Gigant (Giant) which could carry up to 130 armed troops: it was towed by three Me 110s.

The helicopter, comparatively neglected since the success of the Focke-Achgelis, came rapidly to a mature, fully controllable and practical form in the USA, and soon became an indispensable type of aircraft.[2] In Germany, as noted before, the Fa 223 had flown in 1940 and had then been built in limited numbers: it was thus the first production helicopter of history. But the subsequent and sudden development of the mature helicopter – which put an end to the Autogiro family – was due largely to the work of the Russian-born American Igor Sikorsky, who had abandoned his concern with multi-engine aeroplanes and returned to the subject of his earliest enthusiasm, the rotating-wing aircraft, first inspired by Da Vinci.

From the first, Sikorsky concentrated on the single-rotor configuration for his helicopters – with the small anti-torque rotor at the tail – and in 1939 the first of his machines, the VS-300, was completed and tested tethered: it had full cyclic-pitch control and a 75-hp engine, but was not successful.[3] In 1940, the cyclic-pitch control was temporarily abandoned, and two small horizontal rotors on outriggers were provided for fore-and-aft control (including forward motion) and lateral control: this machine made its first successful free

flight on 13 May 1940; in May 1941, with a 90-hp engine, it set up
a world's endurance record for helicopters of 1 hour 32 minutes and
26 seconds. Then in June 1941, the VS-300 was again improved by
providing cyclic-pitch lateral control and a single horizontal rotor at
the tail for fore-and-aft control. Finally, in December 1941, full cyclic-
pitch control with the single main rotor was achieved successfully.
The small anti-torque rotor had been retained throughout. In 1942 the
VS-300 proved itself the first fully practical and successful single-rotor-
configuration machine. In the same year was produced the XR-4 with
a 175-hp engine, as well as the production version (the R-4B) which
went into service with the US Army. The 'classic' Sikorsky helicopter,
the R-5 (S-51) went into service in 1946: it had a 450-hp engine, a
cruising speed of 85 mph, endurance of 3 hours, and carried a pilot
and three passengers. It distinguished itself particularly in the Korean
war, as well as in a variety of civil and military roles before and after.

Thus it was 1942 that can be marked as the year in which the
helicopter 'arrived' as a fully practical flying machine. Thereafter it
developed so rapidly – with new constructors continuously entering
the field – that within a decade there were to be some 30 types flying.
In 1943 appeared the first helicopter with a jet-propelled rotor, the
Austrian Doblhoff No. 1, in which compressed air and petrol vapour
were fed through the rotor blades and burnt in combustion chambers
at the tips, where it was expelled through nozzles; this system obviated
the use of the anti-torque rail rotor.

Perhaps it should be emphasised here that the helicopter proper –
as the word is used today – implies a machine which uses its powered
rotor(s) for vertical takeoff and landing, hovering stationary in the
air, and progressing through the air: it should also be capable of flying
backwards and sideways, as well as forwards. The Autogiros, on the
other hand, had freely revolving rotors which only supported the
aircraft in flight, and allowed of vertical descent (until near the ground
when the machine had to move forward as well) and a steep takeoff,
all propulsion being supplied by a conventional tractor propeller.

The obsolescent biplane not only survived the impact of war, but in
a limited way performed valuable services, especially in naval warfare,
where such machines as the Fairey Swordfish and Albacore acted
as torpedo droppers and maids-of-all-work. The excellent Gloster
Gladiator also fought manfully in Norway, Malta and North Africa.
In training, too, the biplane remained in service in all countries,
and a number of prewar biplanes flew throughout the war on
communications and other duties.

The most important aeronautical development of the Second
World War – although it did not materially affect the conflict – was
the inauguration of practical jet propulsion. After the Heinkel He 178
first flew in 1939, the next development – short-lived and abortive
– came in Italy where the second jet, the Caproni-Campini monoplane,
first flew in 1940 with limited success: this aircraft employed a piston
engine to operate a ducted fan, acting as an air compressor: fuel
was injected into the resulting air stream, burnt continuously, and

Figure 18.7 (above) Second jet aeroplane to fly, the Caproni-Campini: 1940.

Figure 18.8 (right) The first British jet-propelled aeroplane, the experimental Gloster E.28/39 with a Whittle engine: 1941.

expanded through the rear nozzle: it was therefore a jet, but not a turbojet machine. It had a speed of some 200–300 mph, and was abandoned after a few flights in 1940 and 1941 (Figure 18.7).

Meanwhile, in Germany and Britain, research and development were pressed ahead, and Frank Whittle (now Air Commodore Sir Frank Whittle) had his first airborne success in 1941 when on 15 May the Gloster E.28/39, driven by a Whittle centrifugal flow turbojet engine, made its first flight (Figures 18.8 and 18.9). The second aircraft powered by a Whittle engine – two of them – was the only Allied aircraft to see operational service in the war, the Gloster Meteor, which was a single-seat twin-jet fighter with a maximum speed of 480 mph and a ceiling of 40,000 feet. The Meteor first flew in 1943 and was in action against German flying bombs in August 1944, before going overseas with the Allied invasion forces.

But it was in Germany, with her growingly desperate need for fighters to attack the mass Allied raids, that were produced the most spectacular and varied wartime jet aeroplanes. Outstanding was the twin-jet Messerschmitt Me 262 (Figure 18.10), which first flew in 1942. However, it was not until 1944 that the Me 262 was in production and service as a fighter, and later – perhaps misguidedly and for political reasons – as a light bomber. It was powered by two axial-flow Jumo engines, had a maximum speed of 525 mph (as against the Meteor's 480 mph) and a service ceiling of 40,000 feet, and was in every way a remarkable aircraft. It was the world's first

Figure 18.9 The Whittle 1 jet engine, disassembled. (Science & Society Picture Library)

as expendable. After unpiloted launchings, one piloted Natter was launched, but the machine crashed and was destroyed (1945).

Also in 1944 arrived an even more ambitious weapon, the second of the 'Vergeltungswaffen' ('Revenge weapons' – hence 'V' weapons) in the A-4 liquid-fuel rocket colloquially called the 'V-2'. This remarkable weapon marked the most decisive step taken towards the conquest of space. It was the publication of 1919 of Dr R H Goddard's *A Method of Reaching Extreme Altitudes* which had marked the birth of modern rocketry, and it was the 'flying' in 1926 of Goddard's first liquid-fuel rocket which may be said to have actually 'ushered in' the rocket era.

However, it was the first successful 'flight' of the German A-4 (V-2) rocket bomb at Peenemünde on 3 October 1942 that provided the pivotal achievement in practical rocketry, and was to confront the world for the first time with the reality of space travel. For the A-4, during its normal performance, reached a height of 60 miles, and attained an upward airspeed of some 3600 mph. It weighed about 12½ tons at takeoff – including a 2000-lb warhead – and landed at about 2000 mph anywhere up to 220 miles from the firing point after 'flying' for 5 minutes. A stub-winged version (the A-7) was under development at the war's end as a test missile for a projected winged vehicle of far greater range.

In addition to these two ingenious weapons, the Germans were making great strides with winged rocket missiles, one of which, the Henschel Hs 293 glider rocket bomb which was launched from an aircraft, was in action in small numbers. Most of the missiles, however, were designed as anti-aircraft weapons, and only one or two had already been successfully test flown by the time Germany surrendered. All modern developments in guided missiles and rockets derive direct from these German inventions; and German personnel, both in the USA and Russia, have been prominent in producing them.

With the far-reaching development of combat aircraft, and the complicated equipment necessary for their flying and communicating, went a comparable development of the civil transport, especially by the United States. Light and medium transports were following a steady progress, but the backbone of Allied transport aircraft throughout the war remained the twin-engine Douglas Dakota (DC-3), paralleled in Germany by the three-engine Junkers Ju 52. It was in the sphere of the large four-engine transport that the particularly significant development took place, and the USA produced aircraft which were to set the whole style of modern heavy transports, and virtually to monopolise the traffic on the world's long-haul airlines for a decade

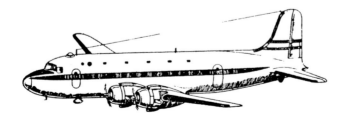

Figure 18.14 Douglas DC-4 Skymaster airliner: 1942.

Figure 18.15 Assembly line at the Douglas Aircraft Company, California: 1940s. (NMPFT/Daily Herald Archive/Science & Society Picture Library)

after the war, making such flights as the Atlantic crossing a mere routine performance. Most important of the new four-engined airliners was the Douglas DC-4 Skymaster (military C-54), which set the standard for four-engine transports for a generation (Figures 18.14 and 18.15). The DC-4 first flew in February 1942, and went into military transport service during 1943: it was smaller than its predecessor with the confusingly similar designation noted before, had a span of 117½ feet, a single fin and rudder, and four 1350-hp Pratt and Whitney radial engines; it carried a crew of six and 42 passengers at a cruising speed of some 200 mph for stage lengths of over 1500 miles. Oddly enough no DC-4s were pressurised. The DC-4 was an immediate success and provided the backbone of Allied long-haul transport, as it did of civil airlines the world over after the war's end.

The DC-6 was a 'stretched' and pressurised development of the DC-4, with reversing propellers for ground braking, which first flew in February 1946, and went into airline service in April 1947.

Second in importance was the Lockheed 049 Constellation (C-69) (Figure 18.16), one of the most graceful aircraft ever to fly, with its sinuous fuselage and triple tail unit: it first flew in January 1943, went into partial military service in April 1944, and full service in April 1945. The Constellation was pressurised, had four 2200-hp radial engines, and carried 51 passengers at a cruising speed of 280 mph for stage lengths of over 2000 miles: like the DC-4E, the Constellation had reversing propellers. Both machines were first employed as military transports. After the war, being well suited to fuselage 'stretching' and other developments, they had a numerous progeny which were consistently successful.

Another large airliner which should be mentioned here was the bulbous Boeing Stratocruiser (Figure 18.17), which was built in small numbers as a civil transport and in considerable quantity as a military transport (C-97): it was developed out of the B-29 and B-50 Superfortress bombers; first flew in November 1944; and went into military service in 1945.

Table of powered takeoffs and flights (c. 1874–1908)

On the following pages is a table showing the best airborne duration times achieved by every man-carrying powered aeroplane which can be said to have made one or more successful takeoffs from about 1874 to the end of 1908. Flight duration was the best indication of sustentation and controllability – thus of success – in those early days; but distances are also given when known. In the case of some well-known machines, two or more entries are given to show their progress.

As may be imagined, the incompleteness and unreliability of contemporary records have made exact details often hard to come by; but after a scrutiny of the circumstances in each case, the calibre of achievement emerges clearly enough, and minor discrepancies do not affect the overall picture.

In assessing the historical importance of many of the early performances (from 1903 onwards), it could be argued that the achievements were so minuscule that they do not even merit the bare inclusion in such a table as this. The reason for their inclusion here is to show the number of machines constructed which were brought to the stage of being at least able to take off. Thus those takeoffs which lasted for less than 15 seconds – they were in no sense proper flights – have not been excluded: their times or distances are also recorded. Even in terms of distance travelled through the air, none of these takeoffs represented more than about 200 metres (say 650 feet) at most: the majority of them were much less.

The durations have been shown in the table to the nearest half minute in flights of up to half an hour; then, after that, to the nearest minute.

The last column gives the approximate number of takeoffs made by each machine, taken to the end of 1908.

The entries are numbered in case it was thought of interest to add a note: these notes will be found following the table pages.

The abbreviations used in the table are as follows:

B	biplane	M	monoplane	ST	semi-triplane
SB	semi-biplane (i.e. what later would have been termed a sesquiplane)	TM	tandem-monoplane	ft	feet
		mod.	modified	hr	hour(s)
		MP	multiplane	m	metre(s)
ctd	continued (i.e. a further flight by an aircraft already included in the table)	P	passenger flight (i.e. pilot plus one passenger)	min	minute(s)
		T	triplane	s	second(s)

Note   If the pilot of a machine was not the man whose name the aircraft bears (i.e. Blériot, Esnault-Pelterie, etc.) his name is recorded immediately beneath the name of the aircraft.

List letter	Date	Location	Duration	Distance	Type	Aircraft and pilot
a	c. 1874	Brest (France)	...	...	M	Du Temple (a sailor)
b	1884 (or 1882)	Krasnoye Sélo, near St Petersburg (Russia)	...	20–30 m (65–98 ft)	M	Mozhaiski (unknown)
c	1890 (9 Oct.)	Armainvilliers (France)	...	50 m (164 ft)	M	Ader
d	1894 (31 July)	Baldwyns Park, Kent (Britain)	...	...	B	Maxim (Maxim and two assistants)
e	1898 (10, 22 Oct.)	St Joseph, Michigan (USA)	...	15, 22 m (50, 73 ft)	B	Herring
f	1903 (7 Oct.)	Widewater, on the River Potomac (USA)	...	...	TM	Langley Aerodrome A (Manly)
g	1903 (Nov.)	Vahrenwalder Heide, near Hanover (Germany)	...	60 m (197 ft)	ST	Jatho
h	1903 (8 Dec.)	Widewater, on the River Potomac (USA)	...	...	TM	Langley Aerodrome A (Manly)

Notes

(a) This steam-powered French tractor monoplane took off for a few metres after a down-ramp takeoff.

(b) Also steam-powered (with a British engine) this Russian machine also ran down a ramp, and was said to have been airborne for some 20–30 metres.

(c) This was the world's first powered aeroplane takeoff from level ground; but it was not a flight in any sense of the term, the machine being incapable of sustaining itself, or of being controlled.

(d) This was really a giant biplane test rig, rather than an aeroplane: it sustained itself for a second or two – until it fouled the restraining rails – but also did not make a flight in any sense of the word: its flight control was primitive to a degree.

(e) A foot-launched hang-glider assisted by a compressed-air motor (see pages 284–5).

(f) This famous tandem monoplane fouled the catapult launching mechanism and plunged into the river: it was both underpowered and weakly constructed, with inadequate flight control.

(g) This very primitive machine probably took off downhill.

(h) This machine again fouled the launching mechanism, or suffered a structural breakage, and again plunged into the Potomac. Manly was luckily rescued unhurt on both occasions.

List no.	Date	Location	Duration	Distance	Type	Aircraft and pilot	Total takeoffs
41	6 July 1908	Issy	8 min 25 s		M	Blériot VIII-bis	20
42	6 July 1908	Issy	20 min 20 s	20 km	B	Voisin-Farman I-bis (H Farman)	60
43	8 July 1908	Turin	15 s	150 m	ctd	Voisin-Delagrange III (Delagrange)	
44	8 Aug. 1908	Hunaudières	1 min 45 s		B	Wright A (France) (Wilbur)	104
45	21 Aug. 1908	Issy	1 min 36 s		M	Antoinette II (Welferinger)	(?)
46	29 Aug. 1908	Hammondsport	3 min	2 miles	ctd	AEA *June Bug* (McCurdy)	
47	12 Sept. 1908	Fort Myer	1 hr 14 min 20 s	50 miles	B	Wright A (Fort Myer) (Orville)	10
48	16 Sept. 1908	Auvours	39 min 18 s		ctd	Wright A (France) (Wilbur)	
49	17 Sept. 1908	Issy	30 min 27 s		B	Voisin-Delagrange III (mod.) (Delagrange)	45
50	17 Sept. 1908	Rocheforte-sur-Loire	40 s	500 m	B	Gasnier	16
51	19 Sept. 1908	Issy	40 s	500 m	B	Ferber IX (Antoinette III)	8
52	21 Sept. 1908	Auvours	1 hr 31 min 25 s	41½ miles	ctd	Wright A (France) (Wilbur)	
53	2 Oct. 1908	Bouy	44 min 31 s	40 km	B	Voisin-Farman I-bis (mod.) (H Farman)	6
54	3 Oct. 1908	Auvours	55 min 37 s	34¾ miles	ctd	Wright A (France) (Wilbur)	
55	10 Oct. 1908	Auvours	1 hr 9 min 45 s	45–50 miles	ctd	Wright A (France) (Wilbur)	
56	16 Oct. 1908	Farnborough	27 s	1390 ft	B	Cody I-B	3
57	25 Oct. 1908	Issy	1 min	800 m	T	De Caters	3
58	29 Oct. 1908	Villacoublay	40 s	500 m	M	Koechlin-de Pischof (Koechlin)	1
59	30 Oct. 1908	Bouy to Reims	20 min	27 km	B	Voisin-Farman I-bis (2nd mod.) (H Farman)	8
60	31 Oct. 1908	Toury to Artenay	11 min	14 km	M	Blériot VIII-ter	6
61	2 Nov. 1908	Magdeburg		60 m	T	Grade I	1
62	17 Nov. 1908	Bouy		10 km	ST	Voisin-Farman I-bis (triplane)	40

List no.	Date	Location	Duration	Distance	Type	Aircraft and pilot	Total takeoffs
63	18 Nov. 1908	Issy	1 min	900 m	M	Antoinette IV (Welferinger)	4
64	1 Dec. 1908	Lyon	1 min	900 m	B	Zipfel	4
65	1 Dec. 1908	Issy		200 m	B	Voisin (Moore-Brabazon)	3
66	7 Dec. 1908	Issy		150 m	T	Goupy I	4
67	17 Dec. 1908	Hammondsport	1 min 30 s	5280 ft	B	AEA *Silver Dart* (McCurdy)	14
68	18 Dec. 1908	Auvours	1 hr 54 min 53 s	62 miles	ctd	Wright A (France) (Wilbur)	
69	21 Dec. 1908	Amiens		10 m	SB	Robart	1
70	25 Dec. 1908	Issy	1 min 30 s	1 km		Antoinette V (Welferinger)	2
71	31 Dec. 1908	Auvours	2 hr 20 min 23 s	78 miles	ctd	Wright A (France) (Wilbur)	

Notes

(The numbers are the list nos. in the tables)

1, 2 These two entries refer to the first and last – of four – flights which constitute the world's first powered, sustained and controlled flights in an aeroplane: 'Orville' and 'Wilbur' refer, of course, to the two Wright brothers. All four of these flights were made from level ground, under engine power alone, and were not assisted either by a downhill run, or by any form of assisted takeoff. The Wrights' weight-and-derrick assisted takeoff device was not introduced until 1904.

3 On 20 September 1904, this machine made the world's first circle by an aeroplane, at the Huffman Prairie, near Dayton.

4–6 This machine was the world's first fully practical aeroplane, which could bank, turn, circle and do figures of eight, all with ease, and could remain airborne for over half an hour at a time; it was the first to fly for half an hour.

7 Although not itself successful, this machine initiated the revival of the monoplane, and strongly influenced both Blériot and Levavasseur.

8 This Ellehammer machine has often been proclaimed as having made the first powered flight in Europe, antedating Santos-Dumont. This claim cannot stand; it did not even make free hop flights, but was tethered to a central pole: it incorporated automatic control, with no rudder, and the 'pilot' was virtually a passenger.

9, 11 The difference between these two was chiefly the important one of the Antoinette engine, the 14-bis having a 24 hp, and the 14-bis (modified) a 50 hp engine: the modified machine also incorporated octagonal ailerons in the outer wing bays. This modified version made the first official hop flights in Europe, in October and November 1906, of which entry No. 11 was the best.

12 The start of the first classic tradition of European powered biplanes, with forward (Wright-derived) elevator, pusher airscrew, and tail unit on an outrigger: the Voisin-built biplanes had no control in roll.

13 This was a 'canard' pusher monoplane of very flimsy construction.

14 Phillips' machine might, with its multiple slats in a

1746 First use of the whirling arm (for ballistic tests, by Robins).

1752–53 Whirling arm used for testing windmill sails (Smeaton).

1754 Lomonosov is said to have flown his helicopter model in Russia.

1764 Bauer designs his fixed-wing monoplane.

1768 Paucton suggests his 'ptérophore' machine, the first idea for a convertiplane with a helicopter screw and a propulsive screw.

1772 Desforges builds his 'voiture volante'.

1781 Meerwein tests his ornithopter-cum-glider. Blanchard builds his 'vaisseau volant'. Restif de la Bretonne publishes his *La Découverte Australe*.

1782 The Montgolfier brothers fly their first model hot-air balloons.

1783

5 June First public demonstration (at Annonay) of a Montgolfier hot-air balloon, unpiloted.

19 Sept. Animals ascend in a Montgolfier hot-air balloon at Versailles.

Oct. Joseph Montgolfier suggests jet propulsion (by hot air) from a balloon, the first idea for reaction propulsion for aircraft.

21 Nov. **The first aerial voyage in history** (de Rozier and d'Arlandes in a Montgolfier hot-air balloon at Paris)

1 Dec. First voyage in a hydrogen balloon (Charles and Robert), also at Paris.

1784 Reinvention of the model helicopter (Launoy and Bienvenu). First test of a full-size propulsive airscrew (Vallet, on a river boat). Designs for ornithopters by Renaux and Gérard. Aries attempts to fly with wings at Embrun.

15 Sept. First aerial voyage in Britain (Lunardi, in his balloon).

16 Oct. First attempt to propel a full-size aircraft with an airscrew (Blanchard on his balloon at London).

1785 Meusnier designs his prophetic airscrew-driven airship.

7 Jan. First Channel crossing by air (Blanchard and Jeffries in a balloon).

15 June First ballooning fatalities (de Rozier and Romain) in a combination hot-air-cum-hydrogen balloon, near Boulogne.

1794 First military aerial reconnaissance by the French army (from a hydrogen balloon at Mauberge).

1796 Cayley flies his model helicopter, adapted from that of Launoy and Bienvenu (see 1809).

1797

22 Oct. First human parachute descent from the air (Garnerin, from a balloon).

1799 First design of a modern-configuration aeroplane, incorporating fixed wings, tail-unit control surfaces, and an auxiliary method of propulsion (Cayley). British army invading India is attacked by rockets from Tipu Sultan's rocket brigade; this news, when it reaches London, leads directly to Congreve's revival of the European war rocket.

1804 Aerofoils first tested on a whirling arm (Cayley). First modern configuration aeroplane flies (Cayley's model glider).

1805 First modern rocket missiles tested (Congreve).

1807 Partial destruction of Copenhagen by Congreve rockets fired from ships of the British Royal Navy.

1807–17 Degen attempts to fly with his flap-valve ornithopter, supported by a balloon (he claims most attention in 1809), when he was the direct cause of Cayley publishing his classic paper (see below).

1808 Invention of the cycle-type tension wheel (Cayley).

1809 Cayley flies his first full-size glider (unmanned). Cayley designs a solid of least resistance, based on the trout.

1809–10 Cayley publishes his classic triple paper on aviation, which lays the foundations of modern aerodynamics; in this, his 1796 helicopter model is also illustrated, and thereafter leads to all subsequent helicopter development.

1811 Berblinger attempts to fly at Ulm, with a Degen-type ornithopter.

1815 First tandem-wing aeroplane design (Cayley), but it is not published.

1816 Cayley attempts to found an aeronautical society.
Degen flies his clockwork helicopter model.

1818 De Lambertye designs his ornithopter and helicopter, with a helicopter 'tender'.

c. 1822 Pocock flies his tentative man-lifting kite.

1827 Pocock's kite-drawn carriage ('char-volant') travels a road successfully.

c. 1830 Artingstall tests his steam-powered model ornithopter.

1831 Walker publishes his tandem-wing designs, which are the first to be published, and influence later inventors.

1837

24 July Cocking killed in his dihedral parachute, derived from a published design by Cayley.

1842 Phillips' steam-driven (from rotor tips) model helicopter flies.

1843 Bourne's helicopter models fly, powered by watch springs.
Illustration of Miller's man-powered ornithopter design published.

March Henson publishes his design for an Aerial Steam Carriage, which has a far-reaching influence owing to its widespread and continuing publication; it is also the first design in history of an airscrew-propelled fixed-wing aeroplane.

April Cayley publishes his design for a convertiplane, which is also the first biplane design in history.

1847 First powered aeroplane model tested (Henson's steam-powered monoplane); it is also the first airscrew-propelled fixed-wing aeroplane in history; but it cannot sustain itself.

1848 Stringfellow's near-successful steam-powered model aeroplane tested; it could not sustain itself.

1849

22 Aug. First bombing raid in history (Austrian pilotless hot-air balloons, carrying bombs, are sent against Venice).
Cayley's full-size 'boy-carrier' glider makes tentative flights.

1852 First aeronautical society founded (in France).

24 Sept. First tentative flight by a manned full-size airship (Giffard), including the first aero

engine – a steam engine – to power an airborne aircraft.

1853 First proper man-carrying flight – but not under control by the occupant – by an aeroplane (Cayley's 'coachman-carrier' glider).
Loup designs his monoplane, the first consistent design in France for an airscrew propelled aeroplane.

c. 1853 First design for stretched-rubber motor for models (Cayley).

1854

27 June Letur is killed on his 'parachute-type' glider.

1856 Carlingford designs his monoplane, in Ireland, which he later built and flew as a kite.

1856–68 Le Bris tests his two full-size gliders, based on the albatross.

1856–96 Mouillard tests his full-size gliders.

c. 1857–58 First successful powered flight by a clockwork-powered model aeroplane (Du Temple).

1858 First tentative aerial photo taken (by Nadar from a captive balloon over Paris).
Jullien tests his rubber-driven model monoplane.

c. 1858–59 Wenham tests his multiplane glider, and demonstrates the superior lifting power of high-aspect-ratio wings.

1859 Cordner flies his tentative man-carrying kite.

1860 Smythies designs his ornithopter-cum-fixed-wing aeroplane.
Invention of the gas engine (Lenoir).

1861 First 'aircraft carrier' in service (for balloon) in US Civil War.

1863 De La Landelle designs his fantasy helicopter.
Ponton d'Amécourt tests his steam-driven model helicopter.
Bourçart builds and tests a full-size man-powered multi-winged ornithopter.
Jules Verne publishes his Five Weeks in a Balloon.
Nadar founds La Société d'Encouragement pour l'Aviation.

1864 Nadar founds the journal L'Aéronaute, which becomes the most important aeronautical journal in the world.

D'Esterno publishes his *Du Vol des Oiseaux*.

1865 First design for a jet-propelled aeroplane (de Louvrié).

1866 Foundation of the Aeronautical Society of Great Britain.

Wenham gives his lecture on 'Aerial Locomotion' to the Society at its first meeting, in which he first announces the results of his 1858–59 tests: the publication of this lecture exerts a great influence on later inventors.

1867 First delta-wing jet aeroplane designs (Butler and Edwards), which include both jet propulsion, and airscrew-jet propulsion proposals, the latter to be rotated by jets from the tips.

1868

June First aeronautical exhibition in history (at the Crystal Palace, near London), where the most important exhibit, Stringfellow's model triplane, is tested (see next entry). First powered model triplane tested (Stringfellow); although unsuccessful, this model is to have great influence and, through widespread publication to lead direct to the first biplanes and triplanes. Ailerons first designed, but in an unpractical form (Boulton). Kaufmann, in Britain, tests steam-driven fixed-wing-cum-ornithopter model, which is unsuccessful. Bourçart tests his full-size ornithopter at Guebwiller. Hunter suggests a jet aeroplane, which also incorporates jet lift.

1870 Pénaud introduces twisted rubber to power models. Harte designs modern flap-type ailerons, but not for proper control in roll. Trouvé's gunpowder-driven model ornithopter flies.

1870s Danjard's tandem-wing model gliders fly.

1871 Pénaud's powered model monoplane (called 'planophore') flies, and demonstrates inherent stability. First wind tunnel used (Wenham and Browning).

1872 First internal combustion engine (gas) drives a full-size aircraft using envelope's gas (Henlein's airship).

1873 Marey publishes his *La Machine Animale*. Renard tests his multi-wing model.

1873–74 Brown tests longitudinal stability of tandem-wing models, which probably influence Langley.

1874

9 July De Groof killed on his semi-ornithopter, at London.

c. **1874** First powered man-carrying aeroplane takes off (Du Temple), but does not fly.

1875 Moy successfully tests his large model tandem-wing Aerial Steamer.

1876 Pénaud patents his full-size aeroplane design, which is also the first design for an amphibian. Cayley's triple paper of 1809–10 is republished by the Aeronautical Society in London. Invention of the four-stroke petrol engine (Otto).

1877 Melikoff designs a gas-turbine helicopter model. Forlanini's steam-driven model helicopter flies. Cayley's triple paper of 1809–10 is republished in *L'Aéronaute*.

1879 Tatin's compressed-air-driven model monoplane flies. Biot tests his full-size glider. Brearey's model 'undulator' flies. Dandrieux flies his 'butterfly' helicopter models.

1881 Mouillard publishes his *L'Empire de l'Air*.

1883 First electric motor to drive a full-size aircraft in flight (Tissandier's airship).

1883–86 Montgomery in USA tests his first gliders, which are unsuccessful.

c. **1884** Second powered man-carrying aeroplane takes off, but does not fly (Mozhaiski).

1884 First near-practical airship flies (Renard and Krebs' *La France*). Phillips takes out first patents for his double-surfaced cambered wings, which are widely published and become very influential. Invention of the steam turbine (Parsons).

Daimler invents the light, high-speed petrol engine.

1885 First practical petrol automobile (Benz).

1886 Daimler builds the second practical petrol automobile.

Jules Verne publishes *Robur le Conquérant* (trans. as *The Clipper of the Clouds*).

1888 First petrol engine to power a full-size aircraft in flight (Wölfert's airship).

1889 Lilienthal publishes his classic *Der Vogelflug als Grundlage der Fliegekunst.*

1890

9 Oct. First full-size piloted aeroplane to leave the ground under its own power (Ader's steam-powered *Éole*), but it does not fly.

1891 Langley in the USA unsuccessfully tests his first steam-driven tandem-wing model.

1891–96 First successful piloted gliding flights, which directly inspire the final phase of aviation which culminated in powered flight (Lilienthal).

1892 Invention of the Diesel engine.

1893 Phillips tests his large powered multi-wing model aeroplane.

Parsons flies his steam-driven model aeroplane.

Invention of the box kite (Hargrave in Australia).

International Conference on Aeronautics is held at Chicago, at which Hargrave's box kites are revealed for the first time.

1894 First semipractical man-lifting kites (Baden-Powell).

Chanute publishes his *Progress in Flying Machines*, the first scientific and authoritative history of aviation to appear.

June Lanchester announces his theory of circulatory flow.

31 July Maxim tests his full-size steam-powered biplane test rig, which just rises from its rails, but does not fly.

1895 First piloted biplane gliders fly (Lilienthal).

Automobile-Club de France founded, which greatly stimulates automobilisme on the Continent.

1895–97 Means in the USA publishes three issues of *The Aeronautical Annual*, which disseminates much useful information.

1895–99 First successful piloted glider flights in

Britain (Pilcher; thus he is the first true British aviator).

1896 Chanute's biplane hang-glider flies successfully and incorporates the Pratt-truss method of rigging, which is to be copied by the Wright brothers.

Lilienthal is killed gliding, the publicity attending which, helps to precipitate the final phase in aviation. He crashes on 9 August, and dies next day.

Automobiles are granted freedom of the roads in Britain, which gives great stimulus to automobilisme.

Langley obtains his first successes with two of his steam-powered tandem-wing models.

1896–97 Tatin and Richet fly their steam-driven model aeroplane successfully.

1897 Ader twice tests his Avion III, on 12 and 14 October, but it does not leave the ground, on either occasion.

First all-metal airship flies (Schwartz).

1898 Aéro Club de France is founded in Paris.

10,22 Oct. Herring makes brief hops at St Joseph, Michigan, on his biplane hang-glider fitted with a compressed-air motor.

1899 Wilbur Wright invents his system of wing warping for control in roll, and flies a kite incorporating it.

Hargrave visits England and gives a lecture demonstration on his box kites.

Pilcher is killed on his *Hawk* glider; he crashes on 30 September, and dies on 2 October.

1900 First Zeppelin flies tentatively.

The Wrights fly their No. 1 glider at Kitty Hawk.

1901 The Wrights fly their No. 2 glider at the Kill Devil Hills, near Kitty Hawk.

Wilbur Wright gives his first lecture, on 18 September (in Chicago), in which he explains his wing warping.

Santos-Dumont flies his airship No. 6 round the Eiffel Tower.

First petrol-driven model aeroplane flies tentatively (Langley).

First full-size petrol-driven aeroplane destroyed when taxiing (Kress' *Seaplane*) in Austria.

Cody's man-lifting box kites are patented.

Aero Club (later Royal) founded in London.

1902 The Wrights make nearly 1000 glides on their No. 3 glider, and invent coordinated warp and rudder control (i.e. combined control in roll and yaw).

The Balzer-Manly radial engine is completed for the full-size Langley Aerodrome (see 1903).

Ferber, after correspondence with Chanute, builds first European Wright-type glider, and starts the revival of European aviation.

1902–03 First practical airship flies (Lebaudy, in France).

1903 Chanute visits France and greatly intensifies the European revival of aviation by lectures and articles on the Wrights.

Jatho, in Germany, tests his powered aeroplane, which is unsuccessful.

7 Oct. Langley's full-size piloted Aerodrome crashes at takeoff.

24 June Wilbur Wright gives his second lecture at Chicago.

8 Dec. Langley's Aerodrome again crashes at takeoff; it is then abandoned.

17 Dec. **The first powered, sustained and controlled aeroplane flights in history** (Wilbur and Orville Wright) at the Kill Devil Hills, near Kitty Hawk; the first of the four flights lasts for 12 seconds, the last for 59 seconds.

1904 Esnault-Pelterie unsuccessfully imitates a Wright glider.

Ailerons (elevons) first used (Esnault-Pelterie), but unsuccessfully.

Archdeacon's Wright-type glider is briefly tested.

Cody's man-lifting kites are adopted by the British army.

Ferber introduces the stable type of biplane glider with a tailplane.

First tentative glide with a passenger (Ferber).

26 May Wrights start flying their powered Flyer II near Dayton.

7 Sept. First use by the Wrights of their weight- and derrick-assisted takeoff method.

20 Sept. First circle flown (Wilbur Wright); this was witnessed and described by A I Root.

9 Nov. First flight of over 5 minutes (Wilbur Wright).

1905 The box-kite concept is first incorporated in an aeroplane (the Voisin-Archdeacon, and Voisin-Blériot float gliders, in France); this starts the stable box-kite aeroplane tradition of Europe.

Cody flies his aileron-equipped glider-kite.

Feb. Exhibition of aeroplane models in Paris.

16 March First glider descent from a balloon (Maloney, on a Montgomery tandem-wing machine); he is killed this year, when flying the same glider.

May Ferber fits an engine and tractor airscrew to his stable tailed type of glider, but it cannot sustain itself.

June First fully practical powered aeroplane flies (Wright Flyer III).

4 Oct. First flight of over half an hour (Orville Wright).

14 Oct. The Fédération Aéronautique Internationale (FAI) is founded by La Vaulx.

6 Oct. Wrights' last flight until 6 May 1908.

1906

Jan. The Wright patent, including description of simultaneous use of wing warping and rudder, is published in *L'Aérophile*.

March First tractor monoplane tested (Vuia), which, although unsuccessful, leads to Blériot and the whole European monoplane tradition.

12 Sept. Ellehammer makes a hop flight of 140 feet, but the machine is tethered to a central post, and no free flight is made.

Oct.–Nov. Santos-Dumont makes the first official powered hop flights in Europe, but the best (12 November) covers 721 feet in 21⅕ seconds.

Nov. Ader, as a result of Santos-Dumont's efforts, suddenly claims – for the first time – that he flew for 300 metres in 1897; this claim is now known to have been deliberately fabricated.

1907 First tentative powered flight in Britain (Phillips), in his multi-slat aeroplane.

Lanchester publishes his *Aerodynamics*, which includes a detailed exposition of his theory of circulatory flow.

Dunne's first swept-wing tail-less biplane tested, unsuccessfully.

Cody's unmanned engined kite flies along a wire.

First full-size powered triplane tested (Ellehammer) in Denmark.

Feb.–Mar. European pusher biplane configuration crystallised (Voisin-Delagrange), but the machine is not successful.

April Exhibition of aeroplane models at London.

April, July First primitive cantilever monoplanes tested (Blériot's 'canard' and *Libellule*).

29 Sept. First man-carrying helicopter rises (Breguet), but not in free flight.

Oct.–Nov. Henri Farman becomes the first successful European pilot.

Nov. First 'light aeroplane' type tested (Santos-Dumont's No. 19), but is not successful. Blériot introduces the modern-configuration tractor monoplane (his No. VII); although very influential, it is not itself successful.

10 Nov. First flight in Europe of over 1 minute (Farman on a Voisin).

3 Nov. First man-carrying helicopter rises vertically in free flight (Cornu), but is not practical.

1908

13 Jan. First official circle flown in Europe (Farman, on his modified Voisin, at Issy).

6 May Wrights fly for the first time since 1905, and first use upright seating at the Kill Devil Hills.

14 May First passenger flight (Wilbur Wright takes C Furnas) at the Kill Devil Hills.

30 May First passenger flight in Europe (Farman takes Archdeacon). First European flight of over ¼ hour (Delagrange on a Voisin).

June–July First flap-type ailerons used (Blériot VIII), but only for stabilising. Roe tests his biplane at Brooklands and makes brief hop flights, almost certainly after downhill runs.

28 June Ellehammer makes the first flight in Germany.

4 July First monoplane flight of 5 minutes (Blériot, on his No. VIII). Curtiss wins the *Scientific American* trophy for the first flight in public in the USA (1 minute 42½ seconds).

8 July First woman to fly as passenger (Mme Peltier, with Delagrange).

8 Aug. Wilbur Wright first flies in public (at Hunaudières, in France) in the first practical two-seat aeroplane, and transforms aviation, chiefly by his display of flight control; he transfers to nearby Auvours and flies there from 21 August to 31 December.

Sept. Lorin publishes in France the first of his designs for jet aeroplanes.

3 Sept. Orville Wright first flies in public at Fort Myer (USA).

6 Sept. First European flight of about ½ hour (29 minutes 53 seconds) (Delagrange on a Voisin).

9 Sept. First flight of over 1 hour (Orville Wright).

17 Sept. First fatality in powered aviation (Selfridge, flying as passenger with Orville Wright, is killed).

21 Sept. First flight of over 1½ hours (Wilbur Wright).

Oct. Grade becomes first native German pilot. First practical aileroned monoplane flies (Antoinette IV).

3 Oct. First passenger flight of over ½ hour (Wilbur Wright takes Reichel).

6 Oct. First passenger flight of over 1 hour (Wilbur Wright takes Fordyce).

8 Oct. First Briton to fly as passenger (G Brewer, with Wilbur Wright).

16 Oct. First powered flight in Britain (Cody – still American – at Farnborough).

30 Oct. First cross-country flight (16½ miles, by Farman from Bouy to Reims).

31 Oct. Farman attains altitude of 80 feet.

Dec. First Briton to become a pilot, excluding Farman (Moore-Brabazon).

18 Dec. Wilbur Wright attains altitude of 360 feet.

31 Dec. First flight of over 2 hours (Wilbur Wright). Wilbur Wright finishes his season at Auvours, having made over 100 flights; having been in the air for over 25 hours, including making six flights of over ½ hour, six of over 1, and one of over 2 hours; he takes up passengers on more than 60 occasions.

1909 Wright brothers are honoured and fêted throughout Europe. First flights take place in Austria, Sweden, Romania, Russia, Turkey, Portugal and Canada.

Weiss flies his bird-form gliders.

Gnome rotary engine first goes into service on Henry Farman III.

First practical wing-warping monoplanes fly (Blériot XI and Antoinette VII).

23 Feb. First flight in the Commonwealth outside Britain (McCurdy on the *Silver Wing* in Canada).

March Goupy II flies and establishes the modern tractor biplane configuration.

April First cinematograph photos taken from the air (from a Wright machine, near Rome).

April–May First practical aileroned biplane flies (Henry Farman III).

First Briton flies in Britain (Moore-Brabazon).

22 May First monoplane flight of over ½ hour (Latham on Antoinette IV).

5 June First monoplane flight of over 1 hour (Latham on Antoinette IV).

13 July Blériot flies cross-country for 26 miles (Étampes to Chevilly).

19 July Latham crashes in his first attempt to fly the Channel, on Antoinette IV.

23 July Roe covers 900 feet on his first triplane.

25 July First Channel crossing by aeroplane (Blériot), from near Calais to Dover, on his No. XI monoplane; this flight has profound effect on world governments as showing that the sea can be conquered by aircraft.

27 July Latham crashes in his second attempt to fly the Channel on Antoinette VII.

Aug. First great aviation meeting is held at Reims, and has widespread influence as showing that the aeroplane was now a practical vehicle.

27 Aug. First flight of over 100 miles, which was also first lasting over 3 hours (Farman, at the Reims meeting).

7 Sept. First powered aeroplane pilot killed (Lefebvre, when testing a new French-built Wright).

8 Sept. First flight of over 1 hour in Britain (Cody).

22 Sept. Second powered aeroplane pilot killed (Ferber on a Voisin, when taxiing, at Boulogne).

Oct. First Short-built Wright machine flies in Britain.

2 Oct. First flight of above 1000 feet altitude (Orville Wright).

30 Oct. Moore-Brabazon wins *Daily Mail* prize for first circular mile by a Briton on an all-British machine, i.e. a Short.

Dec. First successful air-to-ground still photos taken from an aeroplane (of Mourmelon, Camp de Châlons, from an Antoinette).

6 Dec. Third powered aeroplane pilot killed (Fernandez on a self-designed machine).

24 Dec. Roe flies ½ mile on his second triplane.

30 Dec. First flight by a monoplane of over 100 miles, which was also the first by a monoplane to last over 2 hours (Delagrange on a Blériot XI).

1910 Over 20 aviation meetings are held in Europe: also meetings in USA and Egypt.

First flights made in Spain, Switzerland, Argentine, Brazil, Indo-China and China.

First full-size (but unsuccessful) jet-propelled aeroplane is built by Coanda, the jet being produced by a ducted fan.

First air passenger service starts (Zeppelin airships in Germany).

First practical airspeed indicator (Etévé).

Official report on Ader's 1897 trials is released, showing he never flew at all.

Aviation fatalities for the year number 32; this makes 39 since (and including) Lilienthal.

Jan. Los Angeles meeting (USA).

4 Jan. Delagrange killed when flying his Blériot.

Feb. Patent granted to Junkers for a cantilever 'flying-wing' aeroplane.

8 March First woman to become a qualified pilot (Baroness de Laroche).

10 March First night flights (Aubrun on a Blériot, in the Argentine).

28 March First flight by a seaplane (Fabre).

27–28 Apr. London to Manchester air race (won by Paulhan on a Henry Farman).

28 April First night flight in Europe (Grahame-White on a Henry Farman).

2 June First double crossing of the Channel, without landing (Rolls on a Wright).

July First bombing tests made (Curtiss, with dummies over Lake Keuka).

12 July First British pilot to be killed (Rolls, flying a French-built Wright, at Bournemouth).

17 Aug. First cross-Channel passenger flight (Moisant and his mechanic in a Blériot).

27 Aug. First air-to-ground radio, and vice versa, (by McCurdy, from a Curtiss in the USA).

28 Aug. Dufaux, the first Swiss pilot, flies across Lake Geneva.

Sept. Harvard-Boston meeting (USA).

23 Sept. First flight over the Alps (Chavez on a Blériot, but he is killed when about to land at Domodossola).

Oct. Belmont Park Meeting, Long Island, USA.

2 Oct. First midair collision (at Milan).

14 Nov. First takeoff from a ship, marking the true birth of the aircraft carrier (Ely, in the USA, on a Curtiss).

Dec. De Havilland is appointed designer and test pilot at Farnborough.

1911 The year sees the rise of aviation as a popular sport and spectacle, and the establishment of many aerodromes.

First long-distance flights and long-distance races take place.

Military aviation meetings held in Britain and France: various aircraft fitted with guns.

Wright's win action against French manufacturers for patent infringement (see 1913).

First oleo-undercarriages (Farnborough and Esnault-Pelterie).

First air-mail flights in various countries.

First bombsight introduced (Scott, in USA).

Montgomery killed on one of his own gliders.

Jan. First live bombing tests (US Army, from a Wright, at San Francisco).

First practical seaplane flies (Curtiss float plane).

McCurdy, in a Curtiss, flies 90 miles over water from Key West (Florida) to Havana (Cuba).

18 Jan. First landing on, and takeoff from, a ship (Ely), in the USA.

12 April First non-stop flight from London to Paris (Prier on a Blériot).

Aug. Atwood, on a Wright, flies from St Louis to New York via Chicago by stages (1266 miles).

3 Aug. First amphibian flies (Fabre-Voisin).

Sept.–Nov. Rodgers flies his Wright across the USA, from Long Island (NY) to Long Beach (CA) covering some 4000 miles in 82 stages.

22 Oct. First use of the aeroplane in warfare (reconnaissance by the Italians, in a Blériot, against the Turks).

24 Oct. Orville Wright makes record soaring flight of 90 minutes, at the Kill Devil Hills (see 13 Sept. 1921).

Oct.–Nov. First 'Concours Militaire', at Reims.

1912 The Farnborough B.S.1 biplane flies, the prototype of all single-seat scouts and fighters.

Monocoque construction introduced (by the Swiss Ruchonnet, in a French Deperdussin).

First artillery spotting by aeroplane (B.E.1, in Britain).

German military flying is inaugurated.

First flying boat flies (Curtiss).

Military monoplane construction restricted in France and Britain after crashes.

First enclosed cabin aeroplanes fly, monoplane and biplane (Avro).

First all-metal aeroplane flies (the Tubavion of Porche and Primard).

First use of corrugated aluminium wings (Reissner).

Feb. First to fly over 100 mph (Vedrines on a Deperdussin).

1 March First parachute drop from an aeroplane (Berry in USA, using a static line).

March First seaplane meeting (at Monaco).

13 April Royal Flying Corps founded (Royal Warrant signed 13 April, and implemented on 13 May).

30 May Wilbur Wright dies of typhoid.

Aug. First British military aeroplane competition, which is won by Cody.

12 Nov. First successful catapult launch of a powered machine after the Wrights (Curtiss).

1913 The Sopwith Tabloid first flies, and thereafter has much influence.

First practical 'all-round' stable aeroplane flies (the Farnborough B.E.2C).

First race for the Schneider Trophy for seaplanes.

First large multi-engine (four) aeroplane flies (Sikorsky Bolshoi in Russia).

Wrights again win their action (in appeal).

The Avro 504 first flies, and becomes one of the classic aircraft of history.

The tail-less Dunne No. 8 flies from Eastchurch to Paris.

Vedrines flies by stages from Nancy to Cairo (2500 miles).

20 Aug. First looping the loop (Nesterov on a Nieuport, at Kiev).

Sept. Pégoud performs the loop, and other evolutions, and becomes the world's first master of aerobatics.

23 Sept. First non-stop flight across the Mediterranean (Garros).

1914 First tentative scheduled airline opened (by Fansler, in Florida, USA).

First 'Concours de la Sécurité' (held at Buc).

First Zeppelin raid (on Antwerp).

English air attack on Friedrichshafen, using Avro 504s.

1915 First Zeppelin raid on London.

First successful gun firing through propeller fitted with deflector plates (Garros, on his Morane, in April).

First practical interrupter gear invented by the Germans and fitted to Fokker E.1s (July).

First all-metal cantilever aeroplane flies (Junkers J.1).

1916

17 May First aeroplane-from-aeroplane midair launch (Porte Baby caries Bristol Scout).

12 Sept. First pilotless radio-guided flying bomb tested (Hewitt-Sperry, in the USA).

1917 First mass aeroplane raid on London (13 June).

First low-wing cantilever monoplane fighter flies (Junkers J.7/9).

1919 First regular and scheduled commercial air-mail and passenger lines opened.

International Air Traffic Association (IATA) formed.

Junkers invents aerofoil wing flaps.

May US Aerial Mail Service inaugurated.

16–17 May First transatlantic flight, by stages via the Azores (by the US Read et al. in the NC-4 flying boat).

14–15 June First direct non-stop transatlantic flight (by the British Alcock and Brown, in a Vickers Vimy).

2–13 July First direct transatlantic crossing by an airship, and first double crossing by an airship (British R.34).

12 Nov. (12 Nov. – 10 Dec.) First flight from England to Australia (by Ross and Keith Smith et al., in a Vickers Vimy).

1920 First aeroplane flies with practical retractable undercarriage (Dayton–Wright R.B.).

Split flaps invented by Orville Wright and Jacobs.

March First machine flies with Handley Page wing slots.

Sept.–Oct. Completion, and firsts tests, of Zeppelin-Staaken E.4/20 four-engine all metal 18-passenger transport, the forerunner of the modern large all-metal airliner.

1921 Record flying leap (40 feet) by pedal cycle equipped with wings (Poulain, Paris).

22–23 Feb. First coast-to-coast (San Francisco–New York) air-mail flight.

21 July First battleship (ex-German) sunk by bombs, in test (Mitchell of US Army, with Martin bombers).

13 Sept. Hirth, in Germany, breaks 1911 soaring record (established by Orville Wright) with flight of 21 minutes.

1922

18 Aug. First soaring flight of one hour (Martens, in Germany).

1 Oct. First air force to assume complete control of a military command (the RAF in Iraq).

1923 Turnbull variable-pitch propeller demonstrated (in production by Curtiss in mid-1930s).

3 Jan. First soaring flight of over 5 hours (Floret in a Hanriot, at Biskra).

9 Jan. First flight of a practical gyroplane (Cierva's C.3 Autogiro, near Madrid).

2,3 May First non-stop coast-to-coast crossing of USA (Kelly and Macready in a Fokker T-2).

27 June First complete pipeline flight refuelling (in USA, between two DH 4Bs).

1924 Hele Shaw-Beecham variable-pitch, constant-speed, propeller demonstrated (produced by Rotol in late 1930s).

The Fowler wing flap invented.

Trimotor era started by first flight of Junkers G-23 three-engine all-metal monoplane airliner.

1 April   Imperial Airways formed.

7 April   (7 April – 28 Sept.) First round-the-world flight (by American Smith, Nelson, *et al.*).

1925

22 Feb.   DH Moth first flies, and heralds the popularity of the light aeroplane movement.

26 July   First soaring flight of 10 hours (Massaux, in Belgium, on a Poncelet).

16 March   (16 Nov. – 13 March) Cobham makes the first of his pioneering empire flights (to Cape Town).

17 Dec.   Gen. 'Billy' Mitchell (US Army) found guilty at court martial of criticising state of US military aviation.

1926   Proposals for gas-turbine propeller propulsion, by Griffith, lead to a development programme at the Royal Aircraft Establishment at Farnborough. Rohrbach, in USA, gives his influential lecture on stressed skin construction.

16 March   First flight of a liquid-fuel rocket, designed by Goddard in USA, which marks the birth of practical modern rocketry.

9 May   First flight over the North Pole (Byrd and Bennett, of the USA, in a Fokker F.VII/3m).

1927

20–21 May   First solo Atlantic crossing (Lindbergh in a Ryan, from New York to Paris).

4 July   Lockheed Vega first flies, and inaugurates a new era in commercial flying.

1928

12,13 April   First east-to-west aeroplane crossing of the Atlantic (Koehl *et al.*, in a Junkers W.33).

31 May   (31 May – 10 June) First flight across the Pacific (Kingsford Smith *et al.*, in a Fokker F.VII3m, from USA to Australia).

11 June   First rocket-propelled aeroplane flight (Stamer, in an Opel-Stamer).

1929   Melvill Jones publishes his influential paper, 'The Streamline Aeroplane'.

23 Oct.   Dornier Do X, 12-engine flying boat, carries 169 people.

1930   Whittle takes out his first jet-engine patents (published 1932).

5–24 May   Amy Johnson flies solo from England to Australia, in a DH Moth.

1931   First practical delta-wing aeroplane flies (Lippisch).

First application of jet propulsion to a full-size aircraft in flight (Italian airship *Omniadir*, with compressed air).

11 June   Handley Page H.P. 42 biplane airliner enters service with Imperial Airways, and sets new standards of comfort.

13 Sept.   Britain wins Schneider Trophy outright with the Supermarine S.6B, flown by Boothman at 340 mph.

1932   Imperial Airways open London–Cape Town service.

Junkers Ju 52-3m transport first flies, which is to form the backbone of German military transport in the Second World War.

Cobham starts his flight refuelling experiments.

21,22 May   First solo Atlantic crossing by a woman (Earhart in a Vega).

1932

18,19 Aug.   First solo east-to-west Atlantic crossing (Mollison).

1933

8 Feb.   First modern-type monoplane airliner flies (Boeing 247).

3 April   First flight over Mount Everest (Clydesdale *et al.*).

1 July   Douglas DC-1 first flies.

15–22 July   First solo flight round the world (Post).

1934   First practical constant-speed variable-pitch propellers enter airline service.

July   Douglas DC-2 first enters airline service.

Oct.   MacRobertson air race (England–Australia) **1935**.

July   Prototype of the B-17 Flying Fortress first flies (Boeing 299).

July   Breguet helicopter flies successfully.

1935–36   Prototypes of many fighters and bombers of Second World War first fly.

1936

June   Douglas DC-3 twin-engine airliner enters service, and so starts the career of the greatest transport aircraft of history.

26 June   First flight of the first really practical helicopter (Focke-Achgelis Fa 61).

4 July   Short Empire monoplane flying boat first flies.

1937   First helicopter flight of over 1 hour (Focke-Achgelis).

May   First fully-pressurised aeroplane flies (Lockheed XC 35).

6 May Zeppelin *Hindenburg* crashes in flames in USA, and brings virtual end to large airship operation.

August First modern-type, four-engine, transport flies (Junkers Ju 90).

1937–39 Experimental mail-carrying and survey flights across the North and South Atlantic.

1937–38 Spanish Civil War becomes testing ground for German and Italian combat aeroplanes.

1938

31 Dec. First flight of first pressurised transport aeroplane (Boeing 307).

1939

30 June First rocket-propelled (liquid fuel) aeroplane flies (Heinkel He 176).

27 Aug. First turbojet aeroplane flies (Heinkel He 178).

1940

13 May First successful flight by a single-rotor helicopter (Sikorsky VS-300).

27 August Caproni-Campini 'quasi-jet' first flies.

1941

9 Jan. Avro Lancaster heavy bomber first flies.

Feb. First British four-engine bomber enters services (Short Stirling).

15 May First flight of first British turbojet aeroplane (Gloster E.28/39, with Whittle engine).

Sept. Whittle jet engine is flown from Britain to USA, and provides the model for the first practical US jet engines.

1942 First fully-practical single-rotor helicopter flies (Sikorsky VS 300) and inaugurates the modern helicopter age.

Douglas DC-4 first flies, and inaugurates a whole generation of four-engine airliners.

18 July First operational jet combat aeroplane, which was also first production turbojet aeroplane, first flies (Messerschmitt Me 262).

1 Oct. First US turbojet aeroplane flies (Bell XP-59A, with two Whittle-derived engines).

3 Oct. First long-range rocket missile 'flies' (German A-4): this marks the birth of practical space flight.

1943 First jet-propelled-rotor helicopter flies (Doblhoff).

9 Jan. Lockheed Constellation airliner first flies.

15 June Prototype of the first jet bomber flies (German Arado Ar 234B-2).

24 July Prototype of the Gloster jet Meteor first flies.

1944 First practical rocket-propelled aeroplane in service (German Me 163).

First flying bombs in action (German FZG-76).

First long-range rocket bombs in action (German A-4).

1945 First atomic fission bombs dropped (on Japan).

First turboprop aeroplane flies (Gloster Meteor with Rolls-Royce Trents).

1945–46 Regular transatlantic passenger services introduced, with only American machines involved.

Glossary

Aerobatics. Aerial acrobatics.

Aerodonetics. A term, now obsolete, used for the science of gliding and soaring.

Aerodrome (as aircraft). The word mistakenly first used by S P Langley, then by others, for their aeroplanes: the Greek word *dromos* can mean a course, a race or running, or the place where such activities take place; but never the man, animal, or machine that runs or races.

Aerodrome (as airfield). This good old-fashioned word (see also above for etymology) is now slowly disappearing in favour of **Airfield** for all military aerodromes, and for the small civilian aerodromes; and **Airport** for the medium and large civilian aerodromes from which scheduled airlines are operated.

Aerodromics. An early term, used by Langley, for the construction and operation of flying machines (i.e. of 'aerodromes' in his usage).

Aerodynamic missile. See **Missile**.

Aerodynamics. That field of dynamics concerned with the motion of air and other gaseous fluids; a branch of fluid mechanics.

Aerodyne. The seldom-used word for all types of heavier-than-air aircraft, excluding certain missiles and VTOL machines. See also **Aeroplane**.

Aerofoil (Airfoil in USA). A body designed to obtain an aerodynamic reaction normal to its direction of travel through the air (e.g. a wing, propeller blade, fin, etc.).

Aeronaut. Literally an 'air sailor': today generally confined to either pilot, crew member or passenger in a balloon or dirigible airship, especially the former: but the word has, in the past, been applied to airmen in heavier-than-air machines.

Aeronautics. The whole field of man-made aircraft, of whatever type.

Aeronef. An early word (French for 'flying ship') for any kind of aircraft.

Aeroplane (Airplane in USA). Any heavier-than-air aircraft supported by the dynamic reaction of air flowing over or about fixed or rotating plane surfaces; the term has slowly become synonymous with 'powered aeroplane', and most people today would understand it in that sense. Historically, it is used in the first sense. 'Aeroplane' originally meant simply a fixed wing, i.e. an *aero*-plane.

Aerostation. The whole field of lighter-than-air aircraft; as opposed to aviation. A lighter-than-air aircraft is an **Aerostat**, and the science is that of **Aerostatics**.

Ailerons. Movable surfaces to control the rolling movements of an aeroplane, now generally set in or by the trailing edges of wings (near the tips). Some early aeroplanes had between-wing ailerons. See also **Differential ailerons**; **Wing warping**.

Air brake. Any flap or similar device for slowing down an aeroplane in flight, i.e. which increases drag, as opposed to a **Flap** (which see) which increases both lift and drag. See also **Flap**; **Spoiler**; **Air brake (steering)**.

Air brake (steering). A term adopted in this book at the suggestion of the Farnborough authorities, for a device in which a part of either wing can be raised or lowered in order to retard the wing and slew the aeroplane round, thus changing its heading. This concept was never associated with control in roll.

Aircraft. Any kind of man-made airborne vehicle. The word is often used loosely as a synonym for aeroplane, which can be misleading if the machine in question is not identified at first.

Airfield. See **Aerodrome**.

Airflow. The flow of air around an object in flight.

Airfoil. The American spelling of **Aerofoil** (which see).

Airframe. An aeroplane without its engines and their accessories.

Airliner. An unsatisfactory word connoting a medium or large transport aeroplane.

Airplane. The American spelling of 'aeroplane'. This form of the word was officially adopted in the USA in 1911, and also strongly advocated at the time for use in Britain.

Air pocket. See **Bump**.

Airport. See **Aerodrome**.

Airscrew. A screw to effect propulsion through the air: an alternative word to propeller (which see). 'Airscrew' is sometimes the word of choice when discussing the early history of the device, to distinguish it from the marine propeller.

Airscrew disc. See **Propeller disc**.

Airship. A power-driven lighter-than-air aircraft; but often used before 1912 for any kind of powered aircraft, including aeroplanes.

Airspeed. See **Speed**.

Airspeed indicator (ASI). A flight instrument showing the speed of the aircraft relative to the surrounding air. The ordinary ASI comprises a pitot and a static tube which measure the difference between dynamic and static pressures. See also **Mach meter**.

Alighting gear. An elegant but obsolete early term for the undercarriage.

All-up weight. The total weight of an aeroplane together with everybody and everything aboard.

Altimeter. An instrument for indicating altitude, usually an aneroid barometer calibrated to read feet or metres in a standard atmosphere.

Altitude. The elevation of an object above a given level: with aircraft, a given altitude is generally taken to be that above sea level.

Amphibian. An aircraft equipped to take off and land on either land or water.

Angle of attack. See **Attack**; **Incidence**.

Angle of incidence. See **Attack**; **Incidence**.

Anhedral. The generally accepted term for negative dihedral, although etymologically the word 'anhedral' should mean 'positive dihedral': it is not clear how this contradiction arose. See **Cathedral**; **Dihedral**.

Annular wing. A cylindrical wing.

Anti-torque rotor. See **Rotor** (anti-torque).

Artificial horizon. A gyroscopic flight instrument indicating to the pilot the pitching and banking movements of his aircraft.

Aspect ratio. The ratio of the span to chord of an aerofoil: a high-aspect-ratio wing is great in span and small in chord; a low-aspect-ratio wing is small in span and great in chord.

Assisted takeoff. Any method of accelerating an aircraft's takeoff, apart from its integral engine(s). See also **Jet-assisted takeoff.**

Astronautics. The field of space travel.

Attack (angle of). American term of **Incidence** (which see).

Autogiro. A trade name (the Cierva Autogiro) for the first succesful type of gyroplane (which see). The name is often loosely applied to other gyroplanes.

Automatic pilot (**Autopilot** in USA). A gyroscopically operated control mechanism which maintains a preset course and altitude of an aircraft by making automatic corrections of the control surfaces.

Autorotation. The free rotation of rotor blades without engine power: also used of an aeroplane when spinning.

Aviation. The whole field of heavier-than-air aircraft, as opposed to aerostation. It is becoming increasingly used as a synonym for aeronautics (to include all 'man-made' flying) which is to be deplored.

Aviator. The pilot of a glider, powered aeroplane or helicopter; sometimes loosely used of other members of an aircrew, who are better termed 'airmen'.

Avion. The French word for 'aeroplane' invented by Clément Ader.

Axis. A straight line that passes through a body and about which that body may revolve. An aircraft is considered to have three mutually perpendicular axes, each of which passes through the centre of gravity. 1. The **Longitudinal axis**, the nose-to-tail axis, about which the aircraft revolves in rolling; 2. the **Lateral axis**, the side-to-side (spanwise) axis about which it revolves in pitching; and 3. the **Vertical** (or normal) **axis**, which runs in the plane of symmetry (through top and belly), about which it revolves in yawing.

Balance. See **Equilibrium.**

Balancing planes (or tips). An early term for ailerons.

Ballistic missile. See **Missile.**

Balloon. An unpowered aerostat, generally spherical or near-spherical.

Banking. Inclining an aircraft laterally, usually when making a turn, to prevent skidding. Sometimes loosely used for 'turning'.

Barnstorming. An early term for itinerant exhibition flying (especially in USA) where pilots flew at fairs.

Beaufort scale. A scale from 0 to 12 symbolising the strength of wind devised by Sir F Beaufort (1774–1857).

Bernouilli theorem. When applied to a flow of air, the theorem states that as the velocity increases, the pressure decreases.

Biplane. An aeroplane with two main sets of wings, one above the other: the term was sometimes used, in early works on flying, for a tandem-wing monoplane. See also **Wing**(s).

Boost. To supply an engine with more air than it would ordinarily induct, to increase the power obtainable under appropriate conditions.

Boundary layer. A thin layer of fluid adjacent to a surface, in which the viscous (friction) forces are not negligible.

Box kite. A form of kite (see **Kite**), and applied in the early days of flying to many full-size biplanes, often (and unaccountably) those machines which had no trace of box-kite construction, e.g. the so-called Bristol 'Box-Kite'.

Braking parachute. See **Parachute** (braking).

Bump. A violent movement of an aeroplane, generally up or down, due to turbulent air currents: formerly called, colloquially, an 'air pocket'.

Bunt. A manoeuvre in which an aeroplane performs half an outside loop downwards and emerges upside down going in the opposite direction.

Burbling. Separation in the boundary layer of air about a streamlined body, resulting in divergent velocities and pressures, and causing loss of lift and increase in drag.

Camber. The curve of an aerofoil section from leading to trailing edge, either the upper surface, lower surface, or mean line between them.

Canard. The French word for 'duck'. The word unaccountably applied to a 'tail-first' aeroplane, i.e. with the fuselage and elevator forward of the main wings.

Canopy. See **Parachute.**

Cantilever. A wing (or any other member) supported at one end only, without any external bracing.

Cantilever aeroplane. One with cantilever wings.

Cathedral. A corruption of 'Katahedral', sometimes used in early aviation for negative dihedral (anhedral). See **Anhedral.**

Ceiling. The maximum altitude attainable by an aircraft. **Service ceiling** is the altitude at which the rate of climb falls below some specified value.

Centre of gravity. The point at which the combined force (resultant) of all the weight forces in a body are concentrated for any position of the body.

Centre of lift. The point at which a body in equilibrium may be said to be supported.

Centre of pressure. The point on the chord of an aerofoil where the resultant of all pressure forces may be said to act.

Centre section. The central panel or section of an aeroplane's wing(s), often extended to mean the portion of the fuselage involved.

Certificate of Airworthiness (C of A). A certificate issued by the Air Registration Board (in Britain) [now issued by the Civil Aviation Authority] respecting civil aircraft, permitting the machine in question to operate under given conditions, etc.

Chord. The straight-line distance between the leading and trailing edges of an aerofoil (as opposed to **Span**).

Cloche. The French word for 'bell', used to describe the inverted bowl at the base of Blériot's control column, to the edge of which the elevator and warping wires were attached.

Cockpit. The compartment from where an aircraft is controlled, seating the pilot and often other crew members: in large aircraft it is often referred to as the 'flight deck'; sometimes found in early French manuals spelt 'coke-pit'.

C of A. Abbreviation of Certificate of Airworthiness.

Collective pitch control. The helicopter control in which the pitch of all the rotor blades is changed simultaneously for vertical ascent and descent. See also **Cyclic pitch control.**

Constant-speed propeller. See **Propeller** (constant speed).

Control. See **Stability and control.**

Control column. The pilot's control for working elevators and ailerons.

Control surface. Generally used to denote one of the main control surfaces of an aeroplane (i.e. rudder, elevator or ailerons) but including flaps, tabs, etc.

Convertiplane. An aeroplane whose shape is mechanically changed during flight to enable it to land and take off vertically.

Control lever(s). An early word for the control column, when one or more levers were sometimes used.

Crash landing. A forced landing resulting in a crash.

Critical Mach number. See **Mach number.**

Cruising speed. A level flight speed resulting from a power setting recommended by the makers for flying under a given set of conditions, usually the optimum compromise of speed and range.

Cyclic pitch control. A helicopter control by means of which the angle of attack of the rotor blades is changed, to produce a horizontal thrust component, and hence horizontal flight in any direction.

Dead reckoning. The method of estimating an aircraft's position in the air by a calculation involving earlier known position, elapsed time, speed, heading, effect of wind, etc.

Deck. An early word for a wing. See also **Flight deck.**

Delta wing. An aeroplane's wings which in plan form resemble an isosceles triangle, with the trailing edges forming the base.

Differential ailerons. Modern usage confines this term to the special aileron linkage which results in the up-moving aileron travelling farther than the down-moving one. The mere fact of one aileron moving up whilst the other one goes down is best referred to as 'contra-acting'.

Dihedral. The upward inclination of an aeroplane's wings from their roots, making a shallow V from the front view: hence **Dihedral angle**. Strictly speaking this is 'positive dihedral', but the 'positive' is generally omitted. Negative dihedral (downward inclination) is generally called 'anhedral' (which see). Longitudinal dihedral is the angle formed by the chord lines of the wings and tailplane to aid longitudinal stability.

Directional gyro. A gyroscopic flight instrument indicating the aircraft's heading.

Directional stability. See **Stability.**

Dirigible. A dirigible airship (i.e. powered).

Dive brake. A small retractable surface on wing, or fuselage, to retard an aircraft in a dive.

Dorsal. Of, or pertaining to, the back; hence 'dorsal fin', etc., where 'back' is envisaged as the top of the aircraft as distinct from the bottom, where the word 'ventral' would apply.

Downwash. The downward deflection of air by an aerofoil relative to the undisturbed air.

Drag. A resistant force exerted by the air upon a body, in a direction opposite to the direction of motion. In the early days of flying, drag was termed 'drift', or simply 'resistance'. **Profile drag** is a composite drag produced by the lifting surfaces, and comprises **Form drag** (due to the shape of the aerofoil) and **Skin friction**. **Induced drag** is that due to the lift forces produced by the wings. **Parasite drag** is that produced by parts of the aircraft other than the lifting surfaces. **Interference Drag** is that induced by the interaction of wings, fuselage, tail, etc.

Drift. A lateral divergence of an aircraft or missile from the projected line of its heading. Also an early term for drag.

Droop. An early word for 'anhedral' (which see).

Dynamometer. An instrument for measuring the power, thrust or torque of an engine, rocket, etc.

Elevator. A horizontal control surface to control the climb and descent of an aircraft. In early aviation it was usually called the 'horizontal rudder'.

Elevon. A control surface combining the functions of elevator and aileron.

Empennage. The early term for an aeroplane's tail unit, this French word being derived from *empenner*, to feather an arrow.

Engine. The power source of an aircraft (see also **Motor**).

Equilibrium (in flight). The stability achieved when the forces of drag, thrust, lift and weight are acting so as to produce steady flight. See also **Stability.**

FAI. Abbreviation of Fédération Aéronautique Internationale.

Fairing. An auxiliary member or structure shaped to reduce drag.

Fan-type engine. A radial engine having cylinders disposed over not more than half the arc of the circle.

Fillet. A fairing, generally where two surfaces join, to improve the airflow.

Fin. A fixed vertical aerofoil for stabilising purposes. The American term is 'vertical stabiliser'.

Flap. Any control surface designed to increase the lift, or lift and drag combined, of an aeroplane (as opposed to an **Air brake**, which only increases drag); the term is usually applied to those surfaces which either hinge down at the trailing edge of the wings, or are projected from an extension of the trailing edge, curving downwards (Fowler flap): among other types are slotted, split and leading-edge flaps.

Flapper. An ornithoptering winglet, or small beating surface, used to effect either propulsion-cum-lift, or propulsion only.

Flatten out. To level off an aircraft after a dive or climb.

Flier. See **Flyer.**

Flight deck. The takeoff and landing deck of an aircraft carrier: also used for the cockpit of a large aircraft.

Flight path. The path described by an aircraft, etc., in the air; i.e. the hypothetical hole bored by an aircraft through space.

Flight simulator. A device (dummy cockpit, etc.) in which any or all of the conditions and feelings of flight are simulated, for training and other purposes.

Float plane. A seaplane on a float or floats. See also **Amphibian; Flying boat; Seaplane.**

Flutter. A vibrating or oscillating movement caused by aerodynamic forces acting on an aerofoil (etc.) having elastic or inertial qualities.

Flyer. The Wrights' name for their powered aeroplanes. The name was widely used for powered aeroplanes of any make until about 1909–10. First used by Cayley in 1813. Curtiss spelt the word 'Flier'.

Flying boat. A seaplane with a hull on which it floats, takes off and lands. See also **Amphibian; Float plane; Seaplane.**

Flying machine. Strictly speaking all aircraft, whether powered or not, are machines (see Machine); but the term has been confined almost exclusively to powered aeroplanes in the past, but is now dying out of general usage altogether.

Flying speed. See Speed.

Flying tail. A tail plane, the whole of which can have its angle of incidence changed in flight.

Flying wing. An aircraft consisting entirely (or almost so) of a single large aerofoil within which the engines, passengers, etc., are contained.

Flying wires (Lift wires in USA). Wires (generally external) of the rigging which are attached to a wing, etc., to support the fuselage weight during flight.

Forced landing. An involuntary or emergency landing, which may or may not result in a 'crash landing'.

Form drag. See Drag.

Fowler flap. See Flap.

Fuselage. The body or hull of an aeroplane.

Gap. The distance between the two sets of wings of a biplane (or triplane, etc.).

Gas turbine. An engine in which air is compressed by a rotating Compressor, heat is added by burning fuel, and energy extracted from the gas stream by a turbine. Residual energy in the exhaust gas stream can be utilised to provide Jet propulsion. In addition, the turbine may drive an airscrew – the combination forming a Turboprop engine – or a helicopter rotor, or other machinery.

Gauchissement. See Wing warping.

Glider. An unpowered fixed-wing aeroplane, for gliding or soaring. A 'hang-glider' is one in which the pilot hangs by his arms, etc., and controls the machine by movements of his body and legs.

Gliding angle. The angle between an aircraft's flight path relative to the air, and the horizontal, when it is gliding.

Gravity (centre of). See Centre of gravity.

Ground loop. See Loop (ground).

Guided missile. See Missile.

Gyroplane. In English usage a rotorcraft with non-powered rotors, as in the Autogiro, which provide lift, but no propulsion. In American usage 'gyroplane' may refer to any rotorcraft.

Handed propellers. Propellers revolving in opposite directions to cancel out torque reactions.

Hangar. A building for housing aircraft.

Hang-glider. See Glider.

Helicopter. A type of rotorcraft that derives all its lift and thrust from engine-driven rotating aerofoils (i.e. rotor blades) mounted about an approximately vertical axis.

High-wing monoplane. One with its wings attached near or at the top of the fuselage.

Horizon (artificial). See Artificial horizon.

Horizontal rudder. The early term for an elevator.

Horizontal stabiliser. The American term for a tailplane.

Hydro-aeroplane. An early term for a seaplane (translated from the French *hydroavion*): sometimes confusingly shortened to 'hydroplane'.

Hydroplane. (a) A hydrofoil supported in water by hydrodynamic action; (b) a motorboat equipped with hydrofoils, by which it is supported when in motion; (c) a misnomer for a seaplane, as a contraction of 'hydro-aeroplane'.

Incidence (angle of). (a) The angle between the chord of a wing and the direction of the undisturbed airflow. Also referred to as the Angle of attack. (b) The angle between the chord and the horizontal – properly referred to as the Rigging angle of incidence.

Induced drag. See Drag.

Inherent stability. See Stability.

In-line engine. One in which the cylinders are arranged in one or more straight fore-and-aft rows, as distinct from the 'radial' or 'rotary' engines (which see).

Inside loop. See Loop.

Interference drag. See Drag.

Jet-assisted takeoff. A takeoff assisted by one or more small solid, or liquid, fuel rocket units.

Jet ropulsion. See Reaction propulsion.

Jet thrust. See Static thrust.

Joystick. An early term for the control column.

Keel surface. The effective side surface of an aircraft influencing directional stability.

King post. A vertical strut above the wing, from which bracing wires support it.

Kite. The earliest type of heavier-than-air aircraft, in which 'propulsion' is supplied by the pull on the 'tow line', and lift is supplied by the kite being inclined to the wind. The box kite (invented by Hargrave in 1893) comprises two four-sided 'cells' joined by booms, or variations of this configuration. The word 'kite' has also been used as slang for aeroplane (see Chapter 14 Note 3).

Landing flap. See Flap.

Landing wires. Wires (generally external) of the rigging which support the weight of the wings when on the ground.

Lateral axis. See Axis.

Lateral control. A term which is loosely used for control in roll, but should only be used for overall lateral control which involves control in roll, yaw and pitch.

Lateral stability. See Stability.

Leading edge. The edge of an aerofoil (wing, propeller, etc.) which first meets the air in normal flight; as opposed to the 'trailing edge' (which see).

Lift. That component of the total aerodynamic forces acting on an aerofoil (or whole aircraft, etc.) perpendicular to the relative wind; in normal flight, it is exerted in an upward direction, opposing the pull of gravity.

Lift (centre of). See Centre of lift.

Lift/drag ratio. The ratio of lift to drag.

Link trainer. A synthetic training device, comprising a hooded cockpit, for training in instrument flying, radio aids, etc. See also Flight simulator.

Longeron. A longitudinal structural member of the fuselage.

Longitudinal axis. See Axis.

Loop (ground). A violent turn to left or right made by an aeroplane when on the ground (i.e. taxiing, taking off or landing).

Looping the loop (or Loop). A flight manoeuvre in which an aeroplane flies an approximately circular path in a vertical plane; an Inside loop is the normal way of looping the loop, with the top of the aeroplane inside the circle traced: an Outside loop is a loop in which the top of the aircraft is on the outside of the circle traced.

Low-wing monoplane. One with the wings attached at or near the bottom of the fuselage.

Machine. In an aeronautical context, the word is used synonymously with 'aircraft'.

Mach meter. A special airspeed indicator registering the Mach number.

Mach number. The ratio of the airspeed of an aircraft to the speed of sound in the air surrounding it. Mach 1 is the speed of sound; Mach 2 is twice the speed of sound; and so on. The **Critical Mach number** is that representing the speed of a given aircraft at which a Mach number of 1 is attained at any local point of that aircraft: the term has also been used to denote the point at which control is lost in a non-supersonic aircraft. The speed of sound is approximately 760 mph at sea level and approximately 660 mph in the stratosphere.

Main plane(s). The main lifting surface(s) of an aeroplane, i.e. the wings.

Mass balance. A balancing weight attached to a control surface.

Mid-wing monoplane. One with the wings attached midway on the fuselage.

Military aircraft (etc.). When used with a small 'm', 'military' refers to all aircraft used by the armed forces, as distinct from commercial or private owners. When spelt with a capital 'M', 'Military' refers to the Army as such.

Missile. Any object thrown, dropped, projected or propelled, for the purpose of hitting a target. An **Aerodynamic missile** is one which is in effect an aeroplane with aerodynamically supporting surfaces; a **Ballistic missile** is any missile that becomes a free-falling body in the latter stages of its 'flight'; a **Guided missile** is a missile directed to its target either by presetting or self-reacting devices, or by radio or wire command from outside the missile; a **Rocket missile** is one propelled and supported entirely by rocket power. In practice, missiles may combine the characteristics of all four of these classes.

Monocoque construction. From the French word meaning 'eggshell': an idealised concept of a completely hollow shell-like structure. See Chapter 14 Appendix; see also **Stressed skin**.

Motor. A word generally synonymous with 'engine'.

Movable tips. An early term for ailerons.

Multiplane. A general term for any aeroplane with two or more sets of wings mounted one above the other.

Nacelle. The French word for 'a small boat': a separate enclosure on an aircraft for housing crew, engine(s) or other objects. The early pusher biplanes would have their fuselages described as 'nacelles', where the tail was carried separately on outriggers. The most usual modern use of the word is an 'engine nacelle'.

Negative dihedral. See **Anhedral**.

Neutral stability. See **Stability**.

Ornithopter. An aircraft sustained and propelled by flapping wings.

Outrigger(s). A projecting structure to support (on an aircraft) such parts as an elevator, rudder or complete tail unit, etc. The word 'boom' is almost synonymous.

Panels. Another early term for **Side curtains** (which see).

Parachute. A parasol-like aero-nautical device for retarding the movement of whatever is attached to it.

The man-carrying parachute is composed of the **Canopy**, the **Rigging** (or **Shroud**) **lines**, and the **Harness**. In a rip-cord parachute the main canopy is pulled out of the **Pack** by a **Pilot parachute**. Also used for a glider in the last [nineteenth] century.

Parachute (braking). A parachute opened behind an aeroplane to retard it.

Parasol monoplane. One with the wings mounted above, and clear of the fuselage.

Payload. That part of the load of a commercial aircraft that produces revenue (i.e. passengers and cargo).

Pénaud-type tail. An early term for a cruciform tail unit, based on the mistaken belief that such a configuration was introduced by Alphonse Pénaud. It was first used by Cayley in 1804.

Pilot parachute. See **Parachute**.

Pitch. The blade angle of a propeller or rotor blade.

Pilot-static tube. See **Airspeed indicator**.

Plane. (a) Short for 'aeroplane'; (b) a wing; (c) a flat surface.

Plane of symmetry. A vertical plane containing the longitudinal axis of a symmetrical object, such as an aeroplane, where such a plane would cut through the machine from nose to tail leaving the port side and wing on one side of the plane, and the starboard on the other.

Planophore. Alphonse Pénaud's name for his stable model monoplane of 1871; from the Latin *plano* (plane) and the Greek *phoros* (bearing).

Pontoon. An early term for a float.

Powered glider. See **Glider**.

Power plant (or **unit**). In aircraft these terms are generally taken to include the engine, propeller and accessories.

Power/weight ratio. The ratio of the power of an engine to its own weight; or, when used of the whole aircraft, the ratio of power to total weight.

Pressure (centre of). See **Centre of pressure**.

Pressurisation. The keeping of the interior of an aircraft at a higher air pressure than the atmospheric pressure outside.

Prime mover. A source of mechanical power produced entirely from non-mechanical sources of energy, e.g. chemical, electrical.

Production model. Any of a batch of aircraft (etc.) manufactured under standard conditions.

Profile drag. See **Drag**.

Propeller. This word, in aeronautical and marine parlance, only became synonymous with 'airscrew' from about 1845 to 1855. Prior to that it referred to any propelling device.

Propeller (constant-speed). One that tends to maintain the engine revolutions under any flight conditions by automatically increasing or decreasing the pitch of the blades.

Propeller (contra-rotating). A twin unit comprising two coaxial propellers rotating in opposite directions. 'Counter-rotating' is generally applied to two propellers on separate axes, or to two propellers on the same axis but driven independently by two engines.

Propeller (reversible-pitch). One whose blades can be turned to negative pitch to produce reverse thrust to retard an aircraft when landing.

Propeller (variable-pitch). Any propeller the pitch of whose blades can be altered in operation.

Propeller disc. The space covered by a rotating propeller.

Propjet. See **Turboprop**.

Prototype. The first one (or more) complete and working aircraft (or other object) of a new type, class, or series. There may be more than one prototype of a given machine. See also **Production model**.

Pusher propeller. A propeller placed behind its engine, and generally behind the main wings of an aeroplane.

Push-pull. An adjective applied to a combination of pusher and tractor propellers.

Radial engine. One in which one or more rows of cylinders are arranged radially around a common crankshaft: the cylinders are stationary, as distinct from the 'rotary' engine (which see).

Radius of action. The distance between the takeoff point of an aircraft and its point of safe return, allowing for the various conditions en route, at its 'target', etc. applied chiefly to military aircraft.

RAE. Abbreviation of Royal Aircraft Establishment.

RAeC. Abbreviation of Royal Aero Club.

RAeS. Abbreviation of Royal Aeronautical Society.

RAF. Abbreviation originally of the Royal Aircraft Factory (Farnborough); later of the Royal Air Force, (formed 1918).

Range. The overall distance an aircraft can fly under a given set of conditions. See also **Radius of action**.

Rate-of-climb indicator. A flight instrument to show the rate of climb or descent of an aircraft.

Reaction propulsion. Propulsion by means of reaction to a jet of gas or liquid projected rearward (hence 'jet propulsion'), as by a turbojet or rocket engine: in modern usage the term 'jet propulsion' is only applied to air-breathing engines, and not to rocket engines.

REP. The initials of Robert Esnault-Pelterie which he used as a generic name for his aeroplanes, and which was inscribed on his machines, followed by a numeral.

Reversible-pitch propeller. See **Propeller** (reversible-pitch).

RFC. Abbreviation of Royal Flying Corps.

Rib. A chord-wise structural member of a wing, or other component.

RNAS. Abbreviation of Royal Naval Air Service.

Rocket engine. A reaction propulsion engine whose fuel includes an oxidiser, thus making it independent of the atmosphere. Rocket engines may use solid or liquid fuels.

Roll. (a) Any movement about the horizontal axis of an aircraft; (b) a deliberate manoeuvre in which an aeroplane is rolled over: also **Half-roll**; (c) the American equivalent of 'run'; i.e. takeoff, landing or taxiing, roll; also used thus in the early days of British flying.

Roll, control in. Control in an aircraft about its longitudinal axis, usually effected by ailerons or wing warping.

Rotary engine. One in which the crankshaft remains fixed, and the cylinders revolve about it, the propeller revolving with them.

Rotary-wing aircraft. See **Rotorcraft**.

Rotating-wing aircraft. See **Rotorcraft**.

Rotor (of a rotorcraft). An assembly comprising generally two or more long narrow wings (called 'blades') set in a hub on a vertical shaft which provide lift (or lift and thrust).

Rotor (anti-torque). A small rotor on a rotorcraft revolving in the vertical plane which generates thrust to oppose the torque effects of the main rotor.

Rotorcraft. An aircraft which employs rotating aerofoils to provide lift, or both lift and propulsion. In American usage, a 'gyroplane' is the equivalent of a rotorcraft. See also **Autogiro; Gyroplane; Helicopter**.

Rudder. A vertical control surface for guiding an aircraft in the horizontal plane.

Rudder (horizontal). 'Horizontal rudder' was an early term for the elevator.

Rudder bar (or **Rudder pedals**). The foot-operated bar or pedals to which are attached the cables operating the rudder.

Runner. An early term for a skid.

Sail. Word used by Cayley for an aircraft wing.

Sailplane. A glider designed specially for soaring.

Seaplane. Any aeroplane built to operate only from the water: seaplanes are either **Float planes** or **Flying boats**. The word 'seaplane' was introduced by Sir Winston Churchill in 1913. See also **Amphibian**.

Servo-control. A power-assisted control.

Sesquiplane. A biplane, in which one wing (pair of wings) is much smaller than the other, generally half the area, or less.

Shoulder-wing monoplane. One with the wings attached high on the fuselage: in practice often the same as a high-wing monoplane.

Side curtains. The vertical surfaces sometimes placed between the wings of early biplanes to improve lateral stability, and turning the wings into box-kite cells.

Simulator (flight). See **Flight simulator**.

Skid. Flat or curved wooden (or other) member which may be part of an aircraft undercarriage (with or without the addition of wheels); or be in the form of a **Tail skid**.

Skidding. The sidewise sliding of an aircraft away from the centre of the curve when turning.

Skin friction. The friction of the air particles on a surface in motion. See also **Drag**.

Slat. See **Slot**.

Slipstream. The flow of air driven backward by the propeller.

Slot. A gap between the wing and a specially formed slat, through which air is directed over the upper surface of the wing to preserve a smooth airflow, generally at high angles of incidence; the same principle applied to ailerons, etc.

Slotted wing. See **Slot**.

Sonic speed. The speed of sound. See also **Sound**.

Sound (speed of). The speed of sound is approximately 760 mph at sea level, decreasing with height (owing to decrease in temperature): in the stratosphere it is approximately 660 mph. Speed below that of sound is called **Subsonic**; at that of sound **Sonic**; and above, **Supersonic**. See also **Mach number; Transonic speed**.

Sound barrier. A popular but misleading term loosely indicating the rapid rise of drag at transonic speeds.

Span (of wings). The spread of the wing(s), from tip to tip.

Spar. A span-wise structural member of a wing, etc.

Speed. **Flying speed** is the speed necessary for a fixed-wing aeroplane to attain, or maintain, in order to become or remain airborne. Airspeed is the speed of any aircraft through the air, i.e. relative to the air through which it moves. **Ground speed** is the aircraft's speed in relation to the ground. **Sonic speed** is the speed of sound, i.e. about 760 mph at sea level (see **Sound**).

Speed brake. See **Air brake; Flap; Spoiler**.

Spin. An aerial manoeuvre, intentional or not, in which an aeroplane descends vertically in autorotation.

Spinner. A streamlined fairing fitted over the hub of an airscrew.

Spoiler. A projecting member designed to break down airflow around a body, in order to retard its movement; hence an air brake.

Stability and control

Stability. There are two aspects of aircraft stability, longitudinal stability for motion *in* the plane of symmetry, and lateral stability for motion *out* of the plane of symmetry; the former concerns rising, falling and pitching movements; the latter, rolling, yawing and side-slipping movements. Colloquially and descriptively, however, one may also speak of 'directional stability' which is a component of lateral stability.

Control. Where flight control is concerned, one may speak of 'longitudinal control', which is control in pitch; and 'lateral control' which comprises control in both roll and yaw. In practice the term 'lateral control' is often used to refer to control in roll only, and the term 'directional control' for control in yaw. In the present work I have used the term 'lateral control' for control in roll, unless otherwise stated. In early aviation (up to 1908) the Europeans were concerned to ensure: (a) **Longitudinal stability**; via a tailplane at the back; (b) **Longitudinal control**; via an elevator for control in pitch; (c) **Directional stability**; via a keel area and a vertical surface in the rear; (d) **Directional control**; via a rear rudder. As the Europeans neglected the proper function and use of warping and ailerons, they found it difficult to control their machines when they attempted to turn them on rudder alone, with the outer wings producing more lift on the turn than the inner; the pilots could only counteract the inwards rolling momentum by putting on opposite rudder to accelerate the lowered wings and lift them, and – in extreme cases – hoping that this rudder action would be in time to stop the machine heeling right over and crashing. (e) **Stability in roll**; via a dihedral angle of the wings. Until Wilbur Wright started flying in France in August 1908, the use of ailerons or warping to effect control in roll was neither properly understood nor practised by the Europeans; this was initially due to their remaining ignorant of the necessity to achieve proper control in roll when turning, and their belief that the main function of ailerons or warping was to maintain lateral balance in level flight; then, as a result of these considerations, it was due to their ignorance of the use of the rudder to counteract aileron (or warp)

drag. The Wright brothers, on the other hand, were not concerned with any kind of inherent stability, but much concerned from the first with full lateral control (control in roll, yaw and side-slip).

Stabiliser. Any aerofoil used to provide stability.

Stagger. The placing of the upper wing in advance of the lower in a biplane (or progressively of the upper two in a triplane), called 'positive' or 'forward' stagger. If this arrangement is reversed, it is called 'negative' or 'backward' stagger, or 'back-stagger'.

Stall. The behaviour of an aeroplane when, owing to excessive angle of incidence – usually associated with loss of speed – the wings lose lift.

Steering air brakes. See **Air brakes** (steering).

Steering flaps (or **Tips**). Early terms for ailerons.

Step rocket. A multistage rocket.

Stick. Short for 'control stick', 'control column', or 'joystick'.

Stratosphere. The layer of the earth's atmosphere above the tropopause, extending up to 18 miles.

Streamlining. The giving of a specially shaped and smooth contour to an object to decrease its resistance in a fluid flow.

Stressed-skin construction. The use of the outer skin of a structure to carry primary structural loads in addition to local air pressure. See Chapter 14 Appendix; see also **Monocoque**.

Stringer. A longitudinal stiffening member in stressed-skin construction.

Strut. Connecting member, e.g. between the wings of a biplane, etc.; mainly to take compression loads.

Stub wing. A short wing.

Subsonic speed. Speed below that of sound. See also **Sound**.

Supercharger. A pump or compressor for forcing more air or fuel-air mixture into an engine than it would normally induct at the prevailing atmosphere pressure.

Supersonic speed. Speed above the speed of sound. See also **Sound**.

Tab. A small auxiliary control surface set in, or attached to, a larger control surface in order either to correct or aid the latter's movement or position: a **Trim tab** is one that is set to trim the aircraft.

Tachometer. An instrument indicating revolutions per minute of any rotating unit.

Tail (flying). See **Flying tail**.

Tail assembly. Another term for **Tail unit** (which see).

Tail booms. Outrigger members supporting the tail unit.

Tailplane. The fixed horizontal stabilising plane(s) of the tail unit.

Tail unit. The rear assembly of an aircraft comprising, fin, rudder, tailplane, elevator, etc. Also called **Tail assembly** and **Empennage** (which see).

Tandem. An arrangement of units one behind the other.

Taper. The narrowing of an aerofoil (or other object) either in chord length or thickness, generally applied to the former.

Taxi. To drive an aircraft along the ground or water, other than in takeoff or landing runs.

Terminal velocity. The constant velocity of a falling body attained when the resistance of the air has become equal to the force of gravity acting upon the body.

Thrust. The driving force exerted on any aircraft, missile, etc., by its propeller, rotor blades, propulsive jet, or other means.

Torque. A moment that produces, or tends to produce, rotation, twisting or torsion.

Tractor propeller. One that pulls, i.e. in front of its engine and generally to the front of the main wings of an aeroplane.

Trailing edge. The rear edge of an aerofoil, i.e. over which the air passes last.

Transonic speed. The speed of an aircraft in the region of sonic speed, where the surrounding airflow is simultaneously subsonic, sonic, and supersonic over various parts of the machine.

Trim tab. See **Tab**.

Triplane. An aeroplane with three main (sets of) planes set one above the other.

Turbojet. The recognised combine-word for a gas turbine jet propulsion engine; or (loosely) an aeroplane propelled by it: as distinct from a **Turboprop**.

Turboprop. The recognised combine-word for an airscrew/gas turbine engine combination; or (loosely) an aeroplane propelled by it: sometimes referred to as a 'propjet'. See also **Turbojet**.

Turn-and-bank indicator. A gyroscopically controlled flight instrument indicating the rate of turn of an aeroplane, and amount of skidding (if any).

Undercarriage. The collective term for the wheels or other gear supporting an aircraft on land or water, generally the former: also termed 'landing gear'.

Variable-pitch propeller. See **Propeller**.

V (or Vee) engine. One with banks of cylinders arranged in a V, seen from the end.

Ventral. See **Dorsal**.

Venturi tube. A tube with a constricted throat which, when placed in an airflow, brings about (in the throat) an increase in flow velocity with a consequent diminution of pressure (see **Bernouilli theorem**).

Vertical axis. See **Axis**.

Vertical stabiliser. The American term for a fin.

Volplane. An early term (used as a verb or noun) for 'glide'.

Vortex. A rotating airflow.

Warping. See **Wing warping**.

Wash-in and **Wash-out**. 'Wash-in' is an increase in the angle of incidence of a wing towards, or at, the tip; 'wash-out' is a decrease in the angle of incidence towards or at, the wingtip. 'Wash-in' on one side, and 'wash-out' on the other, was provided on the wings of early aeroplanes to counteract the torque effects of propellers and rotary engines. 'Wash-in' is also incorporated at the tips of glider wings to give early warning of a stall.

Wing(s). The main lifting aerofoil(s) of an aeroplane. By bird-derived usage, a monoplane is said to have two wings, even if there is only one connected surface. Hence a biplane has two 'sets' of wings. But, occasionally (as in 'gull-wing', etc.), the singular is used for convenience. In the last [nineteenth] century the word 'wings' was often used technically to denote ornithoptering wings as opposed to fixed wings ('aero planes'). Cayley called a fixed wing a 'sail'.

Wing loading. The gross weight of an aeroplane divided by the wing area.

Wing warping. A twisting or torsion of a wing to increase or decrease its curvature and thus its angle of incidence, and effect control in roll; used first on the Wright machines. This misleading term ('wing warping') was invented by Octave Chanute in 1903 as a kind of shorthand word for the helical twisting of the wings according to the Wrights' practice. It was first literally translated into French (1903–04) by the verb *gauchir*, which did not mean a twisting of the wings, but a literal 'warping' of them.

Yaw. The movement of an aircraft about its vertical axis.

Zoom. To climb briefly at an angle greater than the normal climbing angle.

Addenda

Various claims to powered flight prior to December 1903

(A note by John A Bagley, added January 1984)

A persistent theme in aeronautical history is the claim that some person or another 'flew before the Wright brothers'. Many such claims prove, on investigation, to involve an unmanned model aircraft, or an unpowered glider, or a flight which can be dated to the period between December 1903 and August 1908 when the Wrights' flying prowess was fully revealed to the world.

There remain a number of cases of claimed powered flights which cannot so easily be explained, including several which were of particular concern to the late Charles Gibbs-Smith, and which he had intended to deal with in his projected second volume of this work. Of these, the most important claim was discussed at length in his book *Clement Ader – his flight-claims and his place in history* published in 1968; while the claims of Mozhaiski, Maxim and Jatho are sufficiently covered on pages 66–7, 76–8, and 128–9.

In the following sections, I have summarised the stories of some less important claimants. In doing so, I believe that I have fairly presented the substance of Charles Gibbs-Smith's research, and that he would agree with my conclusions.

It should be observed that between May 1906, when the Wrights' main patent was granted, and 1917, when the American manufacturers accepted a cross-licensing agreement to facilitate wartime production, a number of persons had a clear interest in proving the existence of 'prior art' as a reason for invalidating the Wright patent. This provides an understandable reason to magnify the achievements of earlier would-be aviators. It is more difficult to excuse some claims made in recent years which seem to stem from a form of chauvinism which cannot accept that practical aviation could have been started in such an obscure place as Dayton, Ohio.

It may also be remarked that if each of the claims quoted below were accepted in full without question, the history of the development of practical aviation would not be altered at all. The events of 17 December 1903 would be of little consequence if they had happened in isolation. Their importance is that they represent an easily identified stage in the progress of the Wright brothers from trials with a tethered kite in 1899 to demonstrations of flying in 1908 which convinced the world that the practical flying machine had arrived at last. None of the flights discussed below had any comparable consequence.

Gilmore

Lyman Gilmore, Jr of Nevada City, California, claimed in 1927 that he had flown a steam-powered monoplane for four miles in 1896, and versions of this story are still occasionally published. Ernest L True carried out a careful investigation into Gilmore's history, published in the *Journal* of the American Aviation Historical Society, summer 1967, and found no substance for any such flight. Gilmore built a number of large model gliders between about 1900 and 1907 before setting up the Gilmore Airship Company at Grass Valley, California. He started construction of a large eight-passenger monoplane which was never completed, and a smaller two-seat machine in which he made unsuccessful attempts to fly in 1912.

Herring

A M Herring studied engineering in New York from 1883 to 1888, during which time he built several unsuccessful gliders. Inspired by reading of Lilienthal's activities, he built two more gliders in 1894 with which he made brief flights, and was then hired by Chanute to build and test models of his multi-wing glider designs. From May to November 1895, Herring worked for Langley in Washington, but then returned to Chanute's employment.

It is evident from Chanute's own accounts that Herring had a significant share in the design of Chanute's most successful machine, the triplane hang-glider of August 1896 which was converted to biplane configuration in September (see page 101). Herring was so encouraged by his successful flights (up to 109 metres) on this machine that he prepared drawings for an aircraft powered by a compressed-air engine.

As Chanute was reluctant to support this project, Herring next built a triplane hang-glider which he flew in October 1896, covering distances up to 285 metres. Then, financed by New York banker M C Arnot and assisted by Chanute's carpenter William Avery, Herring produced a biplane glider in August 1897 which so closely resembled the 1896 Chanute-Herring biplane that Chanute used photographs and drawings of the two craft interchangeably, to the confusion of subsequent historians. This glider was flown successfully by Herring and others on numerous occasions in September 1897.

Herring's powered aircraft – another biplane hang-glider with cruciform tail unit, similar to the 1896 design – was finally built in 1898. After unsuccessfully trying to develop a petrol engine, Herring reverted to his original scheme of a compressed-air motor, which was supplied from an air cylinder sufficient for only 15 seconds running. The engine, mounted above the lower wing, drove two propellers on a common shaft, one ahead of and one behind the wings. On 10 and 22 October 1898, Herring was airborne for 15 and 22 metres distance, over the beach at St Joseph, Michigan, in this machine.

These two brief hops were as close as anyone was to come to achieving powered flight before the Wrights. In later years, Herring and others claimed these 'flights' as a major step towards practical aviation, and that Herring had been 'robbed' of the credit due to him. But it is clear that Herring had reached a dead end:[1] his primitive form of control, by shifting body weight alone, constrained the size of his aircraft so that they could not carry the additional weight of an adequate power unit, even if Herring could have built or acquired one. By 1899, he had built several experimental steam engines, but admitted that the powered aircraft introduced many new problems, 'particularly in the area of steering and control'. Subsequently, he turned to other activities, returning to aviation in March 1909 with the short-lived Herring-Curtiss Company established to build machines designed by Curtiss.

Pearse

Richard Pearse was a farmer and mechanic in a remote part of New Zealand who applied in July 1906 for a patent on a high-wing mono-plane with tricycle undercarriage, driven by an engine and propeller and controlled by a combination of aerodynamic surfaces and pilot's weight-shifting. The only contemporary published references to the construction of Pearse's aircraft are local newspaper reports in November 1909 stating that it had recently flown about 25 yards.

Pearse himself, in a letter to the Dunedin *Evening Star* in May 1915, said that he began his experiments in 1904 after reading of Langley's failure; that by 1906 he had 'sufficiently perfected' his monoplane to patent it; that he built only one experimental aircraft; and that he abandoned his work when it became clear that a substantial industry had been established overseas, particularly in France. In another letter published in September 1928, Pearse said that his aircraft 'was uncontrollable and would spin round broadside on directly it left the ground'.

Nevertheless, since 1971 an elaborate hypothesis has been constructed by a group in New Zealand to prove that Pearse flew before the Wright brothers. On the basis of recollections gathered between 1954 and 1978 from various old inhabitants of the area, they postulate that Pearse made several flights in 1902 and 1903: notably one of about 1.2 kilometres on 31 March 1902, and another of over a kilometre exactly one year later on 31 March 1903.

Richard Pearse's own account seems so much more credible that these remarkable claims must be rejected.

Watson

A claim was made in 1953 by James Y Watson that his brother, Preston A Watson, had built and successfully flown a powered aircraft at Erroll, Scotland, in 1903, before the Wright brothers. Charles Gibbs-Smith investigated this claim, and convinced James Watson that it was untenable. Preston's three identifiable machines were built between late 1908 and 1913, but there is some slight evidence that he may have built a Wright-type glider in 1903 and fitted an engine

to it in 1906. Preston Watson himself, in the magazine *Flight* of
15 May 1914, stated that the Wright Brothers 'were the first to fly in
a practical way'.

Whitehead

Gustave Weisskopf, a German mechanic who adopted the name
Whitehead after migrating to the USA, first comes to notice in 1897,
when he built a man-powered ornithopter for the Boston Aeronautical
Society. This was a biplane with cruciform tail unit, with a pair of
panels mounted between the wings which were evidently intended to
be flapped by the pilot. This machine almost certainly never left the
ground.

The powered machine in which Whitehead claimed to have
flown was built at Bridgeport, Connecticut; it was described and
illustrated in *Scientific American* of 8 June 1901 and in *Illustrierte
Aeronautische Mittheilungen* of October 1901. It was a monoplane
with a curious boat-shaped fuselage, a horizontal tail surface, and
two propellers ahead of the wing stated to be driven by a 20-hp two-
cylinder acetylene engine. For movement on the road, the wings and
tail unit were to be folded, and a separate engine of 10 hp drove two
of the four road wheels. (The mysterious acetylene engine, described
by Whitehead as 'a wonder', has never been described in detail and
almost certainly never existed. Contemporary photographs show
Whitehead with a two-cylinder steam engine, but it is not actually
installed in the aircraft.) In the *Scientific American* article, it is said
that flight has not yet been attempted, but in the German magazine
Whitehead states that he has made a flight lasting 1½ minutes
covering 2800 feet (860 metres).

An account of this flight, full of circumstantial detail, was
published in the *Bridgeport Sunday Herald* on 18 August 1901:
this states that the flight was made in the middle of the night, about
02.00 on 14 August, from a rough field outside the town to which the
aircraft was driven on its own wheels. The story was repeated (shorn
of its less credible details) in the *New York Herald* of 19 August.

These reports of successful powered flight of over half a mile
attracted no great attention at the time; and Whitehead's letters to the
American Inventor, in which he claimed two flights on 17 January
1902 of 2 miles and 7½ miles over Long Island Sound, were published
in the issue of 1 April and then, it seems, were totally disregarded until
1937, when a book called *Lost Flights of Gustave Whitehead* written
by Stella Randolph was published. From 1963 onwards, the claims
have been reiterated with increasing vehemence by a small group of
Connecticut patriots, culminating in the book *History by Contract*
by William J O'Dwyer and Stella Randolph published in 1978,
which charges that Whitehead's flight claims have been deliberately
suppressed by a long-standing and widespread conspiracy among
professional aviation historians.

The account of the flight on 14 August 1901 in the *Bridgeport Sunday Herald* reads like a work of juvenile fiction, but Whitehead's frustratingly brief statements are quite straightforward claims for a substantial achievement. They were made in reputable and widely-read journals and could certainly not have been overlooked by contemporary workers. Yet Whitehead continued to work in comparative obscurity, building a variety of aircraft and engines with little success. The acetylene wonder engine was discarded for the flights of January 1902: Whitehead stated that the aircraft used then was similar to his previous machine, but powered by a 40-hp five-cylinder engine fuelled by kerosene. Then both engines and the 'successful' monoplane were abandoned, for his next aircraft was a triplane glider clearly based on Chanute's designs, to which he fitted a 12-hp two-cylinder kerosene engine with hot-bulb ignition. A single 'flight' of 350 metres on this machine was reported in *Scientific American* of 19 September 1903. Then in December 1905 he applied for a patent, in partnership with Stanley Y Beach, on a monoplane hang-glider quite different from any of his previous aircraft. This was built in 1906, with a four-wheeled open car underneath on which the pilot stood, and towed flights behind Beach's car were made. About the end of the year a three-cylinder 15-hp engine was fitted, but there are no reliable reports of flights. Then a large biplane with a 40-hp four-cylinder engine driving two out-rigged propellers was exhibited in unfinished state by the New York Aeronautic Society in November 1908, and failed to fly when tested in the following year; and finally Whitehead's last attempt to fly was a bizarre helicopter with 60 lifting screws in 1911–12. Such a career of retrogression from the successes of 1901 and 1902 is surely inexplicable; the simplest conclusion must be that those flights of ½ mile, 2 miles and 7½ miles were flights of fancy.

Notes

1 By about 1970, modern light-weight materials and engines made powered hang-gliders controlled by movement of the pilot's body alone technically feasible, but these primitive controls were soon augmented or supplanted by aerodynamic controls in a new generation of 'micro-light' aircraft.

Further reading

(Compiled by Brian Riddle, Librarian of the Royal Aeronautical Society, September 2003)

Anderson, J D, *A History of Aerodynamics: And its Impact on Flying Machines*
(Cambridge: Cambridge University Press, 1998)

Anderson, J D, *The Airplane: A History of Its Technology*
(Reston, VA: American Institute of Aeronautics and Astronautics, 2002)

Baker, D, *Flight and Flying – A Chronology* (New York: Facts on File, 1994)

Blake, J, *Flight: The Five Ages of Aviation* (Sparkford: Haynes, 1987)

Boyne, W J, *The Leading Edge* (Macdonald, 1987)

Boyne, W J, *The Smithsonian Book of Flight* (Washington DC: Smithsonian Books, 1987)

Chant, C, *Aviation: An Illustrated History* (London: Orbis, 1983)

Gibbs-Smith, C H, *The Wright Brothers: Aviation Pioneers and Their Work 1899–1911*
(London: Science Museum, 1987, reprinted 2002)

Gunston, B, *Flights of Fantasy – From Leonardo da Vinci to Hotol* (London: Hamlyn, 1990)

Hallion, R P, *Taking Flight: Inventing the Aerial Age from Antiquity through the First World War*
(New York: Oxford University Press, 2003)

Mackworth-Praed, B, *Aviation: The Pioneer Years* (London: Studio Editions, 1990)

Rendall, I, *Reaching for the Skies: The Adventure of Flight* (London: BBC Books, 1988)

Scott, P, *The Pioneers of Flight: A Documentary History*
(Princeton, NJ: Princeton University Press, 1999)

Spick, M, *Milestones of Manned Flight: The Ages of Flight from the Wright Brothers to Stealth Technology*
(London: Salamander Books, 1994)

Aviation Year by Year (London: Dorling Kindersley, 2001)

Index